Handbook of Social Justice in Loss and Grief

The *Handbook of Social Justice in Loss and Grief* is a scholarly work of social criticism, richly grounded in personal experience, evocative case studies, and current multicultural and sociocultural theories and research. It is also consistently practical and reflective, challenging readers to think through responses to ethically complex scenarios in which social justice is undermined by radically uneven opportunity structures, hierarchies of voice and privilege, personal and professional power, and unconscious assumptions, at the very junctures when people are most vulnerable—at points of serious illness, confrontation with end-of-life decision making, and in the throes of grief and bereavement. Harris and Bordere give the reader an active and engaged take on the field, enticing readers to interrogate their own assumptions and practices while increasing, chapter after chapter, their cultural literacy regarding important groups and contexts. The *Handbook of Social Justice in Loss and Grief* deeply and uniquely addresses a hot topic in the helping professions and social sciences and does so with uncommon readability.

Darcy L. Harris, PhD, FT, is an associate professor in the department of interdisciplinary programs at King's University College at the University of Western Ontario in Ontario, Canada, where she is also the coordinator of the thanatology program.

Tashel C. Bordere, PhD, CT, is an assistant professor of human development and family science and state extension specialist in youth development at the University of Missouri–Columbia and a past editor of *The Forum*.

The Series in Death, Dying, and Bereavement

Robert A. Neimeyer, Consulting Editor

Balk—Dealing With Dying, Death, and Grief During Adolescence
Beder—Voices of Bereavement: A Casebook for Grief Counselors
Berger—Music of the Soul: Composing Life Out of Loss
Buckle & Fleming—Parenting After the Death of a Child: A Practitioner's Guide
Davies—Shadows in the Sun: The Experiences of Sibling Bereavement in Childhood
Doka & Martin—Grieving Beyond Gender: Understanding the Ways Men and Women Mourn, Revised Edition
Harris—Counting Our Losses: Reflecting on Change, Loss, and Transition in Everyday Life
Harris & Bordere—Handbook of Social Justice in Loss and Grief: Exploring Diversity, Equity, and Inclusion
Harvey—Perspectives on Loss: A Sourcebook
Jeffreys—Helping Grieving People—When Tears Are Not Enough: A Handbook for Care Providers, Second Edition
Jordan & McIntosh—Grief After Suicide: Understanding the Consequences and Caring for the Survivors
Katz & Johnson—When Professionals Weep: Emotional and Countertransference Responses in Palliative and End-of-Life Care, Second Edition
Kissane & Parnes—Bereavement Care for Families
Klass—The Spiritual Lives of Bereaved Parents
Kosminsky & Jordan—Attachment-Informed Grief Therapy: The Clinician's Guide to Foundations and Applications
Leenaars—Lives and Deaths: Selections from the Works of Edwin S. Shneidman
Leong & Leach—Suicide among Racial and Ethnic Minority Groups: Theory, Research, and Practice
Lester—Katie's Diary: Unlocking the Mystery of a Suicide
Martin & Doka—Men Don't Cry . . . Women Do: Transcending Gender Stereotypes of Grief
Neimeyer—Techniques of Grief Therapy: Creative Practices for Counseling the Bereaved
Neimeyer—Techniques of Grief Therapy: Assessment and Intervention
Neimeyer, Harris, Winokuer, & Thornton—Grief and Bereavement in Contemporary Society: Bridging Research and Practice
Nord—Multiple AIDS-Related Loss: A Handbook for Understanding and Surviving a Perpetual Fall
Rogers—The Art of Grief: The Use of Expressive Arts in a Grief Support Group
Roos—Chronic Sorrow: A Living Loss
Rosenblatt—Parent Grief: Narratives of Loss and Relationship
Rosenblatt & Wallace—African American Grief
Rubin, Malkinson, & Witztum—Working With the Bereaved: Multiple Lenses on Loss and Mourning
Silverman—Widow to Widow, Second Edition
Tedeschi & Calhoun—Helping Bereaved Parents: A Clinician's Guide
Thompson & Neimeyer—Grief and the Expressive Arts: Practices for Creating Meaning
Werth—Contemporary Perspectives on Rational Suicide
Werth & Blevins—Decision Making near the End of Life: Issues, Developments, and Future Directions

Formerly The Series in Death Education, Aging, and Health Care

Hannelore Wass, Consulting Editor

Bard—Medical Ethics in Practice
Benoliel—Death Education for the Health Professional
Bertman—Facing Death: Images, Insights, and Interventions
Brammer—How to Cope with Life Transitions: The Challenge of Personal Change
Cleiren—Bereavement and Adaptation: A Comparative Study of the Aftermath of Death
Corless & Pittman-Lindeman—AIDS: Principles, Practices, and Politics, Abridged Edition
Corless & Pittman-Lindeman—AIDS: Principles, Practices, and Politics, Reference Edition
Curran—Adolescent Suicidal Behavior
Davidson—The Hospice: Development and Administration, Second Edition
Davidson & Linnolla—Risk Factors in Youth Suicide
Degner & Beaton—Life–Death Decisions in Health Care
Doka—AIDS, Fear, and Society: Challenging the Dreaded Disease
Doty—Communication and Assertion Skills for Older Persons
Epting & Neimeyer—Personal Meanings of Death: Applications for Personal Construct Theory to Clinical Practice
Haber—Health Care for an Aging Society: Cost-Conscious Community Care and Self-Care Approaches
Hughes—Bereavement and Support: Healing in a Group Environment
Irish, Lundquist, & Nelsen—Ethnic Variations in Dying, Death, and Grief: Diversity in Universality
Klass, Silverman, & Nickman—Continuing Bonds: New Understanding of Grief
Lair—Counseling the Terminally Ill: Sharing the Journey
Leenaars, Maltsberger, & Neimeyer—Treatment of Suicidal People
Leenaars & Wenckstern—Suicide Prevention in Schools
Leng—Psychological Care in Old Age
Leviton—Horrendous Death, Health, and Well-Being
Leviton—Horrendous Death and Health: Toward Action
Lindeman, Corby, Downing, & Sanborn—Alzheimer's Day Care: A Basic Guide
Lund—Older Bereaved Spouses: Research with Practical Applications
Neimeyer—Death Anxiety Handbook: Research, Instrumentation, and Application
Papadatou & Papadatos—Children and Death
Prunkl & Berry—Death Week: Exploring the Dying Process
Ricker & Myers—Retirement Counseling: A Practical Guide for Action
Samarel—Caring for Life and Death
Sherron & Lumsden—Introduction to Educational Gerontology, Third Edition
Stillion—Death and Sexes: An Examination of Differential Longevity Attitudes, Behaviors, and Coping Skills
Stillion, McDowell, & May—Suicide Across the Life Span: Premature Exits
Vachon—Occupational Stress in the Care of the Critically Ill, the Dying, and the Bereaved
Wass & Corr—Childhood and Death
Wass & Corr—Helping Children Cope with Death: Guidelines and Resource, Second Edition
Wass, Corr, Pacholski, & Forfar—Death Education II: An Annotated Resource Guide
Wass & Neimeyer—Dying: Facing the Facts, Third Edition
Weenolsen—Transcendence of Loss over the Life Span
Werth—Rational Suicide? Implications for Mental Health Professionals

Handbook of Social Justice in Loss and Grief

Exploring Diversity, Equity, and Inclusion

Edited by
Darcy L. Harris and Tashel C. Bordere

NEW YORK AND LONDON

First published 2016
by Routledge
711 Third Avenue, New York, NY 10017

and by Routledge
2 Park Square, Milton Park, Abingdon, Oxon, OX14 4RN

Routledge is an imprint of the Taylor & Francis Group, an informa business

© 2016 Taylor & Francis

The right of the editors to be identified as the authors of the editorial material, and of the authors for their individual chapters, has been asserted in accordance with sections 77 and 78 of the Copyright, Designs and Patents Act 1988.

All rights reserved. No part of this book may be reprinted or reproduced or utilized in any form or by any electronic, mechanical, or other means, now known or hereafter invented, including photocopying and recording, or in any information storage or retrieval system, without permission in writing from the publishers.

Trademark notice: Product or corporate names may be trademarks or registered trademarks, and are used only for identification and explanation without intent to infringe.

Library of Congress Cataloging in Publication Data
Names: Harris, Darcy, editor. | Bordere, Tashel C., editor.
Title: Handbook of social justice in loss and grief: exploring diversity, equity, and inclusion/[edited by] Darcy L. Harris, PhD, FT, Tashel C. Bordere, PhD, CT.
Description: 1 Edition. | New York: Routledge, 2016. | Series: The series in death, dying, and bereavement | Includes bibliographical references and index.
Identifiers: LCCN 2015030081| ISBN 9781138949928 (hardback: alk. paper) | ISBN 9781138949935 (pbk.: alk. paper) | ISBN 9781315659756 (ebook)
Subjects: LCSH: Social justice. | Loss (Psychology) | Grief. | Marginality, Social.
Classification: LCC HM671 .H363 2016 | DDC 303.3/72—dc23
LC record available at http://lccn.loc.gov/2015030081

ISBN: 978-1-138-94992-8 (hbk)
ISBN: 978-1-138-94993-5 (pbk)
ISBN: 978-1-315-65975-6 (ebk)

Typeset in Bembo and Stone Sans
by Florence Production Ltd, Stoodleigh, Devon, UK

We would like to dedicate this book to the memory of Dr. Kay Fowler, who fostered the connection between us. Kay not only had a deep appreciation for how social justice is woven into thanatology contexts, but she was also a wonderful friend and colleague whose love and laughter are sorely missed.

We also wish to honor our dear colleague and friend, Dr. Ronald Barrett, who died just as this book was going to press. Ron graciously contributed the preface for this volume based on his own experience and reflection. We regret that he did not live to see the book through to publication, yet his voice and vision of culturally responsive practices resonate across it, and hence his presence is indeed felt. We remember his passion, open-heartedness, and dedication to those who struggle with injustice.

We both wish to extend our heartfelt thanks to our chapter contributors for their willingness to share their time and expertise in developing this manuscript. Your contributions and shared passion for this field and your topical areas allowed us to bring this project to fruition, and we owe each of you a debt of gratitude!

Contents

Series Editor's Foreword   xiii
Foreword—Situating Social Justice and Diversity Issues within the Context of Loss and Grief—Kenneth J. Doka   xv
Preface—Ronald K. Barrett   xvii
Acknowledgments   xix

    Introduction   1
    Darcy L. Harris and Tashel C. Bordere

PART ONE
Introductory Concepts   7

1 Social Justice Conceptualizations in Grief and Loss   9
    Tashel C. Bordere, U.S.A.

2 Looking Broadly at Grief and Loss: A Critical Stance   21
    Darcy L. Harris, Canada

PART TWO
Issues Related to Social Status, Policy, and Politics   31

3 Living, Suffering, and Dying in a Globalized World   33
    Solomon R. Benatar, South Africa

4 Compassion in a Materialist World   40
    Neil Thompson, Wales, U.K.

5 Inequality, Exclusion, and Infant Mortality: Listening to Bereaved Mothers   50
    Neil Small, Katie Fermor, Ghazala Mir, and members of the HOPE group, U.K.

Contents

PART THREE
Issues Related to Groups   65

6 Cultural Competence and Humility   67
Paul C. Rosenblatt, U.S.A.

7 "Not Gonna Be Laid Out to Dry": Cultural Mistrust in End of
Life Care and Strategies for Trust-Building   75
Tashel C. Bordere, U.S.A.

8 Is Social Justice Elusive for the First Nations Peoples' Loss and Grief?   85
Kekinusuqs—Judith F. Sayers, Canada

9 Protecting Dignity at the End of Life: An Agenda for Human Rights
in an Aging World   100
Andy Hau Yan Ho and Geraldine Xiu Ling Tan, Singapore

PART FOUR
Individual Experiences in Social Contexts   109

10 Medicalizing Grief   111
Leeat Granek, Israel

11 Iatrogenic Harm and Objectification in the Context of Care
Delivery   125
Darcy L. Harris, Canada

12 The Silenced Emotion: Older Women and Grief in Prison   138
Ronald H. Aday and Jennifer J. Krabill, U.S.A.

13 Grief and Developmental Disabilities: Considerations for
Disenfranchised Populations   154
Rebecca S. Morse, Theodore T. Hoch and Thomas Freeman, U.S.A.

14 Social Expectations of the Bereaved   165
Darcy L. Harris, Canada

PART FIVE
Practice Implications   177

15 Transformation Through Socially Sensitive Experiences   179
Doneley Meris, U.S.A.

16 Spirituality and Social Justice   191
Neil Thompson, Wales, U.K.

17	From Violation to Voice, From Pain to Protest: Healing and Transforming Unjust Loss Through the Use of Rituals and Memorials *Carlos Torres and Alfonso M. García-Hernández, U.S./Canary Islands*	202
18	Restorative Justice Principles and Restorative Practice: Museums as Healing Spaces *Carla J. Sofka, U.S.A.*	213
19	Critical Social Work in Action *June Allan, Australia*	225
20	Navigating Social Institutions and Policies as an Advocate and Ally *Sandra Joy, U.S.A.*	240
21	Care for the Caregiver: A Multilayered Exploration *Darcy L. Harris, Canada*	251
22	The Liberating Capacity of Compassion *Mary L. S. Vachon and Darcy L. Harris, Canada*	265
	Conclusion *Darcy L. Harris and Tashel C. Bordere*	282
	Index	*285*

Series Editor's Foreword

A generation ago, professional texts advocating attention to the diversity of ways in which human beings engage death and loss and offering training in "best practices" took two basic forms. On the one hand, they provided coaching in "cultural competence" to practitioners by surveying the beliefs about death and loss and associated rituals and social dynamics characterizing various ethnic, racial, and religious communities, each given its own brief chapter in a more general tone. On the other hand, professional books stressed the importance of both normalizing grief and respecting its individuality, while sometimes bringing to bear particular theoretical, spiritual, or practical perspectives to guide clinicians in working with the dying or with their grieving families. Somewhat curiously, these two orientations—the one essentially anthropological, the other psychological—rarely were joined together to deeply inform practice in a single book.

While not discounting the genuine relevance of understanding of the diversity of human cultures regarding mortality and the importance of maintaining a compassionate, humanistic stance in working with death and loss, the current volume greatly extends these traditional approaches. What Harris and Bordere have done is assemble a remarkable group of contributors who collectively bring to light what conventional treatments of diversity and practice guidelines tend to obscure—namely the sometimes flagrant and often subtle injustices and failures of political, economic, medical, and even human service professions in meeting people of different cultural groups in moments of great need and vulnerability. Following the lead of the editors themselves, several of the authors ground their comments and analysis in personal accounts of empathic failures, therapeutic ruptures, or simple arrogance born of the ignorance of social, educational and cultural factors implicit in crucial interactions between patients, families, or grieving clients on the one hand and governmental or healthcare systems on the other. Moreover, they consistently anchor their advocacy of cultural humility and social action in highly engaging, realistic case studies that reveal both the abuses suffered by marginalized, stigmatized, or relatively powerless groups and the often touching or inspiring shifts in consciousness that can help ameliorate these same pervasive problems. Readers are therefore likely to complete the book with greater discomfort regarding the typical provision of medical and psychosocial services at the end of life and in bereavement, but also with greater capacity to deeply reflect on their own contexts of work, and their role in abetting or resisting oppressive practices.

Augmenting the depth and critical clarity of nearly all of the chapters of this book are its surprising breadth and detail. With a focus on social justice as the consistent leitmotif, individual chapters trace the evolution of various authors' consciousness of the problem; probe distinctive concerns and resources of social groups as diverse as African Americans, First Nations peoples, and the aged; and shed light on the unique needs of vulnerable populations such as incarcerated women, the developmentally disabled, and the dying. Moreover, they challenge "sacred cows" that tacitly or explicitly support inequities in the provision of care and the implicit priorities and prejudices that legitimate them, whether these stem from materialist or religious values. And finally, they offer and

Series Editor's Foreword

illustrate a wide range of practices to hone reflective practice, cultivate community, and promote recognition of systemic failings that complicate the lives of both care providers and those they strive to serve. In short, the Handbook of Social Justice in Loss and Grief lives up to its name, and should make a clarion contribution to the training of death and bereavement professionals for years to come.

Robert A. Neimeyer, Ph.D.
Series Editor

Foreword
Situating Social Justice and Diversity Issues within the Context of Loss and Grief

Kenneth J. Doka

One of the comments I appreciated most when *Disenfranchised Grief: Recognizing Hidden Sorrow* was published in 1989 was that it added a sociological voice into the study of grief—heretofore considered only from an intrapsychic perspective. *Disenfranchised Grief: Recognizing Hidden Sorrow*, after all, reminded us of the many ways that the norms about social support influenced the grieving process.

However, we need to return even further to address the ways that social class influences the care of dying and bereaved individuals. We may have to go back another two decades to the publication of David Sudnow's (1967) *Passing On: The Social Organization of Dying*, in which he introduced the concept of *social value* and reaffirmed that our mothers were right about wearing clean underwear. On a serious note, Sudnow (1967) found that the perceived social value of a patient deeply affected the quality of care. For example, medical staff would place far more effort in saving an unconscious, well-dressed business man than they would a homeless man smelling of alcohol and urine.

That is what makes Harris and Bordere's *Handbook of Social Justice in Loss and Grief* such a valued edition to the field. It adds a significant voice—one that not only promotes a more sociological perspective to a field dominated by intrapsychic models but a perspective that challenges us with advocating for social justice—a perspective that is often dormant. They integrate multicultural, social justice, and feminist perspectives—possibly for the first time—to ask thanatologists to be more critical in assessing the ways that culture, class, gender, and race affect access to care and caring for persons struggling with dying, loss, and grief.

This is a very personal issue. Though my father's side of the family is middle class and white, one of my cousins on that side married a man who could best be described as a drifter/dreamer always looking for the "big break." They moved throughout the country as her husband drifted from one business venture to another. Sometimes they literally were a step ahead of their creditors. Naturally, they never carried any health insurance. My cousin was experiencing varied difficulties but could never afford the tests recommended. When she was finally hospitalized, the suspected cancer was, in fact, diagnosed. It had advanced too far for anything other than palliative care. She died in her early 50s.

Harris and Bordere's *Handbook of Social Justice in Loss and Grief* has many strengths that need to be acknowledged. First they recognize that we simultaneously belong to multiple culture groupings of race, class, gender, ethnicity—and even occupational cultures. As such we juggle varied cultural identities that assume relevance throughout our day. In effect, we move in and out of privilege and power.

The concept of power—evident throughout the book—is a worthy addition to our thinking in thanatology. When I did some of my graduate work at Wayne State University, I had a professor, Constantina Safilos Rothschild, who in the early 1970s, was just beginning to explore and to develop feminist theory in her marriage and family course. I remember then the insights she shared as we investigated the implications of power in family relationships. Harris and Bordere offer a similar gift to thanatology—the need to consider how power and concepts that imply differential power, such as Sudnow's (1967) concept of *social value*, influence palliative care and services to individuals who are grieving.

Another gift of the book is that however ethereal concepts such as *social justice* can sound, the authors of the chapters root them well. Chapters constantly explore case examples as well as offering provocative questions that allow further exploration of the material. In short the book offers a great model of pedagogical practice—bridging theory, research, and practice well.

At the very least, Harris and Bordere's *Handbook of Social Justice in Loss and Grief* asks us to be reflective—constantly questioning ourselves about the ways that our thoughts and experiences of gender, class, race, ethnicity, and occupation influence our perceptions of those we work for and with and how such perceptions shape our care. It reminds us that even the best intentioned actions that are culturally insensitive or indifferent can lead to unforeseen consequences. As I read, I was reminded of Fadiman's (1997) book—*The Spirit Catches You and You Fall Down*. Fadiman (1997) recounts a case study of a young girl, a Hmong child with epilepsy, brought to a California hospital for care. The physician and medical staff are devoted to her care as is the family. Yet cultural miscommunication, the inability to understand each other's perspective, as well as the power of the hospital to enforce its standard of effective care, had disastrous consequences.

Harris and Bordere's *Handbook of Social Justice in Loss and Grief* offers a possible antidote—a call to sensitivity of all the dimensions of diversity—and to a renewed sense of social justice. We can all benefit from the lessons and reminders so evident—and so needed—in *Handbook of Social Justice in Loss and Grief*.

Kenneth J. Doka, PhD
Professor, The College of New Rochelle
Senior Consultant, The Hospice Foundation of America

References

Doka, K. (Ed.). (1989). *Disenfranchised grief: Recognizing hidden sorrow*. Lexington, MA: Lexington Press.
Fadiman, A. (1997). *The spirit catches you and you fall down*. New York, NY: Farrar, Straus, & Giroux.
Sudnow, D. (1967). *Passing on: The social organization of dying*. Englewood Cliffs, NJ: Prentice-Hall.

Preface

Ronald K. Barrett

After a routine physical exam, Dr. Murray noticed some exceptional shifts in Kwabina's labs—especially a jump in his PSA rates from 2.0 to 8.0 and exceptionally high protein levels. Otherwise, there were no other noticeable symptoms. He was advised to get a biopsy and a CT bone scan. The results revealed an aggressive form of cancer on the prostate. His health insurance coverage limited his options for treatment and authorized one referral to a specialist for a consultation. At his first consultation the expert said: "I have good and bad news. The bad news is that you have cancer, but the good news is with a new lifelong treatment you can survive." A few days after recovering from the brutal delivery of the doctor's prognosis, he realized the seriousness of his condition. He was compelled to respect the old adage of getting three expert opinions and sought out the best local experts for a second and third opinion. He utilized monies from his savings to cover the out-of-pocket costs for these two consultations that his health insurance would not cover. He soon learned and was enlightened about important health and treatment options. This information made a major difference in his final decisions about treatment options, risks and side effects, as well as the predicted health outcomes.

This is *my story*. (During my 2000 sabbatical in West Africa I was given the African name "Kwabina" in an official naming ceremony.) While going through every aspect of my personal experience in the health care system I was aware of my privilege—privileged to have a doctor who was thorough enough to notice irregularities in my labs; privileged to have the knowledge about health systems and care to insist on a second and third opinion; privileged to have the means to afford to go out of my health plan to get a second and third medical consultation; privileged to have health insurance to support an immediate treatment plan for an aggressive form of cancer that was otherwise undetectable; privileged to have health insurance support of the final phase of my treatment plan; privileged to have received exceptional care at many levels of care via my perceived social status. In my personal experience as a patient in the health care system I have had a surreal awareness of differences in health, health care, health care access, quality of life, and death for many, both locally and globally. In far too many circumstances, there is what Dr. Harold Washington calls the "green screen" which universally for most, limits their access to quality health care and determines their quality of life as well as their predisposition and risk for other morbidity risk factors, and premature death—typically more painful and earlier than most.

I am also privileged to share my story for this book, which connects concerns of social justice with death, dying, and bereavement, as these are topics I am also personally and professionally passionate about. My personal experiences in the health care system have been humbling and educational, so much so that I would recommend some personal patient experience in the health care system for all health care professionals, educators, and advocates. While I would not wish on

Preface

anyone a diagnosis with anything as fear-provoking as cancer, some hopefully less serious diagnosis can be quite as educational, sensitizing us to the nuances of care and the experiences of navigating health care institutions and systems of care. Just as important to me, my recent experiences teaching in our study abroad programs while studying international health disparities have also sensitized me to privilege, poverty, and inequities in health, quality of life, health care, and mortality rates globally—especially in Europe, West Africa, the Caribbean, South America, and the U.S.A.

This book is recommended for health practitioners, therapists, social workers, and social justice scholars and researchers, educators, advocates, members of professional and paraprofessional associations, community organizers, death educators, students, and scholars in health disparities, cross-cultural medicine, cultural anthropologists, clergy, social scientists, political scientists, legal scholars (the list can continue to many more) to educate and advocate for the important awareness of the role of social inequalities in health, quality of life, health care access, and supportive care that explain personal and cohort health outcomes. For example, mortality rates are related and correlated with certain social, environmental, and societal factors. In addition, both my own personal story and established research all conclude universally that poverty and socioeconomic issues remain the greatest barriers to quality health care and quality of life for many who have no voice, and too few advocates. It is through thoughtful scholarship and study of social justice that we can begin to educate, advocate, and effect social change. The book calls attention to these matters and humanistic social justice concerns that affect many who are marginalized, oppressed, and underserved.

The editors have assembled an impressive list of experts who nicely cover many of the important concerns and global issues related to health, health care, health outcomes, mortality rates, and professional issues within the context of death, dying, and bereavement. I am also privileged to know the editors personally and know that they "walk the talk," and as academics they have personally connected research, scholarship, education, and service with the reality of social inequality and social justice for people who face and work with loss, change, death, and grief. The editors unapologetically address the reality of social inequality and social injustice in relationship to these issues. It is an important conversation that begs for more discourse. This volume is an impressive contribution.

Respectfully,

Ronald Keith ("Kwabina") Barrett

Editors' Note

It was with great sadness that we learned of the death of Ron Barrett just as this book was going to press. We feel very honored that he shared his story with us; it is our hope that this book will carry forward Ron's voice and passion for social justice and social change for those who are marginalized and oppressed.

Acknowledgments

Dr. Harris: I would like to express my gratitude to the following individuals who encouraged me to think critically and broadly about experiences, both professional and personal: Dr. Joan Mason-Grant, Dr. Anne Cummings, Dr. Susan Amussen, Dr. Stanford Searl, and Roshi (Dr.) Joan Halifax. I would also like to express my profound appreciation to Joanna Radbord, LLB, whose understanding about oppression and vulnerability greatly influenced my thinking and writing, as well as my life. I would also like to acknowledge my life partner, Brad Hunter, and the myriad ways that his deep practice and compassionate intention have provided me with a foundation of support and a wellspring of love from which to draw. And, of course, gratitude to my daughter Lauren, for teaching that love involves learning how to hold on and let go at the same time. Finally, I would also express my profound appreciation and admiration for my co-editor, Dr. Tashel Bordere, whose work and life exemplify conscious living and engagement in this world.

Dr. Bordere: I am honored and humbled to be a part of this important undertaking with my dear colleague, friend, mentor, and co-editor, Dr. Darcy Harris, whose work and dedication to social justice issues I so immensely admire. I wish to thank Dr. Harris for her leadership and the opportunity to embark on this transformative and healing journey together in the conceptualization and completion of this book. Special thanks also to my long time mentor, Dr. Ronald "Ron" Barrett for his wisdom and shared belief in the significance of addressing topics covered in this book.

In the realm of family, I am eternally grateful to my grandparents Walter and Edith Price, who were reared in a historical time in which they were not able to exercise many of the rights and privileges that I am afforded. Thanks for preparing me for a world that you could only imagine and for equipping me with a voice through which groups that have been silenced and absent from dominant discourses may be heard. I extend my heartfelt appreciation to my wonderfully thoughtful daughter Zaydie Ann (and LEB—born in my heart). I am constantly motivated and inspired by your keen curiosities, bravery in new experiences, and high expectations of me to complete this important work "plus 1000 more." To my soulmate and partner, Dr. Kate Grossman, I offer profound gratitude for valuing and sharing my commitment to issues of injustice and enfranchisement in grief and loss. Thank you also to Naomi and Floyd Grossman. Finally, I give my greatest thanks and appreciation to the person who has had the most profound influence on my personal and professional development, my mother and best friend, Delores Price. Thank you for constant support and encouragement to think creatively and critically, engage compassionately, respond graciously, and walk courageously with faith and good humor in this world.

Introduction

Darcy L. Harris and Tashel C. Bordere

Introduction—Darcy

As a child, I was exposed to some of the anti-establishment sentiment that was widespread in the 1960s. I was quite young at the time, but I remember feeling curious about the messages of people like Malcolm X, Martin Luther King, and Gloria Steinem. These public figures were passionate, and at times, angry in their speeches, and I wondered what had made them feel this way. I was riveted to the music that emanated from the Woodstock festival, much of which focused on issues that I hadn't even thought about. The television was always on at dinner time in my home when I was growing up. I would watch images of anti-war protests and civil rights marches juxtaposed with popular programs where all the heroes and heroines were white and wore white hats (or white pearl necklaces), with people of color and different ethnic backgrounds portrayed in terms of their usefulness and service to the white protagonists. Being a white girl born into a middle class family, I was, for the most part, oblivious to how I was privileged as well as how I was silenced. It never occurred to me that I could *choose* whether or not to listen to messages about racial equity or gender parity because I did not believe these issues were relevant to me personally.

Growing up in a military home, I was raised to be proud of my country and to defend the values on which the nation was founded—fierce independence, capitalism, individual rights, and freedom of speech. I celebrated these rights and became very accustomed to references to these freedoms in the speeches of public figures and in political arguments. I looked with pity upon others who did not have what I had—and I bought into the belief that every person had the ability to succeed and prosper if s/he simply made the "right" choices in life. My privilege was in my ability to choose and my obliviousness to the places and people where those choices were not an option. I was blind to this privilege for a long time. Much later, I realized that there were many people, even in my small world, whose lives were significantly limited by discrimination, labeling, and dismissive language—all of which had implications for the opportunities that were available to them, their access to needed services, and the ability to determine their lifestyle and everyday life choices.

I completed my undergraduate degree in nursing and practiced in several small cities in the Southeastern United States. I worked in various hospital settings, usually with critically ill or terminally ill patients. Within my first decade of working as a nurse, I learned about many things that were not taught in school. When I worked in critical care, I was aware that despite my best efforts, some of the families of the black patients in my care would not readily offer information to me that I requested. It was apparent that they did not trust me, and I felt that I had done nothing to elicit such a response. I was shocked when I encountered discrimination from black staff members when I was the only white charge nurse on the unit. Of course, it didn't occur to me at the time that I had been placed in the role of the charge nurse of the unit even though I was the least experienced nurse there; most likely this position (with its higher pay scale) was given to me because I was white. When I tried to advocate for changes in staffing because I felt concern that patient care was being compromised, I was told by the (male) director of nursing that it must be my "time of the month" and that I should go home, get some sleep, and I would feel better the next day. It did not occur to me at the time that if I had been a white male doctor complaining about staffing, the issue might have been addressed constructively. Instead, I became concerned about being labeled as a "whiner" or that I could lose my job if I persisted in my efforts to try to increase staffing to levels that would have been more humane to both the patients and the nurses. In addition, I encountered sexual advances and I was frequently the brunt of sexually laden comments about my appearance by male staff—mostly doctors—who were above reproach due to their positions of power within the hospital, and so I learned to endure this treatment and try to act like the comments were funny or somehow flattering so that my job was not threatened.

Interestingly, it was after a series of personal losses that I started looking at my experiences in the context of a larger social and political web. I realized that there were, indeed, some things that sheer determination and fortitude could not change, such as the fact that I was a woman. At first, I felt like a failure for not being able to accomplish all the things that I thought I "should" be able to achieve. I was exhausted. My marriage suffered as I became more aware of (and more resistant to) the requirements of submission to male authority within the faith tradition in which the relationship had initially been founded. My mother died when I was 30 years old. Her message to me when I was growing up was that, as a woman, my appearance could give me social power; it was a means by which I could have a good life. However, in her final days as she was dying of cancer, she began to talk more candidly with me about her own choices, including her realization that life should be about more than looking a certain way or pleasing others.

During this same time, I was also at an impasse in my career. I had made decisions along the way with the idea that my career would be secondary to that of my husband and family commitments. When I was completing my undergraduate degree, my professors and colleagues just assumed that I would be applying to either graduate school or medical school and they were surprised when I did not continue after I completed nursing school. The message that had been engrained in me was that if I furthered my education, I was choosing a career over my family, and this choice would have been considered subversive to the conservative religious system in which I resided at that time. However, as I watched my mother die and came to the painful realization that life was not what I had been told it would be, I began to question many of these underlying values and the social messages that were embedded within them. My life as I had known it came crashing down as my faith was rendered meaningless, my marriage ended, my mother died, and I experienced complete burnout in my job. My ability to function in my personal relationships and my professional role was undermined by very unrealistic expectations and the belief that following all the social rules and messages I had been taught would provide me with happiness and fulfillment, and I was anything but happy or fulfilled. Out of necessity, I finally took time to reflect upon the difference between the values and beliefs that I had been taught when I was growing up versus the reality of how things actually worked in the world . . . and it was a painful time. I felt like a failure and I experienced a profound sense of self-loathing because I was "weak," which was not permitted in my vocabulary when I was growing up. I was a "victim" of sorts, and this identity was highly stigmatizing to me.

During this time of reflection, I realized that many of the constraints that I experienced at that time were not just external to me, but also within me—reflected in how I valued and thought of myself. As I pondered my situation and the losses I had experienced, I also began to look outward. It was almost as if my vulnerability allowed me to see my patients, my coworkers, and many others in a much more holistic way—as people who were part of families, communities, cultures, and social/political systems. I also began to identify the various ways that power was wielded and ascribed within the context of health care settings, religious institutions, and social structures. Slowly, I began to see how many of the so-called individual problems of people were often rooted in social and culturally complex, interconnected, systemic factors. I finally understood the anger that was present in the voices of those public figures who spoke out against injustice when I was a young child. As I began to emerge out of grief and shame over my perceived "failures," I made a promise that I would try to see with fresh eyes—eyes that were open and aware of the realities of discrimination and oppression—and to recognize how many people's daily lives and choices were often affected by systemic forces over which they had very little influence. I also made a commitment that the vision from these eyes would be guided by compassion for others—and for me as well.

While I consider the time in my life when these losses occurred to be very painful, it was also a pivotal time for me in many ways. I began to see the potential and power of human resilience in the face of oppression and loss. I also clearly saw the way I was interconnected with my patients, colleagues, friends, family, and community. The pain and angst from loss and injustice taught me powerful lessons about suffering, compassion, and grace. These lessons have continued to deepen over time, and I am grateful for these experiences and the way they have opened me to suffering, vulnerability, and pain. I also feel a great deal of gratitude for the opportunities that have opened before me as well. I eventually received graduate training as a therapist and later completed my doctoral studies, and I now devote my life's work to teaching those who wish to relieve suffering as their life's work.

Introduction—Tashel

For as long as I can recall, I have been an advocate for social justice. Although some might attribute my propensity toward fairness to my Taurus zodiac sign, I instead assign my commitment to social justice issues and cultural understandings to conscious decision-making grounded in early experiences within the context of my familial and educational settings. In my formative years and beyond, I was exposed to struggle but taught much more about survival, about the ways that people have risen, about the ways that people have been catapulted throughout history to social action and advocacy in the face of egregious discriminatory practices. I was socialized memorizing Langston Hughes' "Mother to Son," and William Ernest Henley's "Invictus" (1888), which emphasized:

> It matters not how strait the gate,
> How charged with punishments the scroll.
> I am the master of my fate:
> I am the captain of my soul.
>
> (p. 56)

The message conveyed to me early on was that many people had worked and continue to work tirelessly to improve social conditions and life opportunities for me, and the spoken and unspoken expectation was that I would continue in the furtherance of these efforts so that my own children and other marginalized groups could also experience a more just life. Prominent songs like Whitney Houston's, "I believe the children are our future" (Masser & Creed, 1985, track 9), which I frequently belted out in the shower and sang almost yearly at elementary school functions, reinforced such beliefs and socialization practices. I was also reared with my two older male siblings by my mother, who modeled strength and resilience, and supported my "gender equality" and "youngest child" advocacy efforts and less than traditional ways of thinking and being in the universe.

During one of my recent trips back home to New Orleans, I ran into a childhood friend. We immediately began reminiscing about our days of bike riding, tag, and the intense tackle football "tournaments" on our neighbor's front lawn in which I was the only girl to play. I began to reflect on how miraculous it was that I made it unscathed through several years of the rough and tough play that was characteristic of tackle football during my formative years without equipment or other protective gear. I was just about to brag about my quick feet and outstanding touchdown record when my dear friend interrupted with laughter, "Your brother wouldn't let anyone NEAR you!" Time stood still. It was not until this precious yet enlightening moment in my adult life that I realized my brother had been blocking for me. All those years, across games too many to count, my brother had blocked for me. I still wish to own that I was indeed a talented football player, not "a girl football player," with very swift and fancy footwork. However, the ways in which my older brother used his privilege to serve as my ally cannot be understated. I was protected through these potentially dangerous experiences because someone more experienced and bigger in stature (and potentially perceived as threatening to opponents), consciously chose to serve as gatekeeper and advocate on my behalf.

As I matured and moved from the safety of my familial setting in childhood to the less secure settings of adolescence and adulthood, many of the protections that had been in place began to seemingly dissipate. It was then that I started to witness and experience more pronounced forms of disenfranchisement from the college course at a southern university in which I earned an "A" but received a "B" because the professor "had never had a black student earn an 'A' in her Religious Studies course before" to the more profound loss of my older living child due to the lack of parental rights in the dissolution of same sex partnerships.

Disenfranchisement feels awful for most anyone who experiences it around anything in which meaning is derived. It is debilitating and can be damaging. In each of these instances, I felt very deceived, angry, and, at times, lost as I was faced with the reality that this power I thought I carried in the palm of my hands "as master of my fate," based on my childhood understandings of justice and power, had certain limits and did not exist to the extent that I had imagined or had been taught. I quickly and painfully learned that social and political power can indeed impose real restrictions on personal power and opportunity structures among people who exist in the margins of society.

This notion was further brought home to me since the time of my adolescence in witnessing the all too frequent loss experiences of youth bereaved by deaths due to gun violence that continue to go unnoticed and unsupported.

So why am I so devoted to this book? As much as the world is improving, we continue to exist in a society colored by nationality, ability, race, class, sex, age, and other cultural variables. However, this book is not about everything that everyone is doing wrong. It is, in fact, written with the premise that most individuals desire to further their knowledge and skills in diversity and social justice, and wish to implement them both in practice and in their everyday lives. In my work as a professor and researcher, and across the workshops and trainings that I have conducted across the country related to culture, I have found that the desires of facilitating social justice efforts among many well-intentioned individuals are sometimes superseded by fears (e.g., of offending), feelings of inadequacy (e.g., not knowing enough), misconceptions about the amount of work required, and/or by thought processes that promote "culture" as optional in work with the bereaved. I am motivated to co-write and co-edit this book because it contains a wealth of information that will help lift those barriers and further efforts in culturally conscientious practice, pedagogy, research, and beyond with otherwise vulnerable and marginalized individuals and families. I think of my work and this book, in particular, as raising the volume of the voices of populations that might not otherwise be heard. This book provides enlightenment around the additional complications of loss when social and political barriers are present and the ways in which we can use this information to be with families from a position of cultural humility and form alliances with, or even "block" for families who may never know our influence.

This Book

Why are we bringing forward a book that explores issues of social justice and diversity in contexts of death, dying, loss, and grief? Because we feel it is needed. The tendency to focus on individual experiences without taking into account the social and political contexts in which they belong is myopic and short-sighted. It is impossible to try to understand someone without an appreciation for how social forces, culture, political messages, and access to resources profoundly shape that person and her/his choices. The ability to look at issues of justice and inclusion requires us to become aware of these contexts so that we can then make conscious choices as care providers, as students, academics, and as people—who choose to demonstrate compassion in a world that is often blind to the painful effects of oppression, discrimination, and lack of access to basic necessities and resources.

Both of us have worked extensively with individuals who have faced terminal illness, experienced significant losses, and who have endured the deaths of loved ones and parts of themselves. Each person's experiences are embedded within the messages, expectations, and political ideation of their social sphere. It is impossible to separate out someone from the social context in which that individual has developed and now lives. If we are committed to compassionate practice in caring for individuals who face death, loss, and grief, then we must commit ourselves to being open to our shared human experience while at the same time, deeply respecting the rich diversity that exists within these same experiences.

The purpose of this book is to provide the reader with an opportunity to reflect on how social and political forces may have an impact upon various individuals who experience issues related to loss and grief. The concept of socially "just" practice is one that incorporates a deeper understanding of individual experiences of marginalization and oppression in relation to class, race, ethnicity, gender, and other forms of social inequality. There is a plethora of information about assisting individuals and families in end of life care, about supporting bereaved individuals, and also on the grieving process. There is also a great deal of literature that explores issues such as class, race, gender, and equality, but very little has been written about the social and political forces that underscore the experiences of loss and grief. It is our hope that the topics presented in this volume will provide an opportunity for the reader to think broadly and more holistically about how individuals experience loss, change, and grief.

We begin with a basic exploration of concepts in the first chapter. Here, we clarify some basic terms and principles, and provide the foundation for learning to look at issues and experiences from this broader "lens." In the next part, we begin to explore issues related to social status, policy, and politics, and how these issues may have a direct impact upon overall health, well-being, and access to resources.

The next part of the book explores issues related to groups. In this part, we look at how differences in social and ethnic backgrounds may significantly impact upon how care is given and received, how to sensitively approach care from a perspective of cultural humility, and we begin to explore loss experiences of specific groups that have traditionally been marginalized and stigmatized in mainstream political and social policies.

Part four addresses issues that are related to specific individual experiences in social contexts. Specifically, how do diagnoses affect grieving individuals in their experience of loss? How are specific experiences and processes affected by social messages regarding who and what outcomes are valued, who is marginalized, and how experiences of aging, disability, and bereavement are often profoundly affected by the social norms and messages that are embedded within the culture?

We close the book with a part that addresses various practical implications and intervention strategies that are oriented toward socially just practices, including the role of engaged spirituality, rituals and advocacy, clinical social work practice that incorporates social justice as a core value, and the ability of caregivers to function within systems that are often at odds with their values of compassionate care. Because we are both educators, we have included a section to identify key terms and questions for discussion at the end of each chapter. We hope these additions will assist readers to more deeply reflect upon and engage with the material that they have just read.

We welcome our readers to embark on this journey with us, and we hope this book will provide an opportunity for reflection, awareness, and necessary change so that we are able to embrace the wide range of human experiences from a deeper and more compassionate stance.

Darcy L. Harris and Tashel C. Bordere

Question for Reflection

The authors state that "each person's experiences are embedded within the messages, expectations, and political ideation of their social sphere." Consider a personal experience of illness or bereavement. In what ways do you see that your experience was influenced by your social/cultural context? How do you imagine it might have differed if you were of a different socioeconomic class, race, gender, or sexual orientation?

References

Henley, W. E. (1888). *A book of verses* (3rd ed.) (p. 56). New York, NY: Scribner & Welford.

Hughes, L. (1994). Mother to Son. In A. Rampersad & D. Roessel (Eds.), *The collected poems of Langston Hughes* (p. 30). New York, NY: Estate of Langston Hughes. (Original work published in 1922, Crisis, p. 87).

Masser, M., & Creed, L. (Songwriters). (1985). Greatest love of all [Recorded by Whitney Houston]. *Whitney Houston* [CD], New York, NY: Arista Records.

Part One
Introductory Concepts

In this part, we provide some foundational material to serve as the context for the rest of the book.

We begin by exploring the elements of social justice and the various issues that are often considered when adopting socially just practices. Some of the terminology that will be used throughout the book is presented here as well, so that the reader will know the precise meaning and usage of these terms as they occur in various chapters.

We then introduce the concepts of critical theory and analysis, providing several case study examples to help the reader begin the process of critical inquiry in situations that may be relevant to loss and grief. Readers are asked at several points to stop and consider how issues related to power dynamics, social status, and cultural/ethnic identification may have an impact upon access to resources, care delivery, and choices in contexts associated with end of life care, loss, and grief.

These two chapters essentially "set the stage" for the subsequent chapters in the book. Readers are invited to return to these two chapters periodically for reinforcement and clarity of terms and a reminder of the overarching theme(s) for this volume.

1

Social Justice Conceptualizations in Grief and Loss

Tashel C. Bordere

Never doubt that a small group of thoughtful committed citizens can change the world; indeed, it's the only thing that ever has.

Margaret Mead

In a game of coed, intramural flag football, during graduate school, and in the absence of my brother who otherwise "blocked" for me, I was tackled and injured by an opponent charging full speed as I ran the ball just short of a touchdown. As I sat with friends in the hospital emergency waiting room, in nearly unbearable pain, I grimaced and dropped my head. And peering down through torrential tears that clouded my vision, I discerned the brightly colored flaps of the orange flag, still intact, blanketed across my lap, ever so tightly fastened around my waist. In that moment, a frown-like smile, like sun through a cloud and brief escape from pain. He broke my leg, I thought in defeat-like pride, but he didn't get my flag.

As we think of social justice, it is common to conjure violent images and associations with protests and other vicious battles. Although such acts may undoubtedly accompany the journey to overcome barriers that further social justice efforts, the actual experience of justice is often felt in the most silent of moments, yielding individuals a deep sense of solace and broadened opportunity structure. It is this solace and quest for equitable opportunities that drive many of us in our work with the bereaved.

Social Justice and Diversity

In this chapter, I explicate social justice and associated concepts, explore applications of these terms, and conclude with a death and loss case scenario. Foundational concepts around social justice, diversity, and loss have distinct meanings yet are inextricably intertwined. An understanding of these concepts gives us a shared language and helps us in our work in bereavement.

Social justice as defined in this chapter is based on Bell's (1997) framing of it which includes:

> Full and equal participation of all groups in a society that is mutually shaped to meet their needs. Social justice includes a vision of society in which the distribution of resources is equitable and all members are physically and psychologically safe and secure.
>
> (p. 3)

Socially just practice intersects with *culturally conscientious practice*, which involves meeting the variant needs of families through an understanding and openness to evolving knowledge of their social locations (e.g., family structure, ability, sexuality, class, nationality, ethnicity, spirituality; Bordere, 2009). When we attend to the social locations in which individuals are situated, we are better positioned to enter into collaborative relationships and engage in community-centered practice that promotes equity and human dignity (Fowler, 2008).

Culture

The concept of *culture* is often equated with *minority status* and hence associated with under-representation (e.g., Latino, female). However, individuals across groups are cultural beings. *Culture* refers to the beliefs, attitudes, values (collectivism vs. individualism), behaviors (family roles), and practices (e.g., death rituals) shared by a group (Gardiner & Kosmitzki, 2011) to support its survival within various contexts (Hoopes, 1979, p. 3). Culture is largely unconscious. That is, we participate in behaviors and decision-making processes each day, often without conscious awareness. In presentations and workshops, I typically encourage individuals (and I assume the same challenge) to unlearn something new each day, to be mindful of everyday behaviors, choices, interactions, and thought processes. Why did I, for example, order my meal before dessert when I went to the restaurant for the bread pudding? In death and bereavement, what thought process has allowed or not allowed me to reach out to an underserved population within the community in which my program is located?

Culture gives people identity and is often transmitted across generations. Some aspects of culture are represented visibly through symbols (e.g., memorial t-shirts and tattoos, New Orleans *Second Line* funeral rituals) while other aspects of culture are not as directly observable (e.g., the meaning of rebuilding a lost home after a natural disaster). There is great diversity *within* and *across* cultural groups. For example, diversity is found *within* disabled populations (individuals with cognitive and/or physical disabilities) and *across* populations of disabled and abled individuals. The same behaviors may have unique symbolic meanings for individuals within and across groups. Thus, being competent in one interaction does not ensure competence in another interaction even with an individual from the same group (Rosenblatt, 2009).

Privilege and Power

Privilege is a phenomenon of which to be aware when exploring dynamics and interactions with bereaved populations. In understanding *privilege*, let us distinguish between *unearned entitlements* and *unearned advantages* (McIntosh, 2007). Unearned entitlements refer to basic things that everyone should have, such as a sense of safety at school or work and accessible health care. Comparatively, an *unearned advantage* is a form of privilege in which *unearned entitlements*, or things that should be available to everyone, are limited to particular groups. That is, people who are part of dominant/power/privilege groups or located in the "center" benefit and have access to things that people in less-power groups or who exist in the margins do not. Rodriguez, McNeal, and Cauce (2008) explain the concept of the "center":

> People at the center or mainstream of a particular social group have the utmost privilege. With every move away from the center, layers of privilege are removed, and persons at the very edge of the margins may be marginalized by people who are themselves marginalized by others.
>
> (p. 226)

We all have personal power. We have the power to determine our thoughts and perceptions of events. However, the power located at the center that dominant or privileged groups are able to access includes social, economic, and political power or the power to determine, make rules that govern society, and ultimately decide for others. This creates *oppression* or the "double-bind" in which

> living one's life is confined and shaped by forces and barriers which are not accidental or occasional . . . but are systematically related to each other in such a way as to catch one between and among them and restrict or penalize motion in any direction.
>
> (Frye, 1998)

A perceived exemption from privileged status and participation in the cycle of oppression is found among some who otherwise exist in dominant/advantaged groups. This happens for a variety reasons, including a misconception of privilege as a worry-free life of wealth ("But I'm not rich!"). Although groups and institutions have and continue to accumulate wealth at the expense of others, privilege is not synonymous with wealth or a challenge-free life. It does, however, include benefits such as being offered pain medication more frequently than individuals from underrepresented groups for the same injury or health condition (white male privilege); being given information about a death (ability privilege); and the ability to share a room with one's life partner in an assisted living facility (heterosexual privilege).

We all have multiple social identities (e.g., age, race, ability, ethnicity, gender, family structure) that intersect. Thus, everyone may experience some degree of privilege and disadvantage. The more characteristics or social identities that connect individuals to privileged statuses, the more access to resources and opportunities they experience. Conversely, the more characteristics that place individuals in less-power or target groups, the less likely they are to share equally in the power base and benefit from accompanying opportunities. An abled, English-speaking, heterosexual male will experience more privilege in American culture than an individual who is underrepresented on those characteristics. Privilege may be gained or lost as a function of cultural shifts, experiences, and developmental transitions. For instance, a young able-bodied female who benefits from advantages associated with youth privilege will be targeted in later life as a consequence of ageism and may struggle to access affordable, quality health care. As civil rights leader, Martin Luther King (1963, Letter from the Birmingham Jail) emphasized, "Injustice anywhere is a threat to justice everywhere."

Individuals may be unaware of their privileged status and its benefits. This ability to not consider or be aware of one's advantaged position in society, or what is described as the "luxury of obliviousness," is a privilege in itself (Johnson, 2006). Think now of dominant or power groups that come to mind for you in the society in which you live and of a characteristic or feature of your social identity that places you in a power group(s). In her section of the book's introduction, Darcy Harris wrote about growing up with this type of privilege. As highlighted, culture is largely unconscious and many norms, particularly advantages, become taken for granted. Thus, it may require some time and thought to bring these aspects of your identity to conscious awareness.

The initial awareness of privilege can be difficult as privilege does mean benefiting at the expense of someone else. A common feeling around privilege includes *guilt* (e.g., white guilt related to white privilege; Iyer, Leach, & Crosby, 2003; Powell, Branscombe, & Schmitt, 2005). Mixed feelings may also come with the recognition of privilege. It may be distressing to realize that one is benefiting at the expense of another. At the same time, privilege or unearned advantages can be hard to relinquish. Who wants to give up extra safety and police protection in their neighborhoods, the ease of shopping without being followed as a result of age or racial profiling, or the ability to have their partner accompany them in the intensive care unit during hospitalization?

Alliances

As a way of breaking down oppressive forces, some individuals in dominant groups recognize their privileged status and form *alliances* or use their unearned advantages to benefit less power groups (Ayvazian, 2007). For example, Angelina Jolie and Brad Pitt, famous American actors, delayed their wedding plans until same-sex couples were also afforded the right to marry in some states and could share in the 1000-plus benefits and protections provided under federal law through the act of marriage (Human Rights Canpaign, n.d.). Ayvazian (2007) highlights that "allied behavior is intentional, overt, consistent activity that challenges prevailing patterns of oppression, makes privileges that are so often invisible visible, and facilitates empowerment of persons targeted by oppression" (p. 724). Where there is privilege, there is disparity. Where there are allies, there is greater hope for change. What are some ways in which you have functioned or wish to function as an ally?

Marginalization

People who are marginalized tend to have some awareness of the limited resources (e.g., social, political, economic, emotional) and opportunities available to them compared to people in the *center* who may or may not recognize their privileged status. Less powerful groups also tend to be cognizant of the ways that they may be perceived (devalued) or treated (exploited) as members of marginalized groups. They are also socialized with an understanding of privilege and dominance or an "outsider-within" perspective (Collins, 1990, p. 12). Survival in the margins is contingent upon such awareness and socialization processes. In *Souls of Black Folk*, DuBois (1903/1969) describes this dual awareness as analogous to navigating life with a *double-consciousness*:

> It is a peculiar sensation, this *double-consciousness*, this sense of always looking at one's self through the eyes of others, of measuring one's soul by the tape of a world that looks on in amused contempt and pity. One ever feels his [her] two-ness, ... two souls, two thoughts, two unreconciled strivings; two warring ideals in one dark body, whose dogged strength alone keeps it from being torn asunder.
>
> (p. 45)

Where less dominant groups are less aware, they are reminded of their marginalized status and disenfranchisement through policies and messages received within their social and political contexts. I was familiar, for example, with the idea that same-sex unions lacked many of the rights or unearned advantages of heterosexual couples (Human Rights Campaign, n. d.). However, I did not understand the full implications until I was denied time with my own child due to an absence of custody rights in the dissolution of same-sex partnerships. In coping with the loss of my older *living* child, I was sent messages from both marginalized and privileged individuals that undermined, minimized, or denied my status as a parent and my loss experience as significant. As I grappled with this harsh reality and most difficult time of my life, I was told in reassuring tones by many well-meaning people, in both GLBTQ and heterosexual communities, that I could have *another* child, and not to worry, that my daughter (age 3 ½) was young and would *forget about me*. As if offering comfort, "Don't worry," a close friend said, "she won't remember you."

A common *fear* in socially just and culturally conscientious practice is that of *offending* (e.g., What if I say the wrong thing? What if I offend the person?). This fear is important yet also reflects an understanding of justice as relegated to an emotional process. It assumes that we will do justice by people if we avoid or minimize hurt feelings. It disregards the fact that social injustices are not as predicated on interpersonal relationships as they are on power hierarchies and inequities therein (Johnson, 2006). Although offensive statements and hurt *feelings* matter and should no doubt be considered, it is actually the diminished opportunity structure related to privilege and oppression that has larger implications. The un-affirming statements simply add another layer to oppressive forces, the icing on the cake, if you will. That is, as painful as it remains, I find ways to cope with insensitive comments and advice about child loss. However, the inability to see my child due to restricted laws has had serious and far reaching implications for me as a parent in the absence of time with my living child; for my younger child in the absence of her sibling; and for my older child in the absence of her parent, sibling, pet, and the many resources that she, as a result, is not able to access.

In work with the bereaved, it is important to explore the *depth* and *breadth* of marginalization (Rodriguez et al., 2008). That is, in what area(s), if any, does the person perceive a lack of resources (e.g., time, emotional support) as a consequence of marginalization and what is the cumulative impact of lacking these resources? In what way(s) have you experienced disenfranchisement or been targeted for a type of oppression and how were you impacted? Of course, the discourse on power dynamics also asks the question, "Who is benefiting from the marginalization of this individual/group and why?"

Stereotyping

Stereotyping involves generalizations and conclusions drawn based on limited information or on what some might call "a grain of truth." The term was originally conceptualized as the image that comes to mind when we think of a particular social group (Lippman, 1922, p. 81). Stereotypes are held without regard for variations that exist within groups (Hilton & Hippel, 1996). They are learned and may be conscious or unconscious, positive or negative, and are often revealed through our language and behaviors. They may function to preserve the energy of the perceiver as mental shortcuts (Gigerenzer, 2008) but be costly to targets of stereotyping who are inappropriately judged or treated unfairly as a result (Khan, Benda, & Stagnaro, 2012). African American youth bereaved by homicide loss, for example, are often *stereotyped* as "desensitized" based on limited information such as that found in the media. Although media images leave little room for seeing these youth as anything but gun wielding, unattached, and unfeeling, African American youth do indeed experience grief around losses they view as significant just as any other faction of society bereaved by similar losses. These youth are uniformly labeled as "desensitized" without a clear understanding of their lived experiences with violent death losses within social, political, and historical contexts. Some youth may, in fact, appear to not care or seem desensitized. However, many more youth are struggling to cope with multiple, sudden losses and are simply trying to allocate their diminishing emotional resources to the losses that matter most to them (Bordere, 2008–2009; Johnson, 2010).

Language

Language affords great power. Although language has been used both historically and in present-day societies to oppress many groups, we all have the power to unlearn, exchange and replace inappropriate terms (e.g., desensitized), like clothing in a store with ones that yield a better fit, with terms that more accurately represent people's lived experiences. Thus, one step toward socially just practice is monitoring the framing of our language, our words, our descriptors, our labels in death and non-death losses, with particular attention to those that are often stigmatized (e.g., replacing "committed suicide"—criminalized concept with "died by suicide"—non-criminalized concept). This may be achieved by gathering information through communication with the people who are living the experience and learning more about their realities from their social locations (e.g., teens' suicide or homicide loss and grief experiences in Detroit vs. Chicago).

Prejudice and Discrimination

Compared to stereotyping, which involves generalizing, *prejudice* is a biased attitude or prejudgment based on faulty thought processes (Allport, 1954). Like stereotyping, prejudice is learned and may be positive or negative. Stereotyping may be used to justify prejudicial attitudes. Prejudice is a precursor to *discrimination* or biased behaviors (actions or inactions) aimed at individuals and groups (Dovidio, Hewstone, Glick, & Esses, 2010) in efforts to oppress or maintain systems of oppression (Jones, 1972). For example, negative ideas about suicide in a religious institution may contribute to an absence of available services for suicide loss survivors. Discrimination is a process extending across generations (e.g., history of services provided). It is complex as it exists on many levels—individual (intentionally and unintentionally), institutional (laws and policies), and through social structures (health care systems, educational systems). Across the varied levels, it is important to keep in mind that discrimination (e.g., classism, racism, ageism, nationalism, heterosexism) is carried out by individuals. Oftentimes, individuals do not recognize their participation in or "the existence of institutional discrimination because laws (typically assumed to be right and moral) and long-standing or ritualized practices seem normal" (Dovidio et al., 2010, p. 11). This is particularly the case for individuals privileged by such laws who lack contact with individuals disenfranchised by these policies.

Disenfranchised Grief and Suffocated Grief

People who exist in the margins of society (e.g., youth in urban areas, death row inmates); have relationships with deceased individuals deemed as peripheral (e.g., friend, co-worker, dating partner) or stigmatized (e.g., interracial unions); or who have losses not viewed as significant (e.g., pet loss, divorce, home foreclosure) often experience grief that is "disenfranchised" or unacknowledged and unsupported both within their sub-cultures and within the larger society (Doka, 1989; 2002). African American youth, for instance, who reside in urban areas are often disenfranchised grievers. Many African American youth cope with numerous profound death losses related to gun violence and non-death losses, including the loss of safety. As previously highlighted, these youth are often inappropriately described as desensitized. Consequently, these losses are dealt with in the absence of recognition or support for their bereavement experience in primary social institutions, including educational settings, where they are expected to continue in math and writing as if a loss has not occurred (Bordere, 2014).

When a loss is disenfranchised or not acknowledged, it follows that it is typically understudied and hence limited information and resources are available for coping or for providing support. In socially just practice, having *access* to information and programs that address diverse perspectives, lived experiences, and concerns is not just important but necessary (Bordere, 2009; Fowler, 2008). For example, bereavement programs should not only be *available* in communities, but they should also be *accessible* (e.g., translator or translated information in brochures) to diverse populations.

Marginalized individuals may also experience "suffocated grief" (Bordere, 2014, p. 169) related to the penalty imposed for their grief and mourning expressions. For example, youth coping with losses by creating street memorials in the location of a peer's violent death may be charged a fine or arrested. When a verdict is read in a court case involving a death row inmate, the inmate's family members and friends must remain silent, as informed by the judge, or they will be penalized (e.g., arrested, removed from the court) for normal reactions (e.g., crying) for the anticipated loss of their cared-about person.

Further, in the absence of student bereavement leave policies at most universities, students lack rights around academic support (e.g., right to make up exams or missed assignments for funeral attendance) in cases of death and non-death losses, making them vulnerable for both disenfranchised (Doka, 1989; 2002) and suffocated grief experiences (Bordere, 2014). I recently met with a student who told of her distressing experience with a professor in which the penalty for her death loss and grief experience was a lowered grade. The student was not permitted a make-up exam and thus had to take it on the scheduled date, the day after her mother's funeral. At the semester's end, the professor told the student, "I'm sorry that the loss of your mother *caused* you to get a 'D' in the course."

This student's experience is illustrative of the impact of oppression. She is "pressed" or caught between options (taking the exam as required or not taking it) that are not only undesirable but costly, leaving her in a "catch-22" of sorts. It is important to note that marginalized groups may be less likely to resist dominant, oppressive forces (e.g., opt to not take the exam due to unfair timing) as needed, because the "cost of noncompliance" can be especially high (Harris, 2009–2010).

Further, what we see in the relationship described above is a *temporary inequality*, where the more skilled person provides a service to the less skilled person (Miller, 2014). The less skilled person is thought to eventually acquire the skills being taught and reach a similar or higher status. Both parties can gain from the interactions. However, the more skilled person has determining power as the person providing the service. With the knowledge that something can always be done in socially just practice, especially by entities with determining power, what could have been done in this situation to balance this temporary inequality? Here the marginalized person is assigned fault for her circumstance where the person of privilege had the power to intervene. How could professor privilege be used to form alliances with bereaved students, such as the aforementioned student, so that they are supported? It is important to note that *support* is not meant to negate or replace accountability. It instead makes fulfillment of responsibilities more reachable (e.g., when death and loss impacts students in educational settings, employees in workplaces).

Socially Just Practice and Thanatology

As an academician and thanatologist, it is refreshing to know of institutions that promote socially just practices, such as those that employ student bereavement leave policies (i.e., Ball State, Purdue University, University of Wisconsin-Green Bay, Illinois State University). It is likewise refreshing to hear stories of colleagues who function as allies in supporting bereaved students where such institutional policies are not yet in place. Some professors, for example, have policies listed in course syllabi that indicate the type of documentation (e.g., obituary, funeral program) required for make-up assignments and excused absences. In addition to enhancing student academic success, sharing this documentation allows for further acknowledgment of the students' loss experience. At the end of one class period, a student submitted a funeral program to me. This otherwise less participatory student proceeded to share details of her cousin's "celebration of life" service and poem that she had written on his behalf. This exchange afforded me the opportunity to acknowledge her loss, the beautifully written tribute to her cousin's life, arrange a future meeting to establish a plan for completing missed tasks, and develop a closer relationship that ultimately enhanced her academic performance and school functioning (e.g., participation, attendance). In a study of bereaved college students, concrete support (i.e., make-up assignments, exams) was found to be particularly important during the semester in which the loss occurred (Servaty-Seib & Hamilton, 2006).

Conclusion

As this chapter on introductory concepts comes to a conclusion, I thank you for your interests and commitment to issues of social justice and diversity in death, dying, loss and bereavement. In the chapters to follow, you will find a wealth of conscious-raising information to promote continued self-growth and a conglomerate of ideas to facilitate effective practices in grief support. Now knowing firsthand what it feels like to "break a leg," I no longer use the phrase to communicate well wishes for success along one's journey for justice. However, in recounting the solace that comes with such justice, as many of you have also witnessed in bereavement, may we continue to promote and look for flags of hope in work with individuals and families and in the institutions that serve and surround them.

Making the Connection

In the scenario to follow, imagine that you are the Director of Culturally Conscientious Practice at the Hospital of Socially Just Care in Texas. Dr. Elena, a first-year practicing doctor, comes to you in tears, clearly distressed, seeking your ideas and feedback about her experience working with a family on her service during and after the death of their family member. As director, we invite you to journey with Dr. Elena as she explains her case, which we will explore from a culturally conscientious and socially just perspective.

Background Demographics

Patient—Abdul = Early twenties, male, Muslim, overdosed on heroin
Doctor—Elena = Early thirties, female, White, Jewish, first-year Doctor out of Residency

Abdul was brought into the emergency room still receiving CPR to sustain his life. After an hour of many interventions, his heart started beating on its own. (Note: It only takes minutes of not receiving oxygen to cause irreversible brain damage.) He was admitted to the intensive care unit where apart from his heart continuing to beat, he was fully supported by machines. He was declared brain dead over the course of 48 hours.

Abdul's family members were very aware of how sick he was and that he was likely brain dead. Throughout his 48-hour hospital stay, there was a steady stream of visitors including his parents, siblings, friends, and extended family. All were devastated. Abdul's mother, Saleema, was a devout Muslim. She was also a huge support to the entire group during the hospital stay. Saleema seemed to have a small group whom she relied on for strength as well. Most people in her support network shared the same faith, although one in particular was a non-practicing physician who was helping Saleema sort through the information we were giving her in the hospital.

After Abdul was declared brain dead, the family decided to withdraw care. I met with Saleema, her support group, and a large portion of the extended family. I explained our protocol for withdrawing care. We agreed that once the family was all gathered and ready we would start a morphine drip, stop all other medications, and remove any life-sustaining machines from Abdul.

I offered the family the choice of being present in the room when Abdul was taken off the ventilator or stepping out and returning once it was removed. They chose to stay. Abdul was surrounded by his family as we removed him from the ventilator. He died 15 minutes later. As part of our protocol we called the medical examiner's (coroner's) office to see if Abdul would be a coroner's case. We were informed that he would, in fact, be a coroner's case. Patients that are coroner's cases are usually individuals that die from a suspicious cause of death (e.g., drug overdoses), deaths from unknown causes, and deaths after being hospitalized for less than 24 hours that are suspicious. The body is sent to the coroner's office for examination by a medical examiner, and if they are still suspicious about the cause of death, they could decide to do an autopsy.

Having finished my residency and only been in practice less than a year, I have never had a patient become a coroner's case. I have called the coroner to see if patients needed to come to their office, and my experience so far had been them replying that the cases did not need to come to them. This law (that the coroners' office has final say in determining the cause of death in suspicious cases) is in place to protect possible victims of crimes, to help figure out the cause of death in unknown cases where patients would not have the ability to speak for themselves.

After Abdul died, his charge nurse (i.e., nurse in charge of the unit) called the coroner's office and also informed the family that Abdul would be a coroner's case (the body would be immediately brought to the coroner's office) before I had a chance to call or deliver the information to the family.

Saleema (mother), who had been very calm throughout the process became very upset (hysterical) and outraged that her son, Abdul's body would have to go to the coroner's office rather than the mosque/funeral home as her religion would dictate. Saleema, with whom I had previously established good rapport, began screaming at me, *"No one will take my son to the medical examiner! He is NOT going to the coroner! No one will cut my baby! No one will interfere with our religion!"*

I asked Saleema to try to stay calm and let me call the coroner's office to find out more details since I had not directly spoken to them yet. I was informed by the supervisor at the medical examiner's office that because the patient's death was a case of drug-overdose that he would have to be examined to officially determine a "cause of death" for the death certificate. I explained what the patient's mother had told me: The family members are practicing Muslims. According to the patient's mother, Saleema, an autopsy would go against their beliefs. In addition, the patient had died in the early afternoon, and according to their beliefs he had to be buried within 24 hours.

The medical examiner's personnel replied that the patient's (Abdul's) body absolutely had to go to the coroner's office for an exam, that it was the law. They explained that they try their best to follow family's religious practices but they could not guarantee with 100 percent certainty that the body would not need an autopsy. In addition, they said the family's funeral director could call first thing in the morning to request the patient be the first case to help facilitate the early funeral service already scheduled.

Saleema began shouting about the lack of respect for her religious beliefs. Her small support group who had been with her throughout her son's hospitalization and death were at her side again, some escalating in their anger along with her but some trying to help explain the reasoning. I asked Saleema if it would help her to speak with the medical examiner's office directly to voice her concerns and then I connected her via phone with the supervisor. The person who seemed to be the mother's main support was the non-practicing physician. She became increasingly aggressive, telling me I should change the cause of death from heroin overdose to something different.

Saleema was not put at ease by speaking with the staff at the medical examiner's office and the situation continued to escalate. She stated she was going to gather the patient's siblings and friends. After gathering everyone, Saleema stated that she and her family planned to carry the patient's body out of the hospital themselves and then she stormed out of the intensive care unit.

Upset by the situation and distressed for the family, I discussed the situation with the charge nurse in the ICU and the hospital administrator on-call. I called the medical-legal department to see what the rights of the family were in this situation and to see if we could help advocate for them. I called a social worker to have further support in talking with the family and to see if they had other ideas of ways to discuss this further to prevent escalation.

I went to the waiting room and asked Saleema if she could discuss the situation with the funeral home she was using to see if they had encountered this issue in the past. She stated the funeral director was on his way to the hospital.

I requested that when the funeral director arrives that we all sit down to make sure we all understood the situation. The family agreed to this. The funeral home was actually through the families' mosque and the funeral director was of the same faith as the patient's mother.

When the funeral director arrived I sat down with him and the family. He was able to assure the family that the medical examiner's office was very respectful of different religious and cultural beliefs. He also assured the family that this trip would in no way affect the purity of the patient's soul (one of their concerns) or interfere with their rituals.

The situation was resolved without any further issues.

Tashel C. Bordere

Key Terms

Culture—the beliefs, attitudes, values, behaviors, and practices shared by a group to support its survival within various contexts.

Culturally conscientious practice—meeting the variant needs of families through an understanding and openness to evolving knowledge of their social locations (e.g., family structure, ability, sexuality, class, nationality, ethnicity, spirituality).

Disenfranchised grief—individual's experience of loss is unacknowledged or unsupported both within their sub-cultures and within the larger society. This may be associated with others' perceptions of the individual (e.g., on the margins of society), the relationship with the deceased (viewed by others as peripheral or stigmatized), or the type of loss (e.g., pet loss, divorce).

Double-bind—a dilemma in communication in which an individual (or group) receives two or more conflicting messages, and one message negates the other. This creates a situation in which a successful response to one message results in a failed response to the other (and vice versa), so that the person (or group) will automatically be wrong regardless of response. Double binds are often used as a form of social control.

Prejudice—a biased attitude or prejudgment based on faulty thought processes. Like stereotyping, prejudice is learned and may be positive or negative. Prejudice is a precursor to discrimination or biased behaviors (actions or inactions) aimed at individuals and in efforts to oppress or maintain systems of oppression.

Social justice—full and equal participation of all groups in a society that is mutually shaped to meet their needs. Social justice includes a vision of society in which the distribution of resources is equitable and all members are physically and psychologically safe and secure.

Stereotypes—generalizations and conclusions drawn based on limited information; the image that comes to mind when we think of a particular social group. They are learned and may be conscious or unconscious, positive or negative.

Suffocated grief—individual expression of grief is punished or constrained when penalties are imposed for this expression.

Unearned advantage—a form of privilege in which unearned entitlements are limited to particular groups.

Unearned entitlement—basic things that everyone should have (e.g., a sense of safety at school or work and accessible health care).

Discussion Questions

1. What did the physician, Dr. Elena, do well in terms of cultural conscientiousness and socially just practice in her work with the bereaved family? Be specific and give examples.
2. Briefly identify the privileged and less power individuals and groups in this case study?
3. Imagine that Dr. Elena, like many people who are privileged, is unaware of her privileged status, and therefore unaware of the implications of her privilege and the role of oppression in struggles with this family following Abdul's death . . . despite her sincere efforts. Explain the concept of *privilege* to Dr. Elena in a culturally sensitive way and tell her of ways in which her privileged status(es) may have impacted her interactions with Saleema and the family.
4. Oppression is complicated in that it operates on many levels. What systems of oppression were present in the context of the hospital (and Intensive Care) area of the hospital? What systems of support were available in the hospital?
5. Which individuals were disenfranchised in this case study and in what ways? Explain. How did these factors related to disenfranchisement influence the behavioral and affective responses of individuals in the case study following Abdul's death?

6. How does the concept of "*suffocated grief*" relate to Abdul's family's experience?
7. Why are allies particularly important for disenfranchised or less power groups such as Abdul's family in death, dying, and grief? Who did Saleema and her family perceive as an ally (ies)? What additional allies would be been useful in this scenario both for Saleema and Dr. Elena?

References

Allport, G. W. (1954). *The nature of prejudice*. Cambridge, MA: Addison-Wesley.

Ayvazian, A. (2007). Interrupting the cycle of oppression: The role of allies as agents of change. In P. S. Rothenberg (Ed.), *Race, class, and gender in the United States* (7th ed.) (p. 724). New York, NY: Worth.

Bell, L. A. (1997). Theoretical foundations for social justice education. In M. Adams, L. Bell, & P. Griffin (Eds.), *Teaching for diversity and social justice: A sourcebook* (pp. 3-15). New York, NY: Routledge.

Bordere, T. C. (2008–2009). "To look at death another way": Black teenage males' perspectives on second-lines and regular funerals in New Orleans. *Omega: Journal of Death and Dying, 58*(3), 213–232.

Bordere, T. C. (2009). Culturally conscientious thanatology. *The Forum, 35*(2), 1& 3–4.

Bordere, T. C. (2014). Adolescents and homicide. In K. Doka & A. Tucci (Eds.), *Helping adolescents cope with loss* (pp. 161–181). Washington, DC: Hospice Foundation of America.

Collins, P. H. (1990). *Black feminist thought: Knowledge, consciousness, and the politics of empowerment* (p. 12). Boston, MA: Unwin Hyman.

Doka, K. J. (1989). *Disenfranchised grief: Recognizing hidden sorrow*. Lexington, MA: Lexington Books.

Doka, K. J. (2002). *Disenfranchised grief: New directions, challenges, and strategies for practice*. Champaign, IL: Research Press.

Dovidio, J. F., Hewstone, M., Glick, P., & Esses, V. M. (Eds.). (2010). Prejudice, stereotying and discrimination: Theoretical and empirical overview. In J. F. Dovidio, M. Hewstone, P. Glick, & V. M. Esses (Eds.), *The SAGE handbook of prejudice, stereotyping and discrimination* (pp. 3–28). Thousand Oaks, CA: Sage Publications.

Du Bois, W. E. B. (1969). Of our spiritual strivings. In WEB Du Bois, *The souls of black folk* (p. 43). New York, NY: Signet Classic—Penguin Books. (Original work published in 1903).

Fowler, K. (2008). "The wholeness of things": Infusing diversity and social justice into death education. *Omega: Journal of Death and Dying, 57*(1), 53–91.

Frye, M. (1998). Oppression. In P. S. Rothenberg (Ed.), *Race, class, and gender: An integrated study* (4th ed.). New York, NY: St. Martin's Press.

Gardiner, H. W., & Kosmitzki, C. (2011). *Lives across cultures: Cross-cultural human development* (p. 5). Boston, MA: Allyn & Bacon.

Gigerenzer, G. (2008). Why heuristics work. *Perspectives on Psychological Science, 3*(1), 20–29.

Harris, D. (2009–2010). Oppression of the bereaved: A critical analysis of grief in western society. *Omega: Journal of Death and Dying, 60*(3), 241–253.

Hilton, J. L., & von Hippel, W. (1996). Stereotypes. *Annual Review of Psychology, 47*, 237–271.

Hoopes, D. S. (1979). Intercultural communication concepts and the psychology of intercultural experiences. In M. Pusch (Ed.), *Multicultural education: A cross-cultural training approach* (pp. 3–33). La Grange Park, IL: Intercultural Press.

Human Rights Campaign. (n.d.). An overview of federal rights and protections granted to married couples. Retrieved from www.hrc.org/resources/entry/an-overview-of-federal-rights-and-protections-granted-to-married-couples

Iyer, A., Leach, C. W., & Crosby, F. J. (2003). White guilt and racial compensation: The benefits and limits of self-focus. *Personality and Social Psychology Bulletin, 29*(1), 117–129.

Johnson, A. G. (2006). We can't heal until the wounding stops. In A. Johnson (Ed.), *Privilege, power, and difference* (2nd ed.) (pp. 66–67). Boston, MA: McGraw Hill.

Johnson, C. (2010). African American teen girls grieve the loss of friends to homicide: Meaning making and resilience. *Omega: Journal of Death and Dying, 61*(2), 121–143.

Jones, J. M. (1972). *Prejudice and racism*. Reading, MA: Addison-Wesley.

Khan, S. R., Benda, T., & Stagnaro, M. N. (2012). Stereotyping from the perspective of perceivers and targets. *Online Readings in Psychology and Culture, 5*(1). Retrieved from www.dx.doi.org/10.9707/2307–0919.1043

King, M. L. (1963). Letter from Birmingham Jail. *The Atlantic Monthly, 212*(2), 78–88.

Lippmann, W. (1922). *Public Opinion* (p. 81). New York, NY: Harcourt, Brace and Company.

McIntosh, P. (2007). White privilege: Unpacking the invisible knapsack. In P. S. Rothenberg (Ed.), *Race, class, and gender in the United States* (7th ed.). New York, NY: Worth.

Miller, J. B. (2014). Domination and subordination. In P. S. Rothenberg & K. S. Mayhew (Eds.), *Race, class, and gender in the United States* (9th ed.). New York, NY: Worth.

Powell, A. A., Branscombe, N. R., & Schmitt, M. T. (2005). Inequality as ingroup privilege or outgroup disadvantage: The impact of group focus on collective guilt and interracial attitudes. *Personality and Social Psychology Bulletin, 31*(4), 508–521.

Rodriguez, M. M. D., McNeal, C. T., & Cauce, A. M. (2008). Counseling with the marginalized. In P. B. Pedersen, J. G., Draguns, W. J. Lonner, & J. E. Trimble (Eds.), *Counseling across cultures* (6th ed.) (pp. 223–238). Los Angeles, CA: Sage Publications.

Rosenblatt, P. C. (2009). The culturally competent practitioner. In K. J. Doka & A. S. Tucci (Eds.), *Diversity and end-of-life care* (p. 21). Washington, DC: Hospice Foundation of America.

Servaty-Seib, H. L., & Hamilton, L. A. (2006). Educational performance and persistence of bereaved college students. *Journal of College Student Development, 47*(2), 225–234.

2
Looking Broadly at Loss and Grief
A Critical Stance

Darcy L. Harris

Most of my training in health care was focused on the patient as an individual. We were taught about the specifics of physical health and illness in the form of an assessment of the patients' symptoms, including their subjective descriptions of pain and stress. In some venues, mostly hospice/palliative care settings, the unit of care extended to the patient's family. For the most part, however, the focus remained on individualized accounts of symptomatology and determining the appropriate diagnostic category followed by a decision regarding the appropriate technical/medical intervention, and then evaluating the outcome using the reports of physical indicators and subjective responses of individual patients. The assessment form we used at that time included specific bodily systems for us to document in our initial patient interview. At the bottom of the form, almost like an afterthought, a small space was allotted for "psychosocial concerns." We listened compassionately and supported the patient and family members' expressions of angst and anxiety as they related to the illness of the patient. We felt good about the care that we offered, and we did care deeply about our patients and their families. However, we rarely explored or even considered the social context of our patients and how their individual experiences were shaped and molded by forces other than just the disease process at hand.

My graduate training program in counseling psychology included an introduction to critical theory and feminist therapy. During my time in this program, I began to piece together an appreciation of the social forces and institutions that are deeply embedded into almost every aspect of an individual's experience. I knew that access to resources was a key issue for those who did not have adequate insurance or funds to cover their care, but up to that point, I had very limited awareness of how class, race, culture, and gender profoundly affect individual experiences. I also had never considered the impact that historical discrimination and oppression might have on the interactions that occurred in my present day world.

The experiences of loss, death, and grief may be universal, but each person's unique perceptions, choices, perspective, and interpretation of meaning are shaped and molded by many socially-mediated factors. A person's idea of what quality of life means will be profoundly influenced by his or her culture, race, gender, and class. For example, if a person with a terminal illness has spent a lifetime being rewarded financially and socially for being highly independent, suffering an illness where there is dependence and debility may have a very different meaning than for someone whose identity has been formed around mutual caregiving and kinship relationships, where interdependence within the community is viewed as normal. Historical contexts also come into play as well. While the current generation of young people in the United States may have many role models that have crossed previous barriers related to race, class, and gender, they have grown up in homes where their parents most likely were affected first hand by civil rights marches, bigotry, discrimination due to race and/or gender, and the feelings that stem from these experiences. The painful memories and associated feelings do not necessarily change because of rhetoric about equality and desegregation in the present day. Below are some examples of how social issues may be relevant to death, loss, and grief:

- Most service sector work is performed by women and is still viewed as "women's work," with lower compensation than in other sectors. In health care, nurses and social workers are now tasked with increasingly larger patient loads and more complex care patients while they also hit against caps on their income and stagnant salaries that don't reflect their essential role in patient care (Rajapaksa & Rothstein, 2009; Reineck & Furino, 2009).
- Allopathic medicine is the dominant model of medicine in Western industrialized countries; other types of medicine (i.e., traditional Chinese medicine, ayurvedic medicine, homeopathic medicine, Native American medicine, and naturopathy) are devalued as "non-scientific," practiced by charlatans and "quacks." However, individuals who use both allopathic and alternative types of medicine together may, at times, have better outcomes than those who access allopathic medical care alone (Baer, 1989; Caspi, Koithan, & Criddle, 2004).
- There is a bias toward funding research and innovation in areas related to the surgical supply industry and pharmacologic development for new (and potentially profitable) pharmaceutical agents (Rothman et al., 2009). Hospice and palliative care as specialties are devalued due to the tendency to view death as failure in the current medical milieu and the fact that most of the equipment and pharmacology associated with terminal care is already out of patent and thus not as lucrative to potential funders.
- There is often a negative association of counseling and therapy with weakness and dependence. Many insurance companies will either not cover expenses related to counseling, or will do so only minimally. However, it is known that individuals who experience complicated grief after a significant loss can benefit from well-timed professional intervention (Shear, Ghesquiere, & Glickman, 2013).
- Individuals with higher incomes have greater access to various care options and choices through their insurance coverage or by social preference due to their status. Individuals at the bottom of society have shorter lives and suffer more illness (Ballatt & Campling, 2011).
- Experiences that involve emotion are devalued; grief and chronic sorrow are only allowed to be expressed and socially supported under certain conditions, for a limited period of time, and in socially acceptable ways (Doka, 1989; Harris, 2009–2010).

Consider the following examples:

Janet was a 43 year-old mother of two young children. She was also a massage therapist and reiki practitioner whose office was in a complementary therapy co-operative. She was diagnosed with breast cancer and underwent a lumpectomy. Her oncologist recommended a regimen of chemotherapy after her surgery. However, Janet said that she "didn't want to pump chemicals" into her body and declined this treatment, opting for alternative medicine and meditation instead. Two years later, Janet was found to have metastatic cancer in her bones and brain. When Janet presented to the oncology clinic at this time for re-evaluation, one of the nurses remarked (out loud where Janet could hear) that "if she had made the responsible choice, her two children wouldn't be facing the loss of their mother." When Janet died, her two children created a mandala together that was placed on her casket at the funeral service.

Janet was a competent adult who did not align herself with the predominant views of allopathic medical care. If you were a health care provider in this situation, what would your feelings be? Why do you think the nurse made the negative comment about Janet?

Amy was a nursing student who lived in the dorm at the university. She would often go to the library to study in the evenings because it was quiet. She had studied hard all evening for an exam that was scheduled early the next morning. At one a.m., Amy was awakened by loud talking, laughing, and music coming from the room across the hall from her. At two a.m., the music and loud talking continued and she was worried that she would not be able to do well on her exam due to lack of sleep. She got up, put on her bathrobe, and knocked on the door where the music was being played. Two young black women answered the door. When Amy told them she needed to sleep and their music and conversation were keeping her awake, one of the young women angrily replied that Amy was a "little rich white girl who needs her beauty sleep," and slammed the door on her. Amy was shocked. She had never spoken ill to these girls before and she had always been taught to be respectful to others. Amy was neither rich nor did she have time to worry about her appearance because she was spending all of her time studying and working at a job to get through school.

Amy had never shown any disrespect or negativity to the two young women who lived across the hall from her. Why do you think they responded to her the way that they did? What assumptions do you think they were making about Amy and what might have informed their assumptions? What historical factors may be influencing the responses of the girls and Amy?

Alma was a 63 year-old black woman who was admitted to the intensive care unit after suffering a stroke at home. Alma was unresponsive and on life support. The doctors (both were male; one was white, and the other Asian in appearance) spoke with her family, telling them that the stroke was massive and that Alma would never be able to breathe on her own or respond to them again. The doctors requested permission to move Alma from life support because her brain was showing no electrical activity and she was essentially brain dead, with the life support machines keeping her body functioning. The family refused, stating that they wanted everything to be done for Alma, including remaining on the ventilator and being fed intravenously. The doctors left the family and went into the unit. The doctors and nurses then talked among themselves about how unreasonable this family was and that they wouldn't listen to "common sense."

Alma's family all heard the doctors tell them that she was brain dead. Why do you think the family chose differently from what the medical providers were recommending? What do you think the doctors and nurses in the unit were feeling toward Alma's family? What might be the implications to the family for not agreeing to the recommendations of the doctors?

Social and Political Underpinnings and Power

When we begin to explore social and political influences, we are essentially talking about how power is distributed within a society. Power in this context can be defined as the ability to have influence, control, superiority, or an advantage over others (Brown, 1994). It is important to see that systemic power relations exist between social groups that are identified in a society. Being ascribed power also means that you have more freedom to choose and more options available to you than someone who is not seen as socially powerful. Individuals or groups who have more social power can afford to be oblivious to other groups' needs or opinions. Power may have a negative connotation, such as "power over" another person or "domination" of the environment. However, it may have a positive side, such as when a person or a group is "empowered" in a way that frees them from oppression, whether the source is internal or external. In the social context, people who are powerful are those who are able to determine the norms for all social groups within their sphere. All interactions between individuals and groups will have a power dynamic at play, whether that dynamic is obvious or not.

If you stop and think about whose opinion matters and what types of people are set up as examples of success, you might identify high-ranking political figures, sports heroes, and movie stars. You might also think of people who have made breakthroughs in medical science or in information technology. Most of these individuals have high incomes, very comfortable or perhaps even lavish lifestyles, expensive clothing, a certain type of appearance that usually sets a trend for others, and/or a significant sense of being very special as a result of their unique accomplishments or public persona. Because of their status, you will often find these individuals being granted credibility in many topics that are completely unrelated to their area of expertise. Sports stars make highly publicized comments on religious teachings and beliefs. Surgeons may provide opinions on public education policy. Movie stars often use their celebrity status to promote products, causes, and political nominees for office. The reason these individuals are given such broad credibility has to do with the fact that they possess social power by virtue of their perceived success and celebrity status.

We are all born into social groups, and these groups pre-exist before us as social structures. The social and political significance of these groups is established and maintained socially (i.e., not by nature or by divine intervention). Group identities are socially elevated or diminished in relation to one another, establishing structural power relationships between these groups. Individuals are oppressed or privileged by virtue of their membership in various social groups, which may be delineated by race, class, gender, religion, culture, or some other category, such as the type of work performed (i.e, "blue collar" versus "white collar" workers). Membership in groups as a result of certain experiences may also lead to oppression or privilege, depending upon the group and the experience. For instance, individuals who win a large amount of money through a lottery may find a great deal of social power and influence that is usually associated with the dominant group that was not theirs prior to the experience of winning the lottery.

Through our early attachments, we learn about how we are valued socially and our "position" in society relative to other individuals and groups. Our assumptive world becomes formed around our attachment system, and this assumptive world provides us with explanations about how the world works, the expectations we have in our interactions with others, and our view of ourselves in relation to others (Harris, 2011; Janoff-Bulman, 1992). Our family system is the first experience of the world beyond ourselves. From our family system, we learn about how to treat others, what is "right" versus "wrong," and what is valued and what is devalued. Our family system may also introduce us to formal or informal religious teaching, which would further delineate a code of values and world view that was most likely implicit in our early years. We then enter into the formal educational system and learn the values that are espoused and socially reinforced there. The school system exists within the larger socio-political system, which determines the content of educational curricula and the amount and designation of funding that is applied to the various educational institutions and programs. At any time along the way, we most likely will have interactions with other social/political structures, such as the health care system and the laws and public policies that have an impact upon our choices and access to resources. We learn to whom we should defer and who defers to us socially. Our history becomes embedded into our identification with our kinship culture and racial groups, typically along gender-identified roles, and is stratified by income, level of influence, and perceived position in relation to others.

After reading this section, go back to the three scenarios we just discussed in the last section with Janet, Amy, and Alma. Think of how the power dynamics in these situations might be playing a role in what has happened. Who in the situation is viewed to have power? What are the responses of individuals who are less powerful because of identification with a non-dominant group, racial discrimination, or lower class? What are the responses of the individuals who are identified with a group that has power or is part of the dominant group? What historical power dynamics might be informing these scenarios? In doing this exercise, you are beginning to think critically about situations, and learning to think and reflect in this way is essential if you wish to become informed, compassionate, and effective in diverse settings.

The Development of Critical Consciousness

Kumagai and Lypson (2009) describe the need to move the delivery of health care beyond the technical components that focus mostly upon laboratory data, differential diagnoses, and treatment options for disease entities to the development of what they term *critical consciousness*. This type of critical inquiry takes into account that individuals do not exist in isolation, but instead, all individuals exist in relationship to others in the world. Critical consciousness involves

> a reflective awareness of the differences in power and privilege and the inequities that are embedded in social relationships—an act that Freire calls "reading the world"—and fostering of a reorientation of perspective toward a commitment to social justice. The development of this type of consciousness—a process that Freire calls "conscientization"—is both cognitive and affective and leads to engaged discourse, collaborative problem-solving, and a "rehumanization" of human relationships.
>
> (Kumagai & Lypson, 2009, p. 783)

The development of a critical consciousness includes not just acquiring knowledge about physical illness and its treatment, or even about the normal course of grief as described by bereavement researchers and theorists. In order to cultivate this type of awareness, the practitioner must be willing to first engage in critical self-reflection, where there is a pause to understand one's core assumptions, biases, and values, and be able to shift that gaze from oneself to others and to the conditions of injustice in our world. Thus, it is imperative that practitioners become aware of how their beliefs and assumptions have been formed, and how these views may have an impact upon their interactions with others. In addition, there also needs to be an understanding of social issues (both relational and systemic) in order to engage in reflective, ethical practice.

Let's look at another case example: Joe was a 66-year-old black man who was diagnosed with metastatic cancer. Joe lived with his wife Ann in a subsidized housing complex. Ann took care of their two grandchildren during the day while their daughter worked. She also looked after two of her neighbor's children during the day for extra income. Joe had developed symptoms two years before his diagnosis. However, he did not seek medical care because they had no medical insurance, and he was concerned about the expense of going to the doctor. His diagnosis came after he collapsed and was taken to the emergency department by a neighbor (they did not have a car and Ann could not leave the children in her care to go with him). After admission to the emergency room, tests were run and Joe was told there was "cancer in many places in his body." He was given an appointment to see an oncologist, who referred Joe to the local hospice.

Joe and Ann were devastated by the news. However, they also felt a sense of relief that the government had something called a "hospice benefit" that would cover all the costs of medications, equipment, and the visits from the nurses and hospice team. Unfortunately, the hospice care in their area was strictly home care, as there was no residential hospice or palliative care unit in their community. This presented difficulties for Ann, who could not care for Joe at home in addition to their grandchildren and the other children who provided her with an important source of income for their household. She knew their daughter would not be able to afford childcare for the two grandchildren that Ann watched for her every day while she worked. Even though the hospice nurses were helpful and responsive, neither Joe nor Ann felt completely comfortable being at home alone as his condition worsened, but they could not afford (nor were they offered) other options.

Looking superficially at this scenario, many people would feel that Joe is fortunate that there is a hospice benefit available to cover his expenses. He now has access to care without the added burden of trying to find a way to pay for it. However, in agreeing to accept this benefit, he and Ann are faced with other issues that the benefit does not address, such as being forced to stay home where they feel isolated. In addition, if Joe stays in the home and Ann becomes the primary caregiver, her source of income and her daughter's work could be placed at risk because she would not be able to be Joe's primary care provider and adequately supervise the children in her care. They do not have other viable options available for Joe's care because they do not have the income or insurance to pay for it. They have not chosen hospice care for its merits; rather, it is a forced choice based upon financial expedience and not upon an understanding or embracing of the hospice philosophy of care for them.

Issues of class, race, and income are all embedded into this scenario. It is unlikely that the hospice nurses and other team members realize that Joe and Ann have signed the hospice papers out of necessity and not out of free choice, and even if they did recognize this fact, they might even assume that they would provide Joe with the best care because of their own belief in the hospice philosophy, indicating that they believe that they know what is best for Joe and Ann.

As you consider this scenario, think about the following:

1. How is social power manifest in this situation?
2. How were Joe and Ann's choices affected by their social status? What were the determinants of their social status?
3. If Joe were a business executive with a high income, how would his situation differ from the Joe that is described here?
4. What is the responsibility of the hospice workers to ensure that Joe and Ann have been able to freely choose the hospice program for Joe's care?
5. How are the hospice care workers limited in their care delivery in this scenario?
6. Why might the hospice care workers feel that they know what is best for Joe and Ann?

As stated previously, most health care professionals would be focused on treating Joe's symptoms and ensuring he had adequate control over the pain related to his cancer. This focus is probably shared by Joe and Ann as well. However, the concept of *total pain*, as identified by Dame Cicely Saunders in her approach to hospice palliative care, refers to the multidimensional nature of pain to include not just the physical, but also the psychological, social, and spiritual domains that are part of the experience of pain (Mehta & Chan, 2008). In this instance, while Joe may be assured of the relief of physical symptoms related to his advancing cancer, there is no addressing the anxiety and angst that are caused by the requisite home care and their feelings of isolation, let alone the concerns regarding the loss of their only remaining source of income through Ann's home daycare.

Ways of Knowing

An important aspect of critical inquiry is to ascertain what kinds of knowledge and information are valued and what is then devalued because it veers away from the socially accepted norm. For instance, most Western industrialized societies place a high value on objectivity, positivism, stoicism, and intellect. People in Western society shy away from knowledge they cannot verify, which leads to exclusionary thinking and privilege toward linear thinking. Professionals whose training has involved higher education and learning focused on the cultivation of intellect typically have higher incomes than those who do not have this level of education. The scientific method is seen as the standard to which all other types of learning and knowing are compared. Individuals who show more emotion, who don't formulate their knowledge by the scientific method, or who do not excel in typical academic pursuits have less social power than those who do. This creates a class system of intellectual privilege and power in relation to other types of knowledge and learning. And yet, intellectual learning alone has limitations when that learning is applied to human interactions. We can all think of individuals who are intellectually very bright, but who do not know how to engage with others in a healthy or meaningful way. Many individuals are admitted into medical school and higher education programs simply on the merits of their academic marks, which are a reflection of intellect, without any consideration of the attributes and relational skills of the person who has earned this academic achievement. The sad result is that we often have medical doctors and educators who are gifted intellectually, but are not able to relate to their patients, students, or others in a humane, compassionate way.

It is important to recognize that Western societies' privileging of intellectual knowing supersedes all other forms of knowing, such as intuitive knowing, common sense knowing, affective knowing (sometimes referred to as emotional intelligence), spiritual knowing, perceptual knowing, and imaginal knowing (Hassel, 2004). Individuals whose primary way of knowing is not intellectual knowing are often considered to not be very smart—or even worse, seen as backward and primitive. In the earlier scenario with Janet, who chose not to accept allopathic medicine (which is based on the scientific method), the nurse makes a derogatory comment about her choice, stating she has been "irresponsible" not to avail herself of the what she views as the "right" choice for Janet. Perhaps not taking in "chemicals" is more important to Janet than the potential to prolong her life. Perhaps this choice was Janet's way of feeling that she is able to make her own choices instead of having them dictated to her. Maybe she wants her children to see her as a role model for thinking independently. Another possibility might be that spiritual knowing was more important to Janet than aligning herself with the values of allopathic medicine. Most important to this scenario is the immediate negative appraisal of Janet by her health care providers and their lack of an attempt to understand Janet's choices and values.

There is a growing body of literature that supports the importance of honoring and cultivating emotional and social intelligence alongside the intellectual knowing that occurs for most health care practitioners (Freshman & Rubino, 2004). Indeed, science alone brings to mind images of a robot performing rote tasks and algorithms, not of one human offering compassionate care and understanding to another. The goal of attaining knowledge should be more than memorizing lists, formulas, and facts. In order to incorporate humanitarian values into health care, those who are training to provide that care need to learn how to critically reflect, engage with others compassionately, and acquire an understanding of social issues and how they affect individual choices and responses (Kumagai & Lypson, 2009).

Cultivating Reflective Practice as Critical Inquiry

Ellen was graduating from university and had been given an award by her faculty for her stellar scholarship while in her program of study. Ellen would receive this award at the end of the year banquet that was hosted by the Dean of the University. While Ellen came from a white upper-middle-class background and her parents had paid for her education, her father had not agreed to her choice of her major. Although he continued to pay for her tuition through a savings plan that he had set up for her university education when she was younger, he made it clear to her that he wanted "nothing to do with these liberal university types." When Ellen was notified of the award, she felt deeply honored. However, the end of the year banquet cost $75 per person, and she could not afford to pay this amount on her own. She was afraid to ask her parents for the money because of the conflict with her father over her academic choices. Ellen was surprised when one of her professors, a middle-aged black woman, handed a banquet ticket to her after one of her classes. Ellen felt embarrassed, but grateful. When she asked how the professor knew that she was struggling with obtaining the money for the dinner, the professor smiled and told her, "now you understand how one person can make a difference." Her professor was capable of looking beyond Ellen's apparent privilege and most likely her own relation to it as a black woman who was similar in age as Ellen's parents. Her ability to do this afforded Ellen an opportunity to do the same.

Many disciplines have now integrated the concepts of reflective practice into their curricula and continuing education programs. To reflect on our practice with the individuals we serve in our professional capacity, we have to be willing to cultivate awareness and understanding of ourselves and how our backgrounds shape our responses, in addition to being willing to "step out" of a situation in order to see things that are happening in a holistic and open way. For many, the ability to reflect is second nature—something that is just an extension of their personality and daily practice. However, for others, reflection needs to be learned and structured (at least in the beginning). Reflective practice has been linked to enhanced professional competence and to more effective delivery of care, which is why it has become a requirement for many professionals in their ongoing practice (Plack & Greenberg, 2005).

All professional settings have a "culture" established within them, whereby certain behaviors are expected, reinforced, and habituated. For example, most professional offices require an appointment for consultation. Patients are expected to disclose sensitive personal information to professionals in exchange for their services and the anticipation of improvement. Hospitals typically have "visiting hours" and intensive care units usually have posted rules regarding who can visit someone in the unit, at what times, and under what circumstances. In all professions, we become attuned to a specific way of thinking and to language and jargon that are associated with our field of knowledge. In nursing and medicine, the use of the scientific model and the ability to accurately and objectively describe findings, symptoms, and data are valued. In therapeutic professions such as social work, psychology, and counseling, the ability to embed experience into theoretical frameworks and models of meaning making are important. Spiritual care professionals become familiar with existential language, religious symbols, and philosophical dilemmas that are relevant to the clinical care settings in which they practice. Most of the rules, jargon, and expectations in these situations are implicit; they are simply understood to be part of the milieu of the professional environment. However, these familiar protocols, terms, and symbols can readily become barriers to individuals not familiar with the language and expectations that are part of the everyday world of the professionals who function within them.

Clinical work that is rooted in social awareness explores how issues of power are manifest in the life of the individual (Aldorondo, 2007). Innate in this exploration is the concept of empowerment, which is described as a process of dialog through which the client/patient is continuously supported to explore the range of possibilities that she or he sees as appropriate to his or her needs. In an empowerment model, the client/patient is identified as the "expert," and his/her subjective experiences and perceptions form the center for all decisions that are made in the therapeutic setting (Rose, 1990). It is important to note that an empowerment model seeks to identify sources of oppression, validates subjective experiences that have been objectified or marginalized through oppressive forces, focuses upon innate strengths and resilience, and supports advocating for social change to address oppression at the structural level (Gerber, 2007; Lee, 2007).

Let's go back to the examples that were given at the beginning of this chapter and consider them from a critical perspective.

Janet's choice not to take chemotherapy after she was diagnosed with breast cancer:

1. What are the power issues in this situation?
2. Are there issues of race, class, or gender, or historical oppression/discrimination in this situation?
3. What might Janet's choice to not utilize allopathic medicine convey to the health care providers?
4. What are the underlying social expectations that would come into play in this situation?

Amy's experience of the two black girls in her dorm:

1. What are the power issues in this situation?
2. Are there issues of race, class, gender, or historical oppression/discrimination in this situation?
3. What explanation might inform Amy further about the girls' response to her?
4. What are the underlying social expectations that would come into play in this situation?

Alma's family's choices regarding her care:

1. What are the power issues in this situation?
2. Are there issues of race, class, gender, or historical oppression/discrimination present in this situation?
3. What might inform the care providers further about the family's decision?
4. What are the underlying social expectations that would come into play in this situation?

Conclusion

There are many ways in which a critical view is important in the context of death, dying, loss, and grief. As you read the rest of the book, we invite you to consider the contextual pressures and elements that exist all around you in your everyday life. Think about how your choices and the choices of those around you are influenced by social forces and shaped by issues of social power dynamics. Thinking critically about all aspects of life and death is not just about applying a set of questions to specific situations, but more about a way of thinking and being in general, where the contextual elements of the everyday life are recognized and understood for their importance. Over time, developing critical consciousness can become second nature. Instead of it being something that you "do," it is becomes a part of who you are. Once you cultivate this level of awareness, you will never see the world (and the people in the world) in the same way as you did before, and this awareness may become one of the most compassionate forces in your work.

Key Terms

Assumptive world—internalized explanations about how the world works, expectations we have in our interactions with others, and our view of ourselves in relation to others; based primarily on early attachment relationships/experiences.

Critical consciousness—reflective awareness of the differences in power and privilege and the inequities that are embedded in social relationships.

Power—within a social context, the ability to have influence, control, superiority, or an advantage over others. On an individual basis, the freedom to choose and/or having access to a larger array of options than is available to those with less power.

Total pain—the multidimensional nature of pain includes the physical, psychological, social, and spiritual domains that are part of the experience.

Questions for Reflection

1. What are some of the power dynamics that are at play in your life? Consider your involvement (direct and indirect) with employers/employees, family members, government, neighbors, faith communities, strangers on the bus, and everyday interactions.
2. At each stage of growth and development we learn things about ourselves and the world, much of which we adopt in a fairly unconscious way . . . unless we are introduced to conflicting information. What are some early beliefs you have changed/challenged through ongoing learning? What led you to challenge this initial information?

3. People in Western society shy away from knowledge they cannot verify, which leads to exclusionary thinking and privilege towards linear thinking. . . . Individuals who show more emotion, who don't formulate their knowledge by the scientific method, or who do not excel in typical academic pursuits have less social power than those who do.

(p. 26)

What is your response to the role of intellectual privilege in Western society? To what extent do you employ other ways of knowing in your daily life? What is your primary way of knowing? What is your experience when interacting with others who seem to draw primarily on a different way of knowing?

References

Aldorondo, E. (2007). Rekindling the reformist spirit in the mental health professions. In E. Aldorondo (Ed.), *Advancing social justice through clinical practice* (pp. 3–17). Mahwah, NJ: Laurence Erlbaum.

Baer, H. (1989). The American dominative medical system as a reflection of social relations in the larger society. *Social Science & Medicine, 28*(11), 1103–1112.

Ballatt, J., & Campling, P. (2011). *Intelligent kindness: Reforming the culture of healthcare*. London: Royal College of Psychiatrists.

Brown, L. S. (1994). Subversive dialogues: Theory in feminist therapy. New York, NY: Basic Books.

Caspi, O., Koithan, M., & Criddle M. W. (2004). Alternative medicine or "alternative" patients: A qualitative study of patient-oriented decision-making processes with respect to complementary and alternative medicine. *Medical Decision-Making, 24*(1), 64–79.

Doka, K. J. (1989). *Disenfranchised grief: Recognizing hidden sorrows*. Lexington, MA: Lexington.

Freshman, B., & Rubino, L. (2004). Emotional intelligence skills for maintaining social networks in healthcare organizations. *Hospital Topics, 82*(3), 2–9.

Gerber, L. A. (2007). Social justice concerns and clinical practice. In E. Aldorondo (Ed.), *Advancing social justice through clinical practice* (pp. 43–71). Mahwah, NJ: Laurence Erlbaum.

Harris, D. L. (2009–10). Oppression of the bereaved: A critical analysis of grief in Western society. *Omega: Journal of Death and Dying, 60*(3), 241–253.

Harris, D. L. (2011). Introduction. In D. L. Harris (Ed.), *Counting our losses: Reflecting on change, loss, and transition in everyday life* (pp. xvii–xxiv). New York, NY: Routledge.

Hassel, C. (2004). Can diversity extend to ways of knowing? Engaging cross-cultural paradigms. *Journal of Extension, 42*(2), 1–4.

Janoff-Bulman, R. (1992). *Shattered assumptions: Towards a new psychology of trauma*. New York, NY: Free Press.

Kumagai, A. K., & Lypson, M. L. (2009). Beyond cultural competence: Critical consciousness, social justice, and multicultural education. *Academic Medicine, 84*(6), 782–787.

Lee, C. C. (2007). A counselor's call to action. In C. C. Lee (Ed.), *Counseling for social justice* (2nd ed., pp. 259–264). Alexandria, VA: American Counseling Association.

Mehta, A., & Chan, L. S. (2008). Understanding of the concept of "total pain": A prerequisite for pain control. *Journal of Hospice & Palliative Nursing, 10*(1), 26–32.

Plack, M. M., & Greenberg, L. (2005). The reflective practitioner: Reaching for excellence in practice. *Pediatrics, 116*(6), 1546–1552.

Rajapaksa, S., & Rothstein, W. (2009). Factors that influence the decisions of men and women nurses to leave nursing. *Nursing Forum 44*(3), 195–206.

Reineck, C., & Furino, A. (2005). Nursing career fulfillment: Statistics and statements from registered nurses. *Nursing Economics, 23*(1), 25–30.

Rose, S. M. (1990). Advocacy/empowerment: An approach to clinical practice for social work. *Journal of Sociology and Social Welfare, 17*(2), 41–51.

Rothman, D. J., McDonald, W. J., Berkowitz, C. D., Chimonas, S. C., DeAngelis, C. D., Hale, R. W., Nissen, S. E., Osborn, J. E., Scully, J. H., Thomson, G. E., & Wofsy, D. (2009). Professional medical associations and their relationships with industry: A proposal for controlling conflict of interest. *JAMA 301*(13) 1367–1372. doi:10.1001/jama.2009.407

Shear, M. K., Ghesquiere, A., & Glickman, K. (2013). Bereavement and complicated grief. *Current Psychiatry Reports, 15*(1). doi: 406. 10.1007/s11920-013-0406-z

Part Two
Issues Related to Social Status, Policy, and Politics

In this part, we begin to explore issues broadly, looking at global, national, and philosophical perspectives that influence social justice and injustice in various contexts.

We begin by looking at the inequities between countries and groups on a global scale, and how these differences have a profound impact upon quality of life, access to resources, and available choices for the majority of people who live in undeveloped parts of the world. The lack of access to adequate medical and health care, as well as inadequate measures to alleviate pain and suffering at the end of life are an extension of the global inequities that occur between developed and undeveloped countries. This chapter serves as a call for awareness and action to humanely address the suffering that occurs as a result of these inequities.

Next, we look at the paradox of care provision within the context of societies whose fundamental values are rooted in materialism and capitalistic values. The author provides an excellent exploration of the effects of materialism and "atomism" on aspects of human experience within contexts of care, including such issues as how care providers are treated, how care is funded, and the tendency to marginalize individuals who are seen as representing failure in societies that value material gain, productivity, and consumerism. At the conclusion of the chapter, the author suggests potential "antidotes" to the damaging effects of this materialistic undercurrent on the cultivation of a compassionate society.

Finally, chapter five explores the impact of discrimination and marginalization of ethnic groups, using differential data on the experience of infant mortality rates, which are disproportionately higher in these groups than in the dominant national group in the United Kingdom. Drawing from the HOPE study, which provided a forum for support for minority/immigrant women who experienced perinatal loss, the authors give voice to these women and their needs, including recommendations for public and political policy changes that would address these needs in a concrete way.

We encourage readers to consider the "big picture" implications of these chapters, including the impact of disparity between groups in specific regions and social groups, and how the issues raised in this section might be applied to political and social policies in various care settings around the world.

3
Living, Suffering, and Dying in a Globalized World

Solomon R. Benatar

Introduction

Those of us who write or read chapters such as those in this book lead greatly privileged lives with access to the best medical treatments and care available, while the majority of the world's population live, suffer, and die in miserable conditions with access to minimal health care (Benatar, 1998; Birn, 2011; Doyal, 2013). These vast differences in lived experiences across the world are symptomatic of deep, extensive, and overlapping complex global crises that increasingly threaten the lives and well-being of us all (Gill & Bakker, 2011; Gill, 2012), and remind us of the deteriorating 'state of health' of our planet.

Population growth, the emergence and spread of new infectious disease (with HIV as the most striking example), the rise of multi-drug resistance, widening disparities in wealth and health within and between nations, inadequate educational systems, war, refugees, widespread social unrest, the recent and still evolving global economic crisis, and crises in food and water security, together with environmental degradation and climate change, are all signs of the increasing fragility of life on our planet. It is arguable that lying at the heart of these overlapping crises is a form of global structural violence resulting from distortions of value systems that demand a re-evaluation of our future and us as global citizens (Benatar, S. R., 2012; Farmer, Kim, Kleinman & Basilico, 2013).

State of Global Health

Widening disparities and inequities in human health are succinctly reflected in the following statistics that show great variation across the world. Life expectancy at birth ranges from 35 yrs to 85 years, under five mortality ranges from 20:1000 to 170:1000 live births, maternal mortality from 1:7 to 1:11,000 pregnancies, and annual per capita expenditure on health care from less than $20 to greater than $8000 (World Bank, 2013). Beyond these quantitative differences, there are vast qualitative differences that we do not adequately consider and cannot measure. For example, reflect on the number of women who suffer for many years as a consequence of rape, genital mutilation, and other forms of violence; the suffering of children and families whose lives are blighted from malnutrition, child labor, displacement from their homes, and persecution on religious grounds (Benatar, 1997); and the more recently articulated suffering of many men and boys from unseen or low-profile abuses in everyday life and in war-like environments (Benatar, D., 2012).

Considerations of global health should also include the deleterious effects of how we live in our natural environment. These include extinction of many species, widespread deforestation and desertification, glacial melting, exhaustion of ocean fisheries and other changes in oceanic ecology (Friel, Butler, & McMichael, 2011; McMichael, 2001) as well as immense suffering inflicted on animals through large-scale commercial farming (Benatar, D., 2011).

The Social and Societal Determinants of Health

The social circumstances influencing health begin with the physical, mental, and nutritional states of women during pregnancy and childbirth and continue throughout life. Care of infants, education and nurturing of children, opportunities for further study during adolescence, and access to jobs are all enhanced by maternal literacy, as demonstrated in some relatively poor countries with high levels of female literacy. Access to adequate nutrition, clean water, sanitation, housing, and basic health care is essential. Additional societal influences that profoundly affect people's lives include the way the global political economy and trade rules are structured through power differentials to benefit those with resources at the expense of those who do not—so that the rich get richer and the poor get poorer (Gill & Bakker, 2011; Pogge, 2002; Pogge, 2005).

With rapid increases in wealth over the past fifty years, relative poverty has become more pronounced. At the beginning of the twentieth century the wealthiest 20 percent of the world's population were nine times richer than the poorest 20 percent. This ratio has grown progressively to 30 times by 1960, 72 times by 1992, and is still increasing (World Centric, n.d.). It is now well established that there are definite relationships between wealth and health and between poverty and disease. However, these relationships are complex and not linear. For example, one of the wealthiest nations in the world (the U.S.A) has worse health statistics (infant mortality and longevity) than some developing countries. Kerala, a particularly poor state in India, has achieved lower infant mortality rates and greater longevity than many wealthier nations (Birn, 2011; Labonte & Schrecker, 2011). Both *absolute wealth* and *relative wealth* influence physical and mental health, longevity, and social well-being. Among the developed countries it is not necessarily the richest societies that have the narrowest disparities in these measures of human flourishing, but rather those with the smallest income differentials between rich and poor (Wilkinson & Picket, 2010).

In the past 150 years, the world's population has grown to seven billion people (more than a seven-fold increase) while human consumption has increased more than 50-fold (Benatar, 1998). Forty-four percent of people (2,735 billion) live below the World Bank's $2 per day international poverty line, most in constant hunger and under squalid conditions. They consume only 1.3 percent of the global product while 955 million citizens of high-income countries consume about 81 percent of the global product (Pogge, 2005). Of the 4.4 billion people in developing countries, over half lack access to sanitation, over 30 percent lack access to clean water and essential drugs, almost a quarter are inadequately nourished, and poverty accounts for 18 million premature deaths each year (Pogge, 2002, UNDP, 2012). The recent global economic crisis, with rapidly rising food prices, committed an additional 100 million people to poverty (Gill & Bakker, 2011).

The U.S.A, with 5 percent of the world's population, accounts for about 24 percent of annual global energy consumption compared with China, where 20 percent of the world's population used 10 percent of global energy in the early 2000s, rising to 20 percent by 2012 and predicted to approach 30 percent by 2020 if China's growth continues at the same pace (Zakaria, 2012). In China, despite massive economic growth, disparities have widened (the Gini coefficient has increased from 0.21 in the 1980s to 0.47 in 2012) with consequent increasing social strife (Hsaio, 2014).

Globally, privileged people have understandably become less aware of the social and societal determinants of health. The focus of medicine and health care has shifted to a biomedical and technological approach to health care that is delivered at great cost. In many countries and especially in the U.S.A, health care has become a marketable commodity within a so-called free market system, where everything is calculated, planned, and delivered from an economic and regimented managerial mindset. Endless expectations and increased orientation towards patients as clients have also changed the concept of medicine from a caring social function, provided through universal access as a social duty to all citizens of equal moral worth, to a profit-driven commercial enterprise run by a medical care industry in the private sectors, and a poorly managed, cost-containment exercise in overwhelmed public sectors.

Some Key Questions About Living and Dying in a Globalizing World

Introspection leads to several key questions that should both be asked and addressed:

1. Why are conditions of living and dying become so increasingly disparate?
2. How can the many crises we face, including the crisis in health, be interpreted in causal terms?
3. What are the implications of upstream causal forces for living and dying with a modicum of dignity?
4. How can we make a difference?

I have noted elsewhere that there are no easy answers to these complex questions and that insight is required into these complexities and their implications for the remainder of the twenty-first century, if we are to shift the trajectory of progress towards improving the lives and health of many millions more people (Benatar S. R., 2011, 2012).

Our dedicated and committed claims to value freedom, human rights, progress based on reason, human dignity, democracy, competitiveness in free markets, and economic growth through consumption have been used to justify strategies and power relations that benefit a small proportion of the world's population, with inadequate regard for their impact on the majority who continue to live in poverty and poor health with little prospect for improvement (Pogge 2002, 2005). Constantly expanding entitlements and living beyond our means have become unsustainable processes. Such problems are, to a considerable extent, linked to individualism carried to extremes (with overemphasis on the freedom of individuals to do as they wish), and to the perpetuation of a narrow conception of human rights with neglect of obligations and needs (Benatar, 2013). Extending to corporations the rights associated with individuals, locking into place international trade rules designed to favor wealthy nations, expectations of endless economic growth, and the drive to increasing consumerism (through popularized economic dogma) have all been part of a deliberately structured global political economy that promotes the ongoing (often corrupt) acquisition of resources by a rich majority at the expense of falling income for a poor majority. A prime example is financial institutions taking advantage of "freedom" to make unwise investments that led to the global financial crisis in which many people in the U.S.A and elsewhere lost their homes and pensions and many more were thrown into poverty (Benatar, Gill, & Bakker, 2011; Gill & Bakker, 2011). Paucity of social solidarity within and between nations, together with lack of moral imagination, may be key factors in allowing us to ignore the contribution of the wealthy to structuring the causal processes for widening disparities (Benatar, 2005).

We also place undue faith in our ability to solve many of these problems through advances in science and technology. The high value placed on knowledge, and especially new knowledge, eclipses the value of already available knowledge as well as considerations of how such knowledge could be applied with wisdom.

Implications for Dying with Dignity

The affluent minority, who has access to the best of medicine, tend to 'deny' death, and the limits of medicine. The final days of their lives are increasingly dominated by technology and they die in hospitals, lonely and connected to "machines" or among "strangers" rather than surrounded by family (Callahan, 1990; Gawande, 2010; Nuland, 1994). For the poor majority who live in squalid circumstances, lacking adequate access to essential living needs, basic medicines, and health care, death often comes in simple overcrowded homes, with intense suffering and no medical care or pain relief. We should try to imagine what it means to suffer one's last weeks and months in deeply impoverished contexts and without access to pain relief that can make such a positive difference to the experience of dying (King & Fraser, 2013; Macpherson & Aarons, 2009).

Acknowledging Our Predicament on a Larger Scale

It is not enough to ask whether those of us who are privileged care about how fellow humans live and die. We should recognize the severity of our current predicament—largely caused by human action—that is resulting in entropy of our planet and destroying the potential for future life. Oreskes and Conway (2013), writing from an anticipated *future* perspective describe this bleakly:

> A second dark age had fallen on Western Civilization, in which denial and self-deception, rooted in an ideological fixation on "free" markets, disabled the world's powerful nations in the face of tragedy.... Historians view 1988 as the start of the Penumbral Period.... By the end of the millennium, denial had spread widely.... By the early 2000s, dangerous anthropogenic interference in the climate system was under way.... By 2040, heat waves and droughts were the norm. Then in the Northern Hemisphere summer of 2041, unprecedented heat waves scorched the planet, destroying food crops around the globe. Mass migration of undernourished and dehydrated individuals, coupled with explosive increases in insect populations led to widespread outbreaks of cholera, dengue fever, yellow fever.... As social order broke down, governments were overthrown.... The US government declared martial law.... To the historian studying this tragic period of human history, the most outstanding fact is that the victims knew what was happening and why.... It is difficult to understand why humans did not respond appropriately in the early Penumbral Period, when preventive measures were still possible.
>
> (pp. 48–49)

Bertolt Brecht's (1949) interpretation of the Buddha's parable of the burning house provides another perspective on our state of denial about such imminent danger. Brecht vividly described a burning house whose inhabitants when urged to leave, asked one inane question after another about safe conditions outside the house, leading to the conclusion that they would burn to death before they stopped asking questions.

Changing perspectives of ourselves should begin with self-examination of our motives and expectations, insights into what we value, and what the opportunity costs may be of blind pursuit of our poorly understood values. Such introspection may lead us to consider the limits of medicine and of life, to recognize our mortality, to reconsider our currently unsustainable entitlements and to work towards developing sustainable lives for individuals and communities.

If we can extend our scholarly critiques and popular education by expanding our discourses on ethics and human rights beyond the individual, to include 'individuals within society,' such a shift in thinking and discourse could contribute to changing our perspectives on life. New insights could promote motives for a range of new social activities, and political actions that have the potential to reduce social injustice (Benatar, S. R., 2012; Benatar, 2013; Benatar, Gill & Bakker, 2009; Benatar, Daar & Singer, 2003).

Do We Have the Resources?

If we consider that $17 trillion were allocated as "economic emergency funds" to bail out banks during the first few months of the 2008 global economic crisis and that this is 22 times as much as pledged for Millennium Development Goals ($750 billion) over a 15 year period, we can hardly claim that resources could not be mobilized to improve the lives of billions of people (Gill & Bakker, 2011). It has been estimated that $35 billion is needed each year to increase the annual per capita health budget of one billion people from $15 to $35 and that this could be raised from a 0.1 percent tax on the income of the richest one billion in the world (Sachs, 2009). Short- to medium-term mechanisms to facilitate redistribution could include reduction in tax evasion (and tax avoidance) by companies and individuals. It has been estimated that $100 billion is lost annually to the U.S. through tax evasion from offshore accounts (Sullivan, 2009).

Longer term social and economic policies are also needed to effectively respond to the challenges of global economic crises. New financing mechanisms could include new imaginative ways of taxation, for example taxes on airline tickets (Brock, 2011). Most resources from such taxes are channeled into UNITAID, which derives around 70 percent of its income from the international solidarity levy on air tickets. Since inception, UNITAID has raised close to US$2 billion to help provide treatment for approximately 47 million people worldwide. The prospects for broadening the implementation of the airline ticket tax are high (United Nations Development Programme, 2012). In addition to re-evaluation of the tax base and new forms of taxation, rethinking social and economic policies in the medium and long terms to promote healthier societies will require effective and prudent economic regulation, the revitalization of public services (health, transport and education), as well as addressing over-consumption (Bakker & Gill, 2011; Brock, 2011). Such action is critical as economic growth does not even remotely trickle down to the extent erroneously believed by many, and philanthropy cannot remove the disjunction between advances in science, technology/medical care and our ability to use these to improve health more widely. Poor leadership in global health aggravates such issues.

Conclusions

The HIV/AIDS pandemic, symptomatic of instability in a globalizing world (Benatar, 2001), has provided insights into the range and intensity of human physical and emotional suffering that varies greatly across gender, ethnic, age, and social status divides (Doyal, 2013). Widespread commitment to relieving this almost unique form of suffering across the globe has led to many advances, including the development of anti-retroviral drugs and making these available at low cost to millions with HIV/AIDS in poor countries. This example of how we have used our intellect and resources to achieve such a remarkable goal serves to encourage us to embark on new means of progress towards better health, less suffering, and less agonizing ways of dying.

Pathways of progress need not, and indeed should not, all be biomedical. In a world in which consumption and entitlement demands exceed resources and we are severely threatened by planetary degradation and entropy, one of the greatest challenges we face is to enable multidisciplinary teams of scholars and others to craft the social, political, and economic innovations that could allow us to do better with less within health care systems specifically and in society more broadly. Herein lies the potential to vastly reduce human suffering, improve the human condition, and to relieve the ailing of a 'sick planet.'

Key Terms

Absolute wealth—the amount of material resources available to, owned, or controlled by an individual or entity (e.g., a business).

Global health—from a human perspective, the extent to which the entire population experiences physical, mental, and emotional well-being and has adequate access to resources needed to maintain health. From an environmental perspective, the extent to which ecosystems exist in balance that promotes well-being for all members.

Relative wealth—the amount of material resources available to, owned, or controlled by an individual or entity (e.g., a business) in comparison to others.

Social determinants of health—external factors that influence the physical, mental, and emotional health of individuals or groups; these influences may arise from social policy or practice at multiple levels (e.g., local infrastructure for sanitation and clean water; opportunities for education based on gender).

Questions for Reflection

1. "Globally, privileged people have understandably become less aware of the social and societal determinants of health" (p. 34). To what extent are you aware of the social and societal determinants of your own state of health? In what ways might your experience be different if you belonged to a different socioeconomic class or lived in a different part of the world?
2. Review Brecht's (1949) interpretation of the Buddha's parable of the burning house. To what extent do you agree or disagree with this depiction of human denial of imminent danger faced by our planet and our species?

References

Bakker, I. C., & Gill, S. (2011). Towards a new common sense: the need for new paradigms for global health. In S. Benatar & G. Brock (Eds.), *Global health and global health ethics* (pp. 329–322). Cambridge, U.K.: Cambridge University Press.

Benatar, D. (2011). Animals, the environment and global health. In S. Benatar & G. Brock (Eds.), *Global health and global health ethics* (pp. 210–220). Cambridge, U.K.: Cambridge University Press.

Benatar, D. (2012). *The second sexism: Discrimination against men and boys.* Sussex, U.K.: Wiley.

Benatar S. R. (1997). Social suffering: Relevance for doctors. *British Medical Journal, 315* (7123), 1634–1635.

Benatar, S. R. (1998). Global disparities in health and human rights: A critical commentary. *American Journal of Public Health, 88,* 295–300.

Benatar S. R. (2001). South Africa's transition in a globalising world: HIV/AIDS as a window and a mirror. *International Affairs, 77*(2), 347–375.

Benatar, S. R. (2005). Moral imagination: The missing component in global health. *PLoS Med 2*(12): e400. doi:10.137

Benatar, S. R. (2011). Global Leadership, Ethics and Global Health: The search for new paradigms. In S. Benatar & G. Brock (Eds.) *Global health and global health ethics* (pp. 127–143). Cambridge, U.K.: Cambridge University Press.

Benatar, S. R. (2012). Needs, obligations and international relations for global health in the21st Century. In J. Coggon & S. Gola (Eds.), *Global health and international community* (pp. 63–80). New York, NY: Bloomsbury Press.

Benatar, S. R. (2013). Global Justice and Health: Re-examining our values. *Bioethics, 27*(6), 297–304.

Benatar S. R., Daar A., & Singer P. A. (2003). Global health ethics: The rationale for mutual caring. *International Affairs, 79*(1), 107–138.

Benatar, S. R., Gill, S. & Bakker I. (2009). Making progress in global health: The need for a new paradigm. *International Affairs 85*(2), 347–371.

Benatar S. R., Gill, S. & Bakker I. C. (2011). Global health and the global economic crisis. *American Journal of Public Health 101*(4), 646–653.

Birn, A. E. (2011). Addressing the societal determinants of health: The key global health ethics imperative. In S. Benatar & G. Brock G. (Eds.), *Global health and global health ethics* (pp. 37–52). Cambridge, U.K.: Cambridge University Press.

Brecht, B. (1949). The Buddha's Parable of the Burning House. Retrieved March 3, 2014 from: www.whatdoesdemocracylooklike.wordpress.com/2011/07/11/bertolt-brechts-interpretation-of-the-buddhas-parable-of-the-burning-house/

Brock, G. (2011). International taxation. In S. Benatar & G. Brock G. (Eds.), *Global health and global health ethics* (pp. 274–284). Cambridge, U.K.: Cambridge University Press.

Callahan, D. (1990). *What kind of life? The limits of medical progress*. New York, NY: Simon & Schuster.

Doyal, L. (2013). *Living with HIV and dying with AIDS: Diversity, inequality and human rights in the Global Pandemic*. Surrey, U.K.: Ashgate Publishing.

Farmer, P., Kim, J. Y., Kleinman, A., & Basilico M. (2013). *Reimagining global health: An introduction*. Berkeley, CA: University of California Press.

Friel, S., Butler, C., & McMichael A. (2011). Climate change and health: Risks and inequities. In S. Benatar & J. Brock (Eds.), *Global health and global health ethics* (pp. 198–209). Cambridge, U.K.: Cambridge University Press.

Gawande, A. (2010, August 2). Letting go: What should medicine do when it cannot save your life? *The New Yorker, 86*(22), 36-49.

Gill, S. (Ed). (2012). *Global crises and the crisis of global governance*. Cambridge, U.K.: Cambridge University Press.

Gill, S., & Bakker, I. C. (2011). The global crisis and global health. In S. Benatar & J. Brock (Eds.), *Global health and global health ethics* (pp. 221–238). Cambridge, U.K.: Cambridge University Press.

Hsiao, W. C. (2014). Correcting past health policy mistakes [in China]. *Daedalus, 143*(2), 59–68.

King, N. B., & Fraser, V. (2013). Untreated pain, narcotics regulation, and global health ideologies. Retrieved May 18, 2014 from: www.plosmedicine.org/article/info%3Adoi%2F10.1371%2Fjournal.pmed.1001411

Labonte, R., & Schreker, T. (2011). The state of global health in a radically unequal world: Patterns and prospects. In S. Benatar & J. Brock (Eds.), *Global health and global health ethics* (pp. 24–36). Cambridge, U.K.: Cambridge University Press.

McMichael, T. (2001). *Human frontiers, environments, and disease*. Cambridge, U.K.: Cambridge University Press.

Macpherson, C., & Aarons, D. (2009). Overcoming barriers to pain relief in the Caribbean. *Developing World Bioethics, 9* (3), 99–104.

Nuland S. (1994). *How we die: Reflections on the last chapter of life*. New York, NY: Knopf.

Oreskes, N., & Conway, E. M. (2013). The collapse of Western Civilization: A view from the future. *Daedalus 142*(1), 40–58.

Pogge, T. (2002). *World poverty and human rights*. Cambridge, U.K.: Polity Press.

Pogge, T. (2005). World poverty and human rights. *Ethics & International Affairs, 19*(1), 1–7.

Sachs, J. A. (2009, October). Statement made by Jeffrey Sachs during a video conference presentation at the Canadian Conference on International Health. Ottawa, Canada.

Sullivan, M. (2009). $100 billion the country could use. Retrieved May 17, 2014 from: www.nytimes.com/2009/03/14/opinion/14sat1.html

United Nations Development Programme. (2012). *Innovative financing for development: A new model for development finance*? Retrieved May 19, 2014 from: www.undp.org/content/dam/undp/library/Poverty%20Reduction/Development%20Cooperation%20and%20Finance/InnovativeFinancing_Web%20ver.pdf

Wilkinson, R. G., & Pickett, K. (2010). *The spirit level: why equality is better for everyone*. London: Penguin.

World Bank. (2013). *Health expenditure per capita (current US$)*. Retrieved May 13, 2014 from: www.data.worldbank.org/indicator/SH.XPD.PCAP

World Centric. (n.d.). *Social and economic security*. Retrieved May 18, 2014 from: www.worldcentric.org/-conscious-living/social-and-economic-injustice

Zakaria, F. (2012). China's economic crisis. *The Washington Post*, May 23. Retrieved October 30, 2015 from: www.washingtonpost.com/opinions/chinas-economic-crisis/2012/05/23/gJQAB9zclU_story.html

4
Compassion in a Materialist World

Neil Thompson

Introduction

Compassion is, of course, at the heart of the helping professions. But it does not occur in a social vacuum. To what extent compassion is encouraged or discouraged, restricted or enabled to flourish will depend on a number of wider socio-political factors. This chapter explores the relationship between, on the one hand, compassion as a basis for professional practice in rising to the challenges presented by loss and grief and, on the other, materialism as a major feature of the socio-political context in which such practice takes place.

I begin by considering the nature of compassion and the nature of materialism before considering a range of problems associated with compassion and materialism. This leads into a discussion of how we can make progress in promoting compassion in a materialist world.

Compassion

Friedrich Nietzsche (1844–1900), one of the most influential Western thinkers, was scornful of the idea of pity. This was because he believed that suffering was something that could strengthen us. Indeed, he was the person who put forward the idea that what does not kill us makes us stronger (Nietzsche, 1990). Helen Keller's comment that, although the world is full of suffering, it is also full of the overcoming of it is well known and widely quoted. However, her comment that a happy life consists not in the absence, but in the mastery, of hardships is less well known, but equally apt (Keller, 1933). In addition, Davies (2012) emphasizes the importance of the role of suffering in developing value and meaning in our lives.

Pity also has negative connotations—to be regarded as an object of pity is to be stigmatized or even patronized. It is therefore important to be clear that compassion is not simply pity by another name. *Webster's Third New International Dictionary* (1986) defines compassion as: "Deep feeling for and understanding of misery or suffering and the concomitant desire to promote its alleviation; spiritual consciousness of the personal tragedy of another or others and selfless tenderness towards it." (p. 462) It is worth exploring each of these components in turn:

Deep feeling for and understanding of misery or suffering

Being able and willing to acknowledge, and respond to, the suffering of others is clearly a key part of what we mean by compassion; it involves recognition that while we are all unique individuals with our own concerns, challenges and problems, there is merit in reaching out to others in supportive ways. This is a key element of the basis of community and society.

Desire to alleviate it

Awareness of, and attunement to, the suffering of others can be a powerful motivator to bring about change, whether in the current circumstances of an experience of suffering or more holistically and proactively in terms of addressing processes and events that bring about such suffering—for example, peace-making initiatives to end or prevent wars; poverty alleviation measures; or campaigns to end discrimination and the oppression and suffering to which these give rise.

Spiritual consciousness

Two key parts of spirituality are meaning and connectedness. Appreciating and responding to the misery and suffering of others can be understood as important sources of meaning. Compassion can give us a strong sense of meaning, purpose, and direction. Similarly, the concept of connectedness has two main dimensions: (i) a recognition that we are social beings (reflecting what Heidegger, 1962, called 'being-toward-others')—we are connected to fellow human beings in a variety of ways; and (ii) the sense that we are part of something bigger than ourselves. For many people, (ii) comes from being a member of a faith community but, of course, religion is not the only basis of spirituality in general and of connectedness in particular. Our sense of being part of something bigger than ourselves can also come from a political commitment to social justice, for example, or to protecting our habitat from the environmental destruction we are in the midst of inflicting. Both these examples, and many more besides, can be seen to be rooted in compassion.

Selfless tenderness towards tragedy

At a superficial level, the idea of putting the alleviation of other people's suffering before our own needs makes sense as a feature of compassion. However, there is a danger of oversimplification here. A more nuanced understanding would take account of the notion of enlightened self-interest put forward by the philosopher Voltaire (1694–1778)—that is, the recognition that helping and supporting others is not a selfless act, but rather, a means of fulfilling our own needs and wishes—not least by giving us a sense of meaning, purpose, direction, and connectedness. According to this analysis, we can meet our own needs regardless of the needs of others (individualistic self-interest) or we can meet our own needs by helping others to meet their need (enlightened self-interest). Compassion, then, is not so much a selfless tenderness as a positive, constructive, and helpful basis of self-interest that provides a platform for community and a caring and humane society. These four dimensions of the definition of compassion give us a sound basis of understanding and I will return to this four-fold conception when I discuss problems associated with materialism.

However, before leaving the topic of compassion, it is also worth remembering Buber's (1923/2004) distinction between I–Thou and I-it, with its recognition of human connection as part of spirituality. The former refers to interactions that are rooted in mutual respect and concern for one another, while the latter refers to interactions that are purely instrumental, solely about "getting the job done"—the other person is treated as simply a means to an end. Buber argues that I–Thou interactions humanize both parties, whereas I-it interactions dehumanize both parties. That is, it is not only the person who is being treated as "it" that is dehumanized, but also the person who is treating the other party in this way—a process of self-dehumanization accompanies the dehumanization of the other. This distinction will also be relevant later when I address problems associated with materialism.

Finally, in relation to compassion, I want to comment on the understanding of vulnerability put forward by the philosopher Gilles Deleuze. Braidotti (2012), in discussing Deleuze's approach to ethics, states that: "The emphasis falls on vulnerability as the potential capacity to be wounded and hence to require the care, solidarity, and love of others. Respect for vulnerability is therefore the basis of the ethical human relation" (p. 171).

This important passage is worth exploring in a little more detail. The vulnerability (the potential capacity to be wounded) that we all face as human beings means that there will be times when we will need to rely on the compassion of others. Deleuze therefore regards this as an ethical matter—the fact that no one is invulnerable means that we have a moral duty to exercise compassion towards one another. To deny compassion to others when we are highly likely to need it ourselves at some point manifests a moral hypocrisy—yet another factor to take into consideration when we explore the difficulties associated with materialism. Furthermore, the notion of "respect for vulnerability" fits perfectly with the idea of compassion.

Materialism

The term "materialism" has different meanings in different contexts. For example, in the philosophical literature, it is used to distinguish between Hegel's (1807/1976) notion of the dialectical interaction of ideas (idealism) as the basis of social reality and Marx's (1867/2013) notion of the dialectic of material forces (such as ownership of the means of production) as the basis of social reality (materialism). However, there is also a more widespread moral and political use of the term "materialism" to refer to an approach to life that prioritizes wealth and economic advantage over other aspects of human existence and other potential sources of reward, fulfillment, and well-being. It is this latter sense that I will be addressing here.

While this is different from Marx's notion of (dialectical) materialism, it is none the less associated with it. This is because of Marx's critique of capitalism. In capitalism, the emphasis, as the name implies, is on the development of economic capital, of vast resources of wealth. While this is not necessarily a problem in itself, it has some consequences that have the potential to be highly problematic, not least that (i) the system, with its emphasis on labor as less important than capital, thereby presents people as a means not an end; and (ii) workers can be alienated from their work because they do not own the results of it—they are selling their labor and thus receive financial reward in the form of wages, but the creative fruits of their endeavors belong not to them, but to the owners of the companies for which they work.

However, there is more to modern-day materialism than this. James (2007) argues for a less materialistic form of capitalism. He puts forward the notion of "affluenza," the malaise that results from the capitalist emphasis on ever-increasing wealth at the expense of other human rewards and needs. This is a point to which we will return below.

Materialism is often contrasted with spirituality, with the latter being seen as more fulfilling, offering more meaning and human connection. It is not insignificant, for example, that communism —an ideology that rejected capitalism (based on a very distorted and problematic understanding of Marx's ideas)—banned religion, but offered no spirituality in its place. The decline of communist systems since the end of the cold war has brought a resurgence of religion as a form of spirituality, but what has come with it has been a strong emphasis on materialism, as the post-communist states have adopted capitalist economic systems, with the priority being given to wealth accumulation (Brown, 2009)—that is, with the notion of "riches" being defined narrowly as financial gain, leaving relatively little scope for wider, more spiritual riches.

Jordan (2008) shares this concern when he argues that the dominance of the economic approach has become more total than could have been predicted. In an earlier work, Jordan (2006) distinguished between the economy, as conventionally understood in financial terms, and what he calls the "interpersonal economy," which is the psychosocial and spiritual wealth we receive from contributing to, and being part of, supportive communities.

A further significant aspect of materialism is inequality. The focus on maximizing wealth can be seen to have the effect of increasing inequality—that is, of widening the gap between the richest and poorest sectors of society. As we shall see below, this has a major detrimental effect at a number of levels (Wilkinson and Pickett, 2009).

Problems with Compassion

Having provided an overview of both compassion and materialism, I will now identify a number of problems associated with each of these, beginning with compassion.

One noted problem associated with compassion is that of "compassion fatigue." This is a term that can apply at two levels, macro and micro. At the macro level, it manifests itself through media coverage whereby there are so many negative and distressing stories that involve misery and suffering that people tend to disengage as a form of defense mechanism, a protection from the constant stream of potentially emotionally demanding news items (Moeller, 1999).

At a micro level it can be a contributor to burnout for members of the helping professions. Burnout is a response to stress in which the person concerned develops a protective skin which filters out emotion (Maslach and Leiter, 1997). Clearly this is a significant problem for any member of the helping professions, but can be especially problematic in circumstances involving loss and grief, where emotional issues are likely to be very much to the fore (Thompson, 2012).

One further problem with compassion is that, in many people, it evokes responses rooted in paternalism. For example, many charitable efforts have been criticized for being based on what is seen as a patronizing attitude towards those who need help and support. It is no coincidence that a major feature of modern-day voluntary sector provision is an emphasis on empowerment and citizen participation, to guard against such criticisms (Adams, 2008). However, it is important to note that there is nothing inherent in the concept of compassion that makes it patronizing.

Problems with Materialism

While there are problems and challenges associated with compassion, these pale into insignificance compared with the difficulties engendered by materialism. Chief among these is "atomism" (Thompson, 2010). This is a philosophical term that refers to the tendency to focus on the individual level and thus neglect consideration of wider socio-political factors. Materialism brings with it competitiveness (competing for scarce resources plus "conspicuous consumption"—aiming not only to be richer than others, but also to show that we are), and this then narrows the focus to the individual level. Someone who is interested primarily in wealth accumulation is likely to have far less of a focus on the wider picture of social problems and social injustices, such as poverty, deprivation, discrimination, oppression, and related matters.

Such atomism, with its focus on individual wealth, lays the foundations for base consumerism to displace nobler social and spiritual concerns. Southerton (2011) argues that the emergence of consumerism has created a culture that projects an image of life as a set of problems to be solved by purchasing the right product or products from the marketplace. In a telling passage, Hames (2007) highlights how significant this is in relation to (the absence of) compassion:

> Watched by millions who are starving to death, developed nations continue to plunder the environment and accumulate obscene wealth, appearing to value selfishness and greed as if these were the peak of sophistication. Consumers everywhere are demanding more and more of everything, fuelling misery in the developing world and perpetuating the gap between those who benefit from global prosperity and those who cannot.
>
> (p. 4)

He goes on to bemoan the fact that meaning and purpose have come to be dominated by concerns about wealth and status. This position is a reinforcement of the previous chapter's exploration of global plundering by developed nations and the detrimental impact upon those who live outside of these prospering economies.

Barry (2005), writing about the importance of social justice, echoes similar concerns. He argues that, the more materialistic a society is, the more it will be believed that money is the only significant goal in life. This will mean that people with a lot of money will see themselves as winners and those with little money will see themselves as losers. This can then be reflected in an ideology which supports the (pathologizing) idea that those who are better off than others are more virtuous (as if material success is an indicator of moral worth). This ideology, supported by media messages, can then be internalized by rich and poor alike, as well as everyone else on the income spectrum.

Atomism can therefore be seen as a significant barrier to compassion, as it distracts attention from the wider picture and restricts the focus to efforts to maximize individual wealth. Ballatt and Campling (2011) reinforce this point when they argue that an individualistic, competitive society is prone to breed unkindness—a barrier to compassion, rather than a basis for it. They go on to point out that there is evidence that people who care about the happiness of others and the relief of misery will themselves be happier. This is, of course, a strong argument for compassion and against materialism.

Underpinning much of the problematic nature of materialism is the political philosophy of neoliberalism (Chomsky, 2011). This ideology emphasizes a commitment to market forces and minimal governmental or collective activity. This feeds both atomism and managerialism, an approach to public policy which relies on targets and performance indicators. In this way, public and social services are: (i) reduced to a marginal role, a residual safety net for those who are not able to afford insurance or other means of securing their own health and social welfare needs; and (ii) run as much like businesses as possible. Neoliberalism is geared towards maximizing wealth and allocates only a safety net role for compassionate endeavors.

Earlier, I mentioned James's (2007) notion of "affluenza." His basic argument is that the self-centered nature of capitalism has a significant detrimental effect on people's mental health. He proposes that, to fill the sense of emptiness and loneliness of a materialistic consumerism, we seek to replace our need for authentic, intimate relationships by resorting to the consumption that is needed to fuel the economic growth and profits on which capitalism relies. This is significant in terms of human misery and distress: "The more anxious or depressed we are, the more we must consume, and the more we consume, the more disturbed we become. Consumption holds out the false promise that an internal lack can be fixed by an external means" (p. 15).

In a similar vein, Ballatt and Campling (2011) draw on the work of Kasser (2002), who argues that placing ourselves in a position whereby our happiness and self-esteem rely on the possession of material goods for their own sake is a danger to our mental health. Consumerist culture leads many people to work excessive hours and go into debt in their efforts to consume more and more, and the price for this is stress. Echoing the ideas of Jordan mentioned earlier, Kasser also argues that those who place a high value on material wealth are unsurprisingly found to place a relatively low emphasis on the value of personal relationships and to make relatively little contribution to their community (that is, to be less focused on I–Thou interactions).

This shift away from community and shared endeavors towards individualism, competitiveness, and social isolation can be seen to have the effect of reducing social capital. This is a term used to refer to the benefits people accrue from having social contacts. Putnam (2001) raised awareness of the significance of this in his book on "bowling alone," in which he commented on how bowling used to be a team effort and a source of a great deal of community and group connection, but now tends to be a largely individualistic pursuit. He uses this as an example of how individualism has led to a reduced level of social capital for a significant number of people. With the reduced level of social capital and social interaction we get a reduction in the scope for compassion.

Barry (2005) continues the theme of the wider and deeper human price we pay for materialism and the consumerism it engenders. He points out that, the more unequal a society becomes in terms of income and wealth, the stronger the connection between wealth and status becomes. This means that people who make valuable contributions to learning, to the arts, or to the well-being of others are likely to be accorded a comparatively lower social standing, unless they are also able to generate wealth through these activities. Such contributions are given relatively little credit in their own right, while people who make large amounts of money without making such contributions tend to become objects of admiration, held in high esteem in large part through media exposure that attaches more importance to wealth than to well-being (Hedges, 2009). Materialism can therefore be seen to reduce both social capital and the scope for social status premised on anything other than wealth accumulation.

Materialism is now also a major concern because of not only its deposing of spirituality, but also its impact on our human habitat. As Pickering (2012) argues, our (materialistically based) technologically driven lifestyle is doing untold damage to the environment. This is not only harmful and deeply problematic in relation to our habitat, but also detrimental to our well-being. In this way, we are failing to show compassion towards the earth and to all the people and other living creatures who rely on it for life (Fitzpatrick, 2011).

To conclude this section on the problems associated with materialism, I will now revisit the four elements of the definition of compassion that we encountered earlier and comment briefly on how materialism adversely affects each one of them.

Deep feeling for and understanding of misery or suffering

The concerns raised here in relation to materialism and the consumerism and individualism it engenders paint a worrying picture of an approach to modern life in which concern for the misery and suffering of others is a marginal issue compared with the pursuit of wealth and material goods.

Desire to alleviate it

While materialism continues to be a major feature of Western societies, the desire to alleviate suffering will continue to be a secondary consideration if it features at all. This contrasts sharply with the "enlightened self-interest" mentioned earlier, which allows us to gain satisfaction and pleasure from helping others. Pickering (2012) quotes Gandhi's remark that: "The world has enough for everyone's needs, but not for some people's greed." He goes on to argue that: "Corporate greed, acquired second-hand via the advertising industry, makes people feel insecure. The world cannot seem ever to provide enough" (p. 161).

Materialism can therefore be seen to shift our focus away from compassion and on to material gain.

Spiritual consciousness

As we have noted, connectedness is an important part of spirituality, but we have also noted that materialism undermines our sense of community and human connection of being part of something bigger than ourselves. As Southerton (2011) puts it:

> People have become primarily focused on themselves, and the communities that once surrounded us and provided a sense of identity, belonging and security are systematically destroyed by this self-obsession. As communities are undermined, interpersonal relationships are rendered shallow and superficial.
>
> (p. 138)

By focusing on compassion, in contrast, we can join with others in meaningful ways and feel that we are part of a wider humanitarian concern.

Materialism has become a dominant feature of Western lives. It is as if it is an attempt to fill an existential void, to try and make our lives more meaningful. It is ironic, then, that materialism, which has a tendency to displace spiritual concerns, becomes a (shallow, unsatisfying, and self-defeating) process of providing meaning.

Returning to James's concerns about "affluenza" and the effect of materialism on mental health and well-being, he refers to research carried out by Kasser and Ryan (1993) and notes that "as Erich Fromm predicted, in all the fourteen countries studied so far and regardless of gender or age, materialism increases the risk of depression, anxiety, substance abuse, narcissism and the feeling that your life is joyless" (James, 2008, p. 57).

Selfless tenderness towards tragedy

At the heart of compassion, of course, is caring. It is about recognizing, as my comments above about the work of Deleuze indicate, that we are all vulnerable, that we can all be hurt and need help in healing our wounds. Of course, this is particularly the case in relation to loss and grief, as encountering a major loss, directly or indirectly, brings home very powerfully our existential fragility as human beings. It shows how no amount of consumption or material wealth can take away the fact that we are finite beings that can choose either to support one another in responding to the challenges involved or retreat into our materialistic individualism and leave ourselves more open to the insecurities associated with loss and grief.

Moving Forward

If we are to take seriously the value of, and need for, compassion, then we must clearly look closely at what can be done to address the many and profound problems associated with materialism. I am not naïve enough to think that there are easy or magic answers, nor do I believe that a short essay like this can deliver a comprehensive analysis. However, more realistically, there are some important matters I want to highlight to help us move away from materialism towards a more balanced approach to life which leaves far more room for spirituality, community, shared endeavor, and, of course, compassion—caring and supportive human connection that helps us meet the existential challenges of our vulnerability.

In particular, I want to propose five steps that we can take to help us move in the right direction:

1. *Reaffirming spirituality*: For many people spirituality is automatically associated with religion, but this implies that people who have no religion are not spiritual or do not have spiritual needs. It is therefore important that we find a way to reaffirm spirituality both within and without religious communities to give greater attention to spiritual needs for people of all faiths and none (the Dalai Lama, 2013).

    One advantage we have in a thanatological context is that encounters with death and dying (and indeed with loss and grief more broadly) generally have the effect of helping people engage with spiritual matters—a reminder of our mortality and finitude can so easily trigger a response of spiritual questioning and searching.

    A helpful concept when it comes to reaffirming spirituality is that of "spiritual intelligence" (Zohar & Marshall, 2000). Parallel with the notion of "emotional intelligence," (Goleman, 1996) it refers to our ability to make work meaningful, to give a sense of shape, direction and purpose to our working lives. There is perhaps scope to extend this concept to explore how it could be used more widely to make spirituality a higher priority in our lives.

2. *Promoting reciprocity*: Being able to contribute, to give as well as to receive, can be seen as an important foundation of well-being (Thompson, 2013). However, we can detect a tendency to focus on providing care for people when they are dying or grieving which can, if we are not aware of the dangers, leave little room for such contributions, and so reciprocity—and the

sense of self-worth that goes with it—can be lost (Thompson, 2009). We therefore need to ensure that our efforts to be compassionate do not unwittingly have a counterproductive effect by denying people well-being by blocking off opportunities for reciprocity.

3. *Making a commitment to social justice*: As we have noted, materialism and the neoliberal political ideology which promotes it, have the effect of producing increased inequality which, in turn, produces a wide range of problems. A key part of social justice is the recognition of the need for greater equality. While many people simplistically dismiss equality because they confuse it with uniformity, the need to reduce the gap between the richest and the poorest remains (Thompson, 2011). Compassion is often seen as an individual, micro-level matter, while social justice is seen as a collective, macro-level phenomenon, whereas in reality both compassion and social justice need to be addressed at both micro (ethical) and macro (political) levels.

4. *Leadership*: "Being effective and remaining human" is the subtitle of Peter Gilbert's (2005) book on leadership, and that phrase captures a very important element of what leadership is all about. Supporting people who are dying or grieving is important, demanding work, so it is essential that staff involved are indeed effective in what they are doing, but also remain human. Compassion, for all its strengths, can be wearing, with burnout a possible result.

    Leadership is also about creating a workplace culture where people feel valued, supported, and safe. This is, of course, the sort of culture needed for compassion to flourish. Without positive leadership it will be difficult for staff to maintain a positive focus in difficult and challenging circumstances.

5. *Transformational compassion*: The notion of "transformational grief" is now well established. The idea that we can grow, develop, learn, and be stronger after grieving a major loss (Schneider, 2012) chimes well with the idea of "post-traumatic growth" (Calhoun & Tedeschi, 2006). In addition, Dobson and Wong (2012) argue that a major component of coping with existential challenges (such as loss and trauma) is to learn from suffering and gain some degree of spiritual benefit from adversity. This takes us back to Nietzsche's idea, mentioned earlier, that suffering is something that can make us stronger.

    But what of the notion of transformational compassion? Can being attuned to other people's suffering and reaching out to them in their hour of need bring growth, development, learning, and strength for the compassionate helper? My experience leads me to say a very strong yes, but this is clearly an area that needs further research and consideration.

    Being a compassionate helper brings us into contact with our own mortality, fragility, and vulnerability (Papadatou, 2009), something that can be a heavy burden to bear or which can be a transformational experience that strengthens us spiritually, emotionally and practically. An uncritical acceptance of materialism and consumerism can deny us such an existential transformation.

Conclusion

Professionals who are working with people who are dying or grieving face a number of challenges which, in some ways, echo the challenges of the individuals they seek to support (Thompson, 2012). One of the challenges is maintaining a compassionate approach in their own professional interactions, while also seeking to encourage a wider culture of compassion. This chapter has highlighted that the dominance of an ideology of materialism serves in various ways as an obstacle to compassion. In particular, it has shown that materialism by its very nature acts as a brake on spirituality; it places obstacles in the way of higher levels of well-being at both individual and community levels.

Of course, materialism did not develop overnight, and so it will not die out in the short term. But this does not mean that we have to be defeatist. As we have seen, there are steps we can take to ease the situation by moving away from materialism and promoting spirituality and well-being in general and in relation to the challenges of grief in particular.

In recognizing just how far materialism has taken us away from the sense of community that we need for our well-being, James (2008) makes the important point that: "It is incumbent on our politicians to heed this message and to begin the long journey back towards societies which put well-being before the wealth of a tiny minority" (p. 9). However, while I fully agree with this, I would also argue that it is not just politicians who need to play a part. If we are genuinely to reaffirm our spirituality and the connectedness which is an essential part of it (through a greater level of compassion rooted in the community that comes from having a common sense of humanity), then this needs to be a grassroots movement. Such a movement will require political support, of course, but it would be a mistake to leave such an important undertaking to politicians alone.

Key terms

Affluenza—the malaise that results from the capitalist emphasis on ever-increasing wealth at the expense of other human rewards and needs.

Atomism—the tendency to focus on the individual level and thus neglect consideration of wider socio-political factors.

Compassion—deep feeling for and understanding of misery or suffering of others and the concomitant desire to promote its alleviation.

Compassion fatigue—disengaging from or filtering out emotional information, generally after having become overwhelmed by contact with intense or continuous emotional stimuli. This protective strategy may be enacted at the macro level (e.g., large numbers of people disengaging from media coverage due to overwhelming stories of misery and suffering) or on a micro level (e.g., individual burnout by members of the helping professions).

Conspicuous consumption—aiming not only to be richer than others, but also to outwardly and obviously demonstrate the wealth and disparity between those who have wealth and those who do not.

Interpersonal economy—the psychosocial and spiritual wealth individuals receive from contributing to, and being part of, supportive communities.

Materialism—an approach to life which prioritizes wealth and economic advantage over other aspects of human existence and other potential sources of reward, fulfillment and well-being.

Social capital—the expected collective or economic benefits derived from the preferential treatment and cooperation between individuals and groups; the value of social networks and contacts.

Spiritual intelligence—the ability to make work and life meaningful; involves awareness, integration, and adaptive application of the nonmaterial and transcendent aspects of one's existence into everyday life.

Transformational compassion—spiritual, emotional, and practical growth that arises through the process of being attuned and responding to other people's suffering.

Questions for Reflection

1. How would you differentiate compassion from pity? To what extent do you agree with the claim that compassion is connected with spirituality?
2. "To deny compassion to others when we are highly likely to need it ourselves at some point manifests a moral hypocrisy." However, attempting to be aware of—and respond with compassion toward all the needs of all others may contribute to the development of compassion fatigue. How have you balanced these competing demands in your own life?
3. "The more unequal a society becomes in terms of income and wealth, the stronger the connection between wealth and status becomes" (p. 44). Consider the society in which you live. What evidence do you see supporting or contradicting this claim?

References

Adams, R. (2008). *Empowerment, participation and social work* (4th ed.). Basingstoke, U.K.: Palgrave Macmillan.
Ballatt, J., & Campling, P. (2011). *Intelligent kindness: Reforming the culture of healthcare*, London: The Royal College of Psychiatrists.
Barry, B. (2005). *Why social justice matters*. Cambridge: Polity Press.
Braidotti, R. (2012). Nomadic ethics. In D. W. Smith & H. Somers-Hall (Eds.), *The Cambridge companion to Deleuze*. Cambridge, U.K.: Cambridge University Press.
Brown, A. (2009). *The rise & fall of Communism*. London: Bodley Head.
Buber, M. (2004). *I and Thou*. London: Continuum. (Originally published in German in 1923).
Calhoun L. G., & Tedeschi, R. G. (Eds.). (2006). *Handbook of posttraumatic growth: Research and practice*, New York, NY: Routledge.
Chomsky, N. (2011). *Profit over people: Neoliberalism and global order*. New York, NY: Seven Stories Press.
Dalai Lama (2013). *Beyond religion: Ethics for a whole world*. London: Rider.
Davies, R. (2012). *The importance of suffering: The value and meaning of emotional discontent*. London: Routledge.
Dobson, W. L., & Wong, P. T. P. (2012). Women living with HIV: The role of meaning and spirituality. In A Tomer, G. T. Eliason, & P. T. P. Wong (Eds.), *Existential and spiritual issues in death and dying*. New York, NY: Lawrence Erlbaum Associates.
Fitzpatrick, T. (Ed.). (2011). *Understanding the environment and social policy*. Bristol, U.K.: Policy Press.
Gilbert, P. (2005). *Leadership: Being effective and remaining human*. Lyme Regis, U.K.: Russell House.
Goleman, D. (1996). *Emotional intelligence: Why it can matter more than IQ*. London: Bloomsbury.
Hames, R. D. (2007). *The five literacies of global leadership: What authentic leaders know and you need to find out*. San Francisco, CA: Jossey-Bass.
Hedges, C. (2009). *Empire of illusion: The end of literacy and the triumph of spectacle*. New York, NY: Nation Books.
Hegel, G. W. H. (1976). *Phenomenology of spirit*. Oxford, U.K.: Oxford University Press. (Originally published in German in 1807).
Heidegger, M. (1962). *Being and time*, Oxford U.K.: Blackwell.
Jordan, B. (2006). *Social work and well-being*. Lyme Regis, U.K.: Russell House.
Jordan, B. (2008). *Welfare and well-being: Social value in public policy*. Bristol, U.K.: The Policy Press.
James, O. (2007). *Affluenza: How to be successful and stay sane*. London: Vermilion.
James, O. (2008). *The selfish capitalist: Origins of affluenza*. London: Vermilion.
Kasser, T. (2002). *The high price of materialism*. Cambridge, MA: MIT Press.
Kasser, T., & Ryan, R. (1993). A dark side of the American dream: Correlates of financial success as a central life aspiration. *Journal of Personality and Social Psychology*, 65(2), 410–422.
Keller, H. (1933). The simplest way to be happy. *Home Magazine*, February.
Marx, K. (2013). *Capital*, London: Wordsworth. (Originally published in 1867).
Maslach, C., & Leiter, M. P. (1997). *The truth about burnout: How organizations cause personal stress and what to do about it*. San Francisco, CA: Jossey-Bass.
Moeller, S. D. (1999). *Compassion fatigue: How the media sell disease, famine, war and death*. New York, NY: Routledge.
Nietzsche, F. (1990). *Twilight of the idols*. Harmondsworth, U.K.: Penguin. (Originally published in German in 1888).
Papadatou, D. (2009.) *In the face of death: Professionals who care for the dying and the bereaved*. New York, NY: Springer.
Pickering, J. (2012). Is well-being local or global? A perspective from ecopsychology. In J. Haworth & G. Hart (Eds.), *Well-being: Individual, community and social perspectives*, Basingstoke, U.K.: Palgrave Macmillan.
Putnam, R. D. (2001). *Bowling alone: The collapse and revival of American community*. New York, NY: Simon & Schuster.
Schneider, J. (2012). *Finding my way: From trauma to transformation: The journey through loss and grief*. Traverse City, MI: Seasons Press.
Southerton, D. (2011). Consumer culture and personal life. In V. May (Ed.), *Sociology of Personal Life*, Basingstoke, U.K.: Palgrave Macmillan.
Thompson, N. (2010). *Theorizing social work practice*. Basingstoke, U.K.: Palgrave Macmillan.
Thompson, N. (2011). *Promoting equality: Working with diversity and difference* (3rd ed.). Basingstoke, U.K.: Palgrave Macmillan.
Thompson, N. (2012). *Grief and its challenges*. Basingstoke, U.K.: Palgrave Macmillan.
Thompson, S. (2009). Reciprocity in crisis situations. *Illness, Crisis & Loss*, 17(2), 71–86.
Thompson, S. (2013). *Reciprocity and dependency in old age: UK and Indian perspectives*. New York, NY: Springer.
Webster (1986) *Webster's third new international dictionary*. Chicago, IL: Merriam-Webster.
Wilkinson, R., & Pickett, K. (2009). *The spirit level: Why more equal societies almost always do better*. London: Allen Lane.
Zohar, D., & Marshall, I. (2000). *Connecting with our spiritual intelligence*. New York, NY: Bloomsburg.

5

Inequality, Exclusion, and Infant Mortality
Listening to Bereaved Mothers

Neil Small, Katie Fermor, Ghazala Mir, and members of the HOPE group

Introduction

This chapter will examine issues of social justice by focusing on social exclusion and infant mortality. Infant mortality is defined as the death of a live born child before its first birthday. Social exclusion and infant mortality are both important areas of policy debate in the U.K. and globally (Health Inequalities Unit, 2008). We will examine how they are linked and will focus on ethnic minority populations with higher than average rates of infant mortality. The chapter continues by considering a small group of women who have experienced the death of an infant and who have come together in a group called HOPE. We ask how their experience might inform our understanding of the needs of women at the time of childbirth and in the weeks immediately following it. Their experiences illuminate how feelings of exclusion and injustice can be manifest in and through the structures and processes of engaging with health care professionals. The potential to promote social justice and enhance inclusion via listening to the voices of those who have had this experience of loss is considered.

Structural and Behavioral Influences on Infant Mortality

The U.K.'s National Perinatal Epidemiology Unit has identified three main factors: 1) The direct effects of poverty, 2) variations in behavior, and 3) differential access to services, as combining to cause persistent and wide inequalities in pregnancy outcomes and in the health of babies (D'Souza & Garcia, 2003). More specifically, infant mortality rates in the general population are strongly associated with the social position of women (Maher & Macfarlane, 2004). Women's levels of education and literacy, their socioeconomic status, and the level of relative deprivation in their area of residence are all correlated with the risk that their baby will die in its first year (U.K. National Statistics, 2014). This pattern is observed worldwide (World Health Organization, 2005). Infant mortality is also consistently associated with low birth weight and preterm birth, mother's age, birth spacing, access to a range of maternal health technologies, and lifestyle characteristics of the mother and her household. Most notable 'behavioral' risk factors that will affect significant numbers of women in the U.K. are smoking during pregnancy and poor nutritional status. There is a complex interchange between the behavioral and structural influences upon infant mortality. Smoking rates during pregnancy are higher in women who are more socio-economically deprived, and poor nutritional status is also more evident in deprived groups (Sproston and Primatesta, 2003; Kramer, 1998. Mwatsama & Stewart, 2005).

Just as there is a close correlation between key behavioral influences and structural inequalities, so there are complex associations between different structural dimensions of a person's life. Socio-economic background and ethnicity are separately associated with poor birth outcomes (Graham, 2009). However, there is a close association between these two factors. Infant mortality rates are higher in local authority areas with the highest deprivation indicators. These are also the areas where minority ethnic communities are over-represented (Health Inequalities Unit, 2008). A further compounding of the structural and behavioral is evidenced in relation to higher than average rates of infant mortality in babies born to teenage mothers. Levels of deprivation are high in most minority ethnic groups and they are also high for teenage mothers. In some, but not all, minority ethnic groups rates of teenage pregnancy are higher than average; for example, rates in Caribbean communities are higher and in Pakistani origin communities they are lower (Health Inequalities Unit, 2008, see Figure 5.1).

In addition to both structural and behavioral influences on maternal health and on infant mortality, the configuration of health services can also exert a powerful influence. Improvements in care during pregnancy, labor, and birth significantly affect the health outcomes of mothers (Austerberry & Wiggins, 2007; Oakley, Hickey, & Rigby, 1994; Sosa, Kennell, Klaus, Robertson, & Urrutia, 1980). But improvements to these services, as currently configured, while impacting on maternal health outcomes, may not reduce health inequalities unless services are tailored to meet the specific needs of disadvantaged women. Likewise, risk reduction strategies and public health interventions, such as addressing environmental stressors or health education services advising on behavioral change disproportionately benefit those who already occupy advantageous social positions. As with service provision, these strategies need to be targeted and reconfigured if they are to specifically benefit disadvantaged groups and hence have an impact on health inequalities (Marmot, Adelstein, & Bulusu, 1984).

While there are strong similarities in the patterns and prevalence of structural and behavioral factors having an impact on infant mortality and maternal health at the time of birth, there are also some factors that are likely to have a greater impact on a smaller group of mothers. These are factors that do not affect the generality of mothers and babies, but those they affect do so profoundly. For example, maternal diabetes, HIV positive status, or the use of non-prescribed drugs during pregnancy exert a high risk for the babies of women with these characteristics. A further example is that there

| Recorded as death of live born infants before age 1 per 1000 live births (U. K. National Statistics, 2014) |||
| Overall National rate: 4.2 |||
	Rate	Rate Higher than National rate by
Caribbean mothers	9.7	131%
Pakistani mothers	7.6	81%
W. African mothers	7.4	76%
Teenage mothers	5.4	29%

Figure 5.1 Rates of Infant Death in England and Wales

is a genetic contribution to infant mortality. This is evident in all sections of the population, but affects the Pakistani population to a greater extent and is linked to the increased risk for families in communities who favor consanguineous partnerships (who are genetically related). Consanguineous couples affected by a genetic condition have a higher incidence of babies born with congenital anomalies, some of which may be lethal (Sheridan et al., 2013).

Social Networks and Maternal and Infant Health

The development of research on the impact of social capital on health (Putnam, 2000), on ethnic density as potentially both a health promoting and health limiting phenomena (Pickett & Wilkinson, 2008), and on the significance of the extent of inequality in any society rather than the absolute level of deprivation (Wilkinson & Pickett, 2009) complement more established analytic categories, including poverty and ethnicity in the study of health experiences. There is now an extensive body of literature on social capital providing evidence that both the social environment and the community networks have an impact on health outcomes both through psychosocial and physical mechanisms (Siegrist & Marmot, 2006; Horwitz, Morgenstern, & Berkman, 1985; Balaji et al., 2007; Lai, Lin, & Leung, 1998). The ability to 'bond' with those inside and 'bridge' to those outside one's social group increases access to resources at both personal and community levels. High levels of 'bridging,' or social interaction between diverse social groups increase social cohesion (Putnam, 2000), which, in itself, is a positive determinant of health. At a community level, such interaction can influence health outcomes through promoting healthy norms of behavior, restricting unhealthy behaviors, and diffusing health information. Socially isolated individuals are more likely to have poor health outcomes and be located in communities that are depleted in social capital. Both stress and self-esteem have an impact on social relations and physical well-being (Wilkinson & Pickett, 2009).

But, as with the relationship between structural and behavioral influences on health, socioeconomic status is a key factor mediating the effects of social networks. Access to material resources and contacts promoting health and well-being are facilitated and sustained in networks within economically advantaged communities and a "network of poverty and disadvantage" can perpetuate inequality (Afridi, 2011).

Social Networks and Minority Ethnic Communities

Being part of a minority ethnic group and sharing culture and social support networks may be protective of one's health, even in economically deprived contexts. This is illustrated by research in the U.S.A. on the "Latina paradox"(McGlade, Saha, & Dahlstrom, 2004). Latina women have comparable birth outcomes to white women of better socioeconomic status. McGlade et al. (2004) argue that this is because systems of family, friends, community members, and lay health workers provide support (pp. 2062–2065). However, the same effect was not observed for Black mothers, for whom living in an area of moderate to high same ethnic density was associated with a higher risk of low birth weight, preterm birth and infant mortality (Shaw, Pickett, & Wilkinson, 2010, pp. 707–713).

There has also been concern that racism, a persistent feature in the lives of women from minority ethnic communities, was especially evident during pregnancy, for example, in assumptions made by health care workers that led to them not acknowledging reported pain (Barnes, 2008). The 2010 National Perinatal Epidemiology Unit highlighted how women from minority ethnic groups had their first antenatal contact later than the general population. Other studies have reported less awareness of choices around maternity care, less trust and confidence in staff during labor and birth, and less satisfaction with communication from staff (Redshaw, & Heikkila, 2010). Similar findings were obtained by the Healthcare Commission. Women from minority ethnic groups were more likely to be left alone during labor and reported feeling worried by this. This may be because health care professionals feel poorly equipped to communicate effectively with patients from Black and minority ethnic groups. In regards to training needs, Chevannes (2002) identified shortcomings in addressing the needs of women from these groups, apart from dealing with particular conditions such as sickle cell anemia.

Social Support, Birth, and Postnatal Mental Health

There are specific aspects of social support that are of increased importance around the time of birth. Notwithstanding the contribution of social networks (introduced above), many studies show the significance of partners for a woman's sense of well-being, which is sometimes positive and sometimes negative. In a U.K. study, only a few young women with a supportive partner reported feeling unhappy since the birth, compared with two-thirds of those with no supportive partner (Austerberry & Wiggins, 2007). There is significant evidence that a lack of social support is a risk factor for postnatal depression (Balaji et al., 2007). Essex and Pickett (2008) found that women who did not have a companion at birth were more likely to have their baby admitted to the neonatal ward and for the baby to have a low birth weight. Conversely, the presence of a friendly companion during labor reduced birth complications (Sosa et al., 1980). Pakistani, Black mothers, and women from non-English speaking and deprived households were more likely to deliver alone (National Collaborating Centre for Women's and Children's Health, 2010).

Husbands and male relatives may also be significant in influencing engagement of women with antenatal groups (Karl-Trumme, Krajic Novak-Zezula, & Pelikan, 2006). But strong family ties might also impact negatively on take-up of care. St. Clair, Smeriglio, Alexander, and Celentano (1989) found that stronger family ties among inner-city, low-income women in the U.S. were associated with "underutilizing" prenatal care (pp. 823–832.). Perhaps the bonding associated with these family ties deflects investment in bridging between mothers and health care providers. Further, strong ties can also be problematic. Conflict, stress, and a resulting absence of help can all result from close relationships, and the *presence* of these negative relationships is more predictive of depression than is a *lack* of supportive relationships. There is also a distinction between perceived and received social support. It is perceived support which is most closely tied to health outcomes (Balaji et al., 2007; Oakley et al., 1994).

Supporting Women to Have Their Say

The literature on aspects of inequality in the experience of giving birth and in relation to infant health suggests that a complex interchange between structural factors, social networks, behaviors, and interactions with care providers shape experiences. We now turn to reporting the views of women who were recruited to a research study funded by the U.K.'s Economic and Social Research Council (ESRC) and undertaken between December 2010 and December 2013.[1] This study sought to explore the nature of social networks and consider how far they contribute to maternal and child health for women from diverse communities. The study also provided an opportunity for women who had experienced an infant death to suggest interventions they felt would improve care and then to consider how effectively these suggestions could be translated into practice. It is this second objective that we focus on.

The study was conducted in the cities of Bradford and Leeds in the North of England. These cities have higher rates of infant mortality than the national average and are both multi-ethnic cities with areas of considerable deprivation. Interviews were undertaken with 23 women who were from

African or Pakistani backgrounds or who were teenagers and who had experienced an infant death, as well as 26 women from a range of ethnic backgrounds and ages who had felt well supported throughout pregnancy and the first year of their child's life. Women who were interviewed were offered the opportunity to engage in a further participatory phase of the research centered on the establishment of two project development groups that were aimed at exploring solutions to the problems identified in interviews. Of the 23 bereaved women who took part in the study, 10 took part in the participatory phase, four at one site and six at the other. Women were keen to meet regularly in the groups they named 'HOPE' (derived from the acronym for healing, opportunity, peace, and emotion), motivated by the desire both for mutual support and to make a difference for other women and families in the future. Group members had training and support to develop ideas about service changes that were needed, and to engage with key local professionals.

Accounts from HOPE Members

Members wrote about their experiences and we present summaries from six of them. These summaries identify events linked to their child's death. They offer suggestions for change and they also address the positive results they attribute to their involvement in HOPE, both for themselves and for others.

Rezvana: being listened to

My experience

Being listened to: I am very grateful to the NHS for everything they do. However, through my journey of the hospitals I noted that 'being listened to' is a key factor, but not implemented.

Need for sensitivity: I have lost two sons: Hashim seven years ago and Haider Ali just over a year ago.
My planned Cesarean section for Haider was on the date of Hashim's death anniversary. I explained this to the consultant. How could I celebrate one son's birthday on the date of my other son's death anniversary? But that didn't matter. I had to have the Cesarean.

What needs to change?

Listen and then act: The doctors said my son was ready for discharge even with a chest infection. I explained I had not slept for two days, I had no support on the weekend but even then they stood by their decision. Listening to the concerns is not enough. They need to be acted on. It's hard enough for parents to layout their fears without feeling like they don't matter. Why listen if you're not going to do anything about it?

Being part of HOPE

I have become a member of the Maternity Services Liaison Committee (MSLC) since joining HOPE, and want to be able to influence decisions about maternity care for women in the city. I raised my point about listening and acting at the MSLC meeting and expressed my concerns as a parent. I hope that changes will be made as a result of this.

Naz: delays in admissions

My experience

Listening to mothers: Unfortunately in 2008 my third baby Uzair passed away with congenital myopathy. About five or six weeks before he was due, I rang the hospital delivery suite at 9 a.m. and said I was having sharp pains. I could tell it was labor because I'd had a baby before. They said "Oh, stay at home, you're not ready, take pain killers." A few hours later I rang the hospital again and they said "take pain killers." We went to the hospital ourselves about 5 p.m. By 6:15 p.m. they had to rush me and then they started panicking. They had to rush me to delivery through the corridors into the delivery suite when I delivered Uzair. This also happened to me in 2001 when I had my daughter Elesha, they wouldn't admit me when I knew I was in labor, I wanted to be in hospital.

Being involved in care: When Uzair was born, I knew that he was not going to be with me forever. It was so difficult for me and my husband but we wanted to do everything for our son and make him comfortable. With the supervision from the staff in the neonatal department, I was able to write up the feed charts and medicine charts and have a good cross-infection control around my son's cot area, writing up diaries and keeping daily records. Memories are the best things you can have once you have had the loss. If I look back, I don't regret for one minute that I didn't do anything for him, I did everything as I would do at home, whatever I could do.

What needs to change

Regarding admissions—I feel that the staff should listen to mums because they know their body best. The staff should let the mums come in for an assessment and be reassured. I feel that parents should be encouraged to do more for the baby than sitting and watching and feeling lonely, especially when the child has a short time to live.

Being part of HOPE

For others: HOPE group is working to make some changes: We have met with a consultant midwife to discuss problems with admissions, who will report back to the group. We met with a neonatal consultant and will become members of a service user group for the neonatal unit. We worked to get diaries printed by the neonatal unit for parents with sick children. Through HOPE we have been able to learn about, and work with, lots of local and national organizations like BRI*, Health Visiting, befriender training with SANDS, and BLISS* for parent support.

For myself: I feel like a stronger person and not afraid to speak up. I've had my voice heard at conferences and been able to take a lead role. I've enjoyed doing things that will help other parents to get support that we didn't get. HOPE is like a team where everyone supports each other and we make joint decisions.

* BRI is the local hospital, SANDS and BLISS are national charities (SANDS—Stillbirth and neonatal death charity; BLISS—for babies born too soon, too small, too sick).

Nazreen: genetics

My experience

After my daughter Mariam died, I was told several times that it's because I'm married to my cousin, this is why my daughter was ill. This was really upsetting and shocking to me. When I was marrying my husband we didn't have the intention of having disabled children. There were lots of reasons, apart from children, that we chose each other. It's not our fault—in no way would I want to lose a child. Please don't judge me because I'm married to my cousin. I've had three beautiful baby boys and we've had enough losing a daughter. It doesn't help to be blamed for something that I didn't even know about.

What needs to change

Knowledge and sensitivity: Children can have genetic conditions for lots of different reasons, for example having children when you are older. Sometimes nobody knows for sure what the cause is. It's important to find some kind of way to do tests and find out why this has happened. But don't blame us for something that we didn't even want to happen to us.

Being part of the HOPE

It's helped me: The group has helped me understand this issue more and that I should not be blamed.

Helping others: In the HOPE group we are talking to people who work in the NHS. Some of the group are members of the Maternity Services Liaison Committee that makes decisions about how maternity services are run.

Ansa: discrimination/quality of care

My experience

Racism: I have had both negative and positive experiences, in terms of interaction with hospital and community professionals. During labor when I was losing my daughter, Mariam the midwife made insensitive, derogatory and racist comments to me and my husband. There was no interpreter offered to us, so I had to translate what was happening for my husband when I was trying to come to terms with it myself. There was also no counseling available in our mother tongue.

Ill-timed insensitive care: Two weeks after the loss of my son Tariq, community midwives came to my door asking to weigh my baby, it was a painful heart-wrenching experience, and very distressing for my husband also.

Knowing about risk factors: Antenatal classes are tailored to normal pregnancies and don't give you any information about risk factors or what to do when things don't go well. After I lost two babies a consultant started looking at my case in detail and the problem with my pregnancies was identified

Inequality, Exclusion, and Infant Mortality

and dealt with. I am really grateful that this happened but I feel these issues could have been picked up before I lost Mariam. I now have my son Mustafah who is 9 months old. The care provided throughout my pregnancy was outstanding; I was treated with respect and dignity.

What needs to change

Improvements needed: I would like a referral to be made to a support service as soon as it is established that a woman is going to lose, or has lost, a child. There is a need for support to liaise between families and professionals and advocate for women, to promote good mental and physical health following a loss. This needs to be consistent across the board. In HOPE we are working with the MSLC to improve the bereavement support pathway, and we will have befriender training ourselves. Counseling should be available in other languages and I am looking into training for this myself.

Being part of HOPE

Working for others: The HOPE group is working with public health professionals to adapt the "Fregnancy, Birth and Beyond" antenatal program. We are also aiming to set up a specific antenatal support group for women who have experienced an infant death. The voice of HOPE members has led the Maternity Services Liaison Committee to create a subgroup to improve the bereavement support pathway, using SANDS guidelines.

Changes for me: A journey of many revelations of my own self-awareness, strengthening of my own resolve and becoming very motivated to help other bereaving parents even more by empowering them with the right information, which I have come to learn of through HOPE.

A great opportunity to meet other bereaved mothers and have a support group, a safe and open place where I could share my experiences, feelings and thoughts on improvements needed for the maternity services currently provided in Leeds. The research group empowered me to be motivated to set up a support HOPE group for bereaved parents.

I have also now enrolled on a professional counseling course to further my career in helping others which I have done for many years in my various voluntary roles in my community.

Introduced to community groups and providing contacts such as the MSLC and SANDS.

Shabana: feeling isolated

My experience

I felt isolated after my emergency C-section and after my twins passed away. I was placed at the end of the ward right at the end of the corridor and I didn't get any support from the midwives. They didn't really come to my room much. I felt isolated and a bit angry, all of these mixed emotions. The only support was from my family that came to visit me. I think the hardest thing is leaving the hospital with no baby, and at one point I felt like I wouldn't be able to. I think women need support then.

What needs to change

Support: The thing I'd change is to give more support to those women who are going through a bereavement. If a midwife could come downstairs with you when you leave hospital—just a little support would make a big difference

Being part of HOPE

For myself: More confidence as I was a shy person. Support from other people from the group. Help to deal with the loss and bereavement. Knowing/feeling I can make my voice heard.

Support from and for others: Being involved with the HOPE group has enabled me to meet other women going through similar experiences, helping us in some way to deal with our loss. One thing we are doing is working with health visitors and midwives to create a support pathway for women who have lost a child.

Kim: lack of timely care

My experience

Delays seeing GP: I lost Ashley on 16th December 2004 due to an infection called staphylococcus, which was white spots around the genital area. I was given something by my midwife, like white powder, to use. I tried to make a GP appointment on the Monday but no appointment was available until the following Monday. He passed away the Thursday of that week. He would have been nine years of age this year. It was especially hard as it was the Christmas period.

No care after the death: After my son Ashley passed away, no support or counseling were offered. I did not receive my postnatal check-up, which could have led to depression. I only received one leaflet. All I needed was someone to speak to. I wasn't happy with the overall experience.

Other positive experiences: My first two pregnancies were straightforward and very positive. The hospital was supportive as they knew I was a young mum at the age of 17. My labors were great with no complications. Then I went on to have two more healthy pregnancies, Katelyn and Jayden which, again, were positive experiences.

What needs to change

In the future I would like to see more bereavement groups, a place where children, siblings and family members can talk about their loss. More support in hospitals, more distribution of leaflets and overall a buddy system.

Being part of HOPE

Since I came to the HOPE group I have come a long way, I have come out of my shell because of all the support from mums in the group and the professional help from the team.

The HOPE groups identified key priorities for action and produced documents outlining their ideas for what would help. These key priorities noted were in the areas of relationships, knowledge, and service design. Women at both sites wanted to be listened to and taken seriously by professionals, not to feel judged or stereotyped, and to have access to more bereavement support. In addition, being better informed about warning signs and having honest, clear, and complete information were seen as priorities for improving the quality of services. In terms of service design, women at both sites wanted more involvement in decisions around how services are run. Better provision of interpreting, more resources in other languages, and a better ethnic mix of staff and targeted support for women most at risk were additional priority areas identified. As well as issues relating to health services, members of HOPE also explored other areas where they reported insensitivity and injustice. These related to the social care and criminal justice systems. Group members Cecelia and Shameem argued that it was important that mothers felt supported within these broader encounters following the loss of an infant.

HOPE members were involved in presenting findings about what they saw as gaps in support at two developmental workshops attended by local practitioners and policymakers and designed to stimulate service development. They also presented their thoughts, alongside summaries from the research team, at two conferences, one in Northern Ireland and one in northern England. Other dissemination activities involved group members in media presentations including TV.

Evidence of Impact

At both sites, HOPE members formed links with the Maternity Services Liaison Committee (MSLC), including involvement in an MSLC subgroup tasked with improving bereavement support at the local hospital trust. They also worked with Public Health to tailor antenatal education material for women in higher risk groups. In one city a health visiting/midwifery pathway for women at higher risk was developed and also a neonatal service user forum. Initiatives on interpreting provision, staff diversity, and identifying women at higher risk in delivery-suite triage were also developed.

As is evident in HOPE members' accounts, some of the experiences and perspectives presented were hard for professionals to hear, but those who did engage focused on drawing out lessons and on solutions rather than taking the criticism personally. Some HOPE members found it frustrating that change was slow to happen and that more had not been achieved. But when they felt local practitioners engaged with them, there was more of a sense of tangible achievements. Evaluation of the participatory phase of the research study showed that women who took part appreciated the opportunity to be more involved in the research. All felt that they had been able to have a say in developing the aims and direction of the study. The conferences and the developmental workshops were felt to have been very successful and worthwhile. Even though public presentations and telling one's story to the media were challenging, they were also felt to be worthwhile.

As well as access to professionals afforded in the conferences and workshops and the evidence of local impact in terms of service changes, the work of HOPE has been recognized at a national level In 2012, the policy debate in the U.K. featured a significant intervention, via the Chief Medical Officer's Annual Report, in support of both preventive interventions and the importance of listening to the voices of those with the closest experience of any health problem. The work done by the HOPE groups was cited as an example of good practice (Department of Health, 2012). Consistent with the Chief Medical Officer's position, and prompted by the publication of figures that demonstrated contemporary childhood mortality figures varied three-fold across different U.K. local authorities, Dan Poulter, the Junior Minister responsible for Child Health, said that the government had already started a lot of good work. "We are heavily investing in support for mums, families, and children in the early years," he said. "We are training an extra 4200 health visitors by 2015, and 16,000 of the most vulnerable families will be helped by family nurses. But we know there is still much more to do" (Hawkes, 2013, p. 2). It is clear that as initiatives such as these are implemented, there needs to be vigilance to ensure that specific attention is given to the needs of women from minority ethnic backgrounds. There is still a persuasive case to target these women who experience the highest rates of infant mortality in the U.K. That targeting needs to include recognition of the strengths that can come from appointing additional health visitors and family nurses who are from minority ethnic backgrounds.

While it is clear from HOPE members' accounts that a major motivation for them was to effect the sorts of practical changes that would benefit others, there was also a sense that being in the group offered personal benefits. The growth of self-confidence is clear in these accounts, as are the strengths gained from working with others who have had similar experiences. That strength is at times directed towards the past, acknowledging and reflecting on bereavement for example, and at times towards the future, with group members reporting feeling able to develop new interests and take on new responsibilities. Both the benefits from group membership and the potential to benefit others have been recognized by women at both sites, who indicated they wanted to continue meeting as HOPE after the research ended, by the offer of support to continue by public health partners working on infant mortality in Leeds, and by a charity, the National Childbirth Trust, in Bradford.

Bringing Together Research Literature and Personal Accounts

The participatory research we report was located in a part of the U.K. with high levels of deprivation and with significant numbers of people from minority ethnic communities. Given the research reported above, it is not a surprise that levels of infant mortality in the study areas are higher than national averages. We have noted that seeking to address health inequalities involves reconfiguring and targeting interventions to meet the needs of the more disadvantaged groups (Marmot et al., 1984), and that this recognition is evident in policy documents and pronouncements (Deptartment of Health, 2012; Hawkes, 2013). At a local level, that reconfiguring might involve enhancing services through professional training, health education, and treatment. The overall message from HOPE is to listen to the voices of patients from the outset and to act speedily. This is a message of general relevance. But the particular slant brought to bear when it pertains to members of disadvantaged groups is that the listening has to overcome both entrenched professional reluctance to share decision-making and societal assumptions that can be manifest in dismissive attitudes to disadvantaged groups, and sometimes to what is experienced as racism and blame.

The second theme in the research literature we reviewed is the one that looks at social capital. Here, we considered both bonding with others similar to oneself and bridging to other groups, characteristically with different amounts of social power. We have seen how HOPE gave its members a sense of solidarity with others like themselves; it clearly exhibits an enhancement of bonding social capital. But that solidarity and the personal confidence it inspires also supported constructive contact with health professionals, academics, and the media. We have seen how this contact led to changes locally and so can, with confidence, identify enhanced and effective bridging.

Conclusion

We began with a summary of all the structural, behavioral, and service delivery factors that have an impact on infant health and the realization that the common denominator in all of them was the social position of women (Maher & Macfarlane, 2004). Participatory methods are an empowering way of helping women at higher risk of infant death to have a voice in how health services are run and commissioned (Salway et al., 2013). Thus, they offer a route to enhance the contribution of the structurally deprived while improving group members' self-confidence. This study has shown that groups like HOPE are feasible and can have a considerable impact on service development. If we want to address the social justice implications of inequalities in health we need to engage in redistributive politics at a national level, have a local level reconfiguration of service that privileges the sorts of services that will be of most value to the disadvantaged, and have a planning regime built on listening to the voices of those most involved in any problem.

Key Terms

Bridging—social interaction between diverse social groups.
Social capital—the expected collective or economic benefits derived from the preferential treatment and cooperation between individuals and groups; the value of social networks and contacts.
Infant mortality—the death of a live born child before its first birthday.
Social exclusion—the process by which an individual or group is denied access to resources that are commonly available to other individuals/groups in the same society.

Questions for Reflection

1. "Risk reduction strategies and public health interventions, such as addressing environmental stressors or health education services advising on behavioural change disproportionately benefit those who already occupy advantageous social positions." Why do you suppose this would be the case?

2. What is your experience of 'bridging'—connecting in a meaningful way with individuals beyond your social group? (Consider also: how did you define your group for the purposes of considering this question?)

3. "Listening [to the experience of patients] has to overcome both entrenched professional reluctance to share decision-making and societal assumptions that can be manifest in dismissive attitudes to disadvantaged groups." After reading the stories and suggestions of participants in the HOPE program, do you see one of these concerns as a bigger problem than the other? What is your experience of the barriers to listening?

Note

1   ESRC Grant number RES-061-25-0509. Views expressed here are the authors' and not the ESRC's.

References

Afridi, A. (2011). Social Networks: their role in addressing poverty. *Poverty and Ethnicity*. York, U.K.: Joseph Rowntree Foundation.
Austerberry, H., & Wiggins, M. (2007). Taking a pro-choice perspective on promoting inclusion of teenage mothers: Lessons from an evaluation of the Sure Start Plus programme. *Critical Public Health, 17*, 3–15.
Balaji, A. B., Claussen, A. H., Smith, D. C., Visser, S. N., Morales, M. J., & Perou, R. (2007). Social support networks and maternal mental health and well-being. *Journal of Women's Health, 16*(10), 1386–1396.
Barnes, G. L. (2008). Perspectives of African-American women on infant mortality. *Social Work in Health Care, 47*(3), 293–305.
Chevannes, M. (2002). Issues in educating health professionals to meet the diverse needs of patients and other service users from ethnic minority groups. *Journal of Advanced Nursing, 39*(3), 290–298.
Department of Health. (2012). *Our children deserve better: Prevention pays*. Annual Report of the Chief Medical Officer. London, U.K.: HMSO.

D'Souza L., & Garcia J. (2003). *Limiting the impact of poverty and disadvantage on the health and well-being of low-income pregnant women, new mothers and their babies: Results of a mapping exercise.* Oxford, U.K.: NPEU and Maternity Alliance.

Essex, H. N., & Pickett, K. E. (2008). Mothers without companionship during childbirth: An analysis within the Millennium Cohort Study. *Birth, 35,* 266–76. doi: 10.1111/j.1523-536X.2008.00253.x

Graham, H. (2009).*Understanding health inequalities.* Maidenhead, U.K.: Open University Press.

Hawkes, N. (2013, November 2). Childhood mortality varies threefold across different UK local authorities report shows. *British Medical Journal, 347*(7931), 2.

Health Inequalities Unit, Department of Health (2008). *Tackling health inequalities: 2007 status report on the programme for action.* London: HMSO.

Horwitz, S. M., Morgenstern, H., & Berkman, L. F. (1985). The impact of social stressors and social networks on pediatric medical care use. *Medical Care, 23*(8), 946–959.

Karl-Trumme, U. Krajic, K., Novak-Zezula, S., & Pelikan J. M. (2006, March). Prenatal courses as health promotion intervention for migrant/ethnic minority women: High efforts and good results, but low attendance. *Diversity in Health and Care, 3*(1), 55–58.

Kramer, M. S. (1998). Socioeconomic determinants of intrauterine growth retardation. *European Journal of Clinical Nutrition, 52*(S1), S29–33.

Lai, G., Lin, N., & Leung, S-Y. (1998). Network resources, contact resources, and status attainment. *Social Networks, 20,* 159–178.

McGlade, M. S., Saha, S., & Dahlstrom, M. E. (2004). The Latina paradox: An opportunity for restructuring prenatal care delivery. *American Journal of Public Health, 94*(12), 2062–2065.

Maher J., & Macfarlane A. (2004). Inequalities in infant mortality: Trends by social class, registration status, mother's age and birthweight, England and Wales, *1976–2000. Health Statistics Quarterly, 24,* 14–22.

Marmot, M. G., Adelstein, A. M., & Bulusu, L. (1984). *Immigrant Mortality in England and Wales 1970–78.* London: HMSO.

Mwatsama, M., & Stewart, L. (2005, May). *Food poverty and health.* Briefing Statement. London, U.K.: Faculty of Public Health.

National Collaborating Centre for Women's and Children's Health. (2010). Pregnancy and complex social factors: A model for service provision for pregnant women with complex social factors. London, England: National Institute for Women' and Children's Health

Oakley, A., Hickey, D., & Rigby, A. S. (1994). Love or money? Social support, class inequality and the health of women and children. *European Journal of Public Health, 4,* 265–273.

Pickett, K., & Wilkinson, R. G. (2008). People like us: Ethnic group density effects on health. *Ethnicity and Health, 13*(4), 321–334.

Putnam, R. D. (2000). *Bowling Alone.* New York, NY: Simon & Schuster.

Redshaw, M., & Heikkila, K. (2010). *Delivered with care: a national survey of women's experience of maternity care.* Oxford: National Perinatal Epidemiology Unit, University of Oxford.

Salway, S., Turner, D., Mir, G., Bostan, B., Carter, L., and Skinner J., . . ., & Ellison, G. (2013, December). Towards Equitable commissioning for our multi-ethnic society: a mixed-methods qualitative investigation of evidence utilisation by strategic commissioners and public health managers. *Health Services and Delivery Research, 1*(14). doi: 10.3310/hsdr01140

Shaw, R. J., Pickett, K. E., & Wilkinson, R. G. (2010). Ethnic density effects on birth outcomes and maternal smoking during pregnancy in the US linked birth and infant death data set. *American Journal of Public Health,* 100, 707–713.

Sheridan, E., Wright, J., Small, N., Corry, P., Oddie, S., Whibley, C., . . ., & Parslow, R. (2013). Risk factors for congenital anomaly in a multiethnic birth cohort: an analysis of the Born in Bradford study. *The Lancet.* doi: 10.1016/50140–6736(13)61132–0

Siegrist, J., & Marmot, M. G. (2006). *Social Inequalities in Health: New Evidence and Policy Implications.* Oxford: Oxford University Press.

Sosa, R., Kennell, J., Klaus, M., Robertson, S., & Urrutia, J. (1980). The effect of a supportive companion on perinatal problems, length of labor, and mother-infant interaction. *New England Journal of Medicine, 303*(11), 597–600.

Sproston K., & Primatesta, P. (Eds.). (2003). *Health Survey for England 2002.* Joint Health Surveys Unit National Centre for Social Research Department of Epidemiology and Public Health, and the Royal Free and University College Medical School. London: HMSO.

St. Clair, P. A., Smeriglio, V. L., Alexander, C. S., & Celentano, D. D. (1989). Social network structure and prenatal care utilization. *Medical Care, 27*(8), 823–832.

U.K. National Statistics. (2014). Office for National Statistics series: *Infant and perinatal mortality by social and biological factors*. Retrieved November 5, 2015 from www.ons.gov.uk/ons/dcp171778_350853.pdf.

Wilkinson, R. G., & Pickett, K. (2009). *The Spirit Level. Why more equal societies almost always do better.* London, U.K.: Penguin.

World Health Organization. (2005). *The World Health Report 2005: Make every mother and child count.* Retrieved November 5, 2015 from www.who.inf/who/2005/annex/en/index.html.

Part Three
Issues Related to Groups

Individuals who are not part of the dominant group within the society in which they live are at potential risk to be subjected to oppression, discrimination, and marginalization. Those in the dominant group determine what is "normal" for everyone else in a given society. The dominant group also determines the social norms, values, and ideals by which the worth and value of all groups are determined.

In this backdrop, we begin by exploring interactions between individuals who represent different groups. We felt it was important to challenge the notion of "cultural competence" that is commonly put forward as an ideal in organizational training and to instead offer an approach of "cultural humility" that implies that we will never be experts in someone else's culture—but we can be respectful, humble, and open to learn and share with each other in ways that cultivate respect and sensitivity.

Minority groups and groups that are marginalized routinely encounter difficulties with the validation of important needs, access to necessary services, and interactions with those in authority positions within the dominant culture. The concept of cultural mistrust demonstrates that while we may, in the here and now, have the best intentions when providing services to individuals within these groups, there is a legacy of oppression, racism, and abuse that continue to taint these interactions today.

While the chapter on the treatment of First Nations people is based upon the historical treatment of indigenous peoples in Canada, the losses encountered by the First Nations people of Canada are shared by many other indigenous peoples around the world. Giving voice to these losses and understanding some of the underlying issues provides a start towards healing from the legacy of abuse and trauma suffered as a result of rampant colonial practices that are still perpetuated and reinforced through existing legislation and policies today.

Finally, while those of us who work in the field may take access to palliative care for granted, it is apparent that individuals who are older and who are terminally ill comprise groups across the globe that often do not have their basic needs for care and dignity at the end of life addressed. With an aging demographic in most developed countries and lack of access to basic care in undeveloped countries, end of life care that encompasses the concept of dignity for all human beings is a global issue that cuts across many socioeconomic and political spheres.

6

Cultural Competence and Humility

Paul C. Rosenblatt

A former student brought a man newly arrived in the United States from Timor-Leste to visit me. Because I pay attention to the news, I was certain that he had many losses resulting from the genocide carried out by the Indonesian government against his people. I was sure he knew that the U.S. government, my government, armed and trained the Indonesian military and gave the go ahead to carry out the genocide. I think my first words to the man were, "Oh, Timor-Leste, I am so sorry that you have had to deal with what you have had to deal with." He reacted with words of rage and pain, with a message something like, "Your words mean nothing. What does it mean to say you are sorry? You cannot possibly know what happened and what I have lost." And we never got past that. After two minutes he had had enough of me, and he left. Working in a university and living in a metropolitan area that draws diverse people from around the world, including many people with losses that are entangled in social justice issues, I have had many encounters in which whatever I did in interacting with diverse others who had experienced loss went well enough. I had many interactions with that former student about her own losses entangled in social justice issues, and I thought our history together was why she brought the man from Timor-Leste to visit me. However, interacting with bereaved people from other cultures whose losses are entangled in social justice issues is always challenging. And as my experience with the man from Timor-Leste indicates, even with the best of intentions one can put someone off or offend them. This essay draws on what I think I know about interacting with and understanding people who have experienced losses entangled with issues of social justice and culture. However, as with my encounter with the man from Timor-Leste indicates, I have no magic that guarantees that interactions will go well.

Social Justice and Interactions with People Who Are Grieving

We could in theory ignore the social justice issues that are entangled in grief and loss issues of the people with whom we interact. However, if those issues are present, how can we tune them out and provide anything like genuine empathy, caring, and support? For example, there is my African American friend whose life story and whose stories of his parents and extended family are filled with the grim impacts of racism. There is the colleague who grew up in Laos who witnessed loved ones being killed during the so-called Viet Nam war that the U.S. waged. Many of my women friends, relatives, colleagues, and students talk about difficult struggles with sexism and patriarchy.

To be respectful and caring I must be aware of those issues and take them into account in providing acknowledgment, support, and whatever seems appropriate. To be a responsible member of the communities I am in and a functioning citizen, I must pay attention to social justice issues and resist what I see as oppression in whatever ways I can.

Grief support can be wonderfully helpful. It can also create social justice issues. There are ways that what seems like grief support can police grieving in the sense of demanding certain emotions and words from the bereaved and silencing others (Klass & Chow, 2011; Rosenblatt, 2012). Part of being supportive in a social-justice attuned way is to put aside one's own ideas of what a bereaved person should feel and say and to be fully open to whatever s/he chooses to express and communicate. There are grief experts who argue that the just way to support a bereaved person is to be attuned to what seems to be leading edge understanding of bereavement and best practices in dealing with it. However, those leading edge understandings and best practices come from a particular culture (Gone, 2011). Further, even the research that offers broad generalizations about leading edge understandings and best practices is often not, I think, adequately sensitive to or respectful of cultural differences in grieving or the meanings of losses (Rosenblatt, 2009b; 2012). From my perspective the best grief support is socially just and respects the *other's* sociocultural locations with an openess to the other defining what is appropriate in grief and grief support.

An added complexity to bring to this chapter is that even though I often write about cultural diversity in grief and loss as they are entangled in social justice issues, it is challenging and questionable to write about those matters from an expert stance. That stance has the potential to be oppressive and controlling, to be policing in its own way. "I am the expert, and you, dear reader, are not." I try to avoid that expert stance and to write with humility and respect, even though that makes my writing tentative and qualified in ways that might seem out of place in a literature filled with definitive statements by experts. One way to warn the reader that my expertise has its limits is to give examples like the one at the beginning of this chapter of a failure of mine in dealing with a bereaved person.

Interviewing with Humility

To some extent I do research interviews for a living, in which I am often faced with the challenge of hearing strangers' stories of grief and loss entangled in cultural and social justice issues and meanings. I try to interact and listen with humility as people tell me their stories about grief and loss in the context of what they have to say about culture and social justice. Often I do these interviews well in the sense that people appreciate my listening and my questions, seem to feel comfortable with me, and talk at length. For example, when I was interviewing couples for a book on couple bed sharing (Rosenblatt, 2006) innumerable loss and social justice issues were brought up by interviewees. That does not mean that in instances where I could understand interviewee stories as being about social justice issues that they necessarily understood things that way. I often had to work with a multiple consciousness that respected their realities while not losing track of what I thought were social justice realities. For example, every blue collar worker over 30 in that study had at least one serious injury on the job that undermined his or her sleep and the couples' shared sleeping, in some cases permanently. However, almost none of those who talked about the serious injuries spoke of the social justice issues involved when employers demand dangerous work and do not do much, if anything, to mitigate the risks or pay for the physical harm to the employee let alone to compensate for damage to the couple's relationship. I had to keep my thoughts about long-term loss and social justice from imposing realities on interviewees.

The humility with which I interviewed in this and other studies was partly in gratitude for what people shared with me. From a critical theory perspective, I also must deal with my sense of how much my privilege means that I am part of the system that oppresses people who are less privileged than I (Kincheloe & McLaren, 2000). Among many things, that means that I try not to create more social justice issues by interviewing in a closed-minded, controlling, not-hearing way. Instead I try to interview with openness to what people have to offer.

Since interacting with humility means meeting people where they are, if they say little or nothing about their culture and about social justice issues, that is where my interaction with them remains. That is, when I interview, humility means that I leave alone many issues one would think sensitivity to social justice issues would call for attending to. I will probe for such issues, but if the probing does not engage an interviewee, I am inclined to remain focused on what the interviewee shares as significant. That does not mean that I cannot or do not get to other ways of understanding and writing about what people say than theirs. Although we owe it to people to do our best to understand and respect what they have to say, they are not necessarily experts on their culture, their own social justice contexts, or their own social situation (Shweder, 1996). I want to understand people in their own terms, but I think that does not preclude me using my mind and whatever I know or can learn to try to understand things in ways that are not controlled by what they have said to me.

The Concept of Cultural Competence

The concept of *cultural competence* has quite a range of meanings (Comas-Díaz, 2012; de Chesnay, Peil, & Pamp, 2008). I have mixed feelings about some things that might be called "cultural competence" in dealing with grief and loss issues of people from cultures other than one's own. It would be wonderfully useful to be fluent in the language and culture of another person who is wrestling with issues of loss and grief, and to know the relevant social justice issues, etiquette, and cultural practices. I think it is respectful to be grounded in the culture of the other, and I think that having some grounding has at times helped me in offering grief support, doing research interviews, or just connecting with bereaved people from cultures other than my own. It also can help to know about social justice issues that might be relevant to the other's bereavement (for example, how struggles with racism and white culture might show up in narratives of bereaved African Americans about family members who have died—Rosenblatt & Wallace, 2005a, 2005b). If one tunes into social justice issues, there are very few people dealing with loss and grief for whom oppression, economic inequality, injustice, racism, sexism, homophobia would not be part of what they have to say. Thus, it is good to be knowledgeable, but then a little bit of knowledge is dangerous in that it can lead one to stereotype and be insensitive to how diverse people from a particular culture are (Rosenblatt, 2009b).

One may do a better job at helping, relating to, and learning from people whose cultural background is different from one's own if one is knowledgeable about the person's culture. However, there are false promises in the concept of "cultural competence" that suggest that with more learning, self control, and practice one will be able to do quite well in dealing with someone who is from a culture other than one's own. Each new relationship and, to some extent, each new situation is iffy. You hope you will understand the other, interact respectfully and supportively, and not offend. Yes, if you have spent plenty of time with an assortment of, say, Koreans and you even know a bit of Korean, you have a better start. However, Koreans (like all peoples) are diverse, and you may never have dealt with the Korean woman you are now facing as she talks about her loss. I think no matter what you think you know, you have to listen to her, understand her, and respect what she says. We all have to be learners in each interaction. We all have to allow ourselves to be vulnerable and not knowing in interactions with those we hope to understand and/or help (Gunaratnam, 2008, 2013). I would argue that no matter how much "cultural competence" one brings to a relationship, one is also a beginner and the "cultural competence" one has may get in the way of being respectfully and helpfully tuned into the other. If anything, I think being an open and respectful learner is often the ultimate cultural competence.

What Is Humility and How Might One Acquire It?

I try to have humility as I relate to people dealing with grief and loss. Partly it is a matter of being respectful and ethical, and partly it is a matter of knowing that however much I know I do not know enough. Thus, in humility I have to be open to what they provide as we interact. I have to learn from them. Also, I feel humility in relationship to the magnitude of their loss and grief, humility because of my ignorance about their culture, the relevant social justice issues, and their lives.

Following Bollinger and Hill (2012) and Tangney (2000), for me humility is a respect for and openness to whatever the other chooses to communicate. It involves putting aside my ego and my "expertise" and taking the role of learner. I think the opposite of humility is arrogance, closed mindedness, and a lack of awareness of one's own limits and insignificance. I think when one has humility one is fully open to what others offer as truths. When we have humility we are open to truths about ourselves. When we have "cultural humility" (Tervalon & Murray-Garcia, 1998), we are committed to a life of culturally aware self-evaluation, self-critique, and work at contending against injustice (particularly injustice built into our own culture).

Myths/Stereotypes About Cultural Humility

In cultures I know of where there is the concept of something like humility, it seems to me that people think that humility typically comes from living poor. That means many people think that humility comes from life in a lower socioeconomic status household and community. Included in that, one will have learned about living with less materially and with the emotional pain, frustration, deprivation, loss and suffering that may come from that life situation. One implication is that humility is not easy for a person to achieve who has lived a relatively privileged life. From this perspective, a person who has not developed genuine humility cannot simply put on a veil of humility as a role to play in certain situations. One cannot just turn it on in situations where it seems appropriate. Humility is not about putting on a facial expression, taking a posture, using language in a certain way, responding to others in a certain way, though all those things could be involved in behaving with humility. In order to achieve humility many seem to think that one will need significant life experiences that not all of us will have had. Perhaps some people are not in a place now, and never will be, where they can achieve humility in relationship to another. Related to that it seems to me that for some people humility is not comfortable or is too threatening, and so they are not likely to go there and stay there. That of course means that we should guard against false humility in ourselves. Humility has to come from a genuine place inside of one. It is not simply a self-presentation to use in certain potentially challenging social situations. It is not a posture for warding off potential annoyance or disapproval from the other. It is not a sort of superior status of being extremely expert through claiming to know nothing. It involves something at the core of one that sees the other as of enormous importance and that subordinates oneself. Yet humility does not mean to me that one gives up independent thinking or a capacity to see others from perspectives they do not take and may not be able to take. One can still know one's own limits, respect and honor what others say, and get to perspectives and levels of awareness that they seemingly have not.

There is a psychotherapeutic perspective that sees humility as potentially a defense to deflect wrath (Weiss, 2008). Perhaps there are different kinds of humility such that the defending-against-wrath type is so much about self-protection that it is not easily converted into empathic, caring, respectful relating with people from other cultures dealing with grief and loss. But perhaps it is. Perhaps having experienced terrifying wrath or fearing it is one kind of foothold on the kind of humility this chapter addresses. For example, perhaps humility that is engendered in frightening situations makes it easier to understand others whose grief and loss are connected to oppressive situations.

A humility training program, if that is not an absurdity, might involve doing without in various ways, feeling the sting of bigotry and an oppressive social class system, experiencing directly heavy loss and biting injustice. It might involve being in difficult situations with no escape. It seems to me that in some sense one cannot function with humility until one knows others, has heard them, can appreciate where they have been, what they remember, or what they realize that is far beyond or deeper than one has experienced. A crucial step toward humility is to pay attention to others, get to know them, hunt people out whose lives are different, overhear people on the bus. It might take a long time, even years, for some people to reach whatever underlies humility, if they ever can. This is so not only because one might have to accumulate a number of experiences in order to function with humility in a broad range of situations, but it might also take a long time because humility, I think, demands putting aside certain ego defenses (denial and projection, for example) that perhaps many people are not able or willing to put aside. I think one can see the incapacity for humility, for example, in hospice volunteers who seem not to be emotionally present with dying people and who would best volunteer to do things that allow them the freedom to be who they are without being insensitive to others who need support, caring and understanding.

There are also questions about the limits of humility for a person who has privilege in relationship to many others. Can I as a person with white skin privilege, middle class privilege, the privilege of being a U.S. citizen, male privilege, heterosexual privilege, and the privilege of living a comfortable material life ever "get" what is going on with people who lack those privileges? Some would say the answer is, at best, "not fully" (Kincheloe & McLaren, 2000), that from a critical theory perspective my understanding of their stories and lives is at best limited and provisional for many reasons, including that my consciousness has not been built in the same part of the social system that others have built theirs. From another perspective can I be trusted by others who lack the systemic privileges I have? There are many issues in this, but I think a key one is that many people with privilege seem generally oblivious to their privilege and well-defended against anything that could expose them to the sense that their privilege is unearned and that others have suffered from the same system in which they have gained their privilege (Rosenblatt, 2009a).

It is also possible that humility is situational, so someone can work with humility in one situation and be selfish, insensitive, and egotistical in another. My preference is to think of humility as a way of being that one brings to all situations, but it may be that some people have to learn in each new situation how to achieve humility. Either they do not want to or are too defended to ever achieve it in all situations.

The concept of "humility" has prominence in Christian traditions and Western philosophy, and that means that the idea of humility may be a bad fit in some cross cultural interactions. Can one trust any disposition rooted in one culture to be appropriate in all other cultures? The answer to that question must be "no," which suggests that ideally one would want not to simply take a position of humility in interacting with someone who is culturally different but to explore what kind of stance they might want or most appreciate from one as the interaction goes on. Instead of "doing humility," ideally we have to fit into a role that the other pushes us to fit into, and it may not even have a name in our own language(s), which surely means that that role would require a lot of learning from those for whom the role is not familiar.

Humility Can Make Trouble

I do not want to oversell humility. There are times when humility makes trouble (Bollinger & Hill, 2012). The way I have most often experienced this is when people may want my expertise and are annoyed by my trying to withhold it by deferring to them. Also, there are people who feel that I am insulting them by trying to be in a position of humility. Forty years ago I was in Bali, Indonesia, where people expressed their status relationship by the relative height of their head. So if I was sitting on a chair and someone was talking to me who saw himself as lower status than me, he would sit on the floor or in some other way put his head lower than mine. But I often wanted us to be equals or to put myself at a status lower than the other, so I would slide off my chair to get my head at a level the same or lower than the other, and then the other would lower his head further. I would then do the same until we were both on the ground, and the other was very annoyed and probably insulted. Now, I would accept the other's definition of me as higher status in terms of head height, particularly in his cultural world where attributes of mine, like relative age or assumed relative wealth, mattered immensely. Still another way that humility can make trouble is that with some people and some cultures, it invites diminishment, bullying, or ignoring. That is, some people see humility as a sign of weakness and an invitation to them to dominate, control, or dismiss. Also, Bollinger and Hill (2012) suggest that humility can sometimes lead one to sell oneself short, though their view of humility is that it generally entails accuracy in self-evaluation. But then with humility it is not clear what "accuracy" means, because if one in humility is open to the realities of others, one's standard for self-evaluation shifts depending on with whom one is interacting.

The Cultural and Social Complexities of Any Interaction

Our interactions with others are as much governed by their cultural competence, what they make of social justice issues, and how they choose to interact with us as it is by what we do. For example, when I was trying to offer sympathy to an elderly American Indian woman on the Morongo Reservation in Southern California on the deaths of two of her sons and the long-term imprisonment of the three others, I thought she was trying to respect and take care of me as much as I was trying to respect and take care of her. That is, in addition to my effort to be culturally competent and tuned in to social justice issues as I spoke with her about her sons, I also felt that I needed to be culturally competent and respectful in dealing with the cultural competence and respect she offered me. It seems to me that we both were struggling to be real and not be trapped in cultural scripts (Shapiro, 2002) that would make us each into stereotypes for the other.

Even though I advocate humility and openness to the realities of others, I think we have to realize that social construction is going on in many different ways. What people offer us as they talk about their losses is not real reality but something socially constructed (Loseke & Kusenbach, 2008). They are governed by feeling rules, rules about talk, the vocabulary of emotions, social etiquette, and much else that is drawn from their culture or cultures. Many people, like the woman from the Morongo reservation, are bicultural or multicultural, which means they have more than one set of feeling rules, more than one etiquette and so on to draw on, and quite possibly they could say and perhaps feel quite different things depending on the social context. And then we together are socially constructing realities. I may fool myself in thinking that in my humility I am fully open to what the other says and am a neutral receptacle for what is said, but at every moment in our interaction we are pushing whatever it is that is being said and expressed this way and that. My attention, my words, my reactions, my questions influence the other; and I am influenced by the other. Because of this, at the very least I would say that interacting with someone in humility still requires that we be alert to and smart about the cultural and social dynamics that are in play.

It's a Tough World

We live in an astonishingly unjust, oppression-ridden world. Vast amounts of damage have been done that can never be corrected. Vast amounts of damage is being done all over the world as you read this sentence. It will take much more than humility in dealing with grief and loss cross-culturally to change the world noticeably. From a social justice perspective, I wish I knew what to do to turn things around. I wish I did not feel so powerless. But then I say to myself: Do not scoff at any act of humility and sensitivity to cultural and social justice matters in relationship to someone dealing with grief and loss. Such an act of caring represents something very different from the dreadful status quo. In that sense it is a revolutionary challenge to much that is terrible in the world that is done through the actions of governments, corporations, businesses, and individuals. On the other hand, the story I told at the beginning of this essay about my encounter with the Timorese man is a reminder that with the best of intentions and with great humility and great awareness of social justice issues, one's attempts to be connecting and supportive may be unwelcome, hurtful, and rebuffed.

Key Terms

Cultural competence—ability to engage positively with individuals from cultural backgrounds different from one's own. May involve awareness of social custom, language, or other features of that culture which allow one to navigate interactions more smoothly.

Cultural humility—a commitment to culturally aware self-evaluation, self-critique, and work at contending against injustice (particularly injustice built into one's own culture).

Humility—awareness of one's own limits and insignificance; a willingness to put aside personal ego and or perception of self as "expert" and take the role of learner.

Social justice—full and equal participation of all groups in a society that is mutually shaped to meet their needs. Social justice includes a vision of society in which the distribution of resources is equitable and all members are physically and psychologically safe and secure.

Questions for Reflection

1. In the opening section of this paper, the author identifies his intent to share "what I think I know" about the topic at hand. How is this stance (awareness that knowledge based on previous experience/information may not apply to future encounters) relevant for you when approaching new individuals and situations?
2. "There are ways that what seems like grief support can police grieving in the sense of demanding certain emotions and words from the bereaved and silencing others." How may this occur (can you think of some examples?), and how could it be avoided?
3. "A little bit of knowledge is dangerous in that it can lead one to stereotype and be insensitive to how diverse people from a particular culture are." How might you incorporate knowledge about particular cultures in your work without engaging in stereotyping?

References

Bollinger, R. A., & Hill, P. C. (2012). Humility. In T. G. Plante (Ed.), *Religion, spirituality, and positive psychology* (pp. 31–47). Westport, CT: ABC-CLIO.

Comas-Díaz, L. (2012). *Multicultural care: A clinician's guide to cultural competence*. Washington, DC: American Psychological Association.

de Chesnay, M., Peil, R. W., & Pamp, C. (2008). Cultural competence, resilience, and advocacy. In M. de Chesnay & B. A. Anderson (Eds.), *Caring for the vulnerable: Perspectives in nursing theory, practice, and research* (2nd ed.) (pp. 25–37). Boston, MA: Jones & Bartlett.

Gone, J. P. (2011). Is psychological science a-cultural? *Cultural Diversity and Ethnic Minority Psychology, 17*(3), 234–242.

Gunaratnam, Y. (2008). From competence to vulnerability: Care, ethics, and elders from racialized minorities. *Mortality, 13*(1), 24–41.

Gunaratnam, Y. (2013). Cultural vulnerability: A narrative approach to intercultural care. *Qualitative Social Work, 12*(2), 104–118.

Kincheloe, J. L., & McLaren, P. (2000). Rethinking critical theory and qualitative research. In N. K. Denzin & Y. W. Lincoln (Eds.), *Handbook of qualitative research* (2nd ed.) (pp. 279–313). Thousand Oaks, CA: Sage.

Klass, D., & Chow, A. Y. M. (2011). Culture and ethnicity in experiencing, policing, and handling grief. In R. A. Neimeyer, D. L. Harris, H. R. Winokuer, & G. F. Thornton (Eds.), *Grief and bereavement in contemporary society: Bridging research and practice* (pp. 341–353). New York, NY: Routledge.

Loseke, D. R., & Kusenbach, M. (2008). The social construction of emotion. In J. A. Holstein & J. F. Gubrium (Eds.), *Handbook of constructionist research* (pp. 511–529). New York, NY: Guilford.

Rosenblatt, P. C. (2006). *Two in a bed: The social system of couple bed sharing*. Albany, NY: State University of New York Press.

Rosenblatt, P. C. (2009a). *Shared obliviousness in family systems*. Albany, NY: State University of New York Press.

Rosenblatt, P. C. (2009b). The culturally competent practitioner. In K. Doka & A. S. Tucci (Eds.), *Living with grief: Diversity and end-of-life care* (pp. 21–32). Washington, DC: Hospice Foundation of America.

Rosenblatt, P. C. (2012). The concept of complicated grief: Lessons from other cultures. In H. Schut, P. Boelen, J. van den Bout, & M. Stroebe (Eds.), *Complicated grief: Scientific foundations for health professionals* (pp. 27–39). New York, NY: Routledge.

Rosenblatt, P. C., & Wallace, B. R. (2005a). *African American grief*. New York, NY: Routledge.

Rosenblatt, P. C., & Wallace, B. R. (2005b). Narratives of grieving African-Americans about racism in the lives of deceased family members. *Death Studies, 29*, 217–235.

Shapiro, E. R. (2002). Family bereavement after collective trauma: Private suffering, public meanings, and cultural contexts. *Journal of Systemic Therapies, 21*(3), 81–92.

Shweder, R. A. (1996). True ethnography: The law, the lore, and the lure. In R. Jessor, A. Colby, & R. A. Shweder (Eds.), *Ethnography and human development: Context and meaning in social inquiry* (pp. 15–52). Chicago, IL: University of Chicago Press.

Tangney, J. P. (2000). Humility: Theoretical perspectives, empirical findings and directions for future research. *Journal of Social and Clinical Psychology, 19*(1), 70–82.

Tervalon, M., & Murray-Garcia, J. (1998). Cultural humility versus cultural competence: A critical distinction in defining physician training outcomes in multicultural education. *Journal of Health Care for the Poor and Underserved, 9*(2), 117–125.

Weiss, H. (2008). Grievance, shame and wrath. Reflections about the differentiation of narcissistic states of mind. [German]. *Psyche: Zeitschrift fur Psychoanalyse und ihre Anwendungen, 62*, 866–886.

7

"Not Gonna Be Laid Out to Dry"
Cultural Mistrust in End of Life Care and Strategies for Trust-Building

Tashel C. Bordere

"When the hospice nurse came to finally sign us up, my relief was overwhelming. We could relax as I could trust familiar language, honesty, a philosophy that was ours. In hospice, I know I can relax and let them lead us. To not have to play nurse and decide what's important and when to call the doctor and what to do—amazing relief. We celebrate this hospice referral lol."

(personal communication, August 20, 2012)

As I listened intently to Sarah's testimonial, what joy and empathy I felt for her and her husband in this transition. I shared in her deep sense of relief and celebration and pondered for a moment, how wonderful it must feel to be able to navigate an end of life experience with such blithe confidence. For many underrepresented, marginalized groups, this is just not the case. In fact, the actual concept of *cultural mistrust* (Terrell & Terrell, 1981; Terrell & Terrell, 1984) was originally developed to encapsulate the pronounced worries and fears of African Americans concerning health care settings due to legacies of unjust practices that persist today.

In this chapter, a hospice case countering the opening exemplar is utilized to highlight issues related to cultural mistrust or lack of confidence in a health care provider's ability to act with integrity on the patient's behalf. Barriers to trust will also be highlighted as well as strategies for trust-building and maintenance among marginalized groups.

Case Presentation: "Not Gonna be Laid Out to Dry"

I have years of training and expertise in culture and socially just practices. Yet some of my most affirming complimentary lessons in cultural trust and mistrust have come through experiences with my grandfather in his dying process and eventual death. At the age of 75, he was diagnosed with lymphocytic leukemia, a type of blood cancer common in older age males. He lived the full five-year life expectancy of the disease, walking two miles a day (often in dressy socks), maintaining spiritual practices (e.g., reading the Bible), undergoing chemotherapy, and managing through multiple losses, including home-loss, consequent of Hurricane Katrina. An African American male, reared in the deep south, he lived through segregation, desegregation, integration and re-integration; experienced the loss of one child, seven of eleven siblings, six of which were to cancer; and through it all, lived and worked to see his home, destroyed by Hurricane Katrina, be rebuilt.

On the night of Thanksgiving, in a room filled with family members engaged in various discussions, my grandfather leans forward in his recliner and casually whispers to me, "I won't be here always." At this cue, I asked my grandmother to reach out to the physician to inquire about his health care status and hospice. Prior to this query, the attending physician neither discussed hospice care as an option nor made a referral to such services. This is significant as families often rely on physicians, the entities most knowledgeable about the patient's health status, to initiate such discussions (Weckmann, 2008). In the final months of my grandfather's life, his mind remained sharp but his body grew weaker. With no guidance to the contrary, my family continued in its two-hour commute (each-way) to scheduled appointments in which my grandfather would no longer be seen by the physician in whom he and my family had come to establish a trusting relationship. He was instead seen by unfamiliar medical personnel and at a time in which both he and my family were most dependent on his physician's guidance, if not care.

The physician ultimately made the hospice referral. In my grandfather's transition to hospice, a staff nurse (European American female) met with the family to discuss the type of care hospice provides. Qualified in her profession, still yet a stranger to my family, she walks over to the table where my grandmother is seated, stretches out her arm, and in a single gesture, scoops away eight of ten bottles of medication. "Mr. Price will not be taking these anymore!" she exclaims. She proceeds through her regimented list of changes, next explaining in third person language that he would no longer be seeing his current doctor, but would now be cared for by the hospice team, which included a *new* doctor. At this, my grandfather, frail and docile, hardly speaking above a whisper at this stage of his illness, began to yell out in protest: "I'm not signing NO papers!!! I'm NOT signing 'em. I want MY doctor!" Banging his thin hands on the arms of his leather recliner, he exclaimed, "I don't know these people. I'm not gonna be laid out to dry!"

Startled by my grandfather's reaction, the hospice nurse eased into the kitchen to make a call to the main office. In the interim, I was able to intervene as a gatekeeper, calming my grandfather and providing him the reassurance needed to feel safe and secure in this transitional experience. Meanwhile, I listened as the well-intentioned nurse described my otherwise sharp grandfather as "confused," mistaking his anxiety and disgruntlement about the abrupt changes and perceived threats to his care for "disorientation."

Reflection

- How does the opening example differ from the case presentation? In particular, what is the role of privilege and marginalization in the differing responses to hospice admission?
- What might be goals and concerns for Mr. Price? And for the hospice nurse?
- Identify potential barriers in the interactions between Mr. Price and the hospice nurse. How might those barriers be overcome?
- Can you identify things that went well in interactions among any of the dyads?

Trust: Security or Uncertainty

The foundation for trusting relationships and self-trust typically develop in our formative years, but must be confirmed and reaffirmed throughout our lives (Erikson, 1964, p. 247). Similarly, cultural mistrust does not begin as we near death but rather with betrayals of trust in our daily lives and interactions with individuals and societal institutions. It should be no wonder then why the bereaved and individuals approaching death who have experienced such betrayals, or possess historical memories, are especially hypervigilant when faced with instilling confidence in others at the final stage of life.

Barriers: Factors Contributing to Mistrust

Multiple factors contribute to diminished levels of trust in end of life care among marginalized populations, particularly among African Americans. Factors related to mistrust include education about the historical exploitation and mistreatment of minority groups in health care settings and personal experiences with discrimination in medical systems and other institutions (Krakauer, Crenner, & Fox, 2002). There are many well-documented cases, past and present, of discriminatory practices in medical care and in research (e.g., Tuskegee Syphilis Study) (Brandt, 1978; Washington, 2006). Similarly, my grandfather's fears and mistrust were deeply rooted in personal and historical experiences. After a series of aversive and discriminatory medical-related encounters, he avoided formal health care services for much of his adult life. Cultural mistrust, related to racism and discrimination, has been associated with delayed, avoided, underutilized health care services (Byrne, 2008; Hammond, Matthews, & Corbie-Smith, 2010; Hammond, Matthews, Mohottige, Agyemang, & Corbie-Smith, 2010) patient dissatisfaction (Benker, Peters, Clark, & Keves-Foster, 2006; Sohn & Harada, 2008; Moore, Hamilton, Pierre-Louis, & Jennings, 2013; Moore et al., 2013), lack of adherence, and discontinuity or changes in physician (Jacobs, Rolle, Ferrans, Whitaker, & Warnecke, 2006). Prior to being diagnosed with cancer, my grandfather had not seen a doctor in thirty years. In fairness, the nurse could not have known that.

Further, due to disparities in health care services among marginalized individuals or "medical racism" (Krakauer et al., 2002; Rosenblatt & Wallace, 2005, p. 10) and "medical neglect" (Holloway, 2002, p. 3), issues of trust may be particularly salient for persons from marginalized groups in interactions with culturally dissimilar care providers (Barrett, 2009, p. 89). In a study of African American adults, Rosenblatt and Wallace (2005) found that 40 percent of participants believed their cared about person's death was related to medical racism or "death by medical racism" (p. 10). That is, they believed the death was due in part to injustice in treatment such as delayed (e.g., ambulance took too long to arrive) or substandard care (e.g., high risk procedure). Although racial similarity has been shown to reduce mistrust and increase patient satisfaction, researchers have also found that physician race was less important in trust-building than the physicians' ability to communicate effectively across cultures (Jacobs et al., 2006) and utilize patient-centered communication (Street, O'Malley, Cooper, & Haidet, 2008).

Overcoming Barriers: Strategies for Trust-Building and Maintenance

We know much about mistrust in end of life care and much less about ways to establish and maintain relationships that are approached with increased confidence and responded to with integrity. Thus, the section to follow focuses on strategies for trust-building and maintenance in end of life care.

Self-awareness, Reflection, and Privilege. On the morning following our visit with the hospice nurse, I began a 12-hour commute back to my home thinking, *THIS was disastrous!* I have completely failed my family. With all of my knowledge, I have failed them.

Appropriately so, it rained for much of my drive, heavy drops pounding against my window like good friends sharing in sorrow. A few hours into the commute, my phone rang. It was the hospice nurse. I had given her my contact information following the visit and asked that she call if I could be of assistance or play any role in my grandfather's care from across the miles. That morning she did just that.

Tashel C. Bordere

> Nurse: Hi, Tashel. This is Kathy, the hospice nurse. Is this a good time?
> Tashel: Hi, Kathy. Yes. I could use a short break from driving.
> Nurse: Last night, I was thinking about my time with Mr. Price. I feel really badly that he seemed so upset during our visit yesterday. I wasn't pleased with the way things went during the visit. I'm thinking that more background information about Mr. Price will be helpful, and I'm calling in hopes that you might be able to tell me more about your grandfather. This will help me better reach out to him and best meet his holistic needs.

With that, the rain drops seemed to soften, the clouds to dissipate.

Maya Angelou (as cited in Kelly, 2003) once said, "I've learned that people will forget what you said, people will forget what you did, but people will never forget how you made them feel." This simple gesture of a phone call, as a result of self-reflective practice, was monumental in shaping feelings and perceptions of external care and help-seeking. It completely changed the course of my family's relationship and confidence in hospice services and my grandfather's ability to be a willing recipient and participant in his care. The nurse's ability to self-reflect and then, even more importantly, *act* based on reflection, was admirable and courageous, but not only that; it shifted anxiety to peace, uncertainty to assurance, dissatisfaction to contentment, and distress to comfort.

Replacing Assumptions with Five A's of Culturally Conscientious Care. In socially just and culturally conscientious practice, openness to learning and dialog are useful replacements for making what might otherwise be gross assumptions. I think of this dialog as analogous to communication with my young daughter regarding her paintings where instead of making assumptions about images in her work, I inquire, "Tell me about your picture." In my work with adolescents who wear memorial t-shirts honoring their cared-about persons, I have inquired, "What do you wish people to understand about your t-shirt? Tell me about the significance of the t-shirt for you. Wayne Carter (*Lil Wayne*), a well-known rapper, once said in a televised interview, "Give me a canvas, and I'll give you art" (VH1, 2009). In essence, create the space, and I may share some data from my life with you.

In my collective experiences in bereavement work, I have established and found it effective to use the *Five A's of Culturally Conscientious Care*:

- *Acknowledge* ("You seemed upset when I mentioned that you will have a new doctor.");
- *Ask* ("Is that correct?");
- *Accept* (Accept that he—Mr. Price—is worried about *being betrayed and not properly cared for* at this fragile stage of life, "knowing" that his lens is based on his social location and life experiences; accept also the notion of "not knowing" or fully understanding another's position.);
- *Align* (Align where privilege is operating) ("Mr. Price I would like to learn more about you so that I can work with you and your family to ensure you get the best care possible"); and if needed,
- *Apologize* (It is human to make an error, humane to apologize.) ("I'm so sorry. I think I moved through the information pretty quickly. I can see how this is a lot to take in right now. Please stop me as I move forward if you have any questions. Because it may feel like a lot of information to take in, during each visit I will also leave you with things to read in your own time that relate to items we discuss. Here's also the number to the main office should any other questions come up for you.").

"Not knowing": barrier or opportunity? Helping professionals in bereavement may feel disadvantaged in terms of "not knowing." Yet, this worry of *not knowing* stifles work in bereavement care in neglecting to create and provide services or offer programs for individuals and groups we think we may not understand or know enough about. It is no surprise though that individuals worry about not knowing or uncertainty as it is the antithesis of socialization processes within educational systems where individuals are trained to "know," to have the answer, the "correct" answer, in fact. Yet, we receive minimal, if any, enlightenment around death, bereavement, or cultural practices through our formal educational processes (see Harris, 2009). We forget that the greatest advantage remains in bearing witness to the stories, the pain, the joy, and the triumphs of populations we serve and *could be* serving once the barrier associated with fears of *not knowing* is removed. Not knowing is important to recognize but should not be a deterrent. Opportunities exist in not-knowing. Messages such as "I am worried that I don't know . . ." can be replaced with "I am looking forward to learning more about . . ." *Culturally conscientious* practice is being open to evolving knowledge. The expectation to be "all-knowing" is an impossibility and hence a self-defeating frame from which to work. As emphasized by Marilyn Grey (as cited in Carpenter, Fontanini, & Neiman, 2010, p. 112), "Nobody has it all. That's like trying to eat once and for all."

Symbolic Meaning in Interactions. The same behaviors and interactions may have distinct meanings based on our social locations. Thus, even in attempts to connect, cultural conflicts and misunderstandings may arise. They are, in fact, inevitable in human relationships. For the nurse, for example, reducing the number of medications signified relief and better quality of life for the patient (i.e., fewer pills to swallow, less financial costs). For my grandfather and family, this same behavior was concerning as multiple medications were conceptualized as life sustaining. Thus, did the reduction in medication mean they had *given up*? Clarifying the hospice philosophy and role facilitated a shared understanding and unified goals for care.

According to Kagawa-Singer and Blackhall (2001), "culture shapes the way people make meaning of illness, suffering, and dying, and therefore also influences how they make use of medical services at the end of life." Although accepting of the referral, yielding trust to hospice had a certain cultural meaning within my collectivistic family system, heavily reliant on extended, familiar systems (fictive kin—church family, friends) to meet caregiving needs. Thus, it was important to convey that the family was *sharing* care versus *relinquishing* it to hospice.

In the initial transition to hospice services, my family referred to it as "home health care." As a professional and thanatologist, I wanted my grandfather to understand that he was being assisted by hospice services. I wanted to make sure, in the gentlest way that he knew he was dying, that he realized his death was imminent. If he had to die, I wanted his death to be the most well-orchestrated, most perfect death possible, complete with a life fully reflected upon; free of unfinished business, no bucket, no list. This created its own cultural dilemma. I was caught between respecting my grandfather's process and timetable and with doing what I thought was needed. I had forgotten one of the essentials of culturally conscientious care; individuals and families often know best what they need. If we recognize that our view is only one view, acting with cultural humility, the space for trust-building and sharing may widen.

And so it did, and in a most profound way.

In the last interaction with my grandfather, I asked if he wished me to read to him before I left. He had read the Bible each evening and was now too weak to read for himself. In response, and much to my surprise, feeble eyes outstretched, he looked directly into mine quoting several biblical scriptures from memory including Psalms 23: "Yea though I walk through the shadow of death, I will fear no evil" and John 14:1–3:

1. Let not your heart be troubled. You believe in God, believe also in Me.
2. In my Father's house are many mansions. If it were not so, I would have told you so. I go to prepare a place for you.
3. And if I go and prepare a place for you, I will come again and receive you unto Myself; That where I am, there you may be also.

We were united in silence. He had conveyed his understanding of his impending death in a way that was most meaningful to him. Within African American culture, religious beliefs have historically been identified as sources of support, guidance and associated with increased patient satisfaction (Levin, Chatters, & Taylor, 2005).

The quiet was soon broken with, "You can turn off the light though."

With that, assured, I headed out.

Ownership, Accountability, and Self-advocacy Education. When trust in the environment is diminished, it also impacts self-trust or belief in the ability to accomplish one's aims (Erikson, 1964). As demonstrated in numerous studies, trust is a legitimate concern. Yet, there are significant costs for inaction or delayed action due to mistrust. Lack of attention to health and end of life care needs as a result of mistrust leads to unfavorable outcomes such as later-stage diagnosis and reduced treatment options (Ross, Kohler, Grimley, Green, & Anderson-Lewis, 2007), and hence may be just as deleterious. Allies are invaluable in facilitating social change. However, marginalized individuals must also be equipped with tools to advocate for themselves and for appropriate care. That is, if one service provider proves untrustworthy, it is possible to choose a different care provider. It is analogous to any other life experience. If we do not like the service at one restaurant, we do not stop eating. We are compelled instead to choose a different restaurant. *Self-advocacy education* is needed to promote a similar paradigm of thinking about health care and end of life services.

Education and Training. Education and training are desperately needed for service providers and consumers of health and end of life services. Information not only enlightens but often serves to reduce stigma and puncture stereotypes or misconceptions (e.g., "Hospice killed him with morphine after my visit with him last night.").

Show Results. It is paramount that helping professionals in thanatology and end of life care show *results* to build trust and encourage hopefulness. That is, more visible and documented reasons to trust are needed. For example, like many people enrolled in hospice, my grandfather only benefited from services for a brief period of three weeks. However, in that time, the nurse demonstrated trustworthiness by consistently advocating and acting on his behalf to ensure the best quality of life at the end of his life. It was evident that the nurse was able to transfer cultural knowledge and experience to practice.

In an examination of cultural competence measures most used in medical and health care settings, Kumas-Tan, Beagan, Loppie, MacLeod, and Frank (2007) found that most measures of cultural competence assess knowledge of "other" (i.e., minority racial ethnic groups) with minimal or no focus on white identity (as culture), privilege, and power dynamics nor on the ability to put information into practice. Self-knowledge and awareness (including privilege and disadvantage) are germane to culturally appropriate practice with marginalized individuals (Whaley, 2001; Kraukauer et al., 2002; Barrett, 2003; Kagawa-Singer & Kassim-Lakha, 2003). Thus, in addition to cultural competence measures that assess "other" knowledge, more measures are needed to access understanding of privilege and whether and how knowledge and skills are used in practice (Kumas-Tan et al., 2007). Cultural concepts and communication may be taught in "clinical medicine courses, continuing medical education, and risk-management courses" (Krakauer et al., 2002) as well as in death and bereavement courses.

Trust is also affirmed through inclusive and transparent methods in interactions with families. Although some hospital intensive care units include families on medical rounds (i.e., clinical discussions about the patient between the physician treatment team and nurses), family participation remains understudied. In a study of parent participation in pediatric ICU rounds, inclusive practice was found to reduce anxiety both in parents and children (Cushing, 2005).

Accessibility and Availability of Study Findings to Individuals and Communities

Helicopter research, wherein investigators collect data from marginalized groups and then leave the communities without offering information ("never to be heard of again"; Montour & Macaulay, 1988) should be avoided. It reinforces mistrust and serves as a reminder of unjust historical events in medical research (e.g., Tuskegee study) (Scharff et al., 2010). In socially just practice, information gathered through research in end of life care should be made available both to participants and to the communities that serve them. This may be accomplished in numerous and multi-level ways including: provision of interview transcripts, if applicable, to research participants; dissemination of study findings to community agencies; development of guide sheets (e.g., Myths and Facts about Hospice Care) which convey study findings in language appropriate for lay audiences; development of community workshops or trainings (Hospice Education) that are both available and accessible to marginalized populations and interfacing entities (e.g., health care workers, therapists, educators, policymakers); press releases; and presentation of research findings and implications at professional conferences.

Services Beyond and Within the Margins

Provision of Services Outside of the Community. If supportive services related to end of life care are provided beyond the margins of communities of interests, what methods will be used to provide access to the services or information about the programming (e.g., webinars, pamphlets at churches, "lunch and learns," shuttle to the grief support camp)?

Located versus Present. Conversely, if services are *located* within communities of interests, how will program *presence* be communicated? Recognizing that trust may be an issue, community outreach and rapport building activities that include gatekeepers (e.g., clergy or school teachers and administrators) may help increase awareness and establish trustworthiness.

Trust and Care Satisfaction Beyond Death. Although the literature focuses on cultural mistrust among individuals (e.g., physicians, nurses) in the context of hospice and health care settings (e.g., Winston, Leshner, Kramer, & Allen, 2005; Moseley, Freed, Charrell, & Goold, 2007), it is noteworthy that a myriad of entities interface with families in end of life care (e.g., funeral homes, spiritual and religious institutions, law enforcement). Further, trusting relationships and satisfaction with care remain central for many families when life ends or the death occurs. As survivors create memories and make meaning of loss experiences, entities interfacing with individuals and families in end of life care become part of the dying, death and even the after-death story.

I was not present at the time of my grandfather's death, but based on family accounts there remained a deep respect for his body, the presentation of it, and my family's grief at this most vulnerable time of significant loss. Consistent with the reverence and respect paid to the dead within African American culture (Barrett, 2009, p. 83), the funeral home director and staff, for example, were respectful in the display and procession of his body as he was physically removed from the home for the final time. They proceeded slowly and intentionally past my bereaved family with my grandfather now on a stretcher, resembling a bed. His body was neatly wrapped in a white blanket with his eyes closed as in peaceful transition or death. This image presented on the night of my grandfather's death was not only respectful but also affirming and enfranchising for both my grandfather and surviving family members after a life lived amid many otherwise disenfranchising occurrences. He died a dignified death that I attribute to family goals in communion with entities and allies in end of life and after-death care acting on his behalf. The experience parallels with *death justice* imagery poignantly captured in *Thanatopsis*, a classic work of William Cullen Bryant (1817/2003, p. 166).

> So live, that when thy summons comes to join
> The innumerable caravan, which moves
> To that mysterious realm, where each shall take
> His chamber in the silent halls of death,
> Thou go not, like the quarry-slave at night,
> Scourged to his dungeon; but, sustain'd and sooth'd
> By an unfaltering trust, approach thy grave,
> Like one who wraps the drapery of his couch
> About him, and lies down to pleasant dreams.

Conclusion

As outlined in the case presentation, barriers to trust in end of life care are present and may be numerous for marginalized groups. It is important to enter service-oriented experiences recognizing the role of privilege, power, and oppression in interactions. It is also important to enter such relationships with an understanding that there may be a strong possibility that trust needs to be established; and among the trusting, that it will need to be reinforced in intangible and concrete ways.

Key Terms

Cultural mistrust—term originally developed to encapsulate the pronounced worries and fears of African Americans concerning health care settings due to legacies of unjust practices that persist today; may be extended to include any pattern of fear or distrust by members of a minority culture toward members of the majority culture and toward institutions that are largely controlled by the majority culture.

Helicopter research—studies in which investigators collect data from marginalized groups and then leave the communities without offering information.

Medical racism—injustice in treatment provided to marginalized individuals, including delayed or substandard care.

Questions for Reflection

1. Considering the concepts of "cultural mistrust" and "medical racism" (real and perceived), how would you—as a culturally conscientious practitioner—build trust with a client from another cultural group? To what extent do you believe these concepts are relevant in your interactions? To what extent might your beliefs about relevance/irrelevance influence the interaction?
2. Consider your own areas of "knowing" and "not knowing." Can you identify ways in which you venture into some areas of "not knowing"? What areas do you avoid because of discomfort with "not knowing"?

References

Barrett, R. K. (2003). Dialogs in diversity: An invited series of papers, advance directives, DNRs, and end-of-life care for African Americans. *Omega: Journal of Death and Dying, 52*(3), 249–261.

Barrett, R. K. (2009). Sociocultural considerations: African Americans, grief, and loss. In K. J. Doka & A. S. Tucci (Eds.), *Living with grief: Diversity and end-of-life care* (pp. 79–89). Washington, DC: Hospice Foundation of America.

Benker, R., Peters, R. M., Clark, R., & Keves-Foster, K. (2006). Effects of perceived racism, cultural mistrust, and trust in providers on satisfaction of care. *Journal of the National Medical Association, 98*(9), 1532–1540.

Brandt, A. M. (1978). Racism and research: The case of the Tuskegee Syphilis Study. *Hastings Center Rep*, 8(6), 21–29.

Bryant, W. C. (2003). Thanatopsis. In S. G. Axelrod, C. Roman, & T. Travisano (Eds.), *The new anthology of American poetry: Traditions and revolutions, beginnings to 1900* (p. 166). New Brunswick, NJ: Rutgers University Press.

Byrne, S. K. (2008). Healthcare avoidance. *Holistic Nursing Practice*, 22(5), 280–292.

Carpenter, L. L., Fontanini, J. J., & Neiman, L. V. (2010). *From surviving to thriving: Mastering the art of the elementary classroom* (Marilyn Grey—p. 112). Dayton, OH: Lorenze Educational.

Cushing, A. (2005). Parent participation in care: Bridging the gap in the pediatric ICU. *Newborn Infants Nursing Rev*, 5(4), 179–187.

Erikson, E. H. (1964). *Childhood and society* (2nd ed.) (pp. 247–274). New York. Norton.

Hammond, W. P., Matthews, D., & Corbie-Smith, G. (2010). Psychosocial factors associated with routine health examination scheduling and receipt among African American men. *Journal of the National Medical Association*, 102(4), 276–289.

Hammond, W. P., Matthews, D., Mohottige, D., Agyemang, A., & Corbie-Smith, G. (2010). Masculinity, medical mistrust, and preventive health services delays among community-dwelling African-American men. *Journal of General Internal Medicine*, 25(12), 1300–1308.

Harris, D. (2009). Oppression of the bereaved: A critical Analysis of grief in Western society. *Omega*, 60(3), 241–253.

Holloway, K. F. C. (2002). *Passed on: African American mourning stories* (p. 3). Durham, NC: Duke University Press.

Jacobs, E. A., Rolle, I, Ferrans, C. E., Whitaker, E. E., & Warnecke, R. B. (2006). Understanding African American views of trustworthiness of physicians. *Journal of General Internal Medicine*, 21(6), 642–647.

Kawaga-Singer, M., & Blackhall, L. J. (2001). Negotiating cross-cultural issues at the end of life: "You got to go to where he lives." *Journal of American Medical Association*, 286(23), 2993–3001.

Kawaga-Singer, M., & Kassim-Lakha, S. (2003). A strategy to reduce cross-cultural miscommunication and increase the likelihood of improving health outcomes. *Academic Medicine*, 78(6), 577–587.

Kelly, B. (2003). *Worth Repeating: More than 5,000 classic and contemporary quotes* (Maya Angelou, p. 263). Grand Rapids, MI: Kregal Academic & Professional.

Krakauer, E. L., Crenner, C., & Fox, K. (2002). Barriers to optimum end-of-life care for minority patients. *Journal of American Geriatrics Society*, 50(1), 182–190.

Kumas-Tan, Z., Beagan, B., Loppie, C., MacLeod, A., & Frank, B. (2007). Measures of cultural competence: Examining hidden assumptions. *Academic Medicine*, 82(6), 548–557.

Levin, J., Chatters, L. M., & Taylor, R. J. (2005). Religion, health and medicine in African Americans: Implications for physicians. *Journal of the National Medical Association*, 97(2), 237–249.

Montour, L., & Macaulay, A. C. (1988). Diabetes mellitus and arteriosclerosis: Returning research results to the Mohawk Community. *Canadian Medical Association Journal*, 139, 201–212.

Moore, A. D., Hamilton, J. B., Pierre-Louis, B. J., & Jennings, B. M. (2013). Increasing access to care and reducing mistrust: Important considerations when implementing the patient-centered medical home in army health clinics. *Military medicine*, 178(3), 291.

Moore, A. D., Hamilton, J. B., Knafl, G. J., Godley, P. A., Carpenter, W. R., Benson, J. T., Mohler, J. L. & Mishel, M. (2013). The influence of mistrust, racism, religious participation, and access to care on patient satisfaction for African American men: The North Carolina-Louisiana Prostate Cancer Project. *Journal of the National Medical Association*, 105(1), 59–68.

Moseley, K. L., Freed G. L., Charrell, B. M., & Goold, S. D. (2007). Measuring African-American parents' cultural mistrust while in a healthcare setting: A pilot study. *Journal of the National Medical Association*, 99(1), 15–21.

Rosenblatt, P. C., & Wallace, B. (2005). *African-American grief* (pp. 7–18). New York, NY: Routledge.

Ross, L., Kohler, C. L., Grimley, D. M., Green, B. L., & Anderson-Lewis, C. (2007). Toward a model of prostate cancer information-seeking: Identifying salient behavioral and normative beliefs among African American men. *Health Education Behavior*, 34(3), 422–440.

Scharff, D., Mathews, K. J., Jackson, P., Hoffsuemmer, J., Martin, E., & Edwards, D. (2010). More than Tuskegee: Understanding mistrust about research participation. *Journal of Health Care for the Poor and Underserved*, 21(3), 879–897.

Sohn, L., & Harada, N. D. (2008). Effects of racial/ethnic discrimination on the health status of minority veterans. *Military Medicine*, 173(4), 331–338.

Street, R. L., O'Malley, K. J., Cooper, L. A., & Haidet, P. (2008). Understanding concordance in patient-physician relationships: Personal and ethnic dimensions of shared identity. *Annals of Family Medicine*, 6(3), 198–205.

Terrell, F., & Terrell, S. L. (1981). An inventory to measure cultural mistrust among Blacks. *Western Journal of Black Studies*, *5*(3), 180–185.

Terrell, F., & Terrell, S. L. (1984). Race of counselor, client sex, cultural mistrust level, and premature termination from counseling among Black clients. *Journal of Counseling Psychology*, *31*(3), 371–375.

VH1 (Producer). (2009, September). *Behind the Music: Lil Wayne—part 4/4*. [Video file] Retrieved from www.youtube.com/watch?v=0jvY3LBokus

Washington, H. A. (2006). *Medical apartheid: The dark history of medical experimentation on Black Americans from colonial times to the present.* New York, NY: Harlem Moon.

Weckmann, M. T. (2008). The role of the family physician in the referral and management of hospice patients. *American Family Physician*, *77*(6), 807–812.

Whaley, A. (2001). Cultural mistrust: An important psychological construct for diagnosis and treatment of African Americans. *Professional Psychology, Research and Practice*, *32*(6), 555–562.

Winston, C. A., Leshner, P., Kramer, J., & Allen, G. (2004–2005). Overcoming barriers to access and utilization of hospice and palliative care services in African-American communities. *Omega*, *50*(2), 151–163.

8

Is Social Justice Elusive for the First Nations Peoples' Loss and Grief?

Kekinusuqs—Judith F. Sayers

First Nations[1] people in Canada have endured horrific amounts of loss and grief throughout time since the first explorer arrived on their lands. This loss and grief is in some ways indescribable, as the hurt goes so deeply into the fabric of who First Nations are both as peoples, and as individuals. Every possible method has and is being used by the colonizer[2] to deprive First Nations of their lands, resources, culture, language, way of life and governments. The government's main purpose was to assimilate First Nations[3] to solve the "Indian problem" and take the "Indian out of the child" (Leslie, 1978). The most referred to quote on government policy is as follows:

> I want to get rid of the Indian problem . . . Our objective is to continue until there is not a single Indian in Canada that has not been absorbed into the body politic and there is no Indian question, and no Indian Department, that is the whole object of this Bill.
> (Scott[4] 1920, in Leslie, 1978, p. 114)

This chapter will highlight the major losses and grief that First Nations people have suffered and continue to suffer at the hands of the Canadian government and the struggle that First Nations are undertaking to heal and assert themselves as Nations, as they strive for social, political, legal, and moral justice.

Before the arrival of the colonizer, First Nations were rich in lands and resources and did not want for food except in times of scarcity. First Nation territories were within their jurisdiction and control and their people used every corner of their lands to sustain their lives. Fish, wildlife, plants, berries, and medicines were all abundant and they used their knowledge of the land to manage the resources so they would be plentiful for many generations. First Nations people were a very spiritual people, and prayers, respect, and ceremonies were an important part of their lives. The colonizer did not understand or recognize the First Nations spirituality, so they were labeled as "heathens" and "savages" (Day, 2000, p. 118; Sinclair, 2013). From taking bark from a cedar tree, welcoming back the salmon, and gathering food and medicinal plants, prayers or ceremonies were performed before anything was taken. Every day was greeted with a prayer and thanks to the Creator that provided so much. These practices were viewed as primitive and a sign of simple mindedness to the European settlers.

When the first explorers arrived in Canada, they were greeted by the First Nations peoples, who helped them to survive in a world that was foreign to them. They traded products, taught them how to grow food, and provided them with information of where everything was on the land.

Unfortunately, those explorers were greedy and did not respect what belonged to First Nations, nor their way of life. They wanted land and they wanted the resources and other riches that were so abundant, and so they started taking everything. They encouraged others to come and partake of the bountiful land and First Nations peoples were soon overrun by people who wanted to control them. Through the process of colonization, First Nations were removed from their territories and put on reserves and denied their way of life that had always sustained them. There have been so many great losses over the years, but First Nations peoples are resilient warriors who continue to fight for what is theirs. They have been dealing with the grief and loss of what they had, while striving towards what can be again.

"Indians Are not Persons"—Loss of Respect

The attitude of the government towards First Nations people was very apparent in the Indian Acts[5] from 1868–1951 with the definition of a "person." A person was defined as: "an individual other than an Indian." This was the view of the colonizer and that was the way they treated "Indian" people. You have to ask: If an "Indian" was not a person, what was s/he considered to be? Obviously, their idea was that "Indian" people were less than other people; in other words, they were dehumanized. "Indian" people were not allowed to vote until 1960, when the Citizenship Act was amended to allow Indian people to be citizens of Canada. It always amazes me when I hear that it took until 1960 to allow First Nations people in Canada to vote. No wonder so few First Nations people vote in elections today. "Indian" women were not allowed to vote in First Nations elections, or to run for Chief or Council until 1951. Such demeaning laws reflect the way First Nations were treated by the formalized government and how this government tried to strip the dignity and honor of a proud people. This attitude was an enormous loss to their status as a Nation and a setback to any positive relationships that could have been formed. Such policies have never been addressed, nor have there been apologies for the dehumanization of First Nations people.

Banning of the Potlach, Sun Dance, and Other Ceremonies

One of the biggest losses to First Nations people occurred in the Indian Act of 1884 that banned the potlatch. This section allowed charges of any "Indian" or other person who engaged in celebrating the potlatch. Violations made one guilty of a misdemeanor and you could put be put in jail for two to six months. A potlatch was an important event which was held for many purposes such as naming, coming of age, memorials, or passing on of chieftainships and it could last for many days. It included the host giving away gifts and the richer the gifts, the higher status that person had in the communities. Gifts could include canoes, coppers, jewelry, blankets, cedar boxes, fish, and other food. The government saw this as wrong because they did not understand the significance of these potlatches to the First Nations people as an integral part of their governments and culture. In 1886, sun dances were added to the ban along with other ceremonies and there was also a ban stating that goods, articles, and/or money could not be given away. From the government's perspective, anything not understood was seen as subversive and had to be banned.

In 1889 the first charges for violation of the potlatch law were laid. Chief Justice Matthew Begbie threw out the charges as "potlatch" was not defined in the Indian Act. The Act was amended in 1921 to define "potlatch" and in 1922, 34 people were charged with violation; 22 went to prison for two to six months. Others agreed to give up their regalia and promised not to potlatch again. Later down the road, some of the regalia was given back to the First Nations people, but most regalia and other cultural items were seized. Some of these invaluable items were put in museums; others were sold to private buyers and never seen again. Many headdresses, curtains, and other cultural items had been in families for hundreds of years and were irreplaceable.

The potlatch was banned from 1884 until 1951. For 62 years, First Nations people tried to have potlatches and other ceremonies where they would not be found and charged. The Nuu-chah-nulth elders shared with laughter in their voices that they would gather and sing and dance with lookouts. If an Indian agent came along, they were warned by their lookouts in enough time to stop their songs and dances and start singing "Onward Christian Soldiers" as the agent walked in the door. My own grandmother described to me that she would sing the songs and dance the dances on her own to keep them alive in her mind. When the ban was lifted, she taught others so that these songs, dances, protocols, and laws would not be lost forever. First Nations used many ways to keep their songs and dances in their minds and remember what their regalia looked like. Throughout all these years, songs and dances, protocols, and ceremonies were performed when possible, but with the lack of use, many of these important cultural rituals were lost. The songs, the dances, the ceremonies, and the protocols were the heart of the people; they were part of the governing structures of the nations, and a means of re-distributing of wealth. The inability to carry out rituals that defined the heart of a people for these 62 years was an incredible blow to the continuity of the culture of First Nations. Some regalia held in public museums around the world have been returned, but not enough. If the governments wanted to assimilate First Nations people into their society, this was a serious attempt to kill the core of what made First Nations people what they were. This of course did not fully work and today, First Nations culture, songs and dances are alive and reviving. The dark years without being able to practice their cultures to the fullest extent was a devastating loss, which some still grieve to this day, especially for the knowledge of songs, dances and ceremonies that were forgotten and for the loss of regalia and treasure of the chiefs that were made by ancestors.

The Government of Canada has never apologized to the First Nations people for the banning of the potlatch and the negative impact it had on them. There has never been any sort of restitution paid to the First Nations people who lost their significant regalia or spent time in jail. This had to do with government intolerance of something that was so important to First Nations and was in no way a crime. There has been no social justice for a people simply living their lives within their culture as all other people have been able to do throughout the history of Canada. It is an injustice for which the government has not taken responsibility.

Governance Structures—Loss of Systems of Governments

The federal government was cognizant of how to attack First Nations people in ways that would undermine their strength as a people. Either that, or the white man[6] only wanted to make First Nations people like them and they proceeded to try and do that. They thought they were the superior people who knew what was right and determined every other way was wrong. Paternalism, superiority, and privilege were prevalent then and still are today. They could not understand the way First Nations people governed themselves. There was not one way of choosing leaders for a Nation or the laws that people lived under. Various First Nations across the country chose their leaders as hereditary chiefs—passing chieftainship from chief to eldest son, generation after generation. Some had the clan mothers choose who would lead. All of these methods seemed to not be in keeping with the values of the federal government. In 1869, the Indian Act imposed an elective system of Chiefs and Councils. It took a lot of convincing for First Nations to switch over to the elective system, but many did under extreme pressure. A few First Nations on the West Coast still have hereditary chiefs today that lead the communities and never gave into the election system.[7] Others have an elective system under the Indian Act and hereditary or traditional chiefs that take on other roles in the community. There are often divisions in communities over the elective and traditional systems of government. The imposition of the elective system on First Nations has caused rifts in communities and imposed values and systems that are not in alignment with First Nations culture and values. In an effort to make First Nations like the white man's government, the Federal Government destroyed some traditional forms of government that had worked well since time immemorial, years before the explorers set eyes on First Nations lands. The Government of Canada is young in comparison to the centuries old First Nations governments. At the Nuu-chah-nulth treaty table we referred to them as the junior government, which of course they did not appreciate. This is another example of a great travesty and loss for First Nations people. Our communities continue to struggle against foreign forms of governments that have not worked for the benefit of our peoples.

The Indian Act does provide custom codes for elections, but a referendum is needed to switch the community to their own code. During the negotiations of treaties in the British Columbia Treaty Process (BC Treaty Commission, 2009), negotiation has resulted in forms of governments set by the First Nations that include a combination of traditional and elected governments (Maa-nulth First Nations, 2006). In October, 2013, The Federal Government tabled Bill C-9 within their Parliament. This bill included the First Nations Election Act, which gives communities the power to extend the terms of chiefs to four years, and to impose an election law on a First Nation without their consent if they are having a leadership debate or their election has been set aside. First Nations across this country are opposed to Bill C-9 because they were not fully consulted about what is contained within the Bill. So today, the issue of who governs First Nations continues to be unresolved due to the Federal Government's imposition of laws and values that are not compatible with their ways and values.

Loss of Lands and Resources

As more and more settlers arrived in what is now called Canada, land and resources were taken for the settlers' own use regardless of the First Nations who owned, inhabited, and used the lands and resources. It became such a problem that the Royal Proclamation of 1763 was passed by King George III, which recognized that aboriginal title exists and that the land would be aboriginal land until ceded by treaty. The Proclamation forbade settlers from claiming land from First Nations peoples unless it was first bought by the Crown and then sold to the settlers. The Royal Proclamation further set out that only the Crown could buy land from First Nations. The Crown made itself a fiduciary on behalf of First Nations peoples without seeking their consent to do so.

The Crown was not much of a fiduciary and took the lands and resources for its own benefit, granting settlers pieces of lands under various methods. First Nations were eventually placed on reserves throughout Canada and some treaties were negotiated but these treaties were not included in what is now called British Columbia (Union of BC Indian Chiefs, 1916).

What must be noted is that in taking the lands and resources, the Crown did not beat the First Nations in war and did not obtain title to their lands through war. The Crown did not take the lands by treaty. The numbered treaties were treaties of peace and friendship and were not for the purpose of taking the land. First Nations people have their oral treaty, which differs from the written treaty. Treaties were settled with the use of interpreters and there are no First Nation words for cede, surrender, and release—yet all of these words appear in all of the treaties. First Nations people concluded the treaties on a spiritual basis and lived up to their understandings of these treaties while the Federal Government did everything it could to weaken the spirit and intent of the treaties.

The Crown did not discover these lands, as First Nations people were here first and the doctrine of discovery and *terra nullius*[8] have been discredited by the International Court of Justice in the Western Sahara case (Janis, 1976). First Nations were an organized nation, with laws and governing structures, including their own languages and territories. Their lands could not be considered as belonging to no one as the term *terra nullius* implies. The Crown cannot rely on discovery or *terra nullius* for their taking of all the lands and resources of First Nations.

Throughout history until today, the issue of taking the lands without any legal authority or mechanism causes a huge problem with First Nations. First Nations are trying to resolve these issues through treaty making, court battles, defending the land through protests or occupations, and any other means to get a just settlement of their territories, including having their lands back. The Indian Act of 1927 made it illegal to hire lawyers or raise money for land claims and this law was in place until 1951. This was not good faith on the government's part and again has never been addressed or justified but it must be if the governments and First Nations are to achieve reconciliation.

For many years, First Nations development has been hampered by the small amount of land they have under the reserve system with all the resources in their territories exploited by companies with royalties going to the federal and provincial governments. While Canada has become one of the richest countries in the world, First Nations have remained the poorest of the poor. Poverty, unemployment, overcrowding, high mortality rates (Assembly of First Nations, n.d.), youth suicide, and many health problems (Health Canada, 2014) continue to plague what used to be wealthy nations. The loss of First Nations lands and resources has been the greatest loss of all, which is why First Nations are using all forms of action to get their land back.

First Nations people have a deep, intricate relationship to the land, water, and all living things. If you take away the land and resources, you take away First Nations ways of life, their spirituality, and all that they are. The loss and grief associated with such actions are immeasurable. Urbanization and development has minimized the land that First Nations have access to exercise their rights and continue with their way of life. Development has occurred in areas that First Nations value as sacred sites,[9] burial sites,[10] cultural, or heritage sites. It is devastating to First Nations people to see a site that has been used since time immemorial destroyed for the sake of jobs, revenue, and the good of the governmental economy. If you lose a hunting right, you don't just lose a hunting right, you lose all the teachings that go with hunting, including the values of respecting the land and animals, using all parts of the animal, and so much more.

One of the biggest issues facing First Nations in north-eastern British Columbia is the proposed Site C Dam that will flood 5,500 hectares of land. This dam has been approved by the federal and provincial governments and they are proceeding to build it over First Nations objections. Currently there are seven law suits by First Nations trying to stop its construction. Most of the First Nations in the area are opposed to the dam (Father Theo, 2011). There are approximately 238 recorded archaeological sites in this area, which include burial sites that will be flooded and many more sites that are not recorded. The government has the power to obliterate these sites for the good of the society even though the purpose of their Heritage Conservation Act (BC Laws, 1996) is to protect and conserve these sites. First Nations people have fought these developments through consultations and through the courts and/or tribunals, and the First Nations' constitutionally protected rights always lose to jobs and revenue for the general public.

Within British Columbia, there are two large pipeline projects, the Enbridge pipeline and Kinder Morgan Trans Mountain pipeline, which are being opposed by First Nations. The National Energy Board has recommended the Enbridge project to the government over the objections of First Nations, many environmental groups, concerned individuals, and the government of British Columbia itself. The lack of respect for First Nations rights and values continues today. The continual battle to protect First Nations rights takes a toll on the First Nations peoples, but they will not give up, continuing to fight these projects in whatever way they can. But why must First Nations always struggle to preserve what is important to them, and which is already recognized in section 35 of the Constitution Act?

The issue of aboriginal title in British Columbia has never been fully settled (William v. Her Majesty the Queen, 2014). The burden of proving title is on the First Nations, not the government, even though The Crown has not taken the lands legally. The Crown should be able to prove the right to the land, as there is no legal basis for ownership; however, the courts have said differently.

Aboriginal title means proving continual use of the territory. With development and urbanization, continual use is harder to prove due to the extensive development that has destroyed this use. For instance, in forestry, evidence of use has disappeared with logging the forests through several growths. In the case of sacred sites, First Nations leave no physical proof of use, yet archaeological methods require physical evidence. So other than oral history, there is no proof and the governments approve the abrogation of such significant sites.

As First Nations struggle to prove title to their territories, watching the change of use of lands, resources, and important sites is a crushing loss. The grief that people feel for lands taken or destroyed that their ancestors used—sites that were used by their people for centuries, is deeply felt. Their powerful places are ruined, their cathedrals within the forests are destroyed, and First Nations peoples are left reeling with the onslaught. No matter how hard First Nations people work against the taking of lands, resources, and important sites, First Nations resistance has not been successful, which makes the loss even more excruciating. "The land is our life" is the underlying principle for many First Nations. One solution for First Nations and governments is to negotiate settlements, but the federal and provincial governments make such limited offers with token jurisdiction that First Nations will not accept these offers and the parties are at a standstill. To date, there has been little resolution of this injustice.

Residential Schools—Loss of Culture, Language, and Parenting Models

One cannot talk about grief and loss in First Nations communities without talking about Indian residential schools. Residential schools removed children from their home and placed them in church-run schools. The whole issue of residential schools is an immense one and cannot be done justice in a short chapter, and so I will address the issues generally with reference to more comprehensive reports (Aboriginal Affairs and Northern Development Canada [AANDC], 1996).

The federal government always felt that First Nations people should be assimilated into the greater society. As late as 1969, with the introduction of the White Paper (AANDC, 1969), the government pursued assimilation. Earlier references to taking the Indian out of the child and solving the Indian problem were the policy framework from which residential schools originated. The federal government felt that it could do a better job than First Nations parents in looking after their children. A law was created that required all First Nations children to be taken from their families and forced to go to residential schools. If parents did not comply, the police were sent in to get the children. These schools were established by churches and financially supported by the government. From 1870–1996 approximately 150,000 children were taken from their families and communities (Aboriginal Healing Foundation [AHF], 2014). Ninety to one hundred percent of these children suffered physical, mental, and sexual abuse. There was a forty to sixty percent mortality rate in these schools and many of these children never saw their families again.

In the schools, the children were forbidden to speak their language. If they did, they were physically punished and suffered emotional and mental abuse. These children were not allowed to visit their families even though in some cases, their parents lived only a few miles away. Even worse, brothers and sisters at the same school were not allowed to associate. Christianity was shoved down their throats. Children were forced to work long hours and were given only a little food that was not nutritional; now as adults, some of these individuals suffer from osteoporosis and other diseases that are related to malnutrition. These children did not have a mother or father figure to show them how to parent, and when they became adults, they did not know how to be a parent to their children, leading to child apprehensions, which will be addressed in this chapter. Because of the horrendous abuse suffered in residential schools, many of the children later became addicted to drugs and alcohol in an attempt to forget what happened. They used physical abuse on their children, as this is what they had learned. As leaders, they became controlling and used lateral violence within their communities and perpetuated an environment where fear, intimidation, and lack of a voice for the people were the norm. First Nations communities are still healing from this experience. The federal government never recognized the loss of language as an effect of these schools and has never put sufficient resources into revitalizing languages.

The federal government has put in place many initiatives to try and deal with the multi-generational effects of residential schools such as the Aboriginal Healing Foundation (AHF), the Truth and Reconciliation Commission (Truth and Reconciliation Commission of Canada), Common Experience Payment (Service Canada, 2013) and the Independent Assessment Process (AANDC, 2013). These processes were only put in place after First Nations people lobbied and raised the profile of the effects of residential schools. These processes have had limited funding and have not addressed all the issues such as day schools and only provided payments to people born after a certain date, leaving many families without resolution. No process has ever addressed the impact of residential school survivors who became chiefs/leaders in their communities and how they governed not only their communities, but tribal council and provincial organizations which represent First Nations collectively. On June 11, 2008, Prime Minister Stephen Harper officially apologized for residential schools (AANDC, 2010). Many First Nations people appreciated the apology and others felt there was no sincerity or understanding of the magnitude of what they suffered in residential schools. Certainly the federal government has not lived up to the promises it made, does not show any regret as to what happened, and has not taken positive action to give substance to the apology.

Many First Nations people brought lawsuits[11] against the Canadian government for mental, emotional and physical damages caused by their attendance at the Indian residential schools. There were several class action suits that agreed to a court settlement. As part of that settlement, a Truth and Reconciliation Commission was established that would document the experiences of the residential school survivors, promote reconciliation activities, and educate Canadians on the Indian residential school experience. The work of the Truth and Reconciliation Commission was commenced on June 2, 2008. At the end of its mandate, The Truth and Reconciliation Commission was to produce a report to the Canadian government and all parties to the court actions that would provide recommendations on next steps to continue reconciliation. On June 2, 2015, the Final Report[12] entitled "Honouring the Truth, Reconciling the Future" was released. It was a very important day for all those who attended the residential schools and all those that were impacted by the forced removal of children and assimilation efforts at such schools, which is literally every First Nations person in Canada. The fact that the report documented the stories of the survivors was a critical juncture for those who attended the schools and the multi-generational effects suffered by others. The report had 94 calls to action, which included recommendations for Child Welfare, Education, Language and Culture, Health, Justice, Reconciliation, Equity for Aboriginal People in the Legal System, a National Council for Reconciliation, a Royal Proclamation for Covenant of Reconciliation, Settlement Agreement and the United Nations Declaration on Rights of Indigenous Peoples, Professional Development and Training for Public Services, Church Apologies and Reconciliation, Education for Reconciliation, Youth Programs, Missing Children and Burial Information, National Centre for Truth and Reconciliation, Commemoration, Media and Reconciliation, Sports Reconciliation, Sport and Reconciliation, and Newcomers to Canada.

The need for reconciliation in every aspect of life in Canada is clearly demonstrated with every area where there is a call to action. While all the calls to action deserve attention, I would like to focus on the recommendation that calls for a National Council for Reconciliation. It has been the Canadian experience that when any studies on First Nations people are done such as the Royal Commission on Aboriginal People and many studies on missing and murdered indigenous women, the recommendations are never implemented. This cannot happen with the Truth and Reconciliation Commission's calls to action. The National Council for Reconciliation can be an independent oversight body that can oversee the implementation of the recommendations and annual reporting to Parliament. I would go further than outlined in the report and give the Council the power to compel governments and First Nations people to act so the work is actually done. If true reconciliation is to occur, these 94 calls to action must be executed along with other actions that First Nations require for reconciliation.

Much time and money was put into the truth and reconciliation process and this report cannot be put on the shelf to gather dust. More important than time and money is the need to bring First Nations people and the government together to work collaboratively on finding ways to right the past and pave the road forward in a way that can be beneficial to all people in Canada. Too much conflict exists within Canada between First Nations and the federal and provincial governments. There is too much negative energy and money put into fighting one another in the courts, on the land, and in endless negotiations that result in no agreements. Such conflict and resistance will not lead to a positive future for First Nations peoples. Canadians need to read this report, at the very least the executive summary and calls to action, and act on what they can. All levels of government, institutions, and organizations need to determine what is within their power, embrace the calls to action, and actually do something to change the status quo. The status quo is not acceptable. Constructive action with desired results is acceptable and the objectives of the report of the Truth and Reconciliation Commission and First Nations people that live within Canada must be achieved.

There have been efforts made to address the legacy of Indian residential schools, but there is still a way to go to address the dysfunctions in First Nations communities that were caused by the multi-generational impacts of residential schools. Implementing the calls to action of the Truth and Reconciliation Commission will go a long way to resolving some of this legacy.

Taking of Children: Another Huge Loss to First Nations

Taking away children for the residential schools was not enough for the government. Provincial laws were enacted to take First Nations children away from their families if government officials decided it was not in the best interests of the children to stay in the home. One of the key reasons governments wanted to remove children from their homes was to remove them from their connection to the land and the exercise of their rights, which meant there would be less resistance by First Nations people to the development and taking of more land and resources. The 1960s scoop was when many children were taken from their families and reserves and placed in care; this is still an issue today. The Auditor General of Canada in 2008 stated that:

> between 1997 and 2001 there was a rapid increase in the number of on-reserve children placed in care. Over this period, the total number of children in care increased by 65 percent, from 5,340 to 8,791 children. This number has remained around the same level since then. At the end of March 2007, there were about 8,300 on-reserve children in care, a little over 5 percent of all children aged from 0 to 18 living on reserves. We estimate that this proportion is almost eight times that of children in care living off reserves.
>
> (Office of the Auditor General of Canada, 2008)

Statistics Canada numbers based on the 2011 census shows this trend continues (Statistics Canada, 2011). The National Household Survey (2011) states that "of the approximately 30,000 children in care in Canada in 2011, 14,225 were aboriginal. Overall, four percent of aboriginal children were in care, compared to a scant 0.3 percent of non-aboriginal children, or 15,345 children" (Woods & Kirkey, 2013).

When five percent of your population is taken out of the homes of their families, and largely placed in homes that are not First Nations, the loss to First Nations is incalculable. The 'stolen generations' or 1960s scoop children represent over 16,000 First Nations children who were apprehended and put in non-First Nations homes for adoption. Lawsuits are proceeding today based on the lack of consent, lack of culture, and the pain, suffering, and loss of those children (Chiefs of Ontario, n.d.).

The taking of children did not end with the residential schools. A report done by John Beaucage entitled *Children First* (Ministry of Child and Youth Services, 2011), reports that from 1960–1990 over 11,000 First Nations children in Ontario were placed in care and 70 percent of those children were placed in non-First Nations homes. He goes on to cite government and other reports that show that these people now face cultural and identity issues.

There are so many issues being faced by the children who were put in care away from their families and communities and did not have access to their culture. There was also huge grief within the family and community over the loss of their children—their future leaders and people who would be needed to carry out the work within the Nation. Parents, grandparents, brothers, sisters, aunts, and uncles all mourn for lost children, siblings, nieces, and nephews, not knowing where these children are and what happened to them. There is a large hole in their lives as a result of these unimaginable losses.

Missing and Murdered Women—Loss of Key People Within the First Nations Communities

The Native Women's Association of Canada produced a fact sheet in 2010 that reported:

> NWAC has gathered information about 582 cases of missing and murdered Aboriginal women and girls. Of these:
>
> - 67 percent are murder cases;
> - 20 percent are cases of missing women or girls;
> - 4 percent are cases of suspicious death—considered suspicious by family;
> - 9 percent are cases where the nature of the case is unknown.

The missing and murdered First Nations women within Canada have become a prevalent issue that has now captured mainstream media attention. The number of 582 missing and murdered women has grown, and different data bases have reported different numbers. No person's life goes unaffected by missing and murdered First Nations women. In the past six months, two of my friends have had their sisters murdered and another had her best friend murdered. Things that used to happen to someone else are now happening closer to home. When a young girl gets murdered in a community, everyone is affected. Regularly, there are social media calls to assist with missing First Nations women. Emails come in with pictures asking for help in locating another First Nations woman. The issue is one that affects us on a regular basis.

First Nations have been trying to get governments to act on missing and murdered women to no avail. Calls for a public inquiry into missing and murdered First Nations women have been denied. For over 30 years on Valentine's Day, marches are held across the country in memory of these women who have gone missing, or were murdered. An Amnesty International Report, called *No More Stolen Sisters* (2009), states that aboriginal women aged 25 to 44 are five times more likely to suffer a violent death then other women in Canada. Five times more likely—one has to ask why? It is hoped that answering those kinds of questions can be done through a public inquiry. Is it the same old attitude portrayed in the Indian Act that an "Indian" is not a person, or is it just seen as an "Indian problem"? Is this attitude from the past one that is still adopted by the public today? If this was over 600 non-First Nations people, would this problem still be happening? Would there have been a public inquiry held years ago and positive action to prevent violence against women? Is it racial discrimination on behalf of the justice system? There are so many questions with no real answers but the issue remains that too many First Nations women are missing or victims of violence.

The federal government has not put a national strategy in place to prevent violence against First Nations women. They have put $25 million over 5 years into setting up some mechanisms to help deal with the issue, but no clear overall strategy and no real analysis is in place to determine whether those mechanisms will help to resolve the problem. A special parliamentary committee recently came out with a report entitled, *Invisible Women: A Call to Action* (House of Commons, 2014) but many condemned it as maintaining the status quo and not addressing the necessary actions the government needed to undertake.

In British Columbia, there is a highway that runs from Prince George to Prince Rupert where over 31 women have disappeared since the 1960s. It is called the "Highway of Tears" because families weep without the knowledge of what happened to their loved one; not knowing cuts deeply into their hearts.

The Robert Pickton case drew national attention and surprisingly the government of British Columbia called an inquiry into missing and murdered women from the Downtown Eastside of Vancouver. Pickton was accused of murdering 27 women. He went to trial for six of these women, but the Crown decided not to proceed with the other 21 cases, as Pickton would already be in jail for the rest of his life. This decision was an unsatisfying result for the 21 other women who were loved and cherished by their families.

Enough of a furor was raised in British Colunbia that the Provincial Government established a Missing Women Commission Inquiry (MWCI, 2013) into the missing women of the Downtown Eastside over a five-year period and on aspects of the Pickton case. The report concluded that the police investigations into the murdered and missing women were blatant failures. Sixty-three recommendations were made. Most of these recommendations have not been adopted and implemented. This MWCI was controversial from the start from the choice of the person empowered to carry out the inquiry, to the lack of funds given to aboriginal families to be fully represented. Police forces, lawyers, and others were able to be fully represented, but the inquiry only allocated funds for a couple of lawyers to represent all the First Nations families that wanted to be there.

Inequity after inequity! Such an important issue was given attention for a fleeting time and then not enough resources were put in place to implement the recommendations. Stephen Point was appointed to a committee that would help implement these recommendations, but then the government chose not to proceed with the committee when several of the families decided to take legal action against the government based on their exclusion from the process. Stephen Point, not wanting to get involved in the middle of this controversy, resigned.

This is so frustrating for the families, friends and communities of those women who have gone missing or were murdered. It is difficult enough for them to deal with the loss of their family member, but their losses were exacerbated by the inaction of both the federal and provincial governments. As more and more First Nations women go missing and the issue becomes more apparent, it is the hope of many that positive, strategic action will be taken to prevent violence against First Nations women.

Youth Suicides: Loss of Young People in First Nations Communities

Another issue that causes immense grief for First Nations peoples is youth suicides. Youth suicides vary by community, circumstance, location, and other social factors. A report done by Health Canada in conjunction with youth, the Assembly of First Nations, and experts, concluded that youth suicides are five to six times higher than among the non-First Nation Population (Health Canada, 2013). Suicide rates among male First Nations youth are higher than among female youth. In communities where suicide is an issue, prevention measures are elusive. Losing youth to suicide is devastating as communities scramble to deal with the issue. At times, chiefs have called a state of emergency when youth suicides have gotten to a certain threshold point.[13] First Nations have been working on this issue and have put plans in place using culture and language to assist in their programming (Fraser Health, 2012).

Mortality Rates and Death Rituals

Life expectancy rates for First Nations peoples are five to seven years less than for non-First Nations people, and infant mortality rates are 1.5 times higher among First Nations (Assembly of First Nations, 2011). In First Nations communities, it seems that there are people passing on with great regularity. Deaths come in threes, and once one person passes, you begin to worry who will be second and third. Maybe it is because our communities are so interrelated that we feel there are frequent deaths. When Nuu-chah-nulth was negotiating treaties, it seemed that the death rate was very high. I often wondered whether it was a sign that we should not be in treaty negotiations.

When death occurs, the family, friends, and community gather at the family home. People drop by with food and bring strength to the family in their hard time of grieving for the loss of their loved one. In the Nuu-chah-nulth way, your presence brings the family "medicine" so they are able to carry on.

Organizing what happens after a death is an important process. There are many things done. Some people cut their hair to show they are mourning. There are several things that can be done with this hair to help in the healing process. After the funeral, pictures of the person are put away for a year. It is easier to mourn for someone when you are not constantly seeing their picture. In some First Nations cultures, the mirror is covered in the room that the person stayed in. Clothing and bedding are burned after the funeral. There are certain people who do the burning and carry the casket. It cannot be someone who is pregnant or can still bear children. Young men do not carry the casket, but can be honorary pallbearers. I would like to stress that I speak from my knowledge and experience with death and dying. First Nations people have their own ways of dealing with the business that must be done. I am providing some context for some processes that do exist.

Pregnant woman and children under 12 do not attend the funeral and should not look at the body This may seem to be very harsh to some people, but protecting the unborn infant and young minds is most important in our teachings. Children are kept quiet and indoors at night and you did not sing and dance during the period when the person passed on until they were buried. The spirit of the person passing on remains until the burial and you do not want to attract the death spirit by these activities. At times a rattle is used at the graveside and a chant performed that says "Don't Look Back, Don't Look Back." Chants that are used at a funeral cannot be used again for a year unless they are specific chants for funerals.

For younger people who died without living a full life, a memorial feast is held. There is a drying of the tears and you let go of your mourning. Then you dance and sing again and carry on with life. Following the drying of the tears, you sing happy songs and celebrate life. For people who undertake suicide, a memorial feast is not held as their lives were taken unnaturally.

For hereditary chiefs, a memorial feast is held, and you can do so within four years of their passing. The more important the hereditary chief, the longer you wait. You can then bring out his songs, dances, and his name that were put away when he passed. Ceremonies are used for hereditary chiefs that are not used for anyone else. The chiefs (*Haw'iih*) are much respected. When someone very close to you passes on, you take a year to be quiet, not sing and dance (unless you are preparing for the memorial), and you don't attend other funerals and other public events, or you greatly reduce your attendance. It is a time to gather your strength and respectfully mourn your very close relative. For older people that pass on after living a full life, there is no memorial feast. Their life iscelebrated for all they have done and for how they have touched so many people's lives.

There are many protocols that are utilized that can differ by family or First Nation. What I talk about here is from some of my teachings from my elders from the Hupacasath and other Nuu-chah-nulth Nations, and there are reasons behind all of what is done and not done. Death is treated seriously and respectfully.

Conclusions

Throughout this paper I have discussed the many severe losses that First Nations peoples have had to endure and grieve. From colonial attitudes the Government of Canada (1969) has held about our status as a person or peoples, the intent to assimilate and integrate First Nations into the general populace, to the taking of First Nations lands, resources, children, governance, the First Nations' history has been one of fighting colonialism, negative laws, policies, and actions. With the number of issues I have described (and there are many more that I have not specified), it is apparent that such heavy losses could have caused First Nations peoples to crumble and to succumb to government wishes.

Instead of yielding to government, First Nations people have risen up against the continual injustices heaped upon them. Repeatedly, First Nations people are called upon to speak out and fight against colonialism, the destruction of lands, resources, and sacred sites, and to preserve and protect what they can and reclaim their rightful place on this earth.

The horrific losses suffered through residential schools, apprehension of children, youth suicides, and the high suicide and mortality rates have definitely taken a toll on First Nations people; the grief is still being felt and will take more time to heal. The Government of Canada has tried to take away the most critical parts of First Nations: language and culture through the banning of the potlatch and other cultural ceremonies, and our traditional forms of government. It has tried to turn First Nations into duplicates of its governments and tried to ensure they adopt its values. It has not succeeded. It has tried to make sure that First Nation lives are not valued, as over 500 missing and murdered women have become a prominent news item, while the government refuses to complete a public inquiry; it would be obvious that it would be blamed for the inaction and bureaucratic policies and procedures that have allowed this injustice to continue. Those in the government continue, as always, with the theme of dehumanizing First Nations people.

All of what has happened to First Nations—the quality of life that is less than that of the general public, the lack of funding for adequate housing, the unsafe drinking water, and the lack of prevention of health epidemics, has led to greater mortality rates for both adults and infants. Canada's human rights record was criticized when First Nations people found themselves in crisis over their lack of housing in freezing temperatures (Stastna, 2014), or suffered from unsafe drinking water that causes long evacuation (Parliament of Canada, 2010). Canada is embarrassed in the media. Unfortunately, such embarrassment does not lead to positive action or cause the government to work collaboratively and with the consent of the First Nations. Chief Theresa Spence of the Attawapiskat First Nation had to fast for 44 days (Harper, 2013) to try to bring attention to the housing crisis, which still remains unresolved. The federal government still prefers to think they have the solutions for the "Indian problem." Paternalism is alive and well in Canada.

Much has to happen for social justice to occur to address all the issues explored in this chapter. Some progress has been made in some areas but in most, not enough positive, workable solutions have been found due to the attitudes and inaction of both the federal and provincial governments and their inability to work with First Nations, who know what is needed. Loss and grief are all too commonplace and rampant in First Nations communities and this must change. First Nations have been coping with loss and grief from numerous sources, and it is their resilience and warrior spirit that keeps them going. Fighting for future generations is what drives most First Nations communities, and they will not stop their fight for social, legal, and moral justice until their ends are achieved.

Key Terms

Assimilation—the social process of absorbing one cultural group into another group, which is usually the dominant social group.

Dehumanization—denial of individual human attributes to individuals and groups, making them seem less than human and hence not worthy of humane treatment; often results in behaviors such as exclusion, violence, and support for violence against others.

First Nations—the First Nations are the various Aboriginal peoples in Canada who are neither Inuit (indigenous peoples inhabiting the Arctic regions of Greenland, Canada, and Alaska), nor Métis (Aboriginal peoples in Canada who trace their descent from mixed ancestry of First Nations and Europeans).

Multi-generational impact—in the context of this chapter, behaviors, trauma, and grief that have been passed down and reinforced through many generations of a family or group.

Paternalism—behavior, by a person, organization, or state, which limits some person or group's liberty or autonomy supposedly for that person's or group's own good. Paternalism implies that the behavior is against or regardless of the will of a person, or that the behavior expresses an attitude of superiority of the decision-making party.

Questions for Reflection

1. First Nations peoples speak of a profound loss of cultural identity due to the outlawing of important traditions (e.g., potlatch, sundances) by the Canadian government. Consider your own important traditions. What effect do you think it might have for you, your family, or your community, if these traditions were made illegal?
2. The experience of the First Nations peoples in Canada is not unique in how many indigenous peoples have been treated when other groups have taken over their land and formed nations that pressure these groups to assimilate into the established ruling order. Explore examples from other nations and countries for similar occurrences, including the impact of colonization and treatment of indigenous peoples during these times. What are the losses that have occurred? What are the multi-generational effects for these groups?
3. Consider the effects of loss across multiple generations of family and culture. How would you respond to a present day individual who describes feelings of loss associated with something that happened during their grandparents' lifetime? What do you observe within yourself if you belong to the group that is accused of being responsible for this loss?

Notes

1. In this chapter I will use the term First Nation to refer to First Nations people. I will use "Indian" if I am referring to the term "Indian" in the Indian Act. The term Indian is not First Nations but that of the colonizer and I will use my own preferred use of terms.
2. The term "colonizer" refers to people who were not from North America who arrived primarily from European countries into what is now referred to as Canada, and then settled onto the land that was, at that time, already settled by First Nations people. The colonization of North America (including Canada) by European settlers and the establishment of their government upon these lands were also associated with the subjugation of First Nations peoples and the undermining of their land, resources, and way of life.

3. The Act to Encourage the Gradual Civilization of Indian Tribes in this Province and to amend the Laws Relating to Indians (commonly known as the Gradual Civilization Act) was a bill passed by the fifth Parliament of the Province of Canada in 1857.
4. Served as deputy superintendent of the Department of Indian Affairs from 1913 to 1932, and is better known today for advocating the assimilation of Canada's First Nations peoples in that capacity.
5. From 1868–1876 there were four Acts that related to "Indian People", the first act, which was called the Indian Act, was passed in 1876. For ease of reference I am referring to them all as Indian Acts
6. My use of the term "white man" refers to the four races in the world, white, yellow, red, and black. The colonizing government consisted almost entirely of white men.
7. First Nations such as Toquaht, Nuchahtlaht, and Lyackson are examples.
8. *Terra nullius* is a Latin expression deriving from Roman law meaning "nobody's land," which is used in international law to describe territory, which has never been subject to the sovereignty of any state, or over which any prior sovereign has expressly or implicitly relinquished sovereignty.
9. Bear Mountain near Victoria, BC is a good example of the desecration of a sacred site.
10. Poets Cove is a good example of a developer that built on a site with human remains and received a very low fine of $50,000 for such an incredible violation to the ancestors. Under the Heritage Conservation Act, the fine goes to the Government and not the First Nations.
11. www.residentialschoolsettlement.ca/IRS%20Settlement%20Agreement-%20ENGLISH.pdf
12. www.justice.gov.za/trc/report/
13. Cowichan First Nation and Ahousaht First Nation are examples of this.

References

Aboriginal Affairs and Northern Development Canada. (1969). *Statement of the Government of Canada on Indian policy: The White Paper*. Retrieved from www.aadnc-aandc.gc.ca/eng/1100100010189/1100100010191

Aboriginal Affairs and Northern Development Canada. (1996). *Royal Commission on Aboriginal People*, Volume 1, Part 2, c. 10. Retrieved from www.aadnc-aandc.gc.ca/eng/1307458586498/1307458751962

Aboriginal Affairs and Northern Development Canada. (2010). *Statement of Apology*. Retrieved from www.aadnc-aandc.gc.ca/eng/1100100015644/1100100015649

Aboriginal Affairs and Northern Development Canada. (2013). *Independent assessment process*. Retrieved from www.servicecanada.gc.ca/eng/goc/cep/index.shtml

Aboriginal Healing Foundation. (2014). A condensed timeline of events. Retrieved from www.ahf.ca/downloads/condensed-timeline.pdf

Amnesty International. (2009, September). *No more stolen sisters: The need for a comprehensive response to discrimination and violence against indigenous women in Canada*. Retrieved from www.amnesty.ca/sites/default/files/amr200122009enstolensistersupdate.pdf

Assembly of First Nations. (n.d.). *Fact Sheet: The reality for First Nations in Canada*. Retrieved from www.64.26.129.156/cmslib/general/RFNC.pdf

Assembly of First Nations. (2011, June). *Fact sheet: Quality of life of First Nations*. Retrieved from www.afn.ca/uploads/files/factsheets/quality_of_life_final_fe.pdf

BC Laws. (1996). *Heritage Conservation Act*, C. 187 S. 2. Retrieved from www.bclaws.ca/EPLibraries/bclaws_new/document/ID/freeside/00_96187_01

BC Treaty Commission. (2009). *The independent facilitator for treaty negotiations*. Retrieved from www.bctreaty.net/files/negotiations.php

Chiefs of Ontario. (n.d.). *60's scoop*. Retrieved from www.chiefs-of-ontario.org/node/373

Day, R. (2000). *Multiculturalism and the history of Canadian diversity*. (pp. 118). Toronto, Canada: University of Toronto Press.

Father Theo. (2011, March 9). *Treaty 8 First Nations Declaration on the Site C Dam Proposal* [Web log post]. Retrieved from www.fathertheo.wordpress.com/2011/03/09/treaty-8-first-nations-declaration-on-the-site-c-dam-proposal/

Fraser Health. (2012, December). *Fraser Region Aboriginal Youth Suicide Prevention Collaborative: Suicide Prevention, Intervention and Postvention Initiative*. Retrieved from www.fraserhealth.ca/media/AH_suicide-prevention.pdf

Government of Canada. (1969). *Statement of the Government on Indian Policy*. Retrieved from www.aadnc-aandc.gc.ca/DAM/DAM-INTER-HQ/STAGING/texte-text/cp1969_1100100010190_eng.pdf

Harper, T. (2013, January 25). *Theresa Spence's unfulfilling end to 44 day fast*. Retrieved from www.thestar.com/news/canada/2013/01/25/tim_harper_theresa_spences_unfulling_end _to_44day_fast.html

Health Canada. (2013, archived). *Acting on what we know: Preventing youth suicide in First Nations: The report of the Advisory Group On Suicide Prevention*. Retrieved from www.hc-sc.gc.ca/fniah-spnia/pubs/promotion/_suicide/prev_youth-jeunes/index-eng.php#s2121

Health Canada. (2014). *First Nations and Inuit health*. Retrieved from www.hc-sc.gc.ca/fniah-spnia/diseases-maladies/index-eng.php

House of Commons. (2014, March). *Invisible women: a call to action (a report on missing and murdered indigenous women in Canada)*. Retrieved from www.parl.gc.ca/HousePublications/Publication.aspx?DocId=6469851&Language=E&Mode=1&Parl=41&Ses=2

Janis, M. W. (1976). International court of justice: advisory opinion on the Western Sahara. *Harvard International Law Journal, 17*(3). Retrieved from www.papers.ssrn.com/sol3/papers.cfm?abstract_id=1103207

Leslie, J. (1978). *The historical development of the Indian Act* (2nd ed). (pp. 114). Ottawa, Canada: Department of Indian Affairs and Northern Development, Treaties and Historical Research Branch.

Maa-nulth First Nations. (2006). *Maa-nulth First Nations Final Agreement*. (S. 13.3.1/13.2.2). Retrieved from www.bctreaty.net/nations/agreements/Maanulth_final_intial_Dec06.pdf

Ministry of Children and Youth Services. (2011). *Children First: The Aboriginal Advisor's Report on the status of Aboriginal child welfare in Ontario*. Retrieved from www.children.gov.on.ca/htdocs/english/documents/topics/aboriginal/child_welfare_EN.pdf

Missing Women Commission of Inquiry. (2013). Retrieved from www.missingwomeninquiry.ca

National Household Survey. (2011). Retrieved from www12.statcan.gc.ca/nhs-enm/2011/rt-td/index-eng.cfm#tabs1

Native Women's Association of Canada. (2010). *Fact sheet: Missing and murdered Aboriginal women and girls*. Retrieved from www.nwac.ca/files/download/NWAC_3D_Toolkit_e_0.pdf

Office of the Auditor General of Canada. (2008, May). *2008 May report of the Auditor General of Canada*, Chapter 4: First Nations child and family services program. Retrieved from www.oag-bvg.gc.ca/internet/English/parl_oag_200805_04_e_30700.html#hd5a

Parliament of Canada. (2010, May). *Safe drinking water in First Nations communities*. Retrieved from www.parl.gc.ca/Content/LOP/researchpublications/prb0843-e.html

Service Canada. (2013). Common experience payment. Retrieved from www.servicecanada.gc.ca/eng/goc/cep/index.shtml

Sinclair, M. (2013, June). Remarks at the National Research Centre Signing Ceremony. University of Manitoba, Canada. Retrieved from www.umanitoba.ca/about/media/Justice_Sinclair_remarks_at_NRC_signing_cerremony_21_June_2013.pdf

Stastna, K. (2014, April 12). First Nations housing in dire need of overhaul: Shortages, overcrowding and ramshackle homes the norm on many reserves. Retrieved from www.cbc.ca/news/canada/first-nations-housing-in-dire-need-of-overhaul-1.981227

Statistics Canada. (2011). Age groups and sex of foster children, for both sexes, for Canada, provinces and territories. Retrieved from www12.statcan.gc.ca/census-ecensement/2011/dp-pd/hlt-fst/fam/Pages/highlight.cfm?TabID+1&Lang=E&Asc=1&PRCode=01&OrderBy=999&Sex=1&tableID=304

Truth and Reconciliation Commission of Canada. (n.d.) Retrieved from www.trc.ca/websites/trcinstitution/index.php?p=3

Union of BC Indian Chiefs. (1916). *McKenna-McBride Royal Commission*. Retrieved from www.ubcic.bc.ca/Resources/final_report.htm#axzz2vmZO6lN8

William v. Her Majesty the Queen, 34986 Supreme Court of Canada (2014). Retrieved from www.scc-csc.gc.ca/case-dossier/info/dock-regi-eng.aspx?cas=34986

Woods, M., & Kirkey, S. (2013, May). 'Tragic' number of aboriginal children in foster care stuns even the experts. Retrieved from www.canada.com/health/Tragic+number+aboriginal+children+foster+care+stuns+even+experts/8354098/story.html

9

Protecting Dignity at the End of Life

An Agenda for Human Rights in an Aging World

Andy Hau Yan Ho and Geraldine Xiu Ling Tan

Introduction

Population aging is a powerful demographic transformation that is rapidly challenging healthcare infrastructure globally. This phenomenon steadily intensified at the turn of the twenty-first century, and we are only beginning to fully comprehend its impacts at national and global levels. The extensive debate of whether we live longer and healthier lives or suffer from poor health and inappropriate treatments continues as we witness the growing service disparities between medical and social care systems that fail to establish high quality palliative care for all. This chapter examines the end-of-life challenges faced by older people suffering from chronic life-limiting illnesses, and argues that the only way to protect their dignity at life's final and most vulnerable moments is to ensure that palliative care becomes a basic human right.

Challenges of an Aging Population

Recent statistics from the World Health Organization (WHO, 2011) showed that 524 million people were aged 65 or older in year 2010, representing 8 percent of the world's total population. This number is projected to surge and reach 1.5 billion by year 2050, accounting for 16 percent of all people in the world. Although most developed countries, such as France, Sweden, the United Kingdom, and the United States have the oldest population profiles, the vast majority of older people and the most rapidly aging populations live in less developed countries. For example, it took over 100 years for France's elderly population to rise from 7 percent to 14 percent, but the same demographic will occur in less than two decades in countries like China and India (Kinsella & He, 2009). Specifically, according to the United Nations (2010), China's population of people aged 65 and older is predicted to increase from 110 million in 2010 to 330 million in 2050; an astounding three-fold increase within a 40 year time span. Similarly, India's older population is expected to surpass 227 million by 2050, highlighting a staggering proliferation of 280 percent from 2010. These rapidly aging countries will inevitably require new policies that ensure the financial security as well as the health and social well-being of older people; however, they lack a period of sustained economic growth to adequately support and maintain such demands. As a result, "some countries may grow old before they grow rich" (WHO, 2011, p. 5).

One of the main driving forces of the remarkable aging phenomenon of our time is the vast improvement in longevity. In fact, the dramatic increase in average life expectancy during the twentieth century is often seen as one of society's greatest achievements. While babies born in the early 1900s were not expected to live beyond 45 to 50 years of age, life expectancy at birth now exceeds 80 years in most developed societies, especially in East Asia where Hong Kong, Japan, and Singapore are among the global leaders in longevity (WHO, 2011). However, despite a consistent rise in global life expectancies marked by the decline of infectious and acute diseases, older people in the contemporary era are not necessarily living healthier lives as their longevity is underlined by the emergence of chronic and degenerative illnesses. Evidence from the Multi-country Global Burden of Disease Project have indicated that in the course of the next three decades, people in every world region will experience more death and disability from non-communicable diseases and chronic conditions such as heart disease, stroke, cancer, and diabetes (WHO, 2004a), all of which are also the leading causes of deaths among the older generations. A more recent cross-national assessment conducted by the Organization for Economic Cooperation and Development further declared that dementia and Alzheimer's disease (AD) will emerge as one of the other leading causes of death and disability among the aged, whereby 115 million people worldwide are projected to be living with dementia or AD by 2050, a four-fold increase from 2010 (Alzheimer's Disease International, 2010).

All of these findings underscore the fact that increased longevity does not translate into increased well-being in old age. With greater prevalence of life-limiting illnesses with extended dying trajectories, the elderly dependency ratio in most countries will rise sharply over the next 40 years, again with greatest increase found in East Asia including Japan, China and Singapore (United Nations Department of Economic and Social Affairs, 2007). Older people with chronic and degenerative diseases, including cancer and dementia, will inevitability suffer the loss of their ability to live independently due to limited mobility, deteriorations in physical and cognitive functioning, and chronic frailty as they approach the end of life. Unable to perform their activities and instrumental activities of daily living, many will become dependent on family caregivers and a large percentage will eventually be placed in some form of long-term-care (LTC) facilities, such as residential care, nursing homes, and long stay hospitals. According to the OECD (2013), approximately 4 to 7 percent of older people in most developed countries around the world reside in nursing homes, and between 60 and 70 percent of elders die in hospital settings. For these institutionalized elders, LTC facilities are often acknowledged as their final residence, a place where they can receive adequate palliative care and live with comfort and dignity before facing their impending mortality. Unfortunately, this is far from the truth.

Challenges to the Provision of Palliative Care

The World Health Organization defined palliative care as

> an approach that improves the quality of life of patients and their families facing the problems associated with life-threatening illness, through the prevention and relief of suffering by means of early identification and impeccable assessment and treatment of pain and other problems, physical, psychosocial and spiritual.
>
> (WHO, 2004b, p. 84)

Embedded in this definition is a commitment to the affirmation of life, an integration of psychological and spiritual aspects of patient care, the provision of support to help patients live as actively as possible until their death, with support being provided to help families cope during their loved one's illness, and their own bereavement (Chochinov, 2004). In essence, palliative care integrates a support system that enriches the quality of life of the family unit as well as heightens the purpose of a dignified death, regardless of the type of disease or the place of care.

Notwithstanding these honorable convictions, substantial evidence has shown that the dignity and quality of life at the end of life for many older dying patients and their families are still being compromised. A 2002 nationwide study in the United States revealed that even with years of research and education that were directed at advancing the understanding of good palliative practices, older individuals with terminal illness living in hospitals or nursing homes could not expect a satisfactory or dignifying experience with end-of-life care services (Last Acts, 2002). This was due in large part to the lack of understanding about the needs and concerns of dying patients among palliative doctors and nurses on issues that ranged from adequate pain control to those concerning psychosocial and spiritual care, as well as the lack of interdisciplinary collaboration that undermines care coordination and care management. In 2004, the WHO reported that despite the presence of palliative care, many older terminally ill elders were still experiencing unnecessary pain and suffering due mainly to the underassessment of pain, the lack of autonomy and involvement in decision-making, as well as the lack of homecare support and specialist services (WHO, 2004a). In 2008, the U.K. Royal College of Nursing also stated that although institutional nursing staff knowledge, awareness, and sensitivity to the needs and concerns older dying patients and their families had gradually increased, the quality of care they rendered had not. They found that nursing staff had inadequate time and limited resources to deliver quality palliative care, due mostly to the poor physical environments of healthcare institutions combined with inferior organizational cultures that featured management bureaucracy, unrealistic expectations, quick fix attitudes, and staff shortages (Baillie, Gallagher, & Wainwright, 2008).

Most recently in 2011, the Care Quality Commission in the United Kingdom testified that despite gradual advancement in palliative care practices and provisions, one in every five U.K. hospitals inspected failed to provide dignified care to older dying patients mainly due to major deficiencies in care coordination and care management across different professional disciplines and service departments. The Parliamentary and Health Services Ombudsman of the U.K. (2011) had also detailed the tragic incidents of ten elderly terminal patients who were left without food or water, and were trapped in their own urine and feces for long periods of time after they suffered a fall within the hospital compounds regulated by the National Health Services (NHS). Furthermore, Francis (2013) reported in many NHS hospitals, "Large numbers of patients were left unprotected, exposed to risk, and subjected to quite unacceptable risks of harm and indignity over a period of years . . . and as a result, dignity, even in death, were denied" (p. 13). Similar reports are also emerging in Asia as mounting evidence has posited that the pitfalls of palliative care in Hong Kong, which resulted in the indignities of older dying patients and their families, lay principally in the disregard for personal autonomy, the disjointed provision of care, the disparity of care quality, and the absence of communications between different care professionals, hospital departments, and elderly service agencies (Chan et al., 2012; Ho, Chan et al., 2013, Ho, Leung et al., 2013).

These parallel findings from cross-national studies highlight the multifaceted nature of quality palliative care, one that not only concerns human agency and professional practice, but also the social values and structures that govern healthcare institutions and their respective stakeholders. Hence, any missing link within the spectrum of palliative care could prove harmful to individuals' quality of life in life's final margin. Not surprisingly, the glaring inadequacies in current palliative care provisions have led to a renewed public discourse that emphasizes the founding philosophies of palliation, and those that are aimed genuinely and compassionately at helping the aged, the sick and the dying, so as to arrive at a renewed commitment to our most basic human right.

Dignity as the Renewed Foundation of Palliative Care

The renewed discourse on palliative care philosophies and practices aspires to ensure that the needs and concerns of dying patients and their families are optimally addressed. Over the past decade, healthcare professionals across the globe have reached the consensus that patients and families must not only be cared for and feel comfortable in the last phases of life, but in a much broader sense, be provided with comfort through holistic and dignified care. That is, palliative care "honors and protects those who are dying, conveys by words and actions that *dignity* resides in people" (McClement & Chochinov, 2006, p. 106), and that dignity "helps people preserve their integrity while coping with unavoidable physical insults and loss" (Preston, Tang, & McCorkle, 2003, p. 147). In 2004, the WHO further emphasized that, "palliative care is an important public health issue. It is concerned with the suffering, the *dignity*, the care needs, and the quality of life of people at the end of their lives" (WHO, 2004b, p. 6).

With these honorable testimonies, it is evident that dignity and dignified care have become the overarching goal that dictates the provision of palliative care for older dying patients and their families in the modern era. The imperative of dignity has also expanded beyond palliative care to include end-of-life care. While palliative care and end-of-life care are often used interchangeably in public discourse, end-of-life care is more expansive and covers a wider range of services for "those with advanced, progressive, incurable illness to live as well as possible until they die" (National Council for Palliative Care, 2008, p. 2). The Social Care Institute of Excellence (2013) further contended that the delivery of dignified end-of-life care entails support for people to have as much control over the decisions, care, and treatment as possible; provides support to minimize pain and suffering; helps people to plan and to say goodbye to loved ones; allows people time for reflection and provides professional support when needed; encourages, as far as possible, meaningful activities and discussions to support a sense of self-worth and purpose; provides support for family and caregivers; and provides support for those receiving care who may experience bereavement.

Clearly, healthcare professionals and policymakers have now embraced the preservation of human dignity as both a clinical goal as well as a policy goal in the provision of palliative care and end of life care (Dresser, 2008). In recent years, international public health communities have published numerous statements to avow that palliative care is a universal human right where dignity must be safeguarded at life's final and most vulnerable moments. In 2004, the WHO cemented its position on the imperative of dignity in palliative care by stating that, "good quality care towards the end of life must be recognized as a basic human right" (WHO, 2004b, p. 16). In the same year, the International Work Group of the European School of Oncology published a position paper entitled, "A New International Framework for Palliative Care", through which the group stated that "there should be free access to palliative care for all people, as a fundamental human right" (Ahmedzai et al., 2004, p. 2912). In 2005, a statement was released from the Second Global Summit of The National Hospice and Palliative Care Association, protesting that governments must "make access to hospice and palliative care a human right" (The Korean Declaration, 2005, p. 1).

Most recently, the Open Society Foundation made one of the strongest statements urging all nations to protect human dignity and human rights through making palliative care accessible to all:

> Palliative care is fundamental to health and human dignity and is a basic human right. Palliative care is highly effective in managing pain and physical symptoms and can improve adherence to medications. It can and should be delivered with curative treatment that begins at the time of diagnosis. But palliative care goes much further than physical care. It is a holistic approach that improves the quality of life for patients and their families by addressing the psychosocial, legal and spiritual problems associated with life-threatening illness.
>
> (Open Society Foundation, 2012, p. 1)

Despite such overwhelming support to advocate for palliative care as a basic human right, not all people are receiving adequate care at the end of life. Traditionally, palliative care is rendered through hospital settings and offered specifically to patients suffering from cancer. The high predictability of cancer disease progression provides an easier pathway in recognizing and planning for the needs of patients and their families. This has resulted in the perception that palliative care is only appropriate in the last few months or weeks of life and can only be provided by specialized care providers (WHO, 2004b). Yet, as the changing epidemiology of disease has shown, not everyone dies from cancer, and the current regime of palliative care often fails to provide support to people with other serious chronic illnesses or multiple chronic problems with variable illness and dying trajectories (Lunney, Lynn, Foley, Lipson, & Guralnik, 2003). As a result, many terminally ill elders and their families suffer needlessly as palliative care remains inaccessible to them.

Apart from accessibility, major attitudinal, behavioral, educational, and institutional barriers have been also described in the literature related to the development of palliative care for non-cancer patients and the elderly population. These obstacles to broadened palliative care service include the difficulty for patients and families to accept palliative treatment due to fear, uncertainty, and misinformation; the reluctance of clinicians to identify the palliative phase; healthcare providers' apprehension of inducing physical or psychological interventions through misconceptions about pain tolerance and assessment biases; and tension in available service providers and resource allocation (Foley, 2000). Moreover, bureaucratic procedures within organizations, the time required for arranging homecare technology, and the difficulties to obtain extra care for dying patients within the community are all real-life impediments for pushing forth a primary palliative care agenda (Groot, Vernooij-Dassen, Verhagen, Crul, & Grol, 2007).

Therefore, integrating palliative care as a normalized healthcare approach for all older people requires not just extensive knowledge or good intentions, but psycho-education for the public and the determination to remove barriers at all levels of the healthcare system (WHO, 2004b). Fundamentally, increasing public life and death education to promote greater death awareness and preparedness, enhancing professional and allied-health training in palliative and end-of-life care, remodeling of care structures and procedures, as well as expanding care provision and support into local communities, are all important facets in which an important transformation can be instituted (Ho, 2013).

Expanding the Compassionate Borders of Palliative Care

The demographic evolution of the world's population has given rise to renewed discourses on cultivating changes in the global healthcare system. The medical and psychosocial complexities that people face in their old age signify an urgent need for palliative care to be made equitably to all, and not just those suffering from cancer. Effective palliative care is essential in enabling older people to uphold their dignity, self-autonomy, and overall quality of life, and it also helps family caregivers cope with the emotional and socioeconomic challenges that they inevitably encounter.

Thus, careful remodeling of the current palliative care provision, based on existing knowledge and projected statistics, could prove to be an invaluable and cost-effective starting point for addressing the rapidly growing needs of palliative care among the aged. In-patient palliative care and designated hospice beds have important and distinct roles, yet they pose great drains on existing resources and unavoidably limit the expansion of palliative care. Community-based care thus becomes an important direction for broadening palliative care provision in meeting the needs of the twenty-first century. Specifically, older terminally ill patients should be encouraged and provided with greater support to stay at home with their families and live actively in their communities. Expanding the provisions of home care services beyond office hours, networking with non-government organizations, and the training of care providers in elderly homes and community centers are all valuable strategies to facilitate living and dying in place.

As health care professionals and frontline workers in acute settings often feel perplexed and poorly equipped in caring for dying patients and families, more consultative services should be developed to extend palliative care services to different ward settings, primary health care institutions, and private clinics. Daycare services which offer opportunities for patients and families to engage in social activities and support groups, receive respite care and other interventions to better cope with death and dying should be expanded beyond the current setup of hospital-attached service units to include community-based independent service units. Moreover, self-help groups and volunteer organizations should be provided with greater patronage, educative and pragmatic, to assist in the delivery of supportive care within the community.

The provision of palliative care for older people in the foreseeable future will also need to be substantially different given the rapid demographic change. The notion that LTC facilities will become the hospice of the future in caring for older people with multiple chronic conditions with a long trajectory to death is quickly becoming a reality (Abbey, Froggatt, Parker, & Abbey, 2006). In LTC settings, the achievement of quality palliative care will require attention to all levels of the health and social care system, in both its formal and informal manifestations. The traditional palliative care including its skills, values and management structure, which were developed mainly for cancer patients, may well exclude some critical aspects of the care required for older people with different illnesses and life circumstances. Thus, the transferability of current practices and philosophies of palliation to the care of older people must be guided by a root cause analysis of their specific palliative care needs, rather than a simple transmission of skill set from one population (e.g., cancer patients) to another.

In essence, the sustainability of palliative care for older people, and all people in general, rests upon health care policies and practices that are rid of the pragmatic piecemeal approach, and compassionately committed to the promotion of healthy living and healthy aging with that of appropriate end-of-life care (Ho, Chan, & Leung, 2014).

Palliative Care as a Human Right and a Public Health Priority

Death is an inevitable event and the comfort care to the dying, regardless of age, gender, ethnic background and nature of the disease, should be seen as a necessity rather than a luxury in modern health care. Hence, palliative care is a basic human right entitled to all members of society. The main process to achieve this goal is by integrating palliative care into all levels of society through a public health strategy (PHS) that facilitates bilateral involvement from a bottom-up approach starting from the community level as well as a top-down approach starting from the public policy level; as it is impossible to develop a comprehensive palliative care system that is separated from the existing health care system and social support network. In order for a public health strategy to be effective, government bodies have to take an active role to integrate the PHS into all levels of public health care as well as the greater social welfare system owned by the community, involving all members of society through collective and social action (Higginson & Koffman, 2005; Stjernsward, Foley, & Ferries, 2007).

The success of the PHS also requires community organizers of palliative care to commit to interacting with policymakers and health care professionals as well as the general public on a consistent basis, starting with the introductory work of educating them on the concepts of death, dying, hospice, and palliative care (Meier & Beresford, 2007). Advocacy that leads to policy change must further be supported and informed by ongoing institutional and community-based research that addresses the specific needs of palliative care professionals as well as the concerns and wishes of dying patients and their families at the end of life. The research is contextually grounded and conducted with an understanding of the local culture's assumptions, positions, references, values, and beliefs.

Ultimately, in order to promote the aspiration of dignity and dignified care for all, there needs to be a common discourse shared among different stakeholders of a healthcare system, one that penetrates all layers of social structures and boundaries within a society. Such a discourse can be achieved through "Health Promoting Palliative Care," which translates the hospice ideals of *whole person care* into broader public languages and practices related to prevention, harm reduction, support, education, and community actions (Kellehear, 1999). The ideas of 'compassion' and 'the universality of death and loss' then become the impetus for public discourse to facilitate and encourage individuals, groups, and communities to discuss and assess their own perceived needs at the end of life and develop strategies to address them. Kellehear (2005) expanded on these ideas and proposed the establishment of compassionate cities for promoting end-of-life care through public community development. He stated that:

> The idea of compassion is able to transcend . . . problems of economy and society, health and welfare, or law and moral conduct will be rearranged to a single discourse about the health, support and well-being of everyone. This will not simply be because some have fragile health, but because life itself is a fragile experience. The ever-present experience of death and loss reminds us of our cultural, spiritual and political responsibilities towards one another because of . . . the shared experience of death and loss.
>
> (Kellehear, 2005, p. 161)

Clearly, the affinity between dignity and compassion is instrumental for breaking through the bondage of health political economy in the modern era, which often undermines the experience of loss and mortality with the need for efficacy and efficiency.

Conclusion

The human body is more than just a vessel for tissue, organs, and bones. Intertwined within this entity are intricate aspects of the self and a multitude of emotions including joy, love, hope, pain, and suffering. How do we separate the physical body from the emotions that are so innately housed? When there is physical discomfort, is there not a degree of emotional suffering as well? The body should no longer be perceived as being detached from the very core elements that make us human. It is important to recognize that just as we cannot isolate the body from the self, we cannot deny the vital union of dignity, compassion, and clinical care.

Once we realize that physical pain and emotional suffering are inherently interdependent, we will understand more comprehensively the significance of assimilating palliative care across all health and social care systems and throughout the dying trajectories of all people, both young and old. It is a basic human right to be relieved from suffering and a great human privilege to help in this alleviation of pain.

Key Terms

Dignity—seeing the value and worth of the individual person and respecting that person's space, way of life, choices, preferences, and needs as they are indicated by that person.

End-of-life care—a wide range of services for those with advanced, progressive, incurable illness to live as fully as possible until they die.

Palliative care—an approach that improves the quality of life of patients and their families facing the problems associated with life-threatening illness, through the prevention and relief of suffering by means of early identification, assessment, and treatment of pain and other physical, psychosocial, and spiritual problems.

Questions for Reflection

1. Much of the discussion of palliative care involves the concepts of "dignity" and "dignified care." What do these terms mean to you? What would you expect to see happening in care that upheld these values?
2. Several organizations have made strong statements regarding the status of palliative and end-of-life care as basic human rights. Do you agree with the statements? What does it mean to you to consider something a "right?"

References

Abbey, J., Froggatt, K., Parker, D., & Abbey, B. (2006). Palliative care in long-term care: A system in change. *International Journal of Older People Nursing, 1*(1), 56–63.

Ahmedzai, S. H., Costa, A., Blengini, C., Bosch, A., Sanz-Ortiz, J., Ventafridda, V., & Vergagen, S. C. (2004). Position paper: A new international framework for palliative care. *European Journal of Cancer, 40*, 2192–2200.

Alzheimer's Disease International (2010). *World Alzheimer report, 2010.* Retrieved June 27, 2015 from www.alz.co.uk/research/files/WorldAlzheimerReport2010.pdf

Baillie, L., Gallagher, A., & Wainwright, P. (2008). *Defending dignity: Challenges and opportunities for nursing.* London: Royal College of Nursing.

Chan, C. L. W., Ho, A. H. Y., Leung, P. P. Y., Chochinov, H. M., Neimeyer, R. A., Pang, S. M. C., & Tse, D. M. W. (2012). The blessing and curses of filial piety on dignity at the end-of-life: Lived experience of Hong Kong Chinese adult children caregivers. *Journal of Ethnic and Cultural Diversity in Social Work, 21*(4), 277–296.

Chochinov, H. M. (2004). Dignity and the eye of the beholder. *Journal of Clinical Oncology, 22*(7), 1136–1340.

Care Quality Commission. (2011). *Dignity and nutrition inspection programme: National overview.* Retrieved November 18, 2015 from http://www.cqc.org.uk/file/4909.

Dresser, R. (2008). Human dignity and seriously ill patients. In *Human dignity and bioethics: Essays by the President's Council on Bioethics* (pp. 505–512). Washington, DC: The President's Council on Bioethics.

Foley, K. (2000). Dismantling the barriers: Providing palliative and pain care. *Journal of the American Medical Association, 283*(1), 115–115.

Francis, R. (2013). *Report of the Mid Staffordshire NHS Foundation Trust Public Inquiry.* London: The Stationery Office.

Groot, M. M., Vernooij-Dassen, M. J. F. J., Verhagen, S. C. A., Crul, B. J. P., & Grol, R. P. T. M. (2007). Obstacles to the delivery of primary palliative care as perceived by GPs. *Palliative Medicine, 21*(8), 697–703.

Higginson, I. J., & Koffman, J. (2005). Public health and palliative care. *Clinics in Geriatric Medicine, 21*(1), 45–55.

Ho, A. H. Y. (2013). *Living and dying with dignity: An interpretive-systemic framework in Hong Kong* (Unpublished doctoral dissertation). The University of Hong Kong, Hong Kong SAR.

Ho, A. H. Y., Chan, C. L. W., & Leung, P. P. Y. (2014). Dignity and quality of life in community palliative care. In K. Fong & K. W. Tong (Eds.), *Community care in Hong Kong: Current practices, practice-research studies and future directions* (pp. 319–341). Hong Kong: City University of Hong Kong Press.

Ho, A. H. Y., Chan, C. L. W., Leung, P. P. Y., Chochinov, H. M., Neimeyer, R. A., Pang, S. M. C., & Tse, D. M. W. (2013). Living and dying with dignity in Chinese society: Perspectives of older palliative care patients in Hong Kong. *Age and Ageing, 42*(4), 455–461.

Ho, A. H. Y., Leung, P. P. Y., Tse, D. M. W., Pang, S. M. C., Chochinov, H. M., Neimeyer, R. A., & Chan, C. L. W. (2013). Dignity amidst liminality: Suffering within healing among Chinese terminal cancer patients. *Death Studies, 37*(10), 953–970.

Kellehear, A. (1999). Health promoting palliative care: Developing a social model for practice. *Mortality, 4*(1), 75–82.

Kellehear, A. (2005). *Compassionate cities: Public health and end of life care.* New York, NY: Routledge.

Kinsella, K., & He, W. (2009). *An aging world: 2008.* Washington, DC: National Institute on Aging and U.S Census Bureau.

Last Acts. (2002). *Means to a better end: A report on dying in American today.* Retrieved from November 18, 2015 from https://scholarworks.iupui.edu/handle/1805/722.

Lunney, J. R., Lynn, J., Foley, D. J., Lipson, F., & Guralnik, J. M. (2003). Patterns of functional decline at the end of life. *Journal of American Medical Association, 289*(18), 2387–2392.

McClement, S. E., & Chochinov, H. M. (2006). Dignity in palliative care. In E. Bruera, I. J. Higginson, C. Ripamonti, & C. von Gunten (Eds.) *Textbook in palliative medicine* (pp. 92–701). Boca Raton, FL: CRC Press.

Meier, D., & Beresford, L. (2007). Advocacy is essential to palliative care's future development. *Journal of Palliative Medicine*, *10*(4), 840–844.

National Council for Palliative Care. (2008). 10 questions to ask if you are scrutinizing end of life care for adults. Retrieved November 18, 2015 from: http://www.ncpc.org.uk/sites/default/files/EndOfLifeCare_TenQuestions.pdf.

Open Society Foundation. (2012). *Public health fact sheet: Palliative care as a human right*. Retrieved November 18, 2015 from https://www.opensocietyfoundations.org/publications/palliative-care-human-right-fact-sheet.

Organization for Economic Co-operation and Development (OECD). (2013). OECD Health Data 2013: Long-term care resources and utilisation. Retrieved from www.oecd-ilibrary.org/

Parliamentary and Health Services Ombudsman. (2011). *Care and compassion? Report of the health service ombudsman on ten investigations into NHS care of older people*. London: The Stationery Office.

Preston, F. A., Tang, S. T., & McCorkle, R. (2003). Symptom management for the terminally ill. In I. Coreless, B. B. Germino, & M. A. Pittman (Eds.), *Dying, death and bereavement* (pp. 145–180). New York, NY: Springer.

Social Care Institute of Excellence (2013). *Dignity in care*. Retrieved November 18, 2015 from http://www.scie.org.uk/publications/guides/guide15/index.asp

Stjernsward, J., Foley, K. M., & Ferries, F. D. (2007). The public health strategy for palliative care. *Journal of Pain and Symptom Management*, *33*(5), 486–493.

The Korean Declaration. (2005). *Declaration on hospice and palliative care. Second Global Summit on National Hospice and Palliative Care*. Retrieved June 21, 2015 from www.coe.int/t/dg3/health/Source/KoreaDeclaration2005_en.pdf

United Nations. (2010). *World population prospects: The 2010 revision*. Retrieved June 27, 2015 from www.esa/un.org/unpd/wpp

United Nations Department of Economic and Social Affairs. (2007). *World population aging*. New York, NY: United Nations, Population Division.

World Health Organization. (2004a). *The solid facts: Palliative care*. Geneva: World Health Organization.

World Health Organization. (2004b). *Better palliative care for older people*. Demark: World Health Organization Regional Office for Europe.

World Health Organization. (2011). *Global health and aging*. US: National Institute on Aging and National Institute of Health.

Part Four
Individual Experiences in Social Contexts

In this part, we explore how individual experiences can be influenced and affected by the social context in which they occur.

We begin with how the experience of grief itself has become politicized and codified. Grief, a normal and universal human experience, has become labeled as a diagnostic entity in many sectors, which means that grieving individuals can easily become pathologized and labeled as deviant from the norm. Granek considers the implications of grief that is somehow seen to "go awry," meaning that it (and the bereaved person's experience) can be compared to a standard of acceptable and "normal" grief that is socially constructed, but not necessarily correct or helpful to bereaved individuals.

Next, we explore the experiences of patients and professionals within the context of health care delivery. The concept of iatrogenic harm is extended to include psychological iatrogenic trauma to patients who are objectified and dehumanized by a health care system that is run on a business-based model. Furthering the concept to health care professionals, we begin to see how the same health care system has the potential to objectify and wound caregivers as well as those who are the recipients of their care.

In Chapter 12, we read about the plight of older women prison inmates whose grief and loss experiences remain in the shadows, typically ignored by administrators, security personnel, clinicians, researchers, and the greater community. People in prison are often treated as non-persons, stripped of their rights and dignity, and often viewed as deserving of such treatment for the acts they have committed prior to imprisonment. The authors describe how the environmental issues prior to incarceration and the prison culture itself combine in ways that significantly suppress inmates' ability to grieve. Lack of recognition of the many social and emotional losses and isolation are frequent companions to these women.

Chapter 13 describes the challenges and needs of individuals with intellectual disabilities (ID) in dealing with death. The authors describe how these individuals represent an underserved minority with highly specialized needs and limited internal resources for coping with significant losses. While many of these individuals may not be able to cognitively comprehend death, they most certainly feel deprivation and loss, and their needs for support are often ignored.

Finally, we look through a critical lens to the social rules of grief that are prevalent in Western society, including the pressure upon bereaved individuals to remain stoic, highly functional, and productive even after the experience of significant, life-changing losses. The intersection of capitalistic values with the human experience of loss can place bereaved individuals in an impossible situation of either denying the importance of their losses in order to satisfy social expectations, or violating these social rules in order to honor their losses.

10
Medicalizing Grief

Leeat Granek

Introduction

In January of 2012, Benedict Carey, a writer for *The New York Times*, introduced an article on the pathologization of grief with the question, "When does a broken heart become a diagnosis?" (Carey, 2012). In the field of psychology and its related disciplines (psychiatry, social work, medicine etc.), the question of what makes grief pathology has been hotly debated in the last several decades. Questions around what grief should look like, how long it should last, and how it should be treated have circulated in the academic spheres and, more recently, in mainstream media outlets like the article in *The Times*. My own work on the pathologization of grief (see: Granek, 2008; 2010; 2013a; 2013b; Granek & O'Rourke, 2012) has asked a broader set of questions. As a critical scholar on grief, I am less interested in what constitutes pathological grief and more interested in asking questions about how grief got medicalized in the first place, what are the motivations for pathologizing grief, and most importantly, what are the implications for contemporary mourners in thinking about and understanding their grief within a medicalized frame. In this chapter, I touch on each of these issues sequentially.

The Medicalization of Grief

What does it mean to medicalize grief? Conrad (2007) described medicalization as the process by which human conditions or problems become medical problems to be solved. Experiences that were once viewed as a normal part of human life such as pregnancy, childbirth, unhappiness, aging, and death and dying have been brought under medical control and scrutiny. Thus, the medicalization of grief, put simply, means that what was once considered a normal human reaction to the loss of a loved one that could last from a few days to many years has now become a medical or psychological problem to be worked through, and in some cases to be treated with medications or therapy if it is going on 'too long' or 'too intensely.' It is important to understand this process of medicalization in an historical, cultural, and social context, but because that is not the focus of this chapter, and because I have written extensively on these topics elsewhere, I refer readers to these publications to learn more about the ways in which grief has become increasingly pathologized in the last century (see: Granek, 2008; 2010; 2013a; 2013b). Before delineating what medicalized grief is, it's important to understand that regardless of the specific criteria for what constitutes pathological grief, the very idea that we can evaluate ourselves on a continuum of normality or abnormality when it comes to grieving has changed the way we understand mourning. That is, a hundred years ago, few people thought about grieving as something that could go awry or that could be healthy or unhealthy. Grief was simply considered a natural part of life and accepted as part of the normal and expected trajectory of one's lifespan as well as an understandable reaction to the loss of a loved one (Granek, 2008; 2010; Granek & O'Rourke, 2011).

What is medicalized grief? As noted, in the current cultural context where all grief is considered *potentially* pathological, some grief is described as disordered or in need of professional monitoring or treatment (Forstmeier & Maercker, 2007; Horowitz, 2005–2006; Prigerson & Jacobs, 2001; Prigerson et al., 2009; Shear & Frank, 2006; Shear et al. 2011). Within the psy-disciplines (i.e., psychology, psychiatry, etc.), there have been several proposals for more extreme forms of pathological grief called Complicated Grief (CG), Prolonged Grief Disorder, traumatic grief, or in some instances simply, pathological grief (Stroebe & Schut, 2005–2006). These variants of pathological grief have been proposed by largely American researchers for inclusion in *The Diagnostic and Statistical Manual of Mental Disorders* that recently had a new edition come out in 2013 (*DSM-5*; APA, 2013). For a review of the proposed symptomology for these disorders, please see Table 10.1. Although pathological grief (and their variants—e.g., complicated grief, prolonged grief disorder etc.) are currently *not* official diagnoses and were *not* accepted as diagnostic criteria in the 2013 version of the *DSM*, they are used widely by researchers and clinicians and are diagnosed in patients and clients alike.

Most proponents of pathological grief agree that "normal grief" and "pathological grief" look almost identical in terms of symptom presentation in mourners, but that it is a matter of duration and intensity that marks the difference between what is pathological and what is normal. For example, Prigerson and Maciejewski (2005–2006) noted,

> The issue is not whether the symptoms themselves fit into seemingly pathological versus seemingly normal symptom clusters. What our results demonstrate is that the set of CG symptoms that we have identified, at persistent (beyond six months post loss) and severe (marked intensity or frequency, such as several times daily) levels, are predictive of many negative outcomes and that is the basis for distinguishing them from normal grief symptoms.
>
> (p. 15)

In other words, researchers in the field claim that while normal grief and pathological grief *look* the same, duration and intensity mark the difference between normality and abnormality. The concern with this conclusion is that if normal grief and pathological grief look the same, then who has the power to determine what is "too long" or "too intense"? The medicalization of grief attempts to put a set of boundaries around normal grieving without taking into consideration the extreme variability in people's mourning experiences, including culture, gender, age, previous loss history, and personal idiosyncrasies. Moreover, as will be described in the next section, many people take much longer than six months to process a major loss and the current diagnostic system makes it very likely that large swaths of people will be diagnosed with pathological grief.

In addition to the proposed diagnoses of pathological grief, one recent change that did go into the *DSM-5* has to do with what was once called the "bereavement exclusion." Until recently, the bereavement exclusion clause in the *DSM* indicated that a person who is experiencing symptoms of depression could not be diagnosed with clinical depression if they had experienced a major loss within the previous two months. In the new edition, this exclusion was removed, and now, people can be diagnosed with clinical depression two weeks after a major loss if they meet all the criteria. Because many people who are grieving look a lot like people who are experiencing depression, it is highly likely that many more people will be given a diagnosis of depression when they are experiencing normal grief (see Table 10.2 for Major Depressive Episode criteria in the *DSM-5*).

Table 10.1 Proposed Criteria for Prolonged Grief Disorder and Complicated Grief

Pathological Grief Proponents	Criteria	Cut Off From Time of Bereavement
Horowitz and colleagues (1997)	A. Bereavement. B. In the last month, any three of the following seven symptoms with a severity that interferes with daily functioning: **Intrusive symptoms:** 1. Unbidden memories or intrusive fantasies related to the lost relationship. 2. Strong spells or pangs of severe emotion related to the lost relationship. 3. Distressingly strong yearnings or wishes that the deceased were there. **Signs of avoidance and failure to adapt:** 4. Feelings of being alone too much or personally empty. 5. Excessively staying away from people, places, or activities that remind the subject of the deceased. 6. Unusual levels of sleep interference. 7. Loss of interest in work, social, caretaking, or recreational activities to a maladaptive degree.	14 months post loss
Prigerson and colleagues (2009)	A. Event: Bereavement (loss of a significant person). B. 'Chronic yearning, pining and longing for the deceased'; physical or emotional suffering as a result of the desired, but unfulfilled, reunion with the deceased, daily or to a disabling degree. C. Five or more out of nine symptoms such as: "confusion in one's role in life," "difficulty accepting the loss," "avoidance of reminders of the reality of the loss," "inability to trust others," "bitterness or anger about the loss," "difficulty about moving on," "numbness," "feeling that life is unfulfilling," and "feeling dazed or shocked about the loss." D. Diagnosis should not be made until at least six months have elapsed since time of death. E. The disturbance causes clinically significant impairment in social, occupational, or other important areas of functioning. F. The disturbance is not better accounted for by major depressive disorder, generalized anxiety disorder, or posttraumatic death disorder.	6 months

continued...

Table 10.1 Continued

Pathological Grief Proponents	Criteria	Cut Off From Time of Bereavement

Shear and colleagues (2011)	A. person has been bereaved.
	B. At least one of the following symptoms of persistent intense acute grief has been present for a period longer than is expected by others in the person's social or cultural environment.
	  1. Persistent intense yearning or longing for the person who has died.
	  2. Frequent intense feelings of loneliness or like life is empty or meaningless without the person who has died.
	  3. Recurrent thoughts that it is unfair, meaningless or unbearable to have lived when the loved one has died, or a recurrent urge to die in order to find or join the deceased.
	  4. Frequent preoccupying thoughts about the person who has died, e.g., thoughts or images of the person intrude on usual activities or interfere with functioning.
	C. At least two of the following symptoms are present for at least a month:
	  1. Frequent troubling rumination about circumstances or consequences of the death, e.g., concerns about how or why the person died, or about not being able to manage without their loved one, thoughts of having let the deceased person down, etc.
	  2. Recurrent feeling of disbelief or inability to accept the death, like the person can't believe or accept that their loved one is really gone.
	  3. Persistent feeling of being shocked, stunned, dazed or emotionally numb since the death.
	  4. Recurrent feelings of anger or bitterness related to the death.
	  5. Persistent difficulty trusting or caring about other people or feeling intensely envious of others who haven't experienced a similar loss.
	  6. Frequently experiencing pain or other symptoms that the deceased person had, or hearing the voice or seeing the deceased person.
	  7. Experiencing intense emotional or physiological reactivity to memories of the person who died or to reminders of the loss.
	  8. Change in behavior due to excessive avoidance or the opposite, excessive proximity seeking, e.g., refraining from going places, doing things, or having contact with things that are reminders of the loss, or feeling drawn to reminders of the person, such as wanting to see, touch, hear or smell things to feel close to the person who has died.
	D. The duration of symptoms and impairment is at least one month.
	E. The symptoms cause clinically significant distress or impairment in social, occupational, or other important areas of functioning, where is not better explained as a culturally appropriate response.
		6 months post loss

Table 10.2 Criteria for Major Depressive Disorder in the DSM-5

A. At least five of the following symptoms have been present during the same two-week period and represent a change from previous functioning: at least one of the symptoms is either 1) depressed mood or 2) loss of interest or pleasure.
  1. Depressed mood most of the day, nearly every day, as indicated either by subjective report (e.g., feels sad or empty) or observation made by others (e.g., appears tearful);
  2. Markedly diminished interest or pleasure in all, or almost all, activities most of the day, nearly every day (as indicated either by subjective account or observation made by others);
  3. Significant weight loss when not dieting or weight gain (e.g., a change of more than 5 percent of body weight in a month), or decrease or increase in appetite nearly every day;
  4. Insomnia or hypersomnia nearly every day;
  5. Psychomotor agitation or retardation nearly every day (observable by others, not merely subjective feelings of restlessness or being slowed down);
  6. Fatigue or loss of energy nearly every day;
  7. Feelings of worthlessness or excessive or inappropriate guilt (which may be delusional) nearly every day (not merely self-reproach or guilt about being sick);
  8. Diminished ability to think or concentrate, or indecisiveness, nearly every day (either by subjective account or as observed by others);
  9. Recurrent thoughts of death (not just fear of dying), recurrent suicidal ideation without a specific plan, or a suicide attempt or specific plan for committing suicide.
B. The symptoms do not meet criteria for a mixed episode.
C. The symptoms cause clinically significant distress or impairment in social, occupational, or other important areas of functioning.
D. The symptoms are not due to the direct physiological effects of a substance (e.g., a drug of abuse, a medication) or a general medical condition (e.g., hypothyroidism).
E. The symptoms are not better accounted for by bereavement, i.e., after the loss of a loved one, the symptoms persist for longer than two weeks or are characterized by marked functional impairment, morbid preoccupation with worthlessness, suicidal ideation, psychotic symptoms, or psychomotor retardation.

In the *Slate* survey, we asked participants to check off the symptoms they had experienced when grieving. In Table 10.3 below, the first column represents the answer options; the second column represents the percentage of people who endorsed the item (*N*= 7,715).

The "*a,b,c*" indicates which of these response options are considered criteria for complicated grief according to the following theorists: a) Horowitz's criteria must be met 14 months post bereavement; b) Prigerson's criteria must be met six months post bereavement and; c) Shear's criteria must be met six months post bereavement.

Motivations to Medicalize Grief

The pathologization of grief has had an effect on how mourning is understood and managed in day-to-day life. The vocabulary of grief has been thoroughly psychologized. Terms such as *coping, recovery, healing, denial,* and *grief work* or *grief process* are all constructions of psychology, psychiatry, and the mental health professions, and today psychotherapy and medication are common ways in which grieving is addressed. For example, the treatment of both large-scale grief (i.e., events such as 9/11, school shootings, or other acts of terrorism) and small-scale grief (individual responses to death) has become the province of psychology and psychiatry (for examples of psychologists intervening and providing grief counseling, see Brown & Goodman, 2005; Metcalf, 2005; Rosenblatt, 2005; Welt Betensky, 2007). Groopman (2004) called this phenomenon "the grief industry" and stated that it is led by professionals who claim that all bereavement requires intervention in order to avoid pathological grief reactions. Whether it is for individuals or groups experiencing loss, the idea is that grief counselors are needed to help initiate the so-called grief work that enables people to express their feelings and begin the process of healing.

Psychological Counseling

Depending on how CG is defined, as many as 80 percent of people who are bereaved should require counseling (Genevro, Marshall, Miller, & Center for the Advancement of Health, 2004). Although there is little evidence that grief counseling helps people cope specifically with grief (Allumbaugh & Hoyt, 1999; Jordan & Neimeyer, 2003; Kato & Mann, 1999; Schut, Stroebe, van den Bout, & Terheggen, 2001), these findings have not stopped the publication of numerous articles on the efficacy of interventions. Various bereaved populations have been targeted, including all people who have experienced a loss through death; those bereaved in specific groups, such as widows or bereaved parents, and those with CG (Genevro et al., 2004). The evidence for counseling those at risk for CG is inconsistent. Some research has shown that cognitive–behavioral therapy is moderately effective for certain symptoms of CG, such as intrusion (intrusive thoughts), avoidance, and failure to adapt; however, the researchers also note that

> The percentage of patients who experienced reliable change was highest for intrusion and failure to adapt, but a considerable number of patients in the control group [who received no treatment] also showed reliable changes and low to moderate effect sizes. This replicates previous findings of natural declines in bereavement-related symptoms.
> (Wagner, Knaevelsrud, & Maercker, 2006, p. 447)

Other studies have shown the potential, but minimal, benefits of using cognitive–behavioral therapy to treat CG (Ehlers, 2006; Matthews & Marwit, 2004). However, another study looking at interpersonal psychotherapy for treating depression-related bereavement showed that the intervention was no better than a placebo in treating traumatic grief (Hensley, 2006a; 2006b).

Finally, Currier, Neimeyer, and Berman (2008) conducted a meta-analysis examining the efficacy of grief counseling. In this ambitious study, the authors examined 61 randomized outcome studies of bereavement interventions (i.e., psychological counseling, professionally organized support groups, crisis intervention, writing therapy, and formal visiting service) that were reported in 64 academic articles. The authors concluded

> Bereavement interventions have a small but statistically significant effect immediately following intervention but that therapeutic outcomes failed to differ reliably from zero to later follow-up assessments . . . On average recipients of bereavement interventions are not appreciably less distressed when compared to those who do not receive any formalized help.
>
> (p. 23)

Although it would seem from this evidence that overall the effectiveness of grief counseling is questionable, professionals working in the field have explained this by arguing that grief counseling may not work in the form in which it is delivered in research studies, and that the positive effects of grief counseling are most likely masked by poor methodology and a need for different design and implementation of treatment (Jordan & Neimeyer, 2003; Schut et al., 2001). Even more striking, Jordan and Neimeyer's (2003) suggestion that psychologists focus their energies on those who are at risk for CG means that everyone who is bereaved comes under the purview of psychological research and intervention, because everyone who is grieving is potentially at risk for CG. This tautological logic stipulates that if the interventions don't work, more research is necessary to find a good treatment for grieving; if the treatments do work, then it is evidence of the necessity of psychological intervention to aid in the grieving process.

The Pharmaceutical Industry

The development of psychiatric categorization in the *DSM* has had a powerful effect on the perception of mental disorders as medical problems to be solved. Moreover, the development of drugs to treat mental disorders further increased the perception that mental disorders are akin to diseases. The data regarding the use of pharmaceutical drugs to treat mental disorders are staggering. In 2007, sales of Paxil, an antidepressant–anti-anxiety drug, exceeded 2.7 billion dollars worldwide. In 2005, eight out of 20 of the most prescribed medications (for all medical conditions, not just mental disorders) in the United States were antidepressants or anti-anxiety medications, with Paxil topping the list (RX list, 2013). Estimates of the efficacy of antidepressants and anti-anxiety drugs are controversial and range from 15 to 45 percent in treating symptoms of depression and anxiety (Barber, 2008; Breggin, 1991, 1998, 2001; Glenmullen, 2000; Healy, 1997, 2003; Solomon, 2002; Stoppard, 2000). Despite the controversy over the efficacy of these drugs, and despite the clear evidence that placebos are often as effective as antidepressants, the drugs are still widely used and are the most common treatment for disorders like depression and anxiety (Barber, 2008; Healy, 2003).

The treatment of grief has been no exception to this trend. The number of people who are given pharmaceuticals to treat their grief is difficult to measure. Even though complicated, pathological, prolonged, or traumatic grief are not official disorders, some psychiatrists have explicitly prescribed medications to treat grief and, as with counseling, have had questionable results. Although these psychiatrists have focused specifically on grief treatment, countless other bereaved people have been prescribed antidepressants and anti-anxiety medications to treat Major Depressive Disorder (MDD). The diagnostic system is de-contextualized, making it impossible to determine why people are depressed and prescribed antidepressants (Horwitz & Wakefield, 2007). It is highly plausible that many of the millions of patients put on antidepressants could have been suffering from context-specific depression that may have had to do with a loss.

For example, Wakefield, Schmitz, First, and Horwitz (2007) looked at a U.S. comorbidity survey of 8,098 people aged 15 to 54. Of those who were diagnosed and treated for MDD, 90 percent attributed their depression to either a bereavement-related loss or another type of loss, such as losing a job or a relationship. The authors used these data to advocate for more stringent criteria for MDD that take into account the social context of why people are depressed before making a diagnosis, and their research is relevant to this argument. The authors found that those who were grieving looked almost identical in terms of symptom presentation (i.e., appetite and weight problems, sleep problems, lack of energy, and so on) to those who were depressed for other reasons. The conflation of grief with MDD is a significant problem, as one is context-specific and should not be pathologized, whereas the other is a clinical diagnosis and is considered to be a pathology.

The conflation of grief and depression and the overuse of medications to treat grief make it significantly more likely that a grieving person will be given an antidepressant to deal with his/her sadness. This is especially true now that the bereavement exclusion has been removed from the *DSM* criteria to diagnosis clinical depression.

The pharmaceutical industry—and the psychiatrists who are dependent on it for their funding—have a vested interest in turning grief into a pathological condition. Medicating people who are grieving not only puts them at serious physical risk, including increased suicidal thoughts (Barber, 2008; Healy, 2003), sexual dysfunction (Modell, Katholi, Modell, & DePalma, 1997; Montejo-Gonzalez et al., 1997; Patterson, 1993), medication dependence, and withdrawal symptoms (Frost & Lal, 1995; Giakas & Davis, 1997; Kent & Laidlaw, 1995; Keuthen et al., 1994; Lejoyeux & Ades, 1997; Pyke, 1995), but also affects their self-understanding and how they make sense of their grieving experience. The pathologization of grief does not represent merely a diagnosis, it is a narrative in which people learn how to understand themselves, and in the process, experience their grief in a new way.

Impact of the Medicalization of Grief on Mourners

In *Discipline and Punish* (1977) Foucault used the metaphor of the panopticon to describe the process by which cultural ideas become internalized by people in a given society. The panopticon is an architectural metaphor that described a way of arranging people so that they seem to be continually observed, but they themselves cannot see the observer. In the example of a prison, the guard has visual access to all the prisoners, while the prisoners themselves cannot see the guard. What this achieves is a sense that one is continually being watched (regardless of whether the guard actually exists) and, as a result, prisoners will begin to self-discipline and monitor themselves in order to avoid punishment (Foucault, 1977). Mills (2003) wrote:

> Discipline consists of a concern with control which is internalised by each individual: it consists of a concern with time-keeping, self-control over one's posture and bodily functions, concentration, sublimation of immediate desires and emotions—all of these elements are the effects of disciplinary pressure and at the same time they are all actions which produce individuals as subjected to a set of procedures which come from outside of themselves but whose aim is the disciplining of the self. These disciplinary norms within Western cultures are not necessarily experienced as originating from institutions, so thoroughly have they been internalised by individuals. Indeed, so innate and 'natural' do these practices appear that we find it hard to conceptualise what life would be like without [them].
>
> (pp. 43–44)

Grief, as has been illustrated throughout this paper, is a prime example of this kind of disciplining. The obligation to be 'normal' in one's expression of grief; the evaluation of oneself on psychological terms of what normal versus pathological grief looks like; the pressure to do one's grief work; and the obligation to seek professional, psychological help if one cannot do this on one's own are forms of self-discipline that come from the cultural messages about medicalized grief (see Granek, in press, for an overview for representations of pathological grief in mainstream media). Not only does this process result in this kind of behavioral discipline, but it also changes the meaning and experience of grieving for the individual. To conceptualize grief as an illness or a disease that can be cured with therapy or medication is to individualize and privatize what used to be a communal responsibility of grieving the dead. The result for the grieving person is profoundly felt on an individual level as is evidenced by all of the things grieving people *need*, and *should* do, but is also felt by the society in which the grieving person lives.

One of the primary outcomes of the psy-construction of grief is the creation of a culture where these kinds of expectations and scripts around grief become the norm regardless of whether they are viable or helpful for those who are grieving. Much of this kind of grief discipline is untenable and places enormous demands on the mourner. As a result, people who believe they *should* meet these grieving milestones feel they need professional help to achieve these goals. The psychological imperative of accepting and resolving one's grief is a good example of this pressure. Many people will never accept or resolve their sadness over losing someone they loved. The pressure on them to do so, however, not only makes them self-conscious about whether they are doing their grief work properly, but also infuses them with a sense of guilt and failure over being unable to meet these enormous demands. The outcome for the mourner is a sense of shame and embarrassment over both their sadness and their inability to overcome it.

In a critical reflection on the grief literature in psychology, Breen and O'Conner (2007) concluded, "there is a plethora of research on grief, including the descriptions of "symptoms," "risk"factors, and outcomes, without significant attendance to the context of the bereavement itself on the resulting grief experience" (p. 209). Kellehear (2007) wrote, "notwithstanding the genuine value of psychological grief theories there are several rather startling features of them that make those theories appear socially irrelevant, medically abnormal, and publicly bizarre" (p. 75).

Indeed, as grief has steadily slipped into the net of the psychological domain, it has also simultaneously moved out of the public communities that once housed its rituals and traditions. When examined in the context of the public's experiences of grief, these psychological theories do appear to be highly disconnected from what people yearn for when it comes to dealing with their grief.

This conclusion came to me with jarring force as a result of an informal survey I conducted with the writer Meghan O'Rourke for the online magazine *Slate.com* (Granek & O'Rourke, 2011; O'Rourke & Granek, 2011). Within a week of mounting a survey asking about people's experiences of grief, we had received nearly 8,000 responses; what respondents had to say was surprising, touching, and fascinating. There were three major themes that arose repeatedly in this survey. The first was that there was a tremendous variation in people's lived experiences of grief that significantly challenges contemporary psychological definitions of what grief should look and feel like, and more important, how long it should last. For example, 60 percent of our respondents (4,629 of $N = 7,715$)[1] had dreams of the deceased and 20 percent reported imagining they had seen the deceased alive—"symptoms" that some health care professionals consider an indicator of CG (Shear et al., 2011). See Table 10.3 for a list of grief symptoms reported by our participants in the context of CG criteria. In terms of duration, 27 percent of our respondents ($n = 7,081$) reported that they never went back to feeling like themselves after their loss, and another 27 percent said they felt normal only one to two years after the loss. Whereas complicated, pathological, or prolonged grief can be diagnosed six months after a loss, our respondents reported that recovering from the death of a loved one can take a year or several years, and 27 percent indicated that it may never happen at all. Indeed, a mere 11 percent of our sample reported feeling normal or symptom free again six months post loss. These results are summarized in Table 10.3.

Table 10.3 Results of the *Slate.com* Survey

Answer Options	Response Percent (N = 7,715)
Sorrow	81 b
Overwhelming sadness	72 b
Yearning or nostalgia	72 a,b,c
Trouble concentrating	63
Dreams of the deceased	60
Trouble sleeping or insomnia	57 a
Longing	57 b,c
Frequent crying	56
Guilt	55 c
Loneliness	55 c
Anger	49 b,c
Disbelief about the loss	49 b,c
Anxiety	48 c
Anguish	46
Overeating or trouble eating	40
Self-pity	37
Sense of disorganization	39 c
Feeling run down or prone to illness	35
Forgetfulness	32
Physical pain or physical tension	30
Feeling of emptiness in stomach	30
Confusion	29 b
Tightness in throat	29
Agitation or a jittery, jumpy feeling	26 b,c
Relief	25
Frequent sighing	25
Imagining you see the deceased alive	20 c
Shortness of breath	17
Physical illness	12
Muscle weakness	11
Searching for the deceased	9 a,b,c
Chills	6
Tremors	5
Hallucinations	4 c

The second major finding from our survey addressed what I have been suggesting throughout this chapter: The process of psychologizing grief has inadvertently created a kind of public culture around mourning in which grievers feel embarrassed, uncomfortable, and unsure about whether their grief is normal. For example, our survey found that 40 percent of respondents ($n = 7,616$) said they felt pressured to "get over it," "move on with their grief," or "stop talking about it" some of the time. More distressing, 23 percent of respondents ($n = 7,616$) said they felt pressured to move on about their grief most or all of the time.

Finally, and perhaps most important, people seemed most of all to want a community in which to grieve but often felt alone with their mourning. Of our sample, 30 percent ($n = 7,563$) reported being strongly encouraged to seek professional help by their families and friends, and 35 percent ($n = 7,683$) turned to a therapist or another professional to deal with their grief. Interestingly, half the sample ($n = 7,283$) reported a desire for more social support and more public and collective ritual around grief and loss.

The grief literature has yielded similar findings regarding the benefits of social support. *Social support* refers to emotional, economic, and practical help or information that family members, friends, neighbors, and coworkers provide to those in need (House & Kahn, 1985). Diamond, Lund, and Caserta (1987) conducted a longitudinal study with bereaved spouses and found that the size and quality of one's social network was associated with lower depression and higher levels of coping and life satisfaction. Goldberg, Comstock, and Harlow (1988) found that larger social networks, particularly friends who the bereaved contacted frequently, were associated with a reduced risk of emotional distress. Research in the field has reported the importance of social support in reducing the intensity of grief and helping the bereaved cope with their loss (Saranson, Saranson, & Gurung, 1997). The value of emotional and practical support from close family, friends, and work colleagues has also been stressed by the bereaved as particularly important to them. They cite comfort, practical help, and physical and social stimulation as being pivotal to their coping with grief (Cohen, 1988; Dyregrov, 2003–2004; Sherkat & Reed, 1992; Thuen, 1997).

Community is therefore a particularly critical resource for the bereaved. The evidence for the effectiveness of the community in providing social support for grievers seems more convincing and more robustly indicated than the evidence for the effectiveness of grief counseling and medications. In agreement with the need for more communal support rather than psychological intervention, Kellehear (2007) argued that we must return to an organized community of compassion to support the bereaved. Judging from the evidence on social support and grief outcomes, this seems like an excellent direction to pursue.

Conclusion

The loss of protocol around how to grieve and how to help or support a mourner has left those grieving bereft not only of their loved ones, but also of any community in which to understand, mediate, and express their sadness. Mental health professionals are not solely responsible for the disappearance of traditional grief practices in North America. In many ways, these professions have filled the need of the listener and the supporter for the bereaved, and one could claim that this has aided sufferers from falling into deeper, more incapacitating depressions. The mental health sciences have been successful in drawing this area of human life into their purview because they provide a framework for how to manage grief in an era of uncertainty, anxiety, and fear around dying and mourning. In this sense, the pathologization of grief can be considered a positive outcome, for it has provided a feeling of orderliness around an area of life that is filled with chaos and insecurity for a lot of people.

At the same time, research has suggested that the boundary around pathological grief is ambiguous, and therefore inclusive of almost anyone who is grieving. There is very little qualitative difference between what is deemed normal versus pathological grief, and it seems from the literature that the diagnosis of pathological grief is arbitrary and based on the clinician's or researcher's determination of what she or he defines as normal. This view ultimately suggests that the particulars of what defines pathology are less relevant than the idea itself that grief can be evaluated on a normal–abnormal continuum (Granek, 2010). The introduction of grief as psychological object has a symbolic value whereby one does not need to be diagnosed to be affected by the diagnostic classification of mental disorder. The self-consciousness around grief is one example of this. In addition to the sorrow and depression that often accompany bereavement, contemporary mourners are also faced with a distinctively modern anxiety about whether they are doing their grief work properly and whether they are on track with their progress. This new self-consciousness often comes with a sense of shame and embarrassment about mourning that has become part of the experience of the modern griever.

Key Terms

Complicated grief, prolonged grief disorder—proposed diagnoses intended to define the point at which grief becomes pathological and warrants medical intervention or professional treatment.

Medicalization—the process by which human conditions or problems become medical problems to be solved.

Pathology—literally means the study of disease. In this context, refers to identification of an entity as a disorder or something that requires treatment.

Social support—emotional, economic, and practical help or information that family members, friends, neighbors, and coworkers provide to those in need.

Questions for Reflection

1. Consider the idea that we can evaluate ourselves on a continuum of normality or abnormality in regard to grieving or any other human behavior. Where do we draw the line delineating these? How do individuals and groups decide on the point that "crosses the line"? What do you consider to be abnormal grief?
2. Each individual internalizes social expectations and self-monitors behavior to comply with these expectations. However, if fully internalized, one may be completely unaware of these influences. Challenge yourself to consider how such influences may shape your day-to-day behavior, perceptions of "normality," and expectations of others.
3. The author proposes that "the pathologization of grief can be considered a positive outcome, for it has provided a feeling of orderliness around an area of life that is filled with chaos and insecurity for a lot of people." Do you agree or disagree with this claim? Does this balance the risks proposed as being associated with the pathologization of grief?

Note

1. The sample size refers to the total number of people who answered the specific question I am reporting on. Some participants skipped some of the questions. For each of the findings I report in this chapter, I provide the total *n* who answered the question.

References

Allumbaugh, D. L., & Hoyt, W. T. (1999). Effectiveness of grief therapy: A meta-analysis. *Journal of Counseling Psychology, 46*(3), 370–380.

American Psychiatric Association. (2013). *Diagnostic and statistical manual of mental disorders* (5th ed.). Arlington, VA: American Psychiatric Publishing.

Barber, C. (2008). *Comfortably numb: How psychiatry is medicating a nation.* New York, NY: Pantheon Books.

Breen, L. J., & O'Connor, M. (2007). The fundamental paradox in grief literature: A critical reflection. *Omega: Journal of Death and Dying, 55*(3),199–218.

Breggin, P. R. (1991). *Toxic psychiatry: Why therapy, empathy, and love must replace the drugs, electroshock, and biochemical theories of the "new psychiatry".* New York, NY: St. Martin's Press.

Breggin, P. R. (1998). *Talking back to Ritalin: What doctors aren't telling you about stimulants for children.* Monroe: Common Courage Press.

Breggin, P. R. (2001). *The antidepressant fact book: What doctors won't tell you about Prozac, Zoloft, Paxil, Celexa, and Luvox.* Cambridge, Mass: Perseus Publishing.

Brown, E. J., & Goodman, R. F. (2005). Childhood traumatic grief: An exploration of the construct in children bereaved on September 11. *Journal of Clinical Child & Adolescent Psychology, 34*(2), 248–259.

Carey, B. (2012). Grief could join the list of disorders: When does a broken heart become a diagnosis. *New York Times,* January, pp. A1, A2.

Cohen, S. (1998). Psychosocial models of social support in the etiology of physical disease. *Health Psychology,* 7(3), 267–97.

Conrad P. (2007). *The Medicalization of society: On the transformation of human conditions into treatable disorders*. Baltimore, MD: Johns Hopkins University Press.

Currier, J. M., Neimeyer, R. A., & Berman, J. S. (2008). The effectiveness of psychotherapeutic interventions for the bereaved: A comprehensive quantitative review. *Psychological Bulletin, 134*(5), 648–661.

Diamond, M. F., Lund, D. A., & Caserta, M. S. (1987). The role of social support in the first two years of bereavement in an elderly sample. *Gerontologist, 27*(5), 599–604.

Dyregrov, K. (2003–2004). Micro-sociological analysis of social support following traumatic bereavement: Unhelpful and avoidant responses from the community. *Omega: Journal of Death and Dying, 48*(1), 23–44.

Ehlers, A. (2006). Understanding and treating complicated grief: What can we learn from posttraumatic stress disorder? *Clinical Psychology: Science and Practice, 13*(2), 135–140.

Forstmeier, S., & Maercker, A. (2007). Comparison of two diagnostic systems for complicated grief. *Journal of Affective Disorders, 99*(1–3), 203–211.

Foucault, M. (1977). *Discipline and punish: The birth of the prison* (1st American ed.). New York, NY: Pantheon Books.

Frost, L., & Lal, F. (1995). Shock like sensations after discontinuation of selective serotonin reuptake inhibitors. *American Journal of Psychiatry, 152*(5), 810.

Genevro, J. L., Marshall, T., Miller, T., & Center for the Advancement of Health. (2004). Report on bereavement and grief research. *Death Studies. Special Issue: Report on Bereavement and Grief Research by the Center for the Advancement of Health, 28*(6), 491–491.

Giakas, W. J., & Davis, J. M. (1997). Intractable withdrawal from Venlafaxine treated with Fluoxetine. *Psychiatric Annals, 27*(2), 85–92.

Glenmullen, J. (2000). *Prozac backlash: Overcoming the dangers of Prozac, Zoloft, Paxil, and other antidepressants with safe, effective alternatives*. New York, NY: Simon & Schuster.

Goldberg, E. L., Comstock, G. W., & Harlow, S. D. (1988). Emotional problems and widowhood. *Journal of Gerontology, 43*(6), 5206–5208.

Granek, L. (2008). *Bottled tears: The pathologization, psychologization, and privatization of grief* (Unpublished Doctoral Dissertation). York University, Toronto.

Granek, L. (2010). Grief as pathology: The evolution of grief theory in psychology from Freud to the present. *History of Psychology, 13*(1), 46–73.

Granek, L. (2013a). The complications of grief: The battle to define modern mourning. In E. Miller (Ed.), *Complicated grief: A critical anthology* (pp. 30–35). Washington, DC: NASW Press.

Granek, L. (2013b). Disciplinary wounds: Has grief become the identified patient for a field gone awry? *Journal of Loss and Trauma 18*(3), 275–288.

Granek, L. (in press). The psychologization of grief and its depictions in mainstream, North American media. In J. Stillion & T. Attig (Eds.), *Death, dying, and bereavement: Contemporary perspectives, institutions, and practices*. New York, NY: Springer Press.

Granek, L., & O'Rourke M. (Spring, 2011). What is Grief Actually Like: Results of the Slate Survey on Grief. *Slate*. Retrieved from www.slate.com/id/2292126/

Granek, L. & O'Rourke, M. (March 12th, 2012). Is Mourning madness? *Slate*. Retrieved from www.slate.com/articles/life/grieving/2012/03/complicated_grief_and_the_dsm_the_wrongheaded_movement_to_list_mourning_as_a_mental_disorder_.html#comments

Groopman, J. (2004, January). The grief industry. *The New Yorker, 26*, 30–38.

Healy, D. (1997). *The antidepressant era*. Cambridge, MA: Harvard University Press.

Healy, D. (2003). *Let them eat Prozac*. Toronto: Lorimer.

Hensley, P. L. (2006a). A review of bereavement-related depression and complicated grief. *Psychiatric Annals, 36*(9), 619–626.

Hensley, P. L. (2006b). Treatment of bereavement-related depression and traumatic grief. *Journal of Affective Disorders, 92*(1), 117–124.

House, J. S. & Kahn, R. L. (1985). Measures and concepts of social support. In S. Cohen & S. L. Syme (Eds.), *Social support and health* (pp. 83–108). Orlando, FL: Academic Press.

Horowitz, M. J. (2005–2006). Meditating on complicated grief disorder as a diagnosis. *Omega: Journal of Death and Dying, 52*(1), 87–89.

Horowitz, M. J., Siegel, B., Holen, A., Bonanno, G., Milbrath, C., & Stinson, C. H. (1997). Diagnostic criteria for complicated grief disorder. *American Journal of Psychiatry, 154*(7), 904–910.

Horwitz, A. V., & Wakefield, J. C. (2007). *The loss of sadness: How psychiatry transformed normal sorrow into depressive disorder*. New York, NY: Oxford University Press.

Jordan, J. R., & Neimeyer, R. A. (2003). Does grief counseling work? *Death Studies, 27*(9), 765–786.

Kato, P. M., & Mann, T. (1999). A synthesis of psychological interventions for the bereaved. *Clinical Psychology Review, 19*(3), 275–296.

Kellehear, A. (2007). The end of death in late modernity: An emerging public health challenge. *Critical Public Health, 17*(1), 71–79.

Kent, L. S. W., & Laidlaw, J. D. D. (1995). Suspected congenital Setraline dependence. *British Journal of Psychiatry, 167*(3), 412–413.

Keuthen, N. J., Cyr, P., Ricciardi, J. A., Minichiello, W. E., Buttolph, M. L., & Jenike, M. A. (1994). Medication withdrawal symptoms in obsessive-compulsive disorder patients treated with paroxetine. *Journal of Clinical Psychopharmacology, 14*(3), 206–7.

Lejoyeux, M., & Ades, J. (1997). Antidepressants discontinuation: A literature review. *Journal of Clinical Psychiatry, 58*(7), 11–17.

Matthews, L. T., & Marwit, S. J. (2004). Complicated grief and the trend toward cognitive-behavioral therapy. *Death Studies, 28*(9), 849–863.

Metcalf, P. (2005). "A passion of grief and fear exasperates us": Death, bereavement, and mourning-what we have learned a year after 9/11. Picsataway, NJ: Transaction.

Mills, S. (2003). *Michel Foucault*. London: Routledge.

Modell, J.G., Katholi, C.R., Modell, J.D., & DePalma, R.L. (1997). Comparative sexual side effects of Bupropion, Fluoxetine, Paroxetine, and Sertraline. *Clinical Pharmacology and Therapeutics, 61*(4), 476–87.

Montejo-Gonzalez, A. L., Llorca, G., Izquierdo, J. A., Ledesma, A., Bousonon, M. Calcedo . . ., & Vicens, E. (1997). SSRI—Induced sexual dysfunction: Fluoxetine, Paroxetine, Sertraline, and Fluvoxamine in a prospective, multicenter, and descriptive clinical study out of 344 patients. *Journal of Sex and Marital Therapy, 23*(3), 176–94.

O'Rourke, M., & Granek, L. (Summer, 2011). How to help Friends in mourning: Condolence notes? Casseroles? What our grief survey revealed. *Slate*. Retrieved from www.slate.com/id/2300735/

Patterson, W. M. (1993). Fluoxetine induced sexual dysfunction. *Journal of Clinical Psychiatry, 54*(4), 71.

Prigerson, H. G., & Jacobs, S. C. (2001). *Traumatic grief as a distinct disorder: A rationale, consensus criteria, and a preliminary empirical test*. Washington, DC: American Psychological Association.

Prigerson, H. G., Horwitz, M. J., Jacobs, S. C., Parkes, C. P., Aslan, M., Goodkin, K., . . ., & Maciejewski, P. K. (2009). Prolonged grief disorder: Validation criteria proposed for DSM-V and ICD-11. *PLOS Medicine, 6*, 8, e10000121.

Prigerson, H. G., & Maciejewski, P. K. (2005–2006). A call for sound empirical testing and evaluation of criteria for complicated grief proposed for DSM-5. *Omega: Journal of Death and Dying, 52*(1), 9–19.

Pyke, R.E. (1995). Paroxetine withdrawal symptoms. *American Journal of Psychiatry, 152*(8), 149–150.

RX list. (2013, December). The Internet drug index for prescription drugs and medications. Retrieved from www.rxlist.com/script/main/hp.asp

Rosenblatt, P. C. (2005). *Grieving families and the 9/11 disaster*. Picsataway, NJ: Transaction.

Saranson, B.R., Saranson, I.G., & Gurung, R.A.R. (1997). Close personal relationships and health outcomes: A key to the role of social support. In S. Duck (Ed.), *Handbook of personal relationships. Theory, research and interventions* (pp. 547–573). New York, NY: John Wiley.

Shear, M. K., Simon, N., Wall, M., et al. (2011), Complicated grief and related bereavement issues for DSM-5. *Depression and Anxiety, 28*(2), 103–117

Sherkat, D. E., & Reed. M. D. (1992). The effects of religion and social support on self-esteem and depression among the suddenly bereaved. *Social Indicators Research, 26*(3), 259–275.

Solomon, A. (2002). *The noonday demon: An atlas of depression* (1st ed.). New York, NY: Simon & Schuster.

Stoppard, J. M. (2000). *Understanding depression: Feminist social constructionist approaches*. London: Routledge.

Schut, H., Stroebe, M. S., van den Bout, J., & Terheggen, M. (2001). *The efficacy of bereavement interventions: Determining who benefits*. Washington, DC: American Psychological Association.

Shear, K., & Frank, E. (2006). *Treatment of complicated grief: Integrating cognitive-behavioral methods with other treatment approaches*. New York, NY: Guilford Press.

Stroebe, M., & Schut, H. (2005–2006). Complicated grief: A conceptual analysis of the field. *Omega: Journal of Death and Dying, 52*(1), 53–70.

Thuen F. (1997). Social support after the loss of an infant child: A long-term perspective. *Scandinavian Journal of Psychology, 38*(2), 103–110.

Wagner, B., Knaevelsrud, C., & Maercker, A. (2006). Internet-based cognitive-behavioral therapy for complicated grief: A randomized controlled trial. *Death Studies, 30*(5), 429–453.

Wakefield, J. C., Schmitz, M. F., First, M. B., & Horwitz, A. V. (2007). Extending the bereavement exclusion for major depression to other losses: Evidence from the National Co-morbidity Survey. *Archives of General Psychiatry, 64*, 433–440.

Welt Betensky, J. L. (2007). The R.A.F.T.: Recovery after family trauma: A manual for a group psychotherapy intervention for children and families experiencing traumatic grief. ProQuest Information & Learning. *Dissertation Abstracts International: Section B: The Sciences and Engineering, 67* (9-B).

11

Iatrogenic Harm and Objectification in the Context of Care Delivery

Darcy L. Harris

Introduction

Numerous books and articles have been written about the negative experiences of patients in health care systems. These accounts are often troubling, not just due to the descriptions of caregivers' insensitivity and apathy to situations of human suffering, but for the implication that people who have dedicated their careers to care for others could demonstrate callousness to those who are vulnerable and in need of their care and compassion. However, a bigger picture perspective of these scenarios needs to occur, allowing for a better understanding of the contextual forces that have an impact upon patients and the professionals who care for them. It is these social, political, and economic influences that often cause significant wounding to the health care providers' caring capacity, which in turn, can further add to the suffering of those in their care. Interestingly, research on the stresses and strains experienced by hospice and palliative care workers has indicated that environmental and structural stresses typically cause much more distress than working with dying patients and their families (Keidel, 2002; Payne, 2001; Vachon, 1995; Weissman, 2009). In this chapter, we will explore how social and contextual factors can have a profound effect upon both patients and health care workers alike in palliative and hospice care settings.

Iatrogenic Harm

In his book, *What Dying People Want*, David Kuhl (2003) conducted in-depth interviews with several people who were dying. He documented many of the main concerns and issues that these patients shared about their disease, their surviving family members, and the joys and regrets about their lives prior to this time. However, a poignant issue pertaining to suffering arose in several of the interviews. While patients often tolerated and even expected to endure some suffering with their illness, many described a different kind of suffering that resulted from the way they were treated by their doctors and other professional staff in the health care setting. In these descriptions of suffering, patients recounted instances where they felt they were not consulted in decisions, where their concerns took a second place to the agendas that were set out by the health care team or institutional policies, where they were ignored or not taken seriously, and times when their needs were simply overlooked because "the professionals" were too busy to listen to them.

When describing these scenarios, Kuhl (2003) used the term *iatrogenic trauma*. The word *iatrogenic* literally means "physician-induced" and usually refers to harm that occurs to patients as a result of entering medical treatment and having a mistake or accident occur, or developing an infection or complication as a result of being in a care facility or having a medical procedure done (Venes, 2013). In the context of the discussion for this chapter, Kuhl's work implies that treating patients without addressing them as whole human beings with their feelings, social needs, spiritual views, and priorities can cause additional suffering and harm, creating a form of *psychological iatrogenic trauma*.

In her exploration of stresses and distress described by patients and families on a pediatric palliative unit, Rees (2011) equated iatrogenic psychological harm with emotional abuse. She cites the following professional behaviors as problematic, with the potential to cause harm:

- the assumption, inadvertent or otherwise, that medical training justifies overriding patients' views;
- failure to listen or distraction by other priorities;
- disregard or dismissal of emotional responses and needs;
- labeling of patients in ways that do not recognize their humanity;
- insensitive handling of family relationships through inattention to their nature and importance;
- talking over patients, careless words, and failure to respond to the concerns that the patient and family may be feeling;
- inadequate time to explain and listen;
- lack of continuity of care by professionals; and
- lack of regard for privacy and personal dignity, for example, overlooking age-related or cultural norms.

In a narrative study of patients' experiences, Peloquin (1993) asserted that many professional caregivers fail to recognize that illness and debility are experiences that are charged with personal meaning. Many of the patients' narratives in her study indicated feelings of increased distress when helpers distanced themselves rather than communicating directly with them. Analysis of the narratives revealed that patients repeatedly struggled with feeling that their professional caregivers withheld information and misused power in the context of care. The author concluded by stating:

> When helpers neglect their patients' heightened sensitivity, they intensify the pain of illness. At a time in their lives when patients need someone to be there, helpers hold them at bay. They press patients, who experience little control and much anxiety, to be good. They ask for compliance even as they become evasive, curt, or arrogant. They then seem startled to stir a patient's anger; they are baffled when a struggle ensues.
>
> (p. 835)

In a study that investigated patients' subjective experiences in the health care system, Anderson (1981) noted that patients who felt excluded or shut out of responsible interactions with professional caregivers reported higher subjective perceptions of stress, which had a negative impact upon their ability to engage with their caregivers and also on their coping abilities. Patients frequently described feeling helpless, self-conscious, and apologetic for their concerns, angry at being dismissed, out of place because they did not understand the medical jargon that was spoken in their presence, and insignificant as a person in relation to their caregivers. Ballatt and Campling (2011) state, "All the evidence from patients themselves is that they want to be seen and known as the people they are, not just as a list of problems" (p. 36). These same authors acknowledge that patients usually appreciate that health care professionals are under a great deal of stress as well, but that "small acts of kindness," where they sense the professionals notice them and care about them can make a big difference to patients' experiences and sense of well-being.

Reality for Health Care Workers

Most professional caregivers enter their profession with a desire to help others. It is not uncommon to overhear individuals who work in hospice/palliative care settings describe their work as a "calling" or a "ministry." It is doubtful that any professional caregiver would intentionally wish for harm to occur to a patient in his or her care. That being said, why are there so many reports of patient suffering documented from the treatment that patients and families receive in these settings?

Many health care providers find a disparity between their desire to help their patients and the bureaucratic, financially-driven nature of the care delivery system (Ballatt & Campling, 2011). While we are conditioned in Western industrialized societies to value our individuality and unique-ness, the institutionalized health care delivery system seems to lump these unique human qualities into prescribed roles, routines, and rules. Budgetary constraints are felt everywhere, as fewer staff are assigned to care for a greater number of patients who are sicker, needier, and require increasingly more complex care. In addition, full-time jobs with benefits in the health care sector are often difficult to secure. Many of the available jobs are often associated with low wages, poor benefits, lack of job security, and little opportunity for advancement (Morgan, Dill, & Kalleberg, 2013), so health care professionals are more likely to accept work in areas where they do not feel as comfortable, or to stay in jobs where they are stressed and stretched because of the need to earn a living and have benefits for themselves and their families.

Case Example

Sharon is a registered nurse (RN) who works on a 16-bed palliative care unit on the day shift. When she is working, the unit also has two licensed practical nurses (LPN) and two personal support workers (PSW). A social worker is also assigned to the unit, but she is also responsible for two other acute care units in the hospital. Most of the patients are unable to ambulate and require total care for their hygiene and other personal needs. Many are taking multiple medications that must be administered several times through the day.

During one afternoon when Sharon is working, one patient on the unit is actively dying. The family of that patient has required a great deal of emotional support as they have watched their loved one decline. Some out-of-town family members arrived two days ago and were very upset to see the patient in her condition, and they have engaged the care team frequently with their questions, concerns, and need for explanations. Recognizing that this family needs additional support at this time, Sharon paged the social worker and asked if she could come to talk with them. However, the social worker told her that she was involved in an organ donation discussion in the ICU, where a young man's family needed support as they discussed whether or not to proceed with donating his organs after he was involved in a motorcycle accident that had left him brain dead. Sharon knew this would take most of the social worker's afternoon. Although she wasn't sure of the family's religious views, she paged the chaplain to see if he might be able to offer additional support for the family of the dying patient on her unit, but he was in an all-day workshop off site.

Candace, one of the licensed practical nurses working with Sharon, needed to complete two dressing changes, and she also was responsible for giving the patients on the unit their medications on time. If she stopped what she was doing at this point to be with the family of the dying patient, many of her other patients would be in pain because she would be late with their medications. The two personal support workers were busy with several patients whose linens needed to be changed due to soiling and distributing meal trays and helping to feed the patients who needed assistance in eating. Already, some of the food was cold because they were so busy trying to complete the personal care of the remaining patients.

Sharon had made rounds with the various doctors and residents on the floor earlier in the day. Many of the patients had new orders written on their charts, and she was responsible for transcribing these orders and ensuring they were implemented expeditiously. Several of the orders were for a change in pain medication or for increased doses of medication because patients said their pain or symptoms were not being controlled well on their current regimen. Sharon knew these patients were waiting on her to get this done so they would feel relief from their discomfort.

Sharon checked on the dying patient and her family and noticed that the patient's breathing had become more irregular. It wouldn't be long now. Some of the family members were crying and holding the patient's hand. A few were visibly distraught and needed support, and Sharon tried to offer herself to them—but her mind kept racing to the work load that was piling up on the desk at the nurses' station, knowing that other patients were uncomfortable and remembering that she needed to expedite the change in their medications and finish the other orders that were waiting on her to be implemented.

While Sharon was walking back from the room of the dying patient, another patient saw her and called out to her. When Sharon stepped in her room, the patient started talking about questions she had forgotten to raise with her doctor when he was in her room. She then began to cry as she told Sharon about her two young daughters and her concerns about leaving them behind when she died. Sharon wanted to sit down and comfort her—or just be with her while she talked—but she heard the phone ringing at the nurses' station and she was also acutely aware that the call buzzer had been ringing and not answered for a long period of time. She was worried that she was needed for an urgent issue with another patient.

When the next shift came to work, Sharon finally sat down at the desk to transcribe the remaining orders. She then went and checked on the young mother who needed her to listen earlier. The patient was sleeping now. She wouldn't know that Sharon came back to check on her. Sharon never made it back to the room of the dying patient because she kept getting interrupted by other calls, doctor visits, and an admission to the unit that occurred near the end of her shift. Sharon left the unit an hour after her shift ended because she needed to get caught up on her paperwork before she could leave. She felt exhausted and frustrated. Sharon's husband was worried about the level of stress she regularly carried home from her work and told her she "cared too much" for her patients and that she needed to treat her work as "just a job." She felt her work with dying patients was important and she cared deeply about her patients and their families. It was not "just a job" to her and it never would be.

As you consider Sharon's experience, you can imagine what it must be like for her to anticipate going to work and most likely, how she feels when she returns home from work. Sharon wants to care for her patients and she frequently experiences unresolvable dilemmas in regards to various priorities. The justifiable needs of her patients for her attention and care, the implicit demands of her workplace for efficiency, and her own expectations of herself as someone who wishes to relieve suffering are in regular conflict with each other. Situations like this have been described in the literature as the "stress of conscience," or moral distress. In a study of stress-related factors in health care workers, Glasberg, Eriksson, and Norberg (2007) found that many caregivers deaden their conscience in order to keep working in health care. In this same study, those who frequently experienced a "stress of conscience" from lack of time to provide the care that was needed, being unable to live up to others' (or their own) expectations of their work, and having work so demanding that it influenced their home life had very high levels of emotional exhaustion.

Moral distress occurs when one knows the ethically correct action to take but feels powerless to take that action, typically due to institutional constraints that make it nearly impossible to pursue the right course of action. More recently, this definition has been expanded by defining moral distress as the painful psychological disequilibrium that results from recognizing the ethically appropriate action, yet not taking it because of such obstacles as lack of time, supervisory reluctance, an inhibiting medical power structure, institutional policies, or legal considerations (Weissman, 2009). The moral conflicts experienced by health care providers have been described as outcomes of their commitment to, and empathy for the experience of patients, and their desire to alleviate suffering. Situations of moral conflict can engender acute distress in caregivers, resulting from a disparity between the correct action that a professional wishes to take, but is prevented in the implementation of this action by constraints outside of his/her control (Brazil, Kassalainen, Ploeg, & Marshall, 2010). There is a unique stress that occurs when a professional caregiver feels a heightened sense of responsibility in a situation where that same individual has no authority over the decisions and structure of how caregiving is implemented. Moral distress can cause physical and emotional suffering for the care provider that is caught in the dilemma.

For caregivers who are highly invested in providing high quality care and whose identity is defined by their caring capacity, repeated exposure to situations of moral distress can result in deep feelings of failure, erosion of one's sense of self, and deep psychological and emotional pain (Brazil et al., 2010). In an editorial on the topic of moral distress in palliative care, Weissman (2009) described working as part of a palliative care consultation team. During that time, he stated that compassion fatigue and burnout occurred with numbing regularity among team members. He named this response of his colleagues as "being done." In his description, he quoted the words of one of the team members who left: "I just can't do it anymore, I am so angry with the system . . . I can't meet the needs of patients in a manner that lets me sleep at night" (p. 865).

In our case study, Sharon knew many things were "right" to do and wanted to do them, but was not able to do so because of lack of time, an inability to modify the staffing ratios, and rigidity in defining the work roles and responsibilities for the care providers on her unit. Emotional distancing and withdrawal are common ways of coping with this disparity; as we explored in the work by Kuhl (2003), this way of coping by caregivers can have an acute negative impact upon those in their care. A vicious cycle can occur where caregivers feel helpless to implement care in ways that would be congruent with their values and they often cope with this helplessness by pulling back and trying not to care in order to avoid feeling distress. Meanwhile, the patients in their care experience heightened anxiety and increased suffering because they are being treated in a way that does not acknowledge their personhood and vulnerable position. For the caregivers and patients alike, wounding occurs from causes that are external to both. In essence, the caregiver and the patient are both victims to larger, social-political forces that undermine their human dignity and value (Thompson, 2010). In looking at this dynamic, Rees (2011) refers to the "swing of the pendulum," where the overarching systemic issues cause harm to both caregivers and patients.

Objectification in Health Care Contexts

The term *objectification* refers to the denial of a person's subjective traits, such as his/her thoughts, feelings, desires, and experiences. To objectify someone implies that person is treated as either a means to an end, or as a physical entity without acknowledgment of the presence of feelings, goals, social needs, and preferences. When a person is objectified, it is assumed that the individual is being seen as a physical thing (an object) deprived of personal qualities or individuality. In the context of care delivery that is under the auspices of an institution or governmental body, it is important to consider objectification in relation to both the professional caregiver as well as the patient that seeks care. In her exploration of objectification, Nussbaum (1995) stated that a person is objectified if s/he is treated:

- as a tool for another's purposes (instrumentality);
- as if lacking in agency or self-determination (denial of autonomy);
- as if owned by another (ownership);

- as if interchangeable with objects of a similar or different type (fungibility);
- as if permissible to damage or destroy (violability); or
- as if there is no need for concern for their feelings and experiences (denial of subjectivity).

There is a great deal written on the objectification of patients in the health care system, but there is very little written about this same experience as it occurs to the health care workers within these same institutions. We will now explore the ways that both patients and health care workers can be objectified in the health care setting.

Patient's Experiences

Sam was a 78-year-old retired university professor with prostate cancer that had metastasized (spread) to many of his bones and to his brain. He was admitted to the palliative care unit for symptom management and respite care. His wife, Joan, had been his primary caregiver in their home, and she had spent the past two weeks feeling helpless while Sam struggled with rapidly declining functionality. Sam was often confused and incontinent. He was on medication that caused his urine to turn a bright orange color that stained all his clothes and bed sheets when he missed the urinal or was incontinent. Trying to use the urinal created a great deal of stress for both Sam and Joan because he needed to stand up to urinate, but he was also unsteady and at risk for falling. However, when someone tried to assist him, Sam often became irritated because he felt humiliated by people attending to him for such a private bodily function. Twice, a nurse had come to the home and inserted a catheter to try to keep Sam's skin and bed sheets dry. However, in episodes of confusion, Sam had pulled the catheter out twice, causing more pain and trauma to his urethra. Sam was admitted to the palliative care unit for respite care because Joan became exhausted caring for him day and night.

Once on the unit, Joan frequently used the call button to ask for help from the nurses. Sometimes, Sam would be moaning in his sleep and she would be concerned that he was in pain. Other times, Sam would be trying to use the urinal and he would push her away when she tried to help him. Some of the nurses began to resent the frequent calls to assuage Joan's anxiety. To them, Sam's behavior and confusion were to be expected given his disease and how it had progressed. They had many patients who were also very ill; even though they recognized that Joan was stressed and afraid, they could not spend the time with her that she seemed to need. It began to take longer for them to respond to the call bell from Sam's room. Sam would then sometimes end up lying in soiled bed sheets until the nurses came to his room to help. They rotated staff so that the same nurse would not be caring for Sam each day because they felt that Joan was demanding and Sam's care was very time consuming as a result.

Joan began to sense that the nurses resented her neediness. She would pace in the room and try to wait before calling for a nurse when Sam needed help because she was afraid of being seen as "a problem" to them. She was exhausted, but afraid to leave Sam alone because she was concerned the nurses would either not know or not be available when Sam needed help. She never knew who "his" nurse was because it was different every day, and she didn't know if the "new" nurses would take the time to know what Sam needed and how he communicated. Although the main reason for Sam's admission to the palliative care unit was to give Joan respite, she was not able to rest because of her concerns that Sam would not receive care when he needed it without her there to intervene with the nursing staff.

One day, Janet, a student nurse, was assigned to care for Sam. In report, she was told that Joan was "difficult" and that Sam was often agitated. When she walked into the room, Joan was dozing in the easy chair beside Sam's bed. She saw the pictures that Joan had brought in and placed on the shelf behind Sam's bed—one was a picture of the two of them when they were married and another of Sam when he was given an award for his academic accomplishments, with Joan smiling beside him. In these pictures, they both looked relaxed, happy, and close. She then looked at Joan and Sam now in the room and felt the great disparity between their earlier life together and this difficult time now. Joan awoke and saw Janet looking at the pictures. Janet said, "I can't imagine what this must be like for the two of you now. It must be so very hard." Joan began to cry and Janet placed her hand on Joan's arm and let her weep. Through the rest of the day, Janet checked on Joan and Sam every hour, which meant that Joan only had to use the call bell for assistance once during that shift. At the end of the day, the charge nurse commented during her report to the oncoming staff that it was amazing that Joan had "calmed down." Nobody stopped to think that perhaps Janet's acknowledgment of Joan and Sam's personhood and her willingness to be proactive by checking on them without Joan having to call for her might have made a huge difference for both of them that day.

There is much written about the objectification of patients in the health care system. Think of patients being referred to as "the gallbladder in room 201" or the simplistic focus on a patient's disease or behavior while the patient and family's concerns and feelings are seen as irrelevant, secondary, or judged as inappropriate. In the scenario with Sam and Joan, Sam's needs (and Joan's as well) were dismissed because Joan became seen as "a problem" by the staff. Being labeled as such meant that the feelings, thoughts, and subjective experience of both Sam and Joan were not considered in the care that was being offered. The situation was not helped by rotating the nurses, which only increased Joan's anxiety and intensified the problems with Sam's care. Janet's simple acknowledgment of Joan and Sam as people first, followed by a proactive stance taken to address Joan's anxiety rather than ignore it made a big difference in the quality of both Joan and Sam's experience that day. Prior to Janet's involvement with them, Joan and Sam were seen as problems rather than people. Many health care advocates state that without a relational context to care, patients are robbed of their agency and subjective experience, much in line with the descriptions of objectification as described earlier (McLeod, 2002).

Health Care Workers' Experiences

John was a social worker on a hospice community outreach team, where care was provided in patients' homes. John often became close to the families that he would visit, and many of the patients and family members viewed him as a significant source of support and comfort during a very difficult time. Occasionally, John and other members of the team attended the funeral service of a patient when a particularly strong bond had been forged with the patient and family. Attending these funerals provided John with an opportunity to reflect on the value of the work he did and to support the family in a way that they often greatly appreciated. It also allowed him to acknowledge the grief he felt when some of his patients died.

One day, a memo was sent out by the hospice administration to the staff indicating that they were not to attend funerals of patients during regular office hours, when they were expected to be visiting with the patients on the current roster. Based on the new policy, John would no longer be able to attend most of the funerals, even if he wished to do so. John went to the executive director and explained that while he didn't attend many funerals, those that he did attend helped him to deal with the losses that he experienced on a regular basis in the work, and that most funerals were scheduled during regular daytime hours. He also reminded the director that hospice care includes bereavement follow up after a patient died, and he felt that his attendance at these funerals benefited the bereaved family members as well. The executive director told John that he was hired to see clients during regular office hours and that his focus needed to be on those patients who were still living. He was reminded that the bereavement coordinator oversaw the aftercare of families and this part of the work was not his responsibility. John left the director's office feeling that he was being robbed of an important source of meaning and satisfaction in his work, which was also an extension of the close relationships that he often formed with his patients and their families.

In this situation, John was expected to 1) dismiss the importance of the relationships that he formed with his patients and families, 2) deny the presence of his own grief when he experienced the loss of patients in his care, 3) turn over care of the families with whom he has a strong relationship to the bereavement coordinator after his patients died because it was not his role, and 4) focus on efficiency rather than upon relational needs and values. If John repeatedly feels pressured to relinquish the relational context of the care he provides, he most likely will either have to adjust how he cares for patients by being less emotionally available to them (which may be impossible for someone whose professional role is an extension of himself as a person), or find another place to work that does not place him in a dilemma between his professional role and his personhood (which is not likely to be easy).

The concept of burnout was described by Maslach, who developed the Maslach Burnout Inventory (Poghoshyan, Aiken, & Sloan, 2009). The inventory includes subscales related to depersonalization, which is a related concept to objectification. The objectification of care providers within the context of health care systems is an insidious process, where the health care worker is also robbed of his/her voice, feelings, agency, and personhood (as described by Nussbaum earlier) within the context of the workplace. John was expected to immediately remove himself from the family of a patient who died and replace that patient with another terminally ill individual. Likewise, the family was expected to immediately replace John with the bereavement coordinator, whom they had not met, at a time of acute grief and vulnerability. John rightfully felt that something was wrong with the administration's lack of recognition of the relational component of the care that he provided.

In contrast to the literature written about objectification of patients in the health care system, very little is written about the objectification of health care workers in the context of their workplace. This objectification may not be overtly apparent because of the overarching logistics involved in care provision. For example, while caregivers often form meaningful relationships with patients and family members in the context of care delivery, the "relationship" has a boundary defined by the working hours of the care provider and the staffing needs of the care system in general. In areas where care provision occurs around the clock and on weekends, staff must be rotated out of necessity. However, the way that staffing is implemented should allow for as much continuity between a primary provider and the patient and family as possible. Many staffing arrangements are set up based upon the credentials and training of the various care providers. For example, in the 16-bed palliative care unit where Sharon works, there are a total of 13 different RNs who work across the various shifts and days of the week. The staffing requirement for this unit posits that there is one RN, two LPNs, and two PSWs for the day shift. The policy doesn't specify who the workers are, as long as their professional designation and training is the same, which could potentially fit the concept of fungibility as defined by Nussbaum (1995) and commodification of the person by Kaveny (1999). One registered nurse is replaceable by another. One licensed practical nurse is interchangeable with another. Sharon has a strong relationship with several of the patients and families on the unit, and her presence with them is integral to their adjustment. However, the staffing policy identifies her as completely "replaceable" to these families by any other RN who works on the unit, and very few people in the health care system would scrutinize this perspective. This way of looking at care implies an instrumental rather than an intrinsic valuing of the people who are the care providers and those in their care, resulting in the potential commodification of care and objectification of care providers. Kaveny (1999) explains that "fungibility and instrumentality are mutually reinforcing aspects of commodities" (p. 211). Thus, care providers who are seen as interchangeable and replaceable and who are not valued for their relational abilities and intrinsic human qualities are essentially being seen as objects and commodities. In contrast, Ballatt and Campling (2011) make the point that patients may not remember names of medications, medical jargon, or even intricacies about their diagnoses and treatments—but they often vividly recall the tone and demeanor of their care providers. The relational context of the care matters a great deal to both the patients and those who care for them.

It is within the context of the relationship between the caregiver and the patient/family that the social, emotional, relational, and existential aspects of pain are addressed, and where care providers also experience the satisfaction that their work is meaningful and important. Addressing the patient's needs holistically is referred in the hospice literature as treating the "total pain" of the patient, which is seen as a necessary requirement for good palliative care (Mehta & Chan, 2008). Being treated as if you are replaceable (fungible) can undermine the importance of this relational context in care, which is also foundational to the hospice philosophy of care.

Kaveny (1999) explored the ways in which health care delivery systems commodify both patients and practitioners. She describes three main purposes of the health care delivery system. The first is to intervene in order to enhance the health of populations, and the second is to provide care to individuals in order to cure disease and improve functionality. She then states:

> The third purpose of health care is also focused on the individual, but not on measurable improvements in health status that are the focus of the second category. It is best described in the language of the corporal works of mercy; as providing companionship, guidance, and some measure of comfort to persons who are faced with the limitations of their own mortality. While this is an important aspect of the treatment of all sick persons, it is particularly crucial in the case of those who are dying. For this class of patients the outcome of all care will be the same—death. It is not the result of the care, but the nature, shape, and quality of the caring process itself that assumes paramount importance in these instances.
>
> (p. 213)

Without the establishment of a relational context to care, generic practitioners perform technical procedures to faceless objects (patients) by interchangeable staff with prescribed roles. It sounds more like an assembly line in a factory than a place where humane care is provided. The point here is that there is a relational context to the care delivery in which the *caring process* occurs, not just in regards to how patients are treated, but also in relation to how care providers are treated in the same system. Professional caregivers who are treated as objects without feelings, needs, and preferences are more likely to turn around and treat patients in a similar way (Browning, Meyer, Truog, & Solomon, 2007; Sherwin, 2012). Adding to this problem is that most medical training is focused on the mastery of technical skills and procedures. This procedural orientation is reinforced by fee-for-service reimbursement for specific procedures and fee scales that are tied into the assignment of specific diagnoses (Kaveny, 1999).

Although the correct and effective diagnosis and treatment of disease is important, the decisions and care that occur in conjunction with this treatment must happen in the context of a relationship between the care provider and the recipient of that care. This relational component is the crucial aspect of care that is often lacking for both the patient and the care provider, especially in the existential circumstances that are commonly present in palliative care settings (Brazil et al., 2010; McLeod, 2002). Terminally ill/palliative patients and the subspecialty of palliative medicine are often devalued because there are no more "procedures" to be performed, leading to a mentality that there is "nothing more to be done." This focus on tasks and procedures (and reimbursement based upon the performance of such) means there is often a lack of appreciation for the aspects of care that involve being emotionally present and journeying alongside another human being in the midst of a time of suffering.

Darcy L. Harris

Looking Critically at Common Experiences in Palliative Care

Many common practices in health care settings have become so widespread that the need for caution around their implementation is rarely explored. Below are some areas where the potential for harmful objectification and depersonalization can occur in the delivery of palliative care for both patients and care providers.

The Use of the Team Approach

The multidisciplinary team approach is mandated for the appropriate delivery of hospice/palliative care services. In this approach, the care of a patient is shared by a group of professionals represented by several different professional backgrounds, such as doctors, nurses, social workers, chaplains, volunteers, and specialty care providers (Downing, 2013). How could patients and families not be pleased with an entire group of people representing a wide variety of professions being dedicated to their care? The rub here is that there still needs to be a point of accountability to the patient and his/her family to know who is ultimately responsible for engaging with them regarding decisions and care. In addition, as stated previously, under the guise of a "team approach," there should not be a sacrifice of the relational component of that care with the patient and his/her family—i.e., today you have nurse A, tomorrow you have nurse B, and the next day you have nurse C., but you are always assured of "a nurse" because there is always a nurse assigned to your team. What is important here is the realization that for many patients, having continuity of care with at least one team member provides a sense of security and trust for approaching the team with concerns and making important decisions about end of life care.

The team approach must also include disclosure to patients and families about the limits of confidentiality. For example, a patient or a family member discloses a very sensitive issue to the social worker on the team when the two of them are talking alone, and then the social worker shares this information with the other team members as part of routine disclosure within the team. Did the patient understand that whatever is shared with the social worker in a private moment would become shared information with everyone else on the team?

Accurately Identifying "the Problem"

Patients and family members may be very focused on their own needs and issues when they are in such an intense and difficult time. At the same time, it is important to keep in mind that even though health care workers may be committed to caring for the patient and family in a holistic way, the reality is that staffing issues, bureaucracy, and financial pressures can hinder these good intentions. Every professional has personal vulnerabilities and limits that may manifest in the work environment at various times and in response to various people and situations. The scenario with Joan and Sam demonstrated how labeling can serve the purpose of protective distancing for professional caregivers and also how this type of distancing can be experienced by those in their care. The culture of the care environment must allow for the human reactions and limitations that are present for patients, families, and care providers without shame or labeling being part of the dynamic.

Patients and family members may become acutely aware that they are being perceived negatively by staff. In response, these same patients and families may dismiss their own needs and feelings or not feel safe to share them with members of the care team if they are concerned that in so doing, they will be seen as a "problem" or an additional "burden" to their care providers (Sherwin, 2012). Care providers also have human limitations in regards to how far their ability to care can be stretched without reprieve. The difference here is that professional care providers have an obligation to engage in self-care behaviors and reflective practice. Some professionals may try to advocate for better conditions in their workplace. Power imbalances exist in care systems, with care providers having power by virtue of their expertise and the dependence of patients and families upon them to administer care that is necessary for symptom control and support. The vulnerability and needs of the patient and family must be respected. Hindrances to the ability to meet patient/family needs should be identified and addressed from all levels, whether they originate with an individual, team, organization, and/or political system.

One-Sided Conversations

It is easy to fall into the trap of interactions with patients that tend to be one-sided conversations for the purpose of information exchange. Health care providers become very accustomed to sharing information about test results, medication effects and side effects, institutional policies, scheduling procedures, and symptom management. But as the interaction between Janet and Joan demonstrates, when a caregiver pauses and allows the patient and family to share their feelings, thoughts, concerns, and perceptions, the door for the kind of open communication that can facilitate healing can occur, in spite of ravaging disease and terminal illness.

The "Piece of Cake Phenomenon"

Gena Corea, a feminist author who has written extensively about the experience of being a patient in Western medical institutions, describes the "piece of cake phenomenon" (Corea, 2005). What she means by this phrase is that health care workers can become desensitized to the procedures they perform because they are often seen as routine or "a piece of cake" to do. They then assume that patients who will be undergoing these procedures understand the routine nature and lack of complexity, and these same care providers may react negatively if the patient (and family) appears overly anxious or "needy" in relation to this procedure. It is important to remember that events that are uniquely personal and highly significant to patients are often part of the daily routine for clinical and administrative staff, leading to a disparity in the subjective appreciation of the meaning of these events for patients (Ballatt & Campling, 2011).

It is easy for trained professionals to lose the perspective of someone who has entered an environment where highly technical jargon is used, where there is an expectation of compliance in order to get better or have symptoms managed, and where your own expertise and feelings are often seen as irrelevant to the decisions that are made. An example in the palliative care context could be related to the use of morphine or other strong opioids to relieve pain. Some patients are hesitant to take morphine for pain because of concerns about the use of these medications and their potential side effects, and yet they are a routinely used and effective class of medication in palliative care settings for symptom relief. Patients' concerns regarding the use of these medications should be thoroughly explored and acknowledged, with the understanding that while their use is a part of everyday care to most palliative care providers, there may be carry significant negative connotations and concerns for patients and their families.

Conclusion

In this chapter, we've explored potentially problematic issues that can occur in the context of health care delivery settings. The focus is not upon a "bad" caregiver or a "problem" patient, but upon the overarching, structural issues that can have a profound deleterious effect upon those who care and those who require care. These structural issues are bigger than an individual, and they are often bigger than even the institutions and agencies where health care workers practice. Public and social policies about how care is delivered, funded, and managed occur at the political level, where decisions about care are often made in the abstract, with fiscal needs taking priority. In the context of health care, we are all aware that whether care is funded publicly or privately, economics and political views often overshadow the structure of how health care will be administered. What often does not occur, however, are the difficult conversations about political values, social expectations, and unequal privilege that may be granted to some groups over marginalized groups of patients (e.g., patients who are professionals versus indigent patients) and some types of care providers in relation to others (e.g, doctors over nurses). Health care workers and patients alike get caught in the web of these decisions, and this bigger-picture perspective is necessary to address these issues from a structural and political stance.

Key Terms

Burnout—long-term exhaustion and diminished interest in work. Burnout has been assumed to result from chronic occupational stress that accumulates over time.

Iatrogenic harm—literally means "physician-induced"; it usually refers to harm that occurs to patients as a result of entering medical treatment and having a mistake or accident occur, or developing an infection or complication as a result of being in a care facility or having a medical procedure done.

Moral distress—painful psychological disequilibrium that results from recognizing the ethically appropriate action yet being unable to take it (e.g., due to institutional constraints that make it nearly impossible to pursue the right course of action).

Objectification—the denial of a person's subjective traits; the person is treated as either a means to an end, or as a physical entity (an object) deprived of personal qualities or individuality.

Questions for Reflection

1. Consider the scope of responsibility of healthcare workers. To what extent do you consider their relationship with patients to be part of their professional responsibility? Assuming all physical-medical care is expertly offered, to what extent do you consider failings in their relationships with patients to be a violation of professional obligation? To what extent should institutions be responsible for considering the need for this relationship in staffing/scheduling considerations?
2. The moral distress experienced by healthcare providers is discussed as arising from conflicts between personal judgment and institutionally imposed demands. Have you experienced such conflict (in any setting)? How would you respond to such conflicting demands and resultant stress/distress?
3. Have you experienced the "piece of cake phenomenon"? What would have been helpful to you at that time? Were you able to communicate this to the professionals involved? Consider how your own experience may be used to help you understand the experience of others.

References

Anderson, N. (1981). Exclusion: A study of depersonalization in health care. *Journal of Humanistic Psychology*, 21(3), 67–78.

Ballatt, J., & Campling, P. (2011). *Intelligent kindness: Reforming the culture of healthcare*. U.K.: RCPsych Publications.

Brazil, K., Kassalainen, S., Ploeg, J., & Marshall, D. (2010). Moral distress experienced by health care professionals who provide home-based palliative care. *Social Science & Medicine*, 71(9), 1687–1691.

Browning, D. M., Meyer, E. C., Truog, R. D., & Solomon, M. Z. (2007). Difficult conversations in health care: Cultivating relational learning to address the hidden curriculum. *Academic Medicine*, 82(9), 905–913.

Corea, G. (2005). The artificial womb: An escape from the "dark and dangerous place." *The Mother Machine: Reproductive Technologies from Artificial Insemination to Artificial Wombs*. New York, NY: HarperCollins.

Downing, J. (2013). One feature common to all models of palliative care. *International Journal of Palliative Nursing*, 19(7), 315.

Glasberg, A. L., Eriksson, S., & Norberg, A. (2007). Burnout and "stress of conscience"among healthcare personnel. *Journal of Advanced Nursing*, 57(4), 392–403.

Kaveny, M. C. (1999). Commodifying the polyvalent good of health care. *Journal of Medicine and Philosophy* 24(3), 207–223.

Keidel, G. C. (2002). Burnout and compassion fatigue among hospice caregivers. *American Journal of Hospice and Palliative Medicine*, 19(3), 200–205.

Kuhl, D. (2003). *What dying people want: Lessons for living from people who are dying*. Toronto: Doubelday.

McLeod, C. (2002). *Self-trust and reproductive autonomy*. Cambridge, MA: MIT.

Mehta, A., & Chan, L.S. (2008). Understanding of the concept of "total pain": A prerequisite for pain control. *Journal of Hospice and Palliative Nursing*, 10(1), 26–32.

Morgan, J. C., Dill, J., & Kalleberg, A. L. (2013). The quality of healthcare jobs: Can intrinsic rewards compensate for low extrinsic rewards? *Work, Employment & Society*, 27(5), 802–822.

Nussbaum, M. C. (1995). Objectification. *Philosophy & Public Affairs*, 24(4), 249–291.

Payne, N. (2001). Occupational stressors and coping as determinants of burnout in female hospice nurses. *Journal of Advanced Nursing*, 33(3), 396–405.

Peloquin, S. M. (1993).The depersonalization of patients: A profile gleaned from narratives. *The American Journal of Occupational Therapy*, 47(9), 830–837.

Poghosyan, L., Aiken, L. H., & Sloane, D. M. (2009). Factor structure of the Maslach burnout inventory: An analysis of data from large scale cross-sectional surveys of nurses from eight countries. *International Journal of Nursing Studies*, 46(7), 894–902.

Rees, C. (2011). Iatrogenic psychological harm. *Archives of Disease in Childhood*, 97(5), 440–446.

Sherwin, S. (2012). A relational approach to autonomy in health care. In E. Gedge & W. J. Walucho (Eds.), *Readings in Health Care Ethics* (2nd ed.), pp. 14–32. Peterborough, ON: Broadview Press.

Thompson, N.(2010). *Theorizing social work practice*. Basingstoke, U.K.: Palgrave Macmillan.

Vachon, M. L. S. (1995). Staff stress in hospice/palliative care: A review. *Palliative Medicine*, 9(2), 91–122.

Venes, D. (2013). *Taber's cyclopedic medical dictionary* (22nd Ed.). Philadelphia: PA Davis.

Weissman, D. E. (2009). Moral distress in palliative care. *Journal of Palliative Medicine*, 12(10), 865–866.

12

The Silenced Emotion

Older Women and Grief in Prison

Ronald H. Aday and Jennifer J. Krabill

The U.S. prison population has experienced a dramatic growth over the past several decades. With the introduction of stiff anti-drug laws and the implementation of tougher sentencing laws including mandatory minimum sentences, the prison population has grown to record highs. With the additional growth of the baby boom generation, the older adults are the fastest growing segment of the prison population including a steady increase in aging female offenders. Today, over 108,000 women are incarcerated in state and federal institutions (Carson & Golinelli, 2013). Of this group of incarcerated women, an increasing number are now among the rapidly growing population of aging prisoners. According to the most recent Bureau of Justice figures, over 13,640 women age 50 and over are housed in U.S. prisons (Carson & Golinelli, 2013). Almost 30,000 female prisoners currently in their 40s are set to join the ranks of aging inmates (Wahidin & Aday, 2013).

Another contributing factor to the challenges of an aging prison population is the increasing number of long-term inmates. Currently, approximately 40 percent of all inmates over 50 are serving 20-plus year sentences with sentence lengths greatest for inmates in the oldest age brackets (Fellner, 2012). This stacking effect, without question, is increasing interest in aging prisoners' adaptations to a variety of life issues including social losses, death, dying, grief, and bereavement as they age *in place* behind bars. Not only are inmates confronted with the deaths of loved ones on the outside, they must also endure a variety of other multiple losses associated with incarceration. These losses must be dealt with concurrently and can complicate the grieving process sometimes evolving into a full blown crisis stage or grief pileup. For example, Judy's story presented below illustrates the lifetime of losses that can have a cumulative effect on a person's ability to process grief. While disheartening, her story is not unique as she is only one of the many women aging in prison coping with a myriad of losses and heartaches.

Social, Environmental, and Personal Losses in a Correctional Institution

Freedom and Control—the loss of freedom, comforts of home, and ability to fully participate in life associated with the outside world. Prison life is heavily regulated, controlled and unpredictable and, following incarceration, inmates lose the basic freedoms to define and manage their personal schedules, move about at will, and make basic decisions such as who and when they visit loved ones.

Privacy—the inability to escape a crowded social world filled with loud noises, invasion of personal space, sharing of bathroom/shower facilities, and lack of privacy when making private phone calls or writing discreet letters. Lack of safety and threats of victimization make the lack of privacy even more undesirable to older women.

Material Possessions—the necessity of giving up personal effects such as clothes, jewelry, shoes, nail polish, lotions, favorite foods, cell phones, computers, pictures, transportation, family artifacts.

Outside Connections—loss of frequent contacts with children, partners, or other family/friends and opportunities to share special occasions such as birthdays or holidays with loved ones. Lost connections to family may be attributable to one's criminal behavior whereas others are from close prison friends who have been paroled. The realization that these losses may be irreversible can be particularly difficult to accept.

Social Roles/Identity—loss of work roles and accompanying social status, loss of being able to function daily as a parent, child, or grandparent, old titles from the free world and now reduced to inmate status/number.

Self and Past life—loss of a sense that you matter, loss of future hope and dreams, loss as a sexual being and lack of opportunity for touch and intimacy, loss of the person you used to be and the one you wanted for the future.

Health—loss of choice over one's own medical or dental care, which may result in gradual deterioration of health outcomes. Loss of appetite, sensory processes, memory, and ability to complete activities of daily living such as walking independently, climbing stairs, working a regular job.

The primary aim of this chapter will be to provide a voice to older women offenders whose grief and loss experiences remain in the shadow of men and ignored by administrators, security personnel, clinicians, researchers, and the greater community. In the process, the authors acknowledge the impact of pre-prison experiences, a harsh prison environment, and post-prison losses on the inmates' ability to grieve. We further apply Doka's (1989; 2002) notion of *disenfranchised grief* to the context, identifying specific constraints these women confront as they strive to restore order and meaning to their lives following significant social losses or the death of family members, friends, and acquaintances. This chapter will also explore the role of grief rituals, therapeutic programming, and other best practice models introduced as important strategies for assisting inmates with finding suitable alternatives for processing their grief following various types of losses.

The Prison Environment

Understanding the impact of loss for aging female prisoners requires an understanding of the social context in which such life changes occur. It has been suggested that the harshness of prison creates heightened feelings of deprivation and loss (Dhami, Ayton, & Loewenstein, 2007). The "deprivation" model developed around the "pains of imprisonment" was introduced over a half century ago as a framework from which to capture the experience of incarceration (Sykes, 1958). With a recent emphasis on mass incarceration, longer sentences, overcrowded conditions, and little empathy for rehabilitative programs, nothing substantial has occurred inside contemporary prisons to alter this view (Clear & Frost, 2014). Extreme deprivations leading to a "mortification and curtailment of self" (Goffman, 1961), "depersonalization" (Townsend, 1962), and "institutional neurosis" (Ham, 1980) are all conditions which provoke a wide range of sociopsychological reactions. Prison confinement frequently leads to feelings of frustration, anger, powerlessness, fear, sadness, and resentment (Haney, 2006). With the many restrictions found in prison settings, individuals tend to subsist in a defensive shell characterized by isolation and resulting in a gradual process of depersonalization. As such, prison is a place not of rehabilitation but rather one of punishment, custody, strict rules, and discipline (Stoller, 2003). In such a strict living environment, offenders often find such a place unreceptive for processing the painful emotions related to grief and loss.

Non-Death Losses

Many of the psychological and social issues surrounding grief and loss in a prison setting are considered to be quite different than for those who live on the outside (Levine, 2005). It has been suggested that one of the major differences is the degree to which people have control over their lives (Stevenson & McCutchen, 2006). Getting in touch with the profound loss and sadness that results from going to prison, especially if you are in for a long time, is hard in a culture that has little compassion for the pain and suffering of prisoners. In prison, every aspect of an inmate's life including end-of-life issues is generally controlled by others. As a result, inmates frequently have little control over their own lives and the prospect of dying in a foreign place or coping with the loss of others is likely to be a very distressing thought for older adults. The scope and depth of loss for prisoners is enormous and can be particularly difficult for older females (Junior, 2003). Policymakers and practitioners must recognize that geriatric female offenders have often experienced a multitude of losses over the life course that, when taken together, significantly impact their ability to successfully process grief in a prison environment.

The case vignette below was created to provide a summary of the multiplicity of non-death losses many of the women have encountered in their lives. Drawing on life course, stress process, and cumulative disadvantage theories, recent research identifies 70 percent of inmates 55 and older as having survived negative life events, with current losses only intensifying the pain (Maschi, Viola, Morgen, & Kosikinen, 2013). Negative background experiences of older offenders are frequently characterized by exposure to high rates of violence and victimization, limited educational/vocational opportunities, low socioeconomic statuses, addictions, inadequate access to nutrition and preventive health care (Fellner, 2012; Kerbs & Jolley, 2014). As a result, women enter prison much maligned having suffered from a variety of personal losses, stress, trauma, and fear in many stages of their lives (Aday & Krabill, 2011). Non-death losses and transitions such as the experience of parental divorce during childhood or the loss of innocence following victimization can be particularly significant. If these experiences remain unaddressed and unsupported, they can reverberate through an individual's entire life (Leach, Burgess, & Holmwood, 2008).

Case Vignette

Judy Holbird is a 67-year-old Caucasian woman who has been incarcerated in the Arkansas prison system for over 25 years of a 166 year prison sentence. Judy married at the age of 16 to an older and very controlling man who periodically was physically and sexually abusive. After years of suffering from pain, anguish, and feelings of rejection, Judy sought a divorce after 17 years of marriage. Because of the distance, Judy has not had any in-person visits with her family members in years, but corresponds frequently by mail with her two adult children, sister, grandchildren, and close personal friends.

In prison, Judy has been challenged with deprivations of personal autonomy and independence, material possessions, routine contact with the outside world, and social status. However, personal loss, for Judy, began many years before her sentence when she experienced the sudden death of her three-month old child, Erick. Shortly thereafter at age 21, Judy was forced to cope with the traumatic loss of her father who, by all accounts, was murdered execution style in his driveway with a shotgun blast to the back of his head on January 23, 1968. In addition to this tragedy, as a poverty-stricken victim of child and spousal abuse, her story mirrors the life experiences of many incarcerated women today. Over the years, relatives and dear friends she has made while incarcerated have died. For example, since her incarceration, Judy has been notified of the deaths of a half sister, a grandmother, two uncles, one aunt, a cousin, one brother in law, one sister in law, her father in law and mother in law, and a nephew as well as three close friends on the outside of whom she was very fond. In 2012, Judy found herself grieving the loss of yet another child, Penny, who died at the age of 41. Judy takes some comfort in knowing that Penny is so longer suffering from her chronic and painful health condition, but her loss remains immense since Penny was the child that consistently kept Judy informed of family matters.

One of the most emotionally draining losses, without question, has been the dream and anticipation of freedom followed by repeated denials from the parole board. Two years ago Judy's dreams were literally shattered when she was led to believe by the governor that she had spent ample time in prison. Like the majority of lifers and other long-term inmates who seek redemption, Judy acknowledged the pain and agony that she felt when her hopes were dashed. Now forced to endure the emotional struggle of an extended prison stay, the mourning process must yet again be revisited. In Judy's words "it has been a long, long, long time since the grief in my heart has hurt to the deepest corners of my very soul."

The act of imprisonment itself has an immediate and dramatic effect on an individual's social life. The prospect of being separated from family members, missing friends and outside social activities, or coping with family members who have forgotten them are constant worries for older women serving time (Aday & Krabill, 2011). The resulting social losses associated with incarceration can have a devastating and lasting impact on their lives, especially if they leave children or aging parents behind who must now rely on others for support (Krabill & Aday, 2005; Poehlmann, 2005; Pollock, 2004). The notion of a "disrupted life course" results in continued grief reactions as the offenders begin to realize they must forgo important developmental milestones in children or grandchildren's lives such as birthdays, special holidays, graduation, weddings, and newborn grandchildren (Jewkes, 2006). The challenge for inmates to deal with such significant losses is expressed by this 54-year-old *lifer* when she states (George, 2010, p. 98):

> Without a doubt, my great, unabating source of grief is the separation from the people I love. I yearn for the joys I shared with my family, and my memories of our times together make me long for them. I remember our annual Easter feast complete with the coconut Easter bunny cake with licorice whiskers that Aunt Eileen would bake each year. . . . The hardest deprivations inside are the small daily losses, the minutia of my family's experiences from which I will always be barred. So many seemingly insignificant aspects of my life are now desperately mourned. I don't really miss driving a car or being able to wear attractive properly fitting clothes. Everything I miss deeply revolves around the relationships I shared with my family.

However, some inmates may be shunned by relatives who are shamed by their crimes, and in some cases may have their parental rights terminated (Schetky, 1998). Also, some long-term inmates have reported losing all contact with siblings with whom they once shared a close relationship while others may have no knowledge of family or their whereabouts (Luke, 2002).

One of the major consequences of imprisonment is a loss of the prisoners' sense of self-governance. Michel Foucault (1995) has stressed the role of prison as the management of its inmates through continual surveillance, monitoring of spatial activity, and classification. Prisoners are deprived of their identity and loss of liberty, which consists not only of inmates' confinement to but also restrictive movement within the institution (Aday & Krabill, 2011; Stevenson & McCutchen, 2006). Once incarcerated, prisoners are told where to live and what to wear; an indifferent prison system prepares their food and forces them to work in jobs unrelated to their skills. As one older woman commented on her controlled prison experience (Aday & Krabill, 2011, p. 32), "It bothers me that my life is wasted by just obeying prison rules, having everything done for me, but society chooses this punishment." Using a model assessing institutional structure, Haney (2006) found some association between the degree of depersonalization of environment and the effects of self-imagery. He further suggested that the more total the institution (based on such items as orientation of activities, scheduling of activities, provisions for dissemination of rules and standards of conduct, and observation of the behavior in inmates, type of sanction system, how personal property is dealt with, decision-making about the use of private property), the greater its depersonalizing effects. According to Santos (1995), the prison system has stripped away inmate identities removing their abilities to fully distinguish themselves as distinct individuals.

For many aging prisoners, the most important "role loss" influencing institutional adjustment is that of health. Aday and Krabill (2011) found that older female offenders suffer from at least four chronic illnesses creating a significant concern with deterioration and accelerated aging. Other researchers have reported that many long-term inmates are obsessively concerned and highly self-conscious about outward signs of deterioration (Genders & Player, 1990; Wahidin, 2004). With an abundance of time to fill and limited opportunities to fill it, inmates often become preoccupied with physical aging and their increasing health problems. As they experience a restricted life, chronically ill persons become cognizant of the fact that they cannot engage in many of the activities they valued and enjoyed in the past. The restrictions the disease imposes on normal daily activities make the individual feel controlled by the disease. For some, this change in lifestyle is overwhelming. In particular, chronic incurable conditions require major adjustment in personal identity as individuals must assimilate the fact that impairment and constraint will be permanent losses.

Long-term and life-sentenced offenders encounter the greatest challenges acknowledging, accepting, and adjusting to these losses. For many, the pain intensifies from the initial arrest to courtroom hearings, incarceration and appeals processes (Jones & Beck, 2007). Unlike other contexts within which individuals may experience extreme distress, long-term incarceration is unique in the fact the pain of losses is nonfinite; it increases in intensity over time. Haney (2012), for example, explains that these offenders undergo processes of re-traumatization as the losses experienced while incarcerated are remarkably similar to their prior losses. Pains such as conflict-ridden interpersonal relationships do not end when one arrives at prison, but rather, take on the form of friction with prison peers and correctional personnel. In prison, moreover, inmates will have very few options available to pursue activities (school, work, rehabilitative programming) that provide life with a sense of purpose. This is particularly problematic for older offenders who may have "programmed out" of available activities.

Death-Related Losses

Coping with the death of a loved one is an event that nearly half of all women in prison encounter while incarcerated (Harner, Hentz, & Evangelista, 2011). Death-related losses are considered to be the ultimate injustice that threatens the self-esteem for aging female prisoners. Similar to the multitude of personal loses shared by the case study presented earlier, loss of loved ones while incarcerated is a common occurrence, especially for those doing a significant amount of time. Losing family members often translates into losing the daily interactions that serve to normalize one's existence behind bars. The regular phone calls, the letters, and cards sent on special occasions, the simple fact of just knowing someone is on the outside doing your time with you are all significant losses that shrink the inmate's social world. Facing the fact that their lives are different is especially true for aging prisoners who may have outlived family and friends on the outside and now must either turn to others for social support or simply go at it alone. Once again, Erin George (2010, p. 99) illustrates the significant loss of loved ones on the outside:

> I feel the separation from my family more keenly when it comes to the losses. Some of them singularly awful, like the death of my Aunt Marianne. . . . She had been diagnosed with cancer just after my arrest, so this was my first tragedy inside. Her death and the unexpected passing of my old friend Tia—as terrible as those things were, they were made worst by enduring them without my family to hold and comfort me.

Sometimes death-related losses can also trigger other painful emotions associated with previous experiences prior to incarceration. Older women who are serving life sentences have shared with the authors such experiences which frequently make the grieving process even more complicated because of the re-traumatization. As one older woman in her early sixties explains:

> Yesterday I received some photos from my mother of my little sister's memorial service . . . and it was devastating for me to see all of these pictures. . . . Some were from family I have not seen in years . . . and some reminded me of ones who have hurt me . . . my heart was really heavy with pain last night.

When combined with their own personal fears of dying and declining health, these losses can be devastating. Older adults first confront their own mortality, which may lead to greater uncertainty and profound fear. Inmates housed in correctional facilities at some institutions in remote areas may fear having a heart attack or some other sudden life-threatening symptom and the response time of getting them to a medical facility where they could receive proper treatment. The presence of chronic illnesses can create a sense of vulnerability among aging inmates who frequently have to rely on an unfamiliar or untrusting medical system for critical care. In this sense, older inmates are not only grieving their own deterioration, but also mourning the loss of others.

The loss of close friends is one of the most under-researched topics in the bereavement literature. Empirical research, however, indicates that survivors experience many of the same challenges adjusting to life without the close friend as they would the death of a spouse, siblings, children, and other family members (Lalive d'Epinay, Cavalli, & Guillet, 2009–2010). Bereaved friends may report heightened levels of illness, somatization, depression and other mental health concerns occurring near anniversaries, birthdays or significant life events (Sklar & Hartley, 1990). Loss may require survivors to redefine their roles and responsibilities within the support network (Deck & Folta, 1989). Death of friends may also heighten older women's awareness about the meaning of life, the value of friendships, the aging process, and one's own mortality (Roberto & Stanis, 1994).

The impact may be greatest in institutional settings as staff members are often insensitive to residents, restrict their access to information about serious illness, and provide few opportunities for open discussion following death (Lavigne-pley & Lévesque, 1992). Although community-dwelling elders have a wide range of supports and coping mechanisms (e.g., family, other friends, religion, leisure activities) they can utilize for adjustment, these are not as readily available in institutional settings. Deaton, Aday, and Wahidin (2009–2010) specifically illustrate how such events can heighten levels of death anxiety for aging female prisoners. Losing close friends in prison, in fact, may be a harrowing experience as inmates frequently establish close *fictive kin* relations with prison peers, which in many cases is considered more significant than family on the outside (Aday & Krabill, 2011). Prisoners may personally witness their friend's denials for health care, are physically present at the time of deterioration and death, and immediately after the death must return to normal prison routine without the opportunity to mourn the loss.

Processing Grief and Loss in Prison

Each person's journey through grief is unique since it relates to her/his personal experience and relationships. Although certain behaviors are expected for grief related to a loss through death, no particular guidelines exist for non-death related losses (Harner et al., 2011). Social dimensions that may affect grief reactions and mourning in prison include the relationship between deceased and bereaved, whether the loss is acknowledged, the meaning attached to the circumstances of the loss, the type and availability of social support, and whether the public expression of grief is acceptable are some of the more significant factors (Vera, 2007). Although a variety of grief expressions may be found across genders, findings indicate trends in gender differences related to how men and women have been socialized to approach the grief process. Grief that is more often characterized by open displays of intense affect, support seeking, and sharing of emotions with others is often feminized and associated with women whereas grief expressed in more instrumental or active ways (e.g., behavioral expressions) is often associated with males (Doka & Martin, 2010). Again, it is important to note that although these are common patterns, there is also great diversity in grief expressions among individuals (i.e., females may express grief instrumentally and males may employ an expressive/intuitive style).

Even under the best conditions, grieving is a complex and individualistic experience and yet when such a task presents itself in the surroundings of a total institution this creates circumstances of even greater pain for the bereaved. Although social sanctions "enfranchise" women's feminine expression of grief emotions in the general community (Versalle & McDowell, 2004, p. 55), prison is a place that discourages such expressions. For example, one primary reason for not expressing emotions in prison has been linked to the "pervasive interpersonal mistrust" found inside the institution (Greer, 2002, p. 124). More specifically, Greer found that women offenders viewed the notion of expressing emotions of sadness or grief as demonstrating a personal weakness. Portraying a "masculine" position on grief, this point is well illustrated with the following comment:

> Crying is a sign of weakness in here for some stupid reason. They'd think you're soft or something ... when you feel that way, you just stay to yourself. In here you have to put on a whole new face from what you were with your family and friends on the streets.
>
> (Greer 2002, p. 125)

While acknowledging the reality of the death is the first step in grieving, the lack of an opportunity to publicly mourn the loss of a loved one in prison prevents the commencement of the healing process (Junior, 2003). Because of the restraints of openly expressing emotions, research has shown that incarcerated women will often socially withdraw and grieve alone (Ferszt, 2002).

Aday and Krabill (2011) also reported that older women when expressing their grief reactions to the losses associated with incarceration would often conceal their emotions by remaining stoic in public while crying alone in the shower where the noise would be muffled or shedding tears silently after the lights were turned out.

Despite the prevalence of loss in correctional settings, prison administrators have been slow to develop and implement structured policies and programming to facilitate the adjustment process. Mirroring mainstream society, correctional facilities recognize specific "grieving rules" defining the parameters of acceptable grief reactions. Doka (1989) coined the term "disenfranchised grief," which recognizes certain relationships, losses, and grievers are excluded from the routines typically allowed following loss (e.g., Attig, 2004; Corr, 1998; Robson & Walter, 2012) with one of the major contexts for its emergence being correctional facilities (Harner, Hentz, & Evangelista, 2011; Jones & Beck, 2007; Leach et al., 2008; Schetky, 1998). Grieving rights, in most social contexts (including prisons), are typically reserved exclusively for individuals related to the deceased by blood or marriage—denying a relatively large circle of survivors (i.e., partners in non-traditional relationships, ex-spouses or lovers, close friends) opportunities to place closure on relationships. Social norms, further, may disenfranchise grievers by identifying which feelings, somatic symptoms, or behavioral reactions survivors may utilize in coping with stress, pre-selecting the rituals for survivors, and defining the time frame within which the grieving process is completed (Corr, 1998, 2002). In discussion of mourning, without question, too much emphasis is placed on "getting over" the loss rather than engaging in intrapsychic work needed to derive meaning from the experience and restore order to one's social world.

One obstacle to grieving behind bars is the fact that prisoners face policies restricting their access to rituals (i.e., funerals, memorial services, cemetery visits), memorabilia from the deceased, space and privacy to grieve, and safe forums for ventilation, self-disclosure, and social support (Ferszt, 2002; Harner et al., 2011; Young, 2003). Findings from a recent analysis of state-level correctional policies for emergency releases for deathbed visits and funeral attendance revealed that 45 states permitted emergency furloughs (Alladin, Truesdale-More, & Gabbidon, 2008). However, strict eligibility criteria for temporary furloughs may systematically exclude many inmates from fully experiencing grief due to their security classification level, relationship to the deceased, prison conduct or activities, physical and mental health statuses, geographic proximity to the critically ill, and personal finances. In most states, policy narrowly defines family as parents, siblings, spouses, children, in-laws, aunts/uncle, or cousins—failing to acknowledge that many aging female prisoners retain strong connections to former prison peers who had become closer than their own biological kin. State policy may also require inmates to select only one of two furloughs (i.e., bedside visits or funeral attendance), a practice preventing inmates from both resolving unfinished business (i.e., past regrets, relationship conflicts) and physically viewing the body at services. Others may exclude full participation in rituals by permitting inmates to visit the funeral home only before the services.

Although furlough policy decisions are made on a case-by-case basis and may also vary from state to state, the following illustrations highlight the logistical and pragmatic barriers inmates must negotiate in order to engage in activities necessary to fully process and comprehend the finality of the loss (Alladin et al., 2008):

- *Bedside visits.* Normally requires documentation from the relatives' physicians verifying the severity of the condition and likelihood of imminent death. Visits normally are conducted in nursing homes, hospices, convalescence centers, hospitals, or other total institutions, with inmates having no option of visiting chronically/terminally ill inmates in their personal homes.
- *Funerals.* Various policies exist which include the type of service (ie., no closed caskets, cremations), level of contact permitted with other mourners, restrictions on viewing/touching the body, conduct during the service, etc.
- *Finances.* The cost of the furlough is normally the responsibility of the inmate and family, with many states requiring the payment for security, transportation, lodging, meals prior to the furlough. Although some states may permit inmates to use discretionary funds or deduct against future earnings in their accounts, the inability to finance a long-distance trip may strongly discourage inmates from participation in standard rituals. Regulations restricting the amount of money inmates may have on possession while on leave can also be major deterrents to travel.
- *Distance.* Normally travel is restricted on an instate basis, with many states further indicating a maximum number of miles inmates may travel round-trip.
- *Time.* A narrow time frame is the general rule within which trips must be completed. Although the window may vary by state, institution, and travel distance, the awareness that one may only be permitted to spend a few minutes to hours with loved ones lessens desires to participate. In some states, inmates may even face serious repercussions (i.e., treatment as an escape) if they return to the facility late without contacting administration.
- *Security.* Most states designate a minimum number of guards who must be present with the inmate the entire duration of the trip. Restrictions for furlough may also apply to inmates other than those in minimum custody. Restraints, as well, may be required—further attracting excessive, unwanted attention to the inmate.

Additional research, which has examined the grief experiences of female prisoners, reinforces the difficulty to process grief in the criminal justice system. For example, these women have expressed that furlough experiences were constrained and isolated, and viewing was only permitted in isolation from other family members (Freszt, 2002). In this regard, grief work in prison is most difficult even when utilizing the furlough option especially in cases where prisoners are unable to share the loss with family members.

Although grief is a normal reaction to death, aging female inmates frequently experience complicated grief, a condition recognized by symptoms, intensity, and duration deviating from socially recognized norms. Complicated grief, in brief, involves difficulties acknowledging permanent separation from attachment figures and/or adjusting to life without the deceased (Prigerson et al., 1995; Prigerson & Maciejewski 2006). The condition may succeed death or any other form of permanent separation including incarceration (Leach et al., 2008). Given that long-term offenders, in particular, report a gradual deterioration of relationships over time, the awareness that one has aging parents, siblings, or spouses, who cannot physically travel to visit them, can cause similar grief reactions (Aday & Krabill, 2011). In correctional facilities, complicated grief is also closely interconnected with negative pre-incarceration life events and the pains of imprisonment (Hammersley & Ayling, 2006). Specific types include prolonged, delayed, inhibited, and absent grief (e.g., Parkes, 1998; Parkes & Weiss, 1983; Raphael, 1983).

The most common type clinicians will encounter in correctional facilities is delayed grief, a defense mechanism characterized by intentional decisions survivors make to postpone grief until they have the time, space, and resources to fully process the loss. Survivors may suspend grief in response to other obligations, stress overload, pain, fear, or perceived lack of available social support (Rando, 1993). In prisons, low levels of educational attainment (e.g., poor vocabulary), weak interpersonal skills, lack of experience expressing emotions (except anger/hostility), privacy concerns, unwritten codes of inmate conduct, trust issues, and desires to maintain control over situations all inform decisions (Finlay & Jones, 2000; Schetky, 1998; Stevenson & McCutchen, 2006). Incarcerated women, in particular, delay grief to maintain a sense of agency in an environment where surveillance is constant and empathy from administration, staff, or peers is inadequate (Harner et al., 2011; Tate & Wahidin, 2013). Under these circumstances, suspending grief until release and community re-integration appears to be the most rational decision.

Programming for Grief/Bereavement

Various forms of grief and bereavement work may prove effective in this environment, with the efficacy determined by the population, security level, institutional regulations, and inmate comfort level. As individuals with complicated grief reactions often report poor outcomes and low satisfaction with group activities (Ghesguiere, Shear, & Duan, 2013–2014; Johnsen, Dyregrov, & Dyregrov, 2010), and with many inmates, in particular, having reservations about self-disclosure in group exercises (Olsen & McEwen, 2004; Schetky, 1998; Wilson, 2011), individual therapy may be ideal for offenders who may not be fully ready to engage with other members. Offenders whose lives have been fraught with pain from abandonment, for example, may first need to gain assurance their participation will not result in further losses, interrogation, scrutiny, and punishment by leaders, or victimization by peers. Establishing trusting relationships with clinicians and potential group facilitators early in the process, in particular, is imperative due to the tendency of inmates to associate them with administration, security, and health care staff who have not always acted in their personal interests (Schetky, 1998).

However, once trust is established, brief, time-limited group sessions may be highly effective for normalizing the experience; reducing anger, blame and despair, and facilitating personal growth (Olsen & McEwen, 2004; Wilson, 2011). Group work may be structured around general loss-related themes including loss of family and friends, changes in living environment, declines in physical and cognitive status, feelings of alienation from mainstream culture (Toseland, 1995). Elders who are frustrated by rapidly changing social roles, isolation from others, or poor interpersonal skills may find opportunities for participation most appealing as healthy group dynamics introduce avenues for ventilation, validation of one's experiences, education, and collaborative problem-solving (Rizzo & Toseland, 2005). Generally, grief groups function most effectively when the group is relatively small, comprised of homogeneous members (i.e., age, type of death, relationship to deceased), semi-structured with input from members on themes, and founded on the notion of resiliency or maintaining hope for the future (Dyregov, Dyregov, & Johnsen, 2013). Although members will certainly explore pains associated with shared losses, the emphasis should focus on preparing them for positive future experiences.

Designing and implementing programming that specifically addresses age-related issues is one of the most important strategies for supporting geriatric female offenders who are coping with loss. Unfortunately, most correctional programs have been designed for younger offenders, failing to acknowledge the unique life experiences and needs of the aged and infirm. Long-standing beliefs that older adults are unassertive, unmotivated, uninterested, or unwilling to participate in any activities offered have resulted in them being systematically excluded from policy (Kerbs & Jolley, 2009). In facilities nationwide, for example, older inmates receive few opportunities to enroll in classes related to chronic disease management, stress reduction/relaxation training, conflict resolution, and community re-integration. Older pre-release offenders, in particular, receive limited assistance with tasks such as obtaining benefits, managing personal finances, preparing wills, and coping with death, dying, grief, and bereavement concerns—each necessary to resume community roles following the pains of imprisonment (Higgins & Severson, 2009; Maschi, Morgen, Zgoba, Courtney & Ristow, 2011).

The True Grit Model at the Northern Nevada Correctional Institution in Carson City Nevada is one of several across the nation to offer group activities concentrating on topics addressing the various physical, emotional, spiritual, social issues geriatric offenders will experience when confronted with loss (Harrison, 2006). Despite constraints with which program administrators must operate the program, the program has been largely successful in enhancing well-being, quality of life, and overall life satisfaction among members (Kopera-Frye et al., 2013). States interested in adopting similar models, however, will need to acquire political and financial support to maintain activities over time (Fellner, 2012). Futhermore, states will likely need to introduce programming that takes into consideration the intersection between age- and gender-related concerns (Aday & Krabill, 2011; Leigey & Hodge, 2012)

In work with incarcerated women, the overall goal of therapeutic programming is to provide the necessary structure and guidance for survivors to identify their feelings about loss and replace maladaptive responses with more effective approaches utilizing strengths already available to them. Although therapeutic programming in women's prisons is substandard to programming offered in men's prisons (i.e., funding, variety, quality of programs), new programs are being developed nationwide using a holistic approach to problem-solving. Through reading, writing, and experiential exercises, women are learning to increase self-efficacy, interpersonal competence, and behavioral skills following long-standing histories of abuse, addictions, and relationship problems (Carp & Schade, 1992; Negy, Woods, & Carlson, 1997; van Wormer, 2001). Cognitive restructuring and exploring new coping mechanisms is considered to have an adaptive function for women who continue to feel unresolved anger/resentment, self-hatred, guilt, and grief following loss (Leigey & Reed, 2010). Ferszt, Salgado, DeFedele, and Levilee (2009) discuss the impact of a 12-week course, *House of Healing*, on the mental health of incarcerated women who had experienced multiple losses—reporting that participation had resulted in reduced levels of depression and anxiety, increased self-esteem, and increased spiritual well-being.

In a time of diminished resources for structured correctional mental health programming, administration strongly encourages clinicians to explore less expensive alternative for treating offenders. Despite the paucity of research conducted in this area, religious activities, in general, attract larger amounts of older women prisoners than any other structured prison activity. As a result, one of the most promising solutions for reaching aging female offenders coping with loss involves capitalizing on their religious/spiritual involvement. As one older female inmate stressed:

> When I receive news of the loss of a loved one, I cannot do the normal things that free citizens do to honor the deceased while letting go too. We cannot have farewell parties, funeral services. Nor can we make connections with others, share tears, laughter, memories, comfort foods or a stiff drink. Typically we receive no condolences even from the administration. Since we must go through the grieving process alone, many of us turn to religion to fill a critical void. I say goodbye to the deceased inmates I have known by paying a private tribute to them in song celebrating and lifting them up with "I'll fly away."
>
> (Aday, Krabill, & Deaton-Owens, 2014)

Moreover, bereavement literature identifies the following measures of religiosity as effective in adjusting to loss: 1) general religiosity, 2) group affiliation, 3) service attendance, 4.) beliefs (i.e., afterlife), 5) social support, and 6) coping mechanisms while identifying a need to further explore how aspects such as forgiveness (i.e., of self, God, others) impact the survivor's well-being and quality of life (Wortmann & Park, 2008). Older women with histories of trauma or abuse, in particular, report a therapeutic value from spiritual seeking, re-assessing God's will for their lives, joining religious communities, and confiding in others who share their faith (Bowland, Biswas, Kyriakakis, & Edmond, 2011).

Conclusions

As the number of aging prisoners continues to expand worldwide, policymakers must increase sensitivity to the unique experiences members of this population face in times of crisis and loss. Consideration, without question, must be given to the diverse needs of older women who are losing external and internal supports while incarcerated. Encouragement and assistance, whenever feasible, should be given to inmates to permit them to spend time with loved ones throughout the entire process. Under circumstances when logistical or pragmatic constraints would not be conducive to travel or face-to-face contact, correctional facilities should seriously consider the development and implementation of new, innovative policies such as video-conferencing or web-based approaches to correspondence. Although communicating with terminally ill relatives before death (or other survivors following the event) via distance does not allow for the human expression of emotion through touch, this alternative to personal visits does satisfy security and financial concerns while allowing offenders to place closure on important relationships.

Sensitivity should be given to the experiences of older women who are simultaneously trying to negotiate losses within the contexts of their pre-incarceration, incarceration, and post-incarceration identities. Despite the tendency to concentrate exclusively on responding to bereavement for one death (typically the physical death) at a time as it occurs, expanding the parameters of how loss is conceptualized to include other losses outlined in this chapter will undoubtedly prove invaluable. Further research is undoubtedly necessary to examine the extent to which older incarcerated women benefit from interventions such as treatment for Post-Traumatic Stress Disorder, individual and group counseling, religious/spiritual activities, and physical exercise. As correctional personnel who work directly with survivors best understand the institutional culture, they are considered "the most powerful change agents" and should be consulted in developing and implementing new interventions (Loeb, Penrod, Hollenbeak, & Smith, 2011). Although clinicians practicing in every environment, to some extent, disenfranchise grief (Simpson, 2013), staff training is needed for medical, mental health, security, and other personnel to better understand how explicit and implicit policy that encourages inmates to maintain a "tough exterior" or "do their own time" inhibits a successful resolution of grief following loss. Additional training, in particular, should educate staff on the intersection between age and gender-related needs (Aday & Krabill, 2011; Jolley, Kerbs, & Linder, 2014).

Even in institutions constrained by limited resources, opportunities can and should be available to disseminate general information about bereavement, grief, and mourning. Without personnel, finances, space, and time to offer specialized programming, members of this population should be encouraged to educate themselves about practical strategies they can engage in to restore order following trying circumstances. Taylor and Ferszt's (2001) pamphlet, *When Death Enters Your Life* and Welo's (1999) workbook *Life Beyond Loss: A Workbook for Incarcerated Men* both intend to educate incarcerated populations about the most common physiological and psychological responses to stress. The first, for example, outlines observable symptoms inmates frequently endure following the event, personalizes the experience with quotes from actual inmates, and actively encourages the bereaved to participate in funerals or other rituals, like journaling, confiding in others, and making time in private whenever possible for themselves (even cry, as needed) to facilitate adjustment. The second, on the other hand, provides inmates with various exercises they can complete in a self-paced format to initiate healing and serves as a foundation for self-discovery and growth.

In concluding our discussion on grief and loss, the authors strongly encourage personnel to comprehensively assess each inmate upon admission for special needs related to losses incurred prior to incarceration and use results as the foundation upon which services will be rendered. It has been recommended that administrators adopt a case management approach to determining the person-environment fit and developing social programming for older incarcerated adults (Aday & Krabill, 2011). Baseline assessments, without question, should include documentation of special needs of non-death losses such as poverty, histories of victimization, addictions, physical and mental health conditions. Follow-up assessments to determine special challenges that may be ongoing during incarceration are imperative to assist older women in coping with the myriad of losses that occur throughout the duration of the sentence.

Finally, the re-evaluation of policies (e.g., emergency furloughs) that would most likely inhibit or delay grief reactions is necessary as are procedures used in informing inmates of unanticipated, traumatic life events. Careful monitoring of older women in the aftermath of death is certainly necessary, with an individualized approach to treating them essential to healing. For offenders who will eventually be released to resume roles in mainstream society during later adulthood, some degree of consideration and preparation must be given to the losses likely to be encountered in the transition. Community re-entry, for example, is often associated with a profound sense of loss of a predictable structure and routine for older adults who have, over time, experienced institutional dependency. Although correctional personnel are limited by available resources in the amount of time, practical assistance, and emotional support they can extend to grieving offenders, creating the conditions for offenders to work through the grieving process is essential to prison adaptation.

Key Terms

Depersonalization—in the context of this chapter, refers to the treatment of individuals as if they are not people or worthy of the same respect and value as other members of a society.

Delayed grief—a defense mechanism characterized by intentional decisions survivors make to postpone grief until they have the time, space, and resources to fully process the loss.

Disenfranchised grief—individual's experience of loss is unacknowledged or unsupported both within their sub-cultures and within the larger society. This may be associated with others' perceptions of the individual (e.g., on the margins of society), the relationship with the deceased (viewed by others as peripheral or stigmatized), or the type of loss (e.g., pet loss, divorce).

Questions for Reflection

1. The author acknowledges a societal tendency for minimal empathy toward those who are incarcerated. Take a moment to reflect on your own attitude toward those in prison. How do your attitudes/beliefs affect your response as you read this chapter?

2. One obstacle to grieving behind bars is the fact that prisoners face policies restricting their access to rituals (i.e., funerals, memorial services, cemetery visits), memorabilia from the deceased, space and privacy to grieve, and safe forums for ventilation, self-disclosure, and social support.

Consider your own experience with bereavement. To what extent has access to/ participation in these activities been important in your own grief? How might your grief experience have differed if you had been excluded from these?

References

Aday, R. H., & Krabill, J. J. (2011). *Women aging in prison: A neglected population in the correctional system*. Boulder, CO: Lynne Rienner Press.
Aday, R. H., Krabill, J. J., & Deaton-Owens, D. (2014). Religion in the lives of older women serving life in prison. *Journal of Women and Aging, 26*(3), 238–256.
Alladin, T., Tresdale-Moore, S., & Gabbidon, S. L. (2008). An analysis of state-level correctional policies for emergency releases for deathbed visits and funeral attendance. *Professional Issues in Criminal Justice, 3*(4), 83–103.
Attig, T. (2004). Disenfranchised grief revisited: Discounting hope and love. *Omega: Journal of Death and Dying, 49*(3), 197–215.
Bowland, S., Biswas, B., Kyriakakis, S., & Edmond, T. (2011). Transcending the negative: Spiritual struggles and resilience in older female trauma survivors. *Journal of Religion, Spirituality & Aging, 23*(4), 318–327.
Carp, S. V., & Schade, L. (1992). Tailoring facility programs to suit female inmates' needs. *Corrections Today, 54*(6), 152–159.
Carson, E. A., & Golinelli, D. (2013). *Prisoners in 2012: Trends in admissions and releases. 1991–2012*: Washington, DC: U.S. Department of Justice.
Clear, T. R., & N. A. Frost. (2014). *The punishment imperative*. New York, NY: NYU Press.
Corr, C. A. (1998). Enhancing the concept of disenfranchised grief. *Omega: Journal of Death and Dying, 38*(1), 1–20.
Corr, C. A. (2002). Revisiting the concept of disenfranchised grief. In K. Doka (Ed.), *Disenfranchised grief: New directions, challenges, and strategies for practice* (pp. 39–60). Champaign, IL: Research Press.
Deaton, D., Aday, R. H., & Wahidin, A. (2009–2010). The effects of health and penal harm on aging female prisoners' views of dying in prison. *Omega: Journal of Death and Dying, 60*(1), 51–70.
Deck, E. S., & Folta, J. R. (1989). The friend griever. In K. J. Doka (Ed.), *Disenfranchised grief: Recognizing hidden sorrow* (pp. 77–90). Lexington, MA: Lexington.
Dhami, M. K., Ayton, P., & Loewenstein, G. (2007). Adaptation to imprisonment: Indigenous or imported. *Criminal Justice and Behavior, 34*(8), 1085–1100.
Doka, K. J. (1989). *Disenfranchised grief: Recognizing hidden sorrow*. Lexington, MA: Lexington.
Doka, K. J. (2002). *Disenfranchised grief: New directions, challenges, and strategies for practice*. Champaign, IL: Research Press.
Doka, K. J., & Martin, T. L. (2010). *Grieving beyond gender: Understanding the ways men and women mourn*. New York, NY: Routledge.
Dyregov, K., Dyregov, A., & Johnsen, I. (2013). Participants' recommendations for the ideal grief group: A qualitative study. *Omega: Journal of Death and Dying, 67*(4), 363–377.
Fellner, J. (2012). *Old behind bars: The aging prison population in the United States*. New York, NY: Human Rights Watch.
Ferszt, G. G. (2002). Grief experiences of women in prison following the death of a loved one. *Illness, Crisis, and Loss, 10*(3), 242–254.
Ferszt, G. G., Salgado, D., DeFedele, S., & Levilee, M. (2009). House of healing: A group intervention for grieving women in prison. *Prison Journal, 89*(1), 49–64.
Finlay, I. G., & Jones, N. J. (2000). Unresolved grief in young offenders in prison. *The British Journal of General Practice, 50*(456), 569–570.

Foucault, M. (1995). *Discipline and Punish: The Birth of the Prison*. New York, NY: Vintage.
Genders, E., & Player, E. (1990). Women lifers: Assessing the experience. *Prison Journal, 80*(1), 46–57.
George, E. (2010). *A woman doing life: Notes from a prison for women*. New York, NY: Oxford University Press.
Ghesquiere, A., Shear, M. K., & Duan, N. (2013–14). Outcomes of bereavement care among widowed older adults with complicated grief and depression. *Journal of Primary Care and Community Health, 4*(4), 256–264.
Goffman, E. (1961). *Asylums: Essays on the social situation of mental patients and other inmates*. New York, NY: Anchor Books.
Greer, K. (2002). Walking an emotional tightrope: Managing emotions in a women's prison. *Symbolic Interaction, 25*(1), 117–139.
Ham, J. N. (1980). Aged and infirm male prison inmates. *Aging*, (July–August), 24–31.
Hammersley, P. & Ayling, D. (2006). Loss intervention project for adult male prisoners. *Prison Service Journal, 66*(1), 22–26.
Haney, C. (2006). *Reforming punishment: Psychological limits to the pains of imprisonment*. Washington, DC: American Psychological Association.
Haney, C. (2012). Prison effects in the age of mass incarceration. *Prison Journal*, doi: 10.1177/0032885512448604.
Harner, H. M., Hentz, P. M., & Evangelista, C. (2011). Grief interrupted: The experience of loss among incarcerated women. *Qualitative Health Research, 21*(4), 454–474.
Harrison, M. T. (2006). True grit: An innovative program for elder inmates. *Corrections Today, 68*(7), 46–49.
Higgins, D., & Severson, M. G. (2009). Community reentry and older adult offenders: Redefining social work roles. *Journal of Gerontological Social Work, 52*(8), 784–802.
Jewkes, Y. (2006). Loss, liminality and the life sentence: Managing identity through a disrupted life course. In A. Liebling & S. Maruna (Eds.), *Effects of imprisonment* (pp. 366–390). Portland, OR: Willan Publishing.
Johnsen, I., Dyregrov, A., & Dyregrov, K. (2010). Participants with prolonged grief—How do they benefit from grief group participation? *Omega: Journal of Death and Dying, 65*(2), 87–105.
Jolley, J. M., Kerbs, J. J., & Linder, J. F. (2014) Women and issues in care. In J. J. Kerbs & J. M. Jolley (Eds.), *Senior citizens behind bars: Challenges for the criminal justice system* (pp. 93–112). Boulder, CO: Lynne Rienner Press.
Jones, S. J., & Beck, E. (2007). Disenfranchised grief and nonfinite loss experienced by family of death row inmates. *Omega: Journal of Death and Dying, 54*(4), 281–299.
Junior, V. Y. (2003). Helping female inmates cope with grief and loss. *Corrections Today, 65*(3), 76–79.
Kerbs, J. J., & Jolley, J. M. (2009). A commentary on age segregation for older prisoners: Philosophical and pragmatic considerations for correctional systems. *Criminal Justice Review, 34*(1), 119–139.
Kerbs, J. J., & Jolley, J. M (2014). *Senior citizens behind bars: Challenges for correctional systems*. Boulder, CO: Lynne Rienner Press.
Kopera-Frye, K., Harrison, M. T., Iribarne, J., Dampsey, E., Adams, M., Grabreck, T., McMullen, T., Peak, K, McCown, W. G., & Harrison, W. O. (2013). Veterans aging in place behind bars: A structured living program that works. *Psychological Services, 10*(1), 79–86.
Krabill, J. J., & Aday, R.H. (2005). Exploring the social world of aging female prisoners. *Women & Criminal Justice, 17*(1), 27–55.
Lalive d'Epinay, C., Cavalli, S., & Guillet, S. (2009–2010). Bereavement in very old age: Impact on health and relationships of the loss of a spouse, a sibling, or a close friend. *Omega: Journal of Death and Dying, 60*(4), 301–325.
Lavigne-pley, C., & Lévesque, L. (1992). Reactions of the institutionalized elderly upon learning of the death of a peer. *Death Studies, 16*(5), 451–461.
Leach, R. M., Burgess, T., & Holmwood, C. (2008). Could recidivism in prisoners be linked to traumatic grief: A review of the evidence. *International Journal of Prisoner Health, 4*(2), 104–109.
Leigey, M. E., & Reed, K. L. (2010). A woman's life before serving life: Examining the negative pre-incarceration life events of female life-sentenced inmates. *Women & Criminal Justice, 20*(4), 302–322.
Leigey, M. E., & Hodge, J. F. (2012). Gray matters: Gender differences in the physical and mental health of older inmates. *Women & Criminal Justice, 22*(3), 289–308.
Leigey, M. E., & Ryder, M. A. (2015). The pains of permanent imprisonment: Examining perceptions of confinement among older life without parole inmates. *International Journal of Offender Therapy and Comparative Criminology, 59*(7), 726–742.
Levine, S. (2005). Improving end-of-life care of prisoners. *Journal of Correctional Health Care*, 11(4), 317–331.
Loeb, S. J., Penrod, J., Hollenbeak, C. S., & Smith, C. A. (2011). End-of-life care and barriers for female inmates. *Journal of Obstetric, Gynecologic, & Neonatal Nursing, 40*(4), 477–485.
Luke, K. P. (2002). Mitigating the ill effects of maternal incarceration on women in prison and their children. *Child Welfare, 81*(6), 929–949.

Maschi, T., Morgen, K., Zgoba, K., Courtney, D., & Ristow, J. (2011). Age, cumulative trauma and stressful life events, and Post Traumatic Stress symptoms among older adults in prison: Do subjective impressions matter? *Gerontologist, 51*(5), 675–686.

Maschi, T., Viola, D., Morgen, K., & Koskinen, L. (2013). Trauma and stress, grief, loss, and separation among older adults in prison: The protective role of coping resources on physical and mental health. *Journal of Crime and Justice, 38*(1), 113–136.

Negy, C., Woods, D. J., & Carlson, R. (1997). The relationship between female inmates' coping and adjustment in a minimum-security prison. *Criminal Justice and Behavior, 24*(2), 224–233.

Olsen, M. J., & McEwen, M. A. (2004). Grief counseling in a medium security prison. *Journal for Specialists in Group Work, 29*(2), 225–236.

Parkes, C. M. (1998). Coping with loss: Bereavement in adult life. *British Medical Journal, 316*, 850–859.

Parkes, C. M., & Weiss, R. S. (1983). *Recovery from bereavement*. New York, NY: Basic Books.

Poehlmann, J. (2005). Representations of attachment relationships in children of incarcerated mothers. *Child Development, 76*(3), 679-696. doi:10.1111/j.1467-8624.2005.00871.x

Pollock, J. M. (2005). *Prisons and prison life: Costs and consequences*. Los Angeles: Roxbury.

Prigerson, H. G., & Maciejewski, P. K. (2006). A call for sound empirical testing and evaluation of criteria for complicated grief proposed for DSM-V. *Omega: Journal of Death and Dying, 52*(1), 9–19.

Prigerson, H. G., Maciejewski, P. K., Reynolds, C. F., Bierhals, A. J., Newsom, J. T., Fasiczka, A., . . ., & Miller, M. (1995). Inventory of complicated grief: A scale to measure maladaptive symptoms of loss. *Psychiatry Research, 59*(1–2), 65–79.

Rando, T. (1993). The increasing prevalence of complicated mourning: The onslaught is just beginning. *Omega: Journal of Death and Dying, 26*(1), 43–59.

Raphael, B. (1983). *The anatomy of bereavement*. New York, NY: Basic Books.

Rizzo, V. M., & Toseland, R. W. (2005). What's different about working with older people in groups? *Journal of Gerontological Social Work, 44*(1–2), 5–23.

Roberto, K. A., & Stanis, D. I. (1994) Reactions of older women to the death of a close friend. *Omega: Journal of Death and Dying, 29*(1), 17–27.

Robson, P., and Walter, T. (2012). Hierarchies of loss: A critique of disenfranchised grief. *Omega: Journal of Death and Dying, 66*(2), 97–119.

Santos, M. G. (1995). Facing long-term imprisonment. In T. J. Flanagan (Ed.), *Long-term imprisonment: Policy, science, and correctional practice* (pp. 36–40). Thousand Oaks, CA: Sage.

Schetky, D. H. (1998). Mourning in prison: Mission impossible. *Journal of the American Academy of Psychiatry and Law, 26*(3), 383–391.

Simpson, J. E. (2013). Grief and loss: A social work perspective. *Journal of Loss and Trauma: International Perspectives on Stress & Coping, 18*(1), 81–90.

Sklar, F., & Hartley, S. T. (1990). Close friends as survivors: Bereavement patterns in a "hidden" population. *Omega: Journal of Death and Dying, 21*(2), 103–112.

Stevenson, R. G., & McCutchen, R. (2006). When meaning has lost its way: Life and loss behind bars. *Illness, Crisis & Loss, 14*(2),103–119.

Stoller, N. (2003). Space, place, and movement as aspects of health care in three women's prisons. *Social Science and Medicine, 56*(11), 2263–2275.

Sykes, G. (1958). *The society of captives: A study of a maximum security prison*. Princeton, NJ: Princeton University Press.

Tate, S., & Wahidin, A. (2013). Extraneare: Pain, loneliness, and the incarcerated female body. *Illness, Crisis, & Loss, 21*(3), 203–217.

Taylor, P., & Ferszt, G. (2001). *When death enters your life: A grief pamphlet for people in prisons or jails*. Philadelphia, PA: National Prison Hospice Association.

Toseland, R. W. (1995). *Group work with the elderly and family caregivers*. New York, NY: Springer Publishing.

Townsend, P. (1962). *The last refuge*. London: Routledge.

van Wormer, K. (2001). *Counseling female offenders and victims: A strengths-restorative approach*. Springer series on family violence. New York, NY: Springer.

Vera, M. (2007). Social dimensions of grief. In C. Bryant (Ed.), *Handbook on death and dying* (pp. 838–846). Thousand Oaks, CA: Sage.

Versalle, A., & McDowell, E. E. (2004). The attitudes of men and women concerning gender differences in grief. *Omega: Journal of Death and Dying, 50*(1), 53–67.

Wahidin, A. (2004). *Older women in the criminal justice system: Running out of time*. London: Jessica Kingsley.

Wahidin, A., & Aday, R. H. (2013). Older female prisoners in the U.K. and U.S.: Finding justice in the criminal justice system. In M. Mulloch (Ed.), *Women, punishment, community sanctions: Human rights and social justice* (pp. 65–78). London: Routledge Press.

Welo, B. (1999). *Life beyond loss: A workbook for incarcerated men.* Alexandria, VA: American Correctional Association.

Wilson, M. (2011). Exploring the efficacy of a bereavement support group for male category C prisoners. *Bereavement Care, 30*(3), 10–16.

Wortmann, J. L., & Park, C. L. (2008). Religion and spirituality in adjustment following bereavement: An integrative review. *Death Studies, 32*(8), 703–736.

Young, V. C. (2003). Helping female inmates cope with grief and loss. *Corrections Today, 65*(3), 76–79.

13

Grief and Developmental Disabilities

Considerations for Disenfranchised Populations

Rebecca S. Morse, Theodore T. Hoch, and Thomas Freeman

"George" was a 54-year-old man who lived his entire life in a suburban home with his mother, who had just turned 84. His father had died six years earlier. George passed time in his basement, watching home movies of family vacations or playing games on the family's antiquated computer. Occasionally, George's mother would hire an employee from a regional congregate care facility to ride the trains of the local public transit system with George. They would ride to the end of the line and back again, for up to six hours at a time. Employed at a sheltered workshop, George spent his time sitting through group activities such as chair exercises or discussions of current events. Uninterested in these activities, George did not participate. George was always impeccably dressed and well-groomed—his mother always ensured that his personal hygiene was maintained. Although George was able to shower himself, his mother continued to shave his face, brush his teeth, apply his deodorant, and comb his hair. She laid out his clothing for him. She cared for his laundry and she shopped, cooked, cleaned, and cared for all of George's daily needs. George and his mother were content with this arrangement.

George's mother died suddenly and unexpectedly. Life changed quickly and drastically for him. He was temporarily placed in several emergency shelters, and then placed in a group home. The home had a good reputation and the staff provided George competent residential service. Despite this good quality care, the staff were not equipped to give him the level of personal care that his mother previously provided. Instead, the residential program focused on teaching George to take care of his own personal needs. In the few years he lived in that home, George had to learn to brush his teeth, shave, comb his hair, and do all the other basic self-care activities of adulthood. He had to pack his lunch before leaving for work and help clear the table after dinner.

In George's new work setting, located closer to his group home, he is provided services related to developing work skills. His days now consist of doing actual work in the area of vocational tasks, and his pay depends on his daily productivity. His productivity remains consistently low, so he earns little money. George no longer rides trains, since his caregivers do not have time to accompany him and he never learned to ride trains on his own. Now, when those who have known George for years see him, they are saddened by his disheveled appearance coupled with a facial expression that nearly always reflects some combination of anxiety, confusion, and sadness.

George suffered a great loss, not only of his mother, but also in many other areas of his life as a result of her death and absence from several roles that she occupied in his life. He suffered these losses with no real professional assistance to aid in his adjustment or to advocate on his behalf so that he would receive maximum benefit from the new opportunities these life changes could offer. Instead, he remains perpetually stuck in hidden grief, and the people in his life do not seem to understand.

The field of *Thanatology* has researched characteristics of bereavement, and has identified supportive approaches to assist those trapped in a grief cycle to re-engage in life. This research has also addressed challenges facing adolescents and children in dealing with the death of a parent or other loved one. However, thanatology has not adequately identified challenges and needs of individuals with intellectual disabilities (ID) in dealing with death. These individuals comprise a hidden and underserved minority in this important area of social and clinical support—even though they often display some of the most limited repertoires of coping skills and abilities to deal with the death of a loved one (author observations). Well-designed research studies with this population are nearly non-existent. This may reflect a failure to understand the full and complex emotional life that these individuals can display to those who know them best—leading to a general but false conclusion that these individuals simply "do not know what is going on around them" due to their intellectual deficits. For people with ID, and for those who provide supportive care to them, death education and targeted grief support is all but non-existent (Cathcart, 1995; Emerson, 1977; Hollins & Esterhuyzen, 1997; Yanok & Beifus, 1993).

Over the last half century, the field of applied behavior analysis has made significant strides in helping improve lives of people with ID (Austin & Carr, 2000; Rojahn, Schroeder, & Hoch, 2008; Sundberg & Partington, 1998). Behavior analysis looks at behavior in its own right as the phenomenon of importance, not as a symptom of some internal state. Whether overt (such as our actions) or covert (such as our thoughts and feelings), behaviors are believed to be functionally related to events occurring both outside and inside the person, and are directly related to each individual's history of learning. Environmental events that affect behavior can occur immediately before (antecedent to) or after (consequences of) the behavior of interest.

The relationship between George and his mother was full of important antecedents and consequences. After his shower, for example, the bathroom was an antecedent for George's standing motionless while his mother completed his grooming and provided social consequences. After her death, the bathroom no longer functioned this way, and he was now faced with learning how to complete his grooming tasks, in his late fifties. Changes that result in a person's life after the death of a loved one are deep and profound, but also may be analyzed behaviorally.

The loss of a loved one represents many actual losses in terms of the survivor's experiences of daily life. Many activities that were once part of the daily routine are suddenly and permanently ended and can never be resumed. The survivor is repeatedly reminded of the person with whom s/he can never again interact. Certain events or objects evoke a need to talk to the deceased individual, but this cannot happen. This is a natural process of learning to live without the loved one and takes time. However, for people with ID, particular behavioral challenges may arise, primarily due to the limited behavioral repertoires that accompany ID. Many consequences that were previously provided by social interaction with the deceased are no longer available. Deprivation of interactions with the deceased loved one begins to grow in strength and can increase the probability of a variety of problems and other behaviors. Other antecedent environment-behavioral relationships are suddenly changed (e.g., a ringing phone on a Sunday afternoon that used to be a call from a survivor's deceased father may evoke an excited response—but lead to disappointment and possible behavioral issues when, of course, the father does not later arrive). Naturally, the behavior of the person with the ID undergoes profound and sometimes unpredictable changes, just as one would expect in anyone suffering a profound loss. But specific challenges are posed for those who have limited behavioral repertoires (and often limited reinforcers as well). A broad and significant research effort is now required to evaluate the nature of these challenges, and the best practices available to address these therapeutic needs.

To ascertain what level of comprehension is required for an individual to have a reality-based perception of death, one needs an instrument capable of capturing nuances of emotions and perceptions of death by those with ID. Grief can be a nebulous concept with variable behavioral characteristics even for adults within the range of typical intellectual functioning and emotional reactions. But for the sub-population of neuro-typical children, or the sub-population of children or adults with ID, characteristics of a complex grief response may not follow the same emotional trajectory as in the typical adult, and may manifest as apparently unrelated maladaptive behaviors and mannerisms (Childers & Wimmer, 1971; Emerson, 1977; Hollins & Esterhuyzen, 1997; Sternlicht, 1980). Caregivers may not identify a correlation between problem behavior of an individual with ID and bereavement that the individual may be experiencing, especially if those behaviors occur days or even weeks after the loss. This lack of understanding can lead to frustration and confusion on the part of the caregiver, and inadequate care from even the most well-intentioned staff and family members (Cathcart, 1995; MacHale & Carey, 2002).

What follows is an examination of several studies that have attempted to gain insight into the important questions relating to bereavement in individuals with ID—and a brief discussion of potentially useful research to provide additional insights and increasingly effective support. Most current, albeit limited, literature in this area has tried to assess the level of death awareness in individuals with ID in two ways. First, the individuals in question are given a "mental age equivalent" score (e.g., an adult may be said to be functioning at the mental age of a 6-year-old). Second, one may try to draw a correlation between the individual's "death concepts" or awareness of death, and that individual's "life-experience equivalents" (Bihm & Elliott, 1982; Lipe-Goodson & Goebel 1983). Researchers Lipe-Goodson and Goebel (1983) examined percentage of life lived in an institution, and individual's age, gender, and IQ as independent variables. They did not find statistically significant effects pertaining to gender or percentage of life institutionalized, but found a correlation between the life experience the individual had with aging and death awareness. However, they did not control for "the number of deaths experienced" by each participant, and thus may have missed some potentially significant results. But they do conclude that, "regardless of age, those individuals with higher IQs did tend to demonstrate higher levels of both age and death concept development" (Lipe-Goodson & Goebel, 1983).

Other studies do not consider IQ, but instead consider an individual's Piagetian stage of development (e.g., *pre-operational*, *concrete operational*, and *formal operational development*) when examining death awareness. Bihm and Elliot (1982) reported that subjects without a disability, in the *concrete operational* stage of development, "displayed significantly more accurate conceptions of death than the *pre-operational* subjects; however, the *concrete* and *formal* groups did not differ in their conceptions" (Bihm & Elliot, 1982, pp. 205–206). Few, if any, of the individuals with disabilities were able to demonstrate an understanding that they could conceptualize death on the cognitive level of formal operations (Bihm & Elliottt, 1982; Lipe-Goodson & Goebel, 1983; Sternlicht, 1980).

However interesting these findings are, they do not appear to get to the heart of the matter—what do people *do* in the face of such severe losses, and especially how do individuals with limited behavioral repertoires cope? Perhaps work on "conceptualizations of death" will have a positive impact on these individuals, but first, we must evaluate what grief and bereavement may look like for people with ID and how we measure the scope of the problem.

The following story may demonstrate the difficulty in using such terms as "conceptions of death" and "cognitive understanding" when discussing the effect of grief, and trying to develop a clinical approach to bereavement among individuals with ID.

"Gerald" was a 49-year-old gentleman living in a congregate care facility. He was placed in an institution when he was three years old due to intense and chronic self-injury. In the 46 years that followed, he learned a great deal, including how to dress, feed, and shower, by himself. He also learned to speak, albeit with a relatively simple verbal repertoire. Gerald received psychiatric, behavior analysis, speech, occupational therapy, and other therapeutic services designed to reduce his problem behavior and increase his functional independence. Through the years, Gerald's parents visited him every Saturday, like clockwork. After some difficulties in the early days, he became relaxed and content whenever his parents were with him. Gerald's mother was diagnosed with cancer and she had to stop visiting, although his father continued. When she died, his family and other caregivers decided that Gerald would not attend her funeral. Weeks after the funeral, Gerald's father explained to him what had happened, and why his mother stopped visiting him. Until that moment, no one had ever explained to Gerald why his mother stopped visiting. Gerald's father continued to visit, and his own health attendant accompanied when his health began to fail. After Gerald's father died, Gerald's siblings and caregivers determined that Gerald should attend his father's funeral. Two of Gerald's residential staff accompanied him to the funeral, and he left immediately after the service. Sunday visits continued, with his brother, sister, and/or occasionally several siblings at once; although they occurred sporadically and less often as time passed. As happened throughout Gerald's life, the level of his self-injury varied, in both frequency and intensity. Additionally, following his father's death, Gerald began refusing to attend work, and a new behavior, property destruction, began to occur with increasing frequency. His residential and vocational staff did their best to support him through these times, while his medical professionals repeatedly altered the medications used (with limited success) to address his increasing behavioral difficulties. These behavioral changes may indeed have been related to loss of his parents (Harper & Wadsworth, 1993; MacHale & Carey, 2002). Perhaps it was the reduced frequency of the treasured Sunday visits with family—or perhaps just the accumulation of loss (bereavement overload), and the profound changes in the predictability of his life. We cannot know precisely, but there are significant hints in this story that bereavement and grief played at least some part in Gerald's eventual behavioral deterioration, even though that deterioration was delayed in its manifestation.

In order to derive an understanding of the depth of death comprehension of people with ID, studies have used both overt and covert methods. Lipe-Goodson and Goebel (1983) detailed a number of more elegant and deceptive studies that implemented a theoretical model by which researchers prompted participants of different cognitive levels and chronological ages to sort a series of pictures of people according to their age group, as perceived by the individuals doing the sorting. Lipe-Goodson and Goebel (1983) provide a justification for replicating a similar study:

> Professionals working with mentally retarded adults have become increasingly sensitive to the need for programs directed toward them and toward improving recognition of changes which take place with age, development of age appropriate behaviors, and the awareness of the impending death of friends, family, and self along with a comprehension of death.
> (Lipe-Goodson & Goebel, 1983, p. 68)

In the same 1983 study, participants arranged a series of pictures of individuals into categories based on age groups, first sorting the pictures of individuals of the same-sex, then pictures of the opposite sex. After this task was completed, the examiner laid out cards with pictures of persons of the same-sex as the participant into a linear array based on increasing chronological age, and then asked the individual to select the card which most closely matched his or her own age. In this way, researchers sought to establish how the individual saw her/himself in relation to the ages of others of the same-sex. Perhaps this activity could even lead to a discussion of aging, and by extension, death. This study also used a more conventional method of ascertaining death perception (Bihm

& Elliot, 1982; Sigelman, Budd, Winer, Schoenrock, & Martin, 1982; Sternlicht, 1980) by evaluating the individual's verbal expression of death awareness through expressive language. Verbal behavior based studies in this area have various designs; however, a cursory review of these studies reveals that most researchers use techniques such as *word association* reactivity, by looking for increased anxiety in the presence of death-related words (e.g., *cemetery*) or by posing a series of death-related questions, such as those listed below:

> What makes things die?
> How can you make dead things come back to life?
> When will you die?
> What will happen then?
>
> (Sternlicht, 1980, p. 157)

Although such questions may appear profoundly simple, participants' answers may allow researchers to categorize that individual along some developmental scale as is often done with younger children. In fact, Sternlicht (1980) discovered that

> the pre-operational retarded Ss [subjects] did not have realistic concepts of when they will die, or of the permanence of death. They did, however, have realistic notions of how things die. It was also found that the types of replies made to these questions were related to their cognitive level.
>
> (p. 157)

Implications of such results are significant if one factors in the likelihood of increased fear that some individuals with ID have, resulting in increased anxiety. The level of increased fear felt by some individuals with ID is likely compounded by life circumstances, such as aging and death of primary caretakers (often parents), which thrusts grieving individuals into a new social reality, and often into an entirely new living environment, perhaps even into some form of institutionalization. This is even more likely if no close family member, friend, or guardian is available to care for that individual (Cathcart, 1995; Hollins and Esterhuyzen, 1997).

Perhaps equally problematic, the individual with ID is often excluded from all death-related activities and preparations (known as the "death surround") prior to death of a primary caregiver. Thus, following a caregiver's death, changes occur in the individual's lifestyle and environment in ways totally beyond the individual's control, influence, or even allowance to state an opinion. This increases fear and subsequent anxiety that an individual experiences (Cathcart, 1995; Hollins & Esterhuyzen, 1997; McHale & Carey, 2002), and may lead to increases in problem behaviors (Summers & Witts, 2003).

Fear and anxiety are difficult emotional experiences for everyone. Sometimes grieving persons experience "out-of-control" feelings, and these may be exacerbated when one has limited skills in coping with strong emotional states. This may be considered analogous to reactions of a young child who has limited life experience and no learning history in this area. Thus, children (or adults with ID) are likely to demonstrate: a) little or no understanding of what is happening to them, given failure of their assumptive model of the world, b) very limited expressive language regarding thoughts or feelings (and similarly, a reduced likelihood that they will engage in appropriate receptive responses to whatever they may be told), and finally c) an inadequate learning history to understand immediate consequences and ramifications of death—permanency, universality, and irreversibility (Lipe-Goodson & Goebel, 1983; Sternlicht, 1980).

Unlike most children, adults with ID are often likely to require professional support, and even training in learning *how* to grieve in a socially appropriate and adaptive way. Staff reports from residential and vocation service facilities for individuals with ID often contain stories of previously calm and generally well-socialized individuals who suffer loss of a loved one and suddenly become agitated or even violent "out of the blue," and who may not necessarily respond to previously successful assistance techniques (Emerson, 1977; Hollins & Esterhuyzen, 1997; MacHale & Carey, 2002; Yanok & Beifus, 1993). "Staff and carers did not usually attribute behavior problems to bereavement and its concomitant life events, nor was there a recognition of psychopathology due to bereavement" (Hollins & Esterhuyzen, 1997). Although one might argue with use of the term "psychopathology," the quote nonetheless demonstrates the fact that persons with ID are often profoundly underestimated in terms of awareness of what is going on around them, while their internal and emotional lives are often trivialized or simply ignored, leading to a disenfranchised grief (Doka, 1989).

A more recent study by Hollins and Esterhuyzen (1997) examined post-loss-through-death behaviors of adults with ID enrolled in day centers. These researchers expressed concern that, "the majority of carers at the day centers did not subjectively perceive the bereaved client's behavior to be affected by the bereavement, in spite of the fact that, objectively, there were significant differences between bereaved and control groups" (p. 500). They emphasized, "Many people with learning disabilities have difficulties with communication, and if they are unable to express themselves verbally, they may be treated as though they experience no feelings" (p. 497). Yanok and Beifus (1993) argue that some professionals may hold the idea that the individual with ID does not understand or "feel" grief in the same way as one who does not have a disability. They go on to identify these as rationalizations, and while they "may serve to simplify the professional responsibilities of practitioners, they conversely can exacerbate the levels of anxiety, distress, and depression experienced by a bereaving student or client" (p. 144).

While the death of one close to a person with ID often correlates with increased depression and anxiety in the individual, and to other well-defined and quantifiable behavioral problems, Stoddart, Burke, and Temple (2002) report that an eight-week course of "bereavement therapy" proved helpful for participants in their study, all of whom displayed some level of ID. Participants included 14 people diagnosed with various levels of ID and seven others who demonstrated borderline intellectual functioning. Each experienced at least one loss of a family member or roommate within the last ten years. Participants who completed the course of bereavement therapy showed declines in depression ratings from pre- to post-therapy assessments. While these results are preliminary, and this experiment would benefit from quantification of specific behaviors rather than use of ratings scales as the independent variable measure, this study nonetheless indicates that direct therapeutic intervention and training may truly help people with intellectual deficits cope more effectively with grief and bereavement.

One loss unique to many individuals with ID is that of a housemate in a group home. Unlike a typical roommate situation, where individuals have autonomy to express their grief around loss and can choose to connect with the deceased's family, or may be included in the funeral/memorial, surviving individuals with ID may be excluded from many or even all important social opportunities that occur throughout the bereavement process. For example, the individual may not be invited to participate in discussions relating to the impending death and/or funeral or memorial planning for that individual. Such dis-inclusions may result from a compassionate but misplaced desire to shield the surviving individual from sadness. Perhaps the family would find the presence of the surviving friend uncomfortable, or if the death is impending, fear that the individual's presence may "possibly upset" the dying individual. These exclusions, and other factors, may further the disenfranchisement of the grief experience for surviving individuals with ID, who may then suffer a more complicated, conflicted grief.

Cathcart (1995) suggested that some individuals living in a group setting may feel closer to the deceased than to their own family members. If this is the case, there is an increased level of importance for individuals to be more fully integrated in the *death surround* process. The family of the deceased may be unaware of this need, or may be simply dismissive of it, understandably focused on their own loss. However, Cathcart (1995) identifies another factor in such situations which may help alleviate some problems. Residential staff are very likely to feel grief over the death of someone who has been in their care. However, even as they cope with their own sense of loss, they are likely well aware of relationships that have developed in the home over the years. Moreover, they are almost certain to be sensitive to the likely (or already occurring) behavioral reactions of each of the housemates. With this knowledge and sensitivity, they are in the best position to gently communicate news of the death to those living in the home, while providing ongoing support. They may also help facilitate inclusion of those housemates who most need to be involved in the *death surround* process. However, facilitating such inclusion is likely to require considerable social finesse and even specialized training for staff.

Our society has recognized the need for early intervention programs, individualized education plans (IEP), individualized habilitation plans (IHP), vocational rehabilitation, and many other services for individuals with various delays and deficits. These services are meant to foster independence and autonomy as they enable persons of various functional levels to reach their full potential, through training in verbal and interpersonal skills, coping mechanisms, activities of daily living, and a wide variety of other skills which we all need to function throughout our day.

In death education and awareness, needs of individuals in various groups are being studied and at least partially met (e.g., family caregivers losing a family member after a long illness, spouses suffering a sudden loss). Considerable research has focused on children losing a parent. Research concerning death awareness education for those with ID is rare at best, even though the needs of these individuals may be unique:

As this population of persons with developmental disabilities ages, new challenges will emerge for both specialists and educators in the areas of gerontology and developmental disabilities. Programs designed for mid-life persons with developmental disabilities will have to be modified to serve older adults. Senior services, too, will have to incorporate the needs of this unique population into their own plans and programs (Lavin & Doka, 1999, p. 1).

Thus, we see that a basic clinical and therapeutic need is not being met. A branch of death education must be dedicated to the study and delivery of services to individuals with ID and, in particular, to meeting the needs of adults in this population subgroup. Indeed, a person with ID must be prepared for the eventual death of a parent, loved one, or other caregiver. Individuals with ID often rely on such caregivers throughout their lives, and this type of loss, while predictable, may have a larger than typical impact on the life of the survivor. Planning for such losses would best begin at a reasonably early age, most likely by the very first IEP These services should continue through adulthood with reviews of progress at each IHP thereafter, where the need for specific training and eventual therapeutic supports can be regularly evaluated. Steady and reliable preparation would, by necessity, involve helping that person develop as many independent skills as possible (e.g., verbal/communication skills, money skills, travel skills, vocational skills, and of course, activity of daily living skills).

How might such an approach have affected George, the individual in our first brief case study? One viewpoint may be that George's transition to a life without his mother may have been fraught with less difficulty had he already been taught to brush his own teeth, shave himself, select his own clothing, and participate in housework and household maintenance. However, it is important to respect the values within his home and work from his current social location and abilities free of such judgment. Following the death of George's mother, working with him early on to find an appropriate and active vocational setting may have lessened some of the challenges related to dislocation that he must have experienced in moving to a new and much more independently functional work setting. Teaching him how to ride the train on his own—or helping him find friends with whom he could have ridden trains or participated in other leisure activities away from home—would have almost allowed for a sense of normalcy and continuity in some of his routines. When an individual loses so much at once, transition from grief back to a new and different life without the loved one can be considerably more difficult.

An adult who has not been exposed to the complete picture of the life–death trajectory can lose a great deal of his functional capabilities following death of a key caregiver, mainly due to lack of instruction. This individual has limited access to coping mechanisms on which to rely, and has little or no experience with the language needed to express one's needs or feelings in this area. Research has provocatively portrayed a general social system for dealing with death that has actually served to further handicap those already affected by intellectual disabilities, and who subsequently are forced to suffer more deeply when they are inevitably faced with the deaths of family members (Cathcart, 1995; Emerson, 1977; MacHale & Carey, 2002).

One might posit that through effective planning and proactive action on the part of primary caretakers, death education for an individual with a disability might begin with an exploration of an individual's experience with death to that point, and proceed into a discussion of what might happen if and when the primary caretaker is no longer around. The individual with ID should, within reason, be allowed and *encouraged* to actively participate in planning where, and with whom, they might live upon the caretaker's death. Through "rehearsal" of future events, something that could be overwhelming may be manageable if addressed one small piece at a time, and in a step-by-step fashion. It could begin with a non-specific discussion of aging (even with pets or other animals) and then move into the area of death. Human aging and death could be introduced in addition to a discussion of what happens to the deceased after death, in terms of funeral and burial rituals and any accompanying spiritual beliefs and practices. Finally, a discussion could begin to address those things that are likely to happen for the survivor (including both losses and any positive life changes that may be possible). Some related events can even be subject to "rehearsal," such as visiting the cemetery before the death, walking through the hospital, or even discussing some suggestions for the funeral ceremony (which were therapeutically effective in the experience of at least two of the authors). Including the individual in the dying process would also promote opportunities for instruction regarding age-appropriate behaviors for dealing with grief, while instilling the notion that experiencing difficult feelings related to death is permissible, normal (Cathcart, 1995), and also likely to be temporary.

Fortunately, death of a loved one or valued caregiver is an infrequent event for most people. This infrequency does not prevent us from helping prepare people with intellectual and developmental disabilities to meaningfully participate in the *death surround* and in the funeral process. Special educators, behavior analysts, and others who work with persons with intellectual disabilities often work to teach these individuals how to handle such rare but important events as fire drills, medical appointments, being approached by strangers, and even becoming lost in the community. In doing this, the instructor or therapist teaches the person many behaviors, such as moving quietly toward an exit, looking for a police officer, and dialing 911. To the extent that the instructor or therapist practices these behaviors with the student in an instructional situation that approximates the target situation, the behaviors are more likely to occur naturally in the actual target situation. Behaviors that are part of everyday activities may increase an individual's proficiency in them. In other words, when we identify behaviors that are beneficial and meaningful during the death surround, we may find that these same behaviors are part of other complex behaviors, which occur in other, more typical life situations. Teaching these behaviors to the student with ID, to a level of high proficiency in more frequently occurring situations, would provide regular practice for the person. This, in turn, would promote their use of these skills upon the actual occurrence of a death surround, assisting the individual with their transition to a life without the loved one.

Yanok and Beifus (1993) devised a curriculum to explore use of such a proactive death education program, which they termed *Communicating About Loss and Mourning* (CALM). This program uses a practical approach to death education, breaking more complex and abstract death concepts into specific lessons. The CALM curriculum is comprised of eight 50-minute sessions.

> Instructional outcomes for this affective educational program included the following: (a) The student will be able to distinguish between living organisms and inanimate objects within the natural environment; (b) The student will be able to demonstrate an understanding that all living things ultimately die; (c) The student will be able to demonstrate an understanding that death is a permanent condition; (d) The student will be able to demonstrate an awareness of fatal accidents, terminal illnesses, and natural causes of death; and (e) The student will be able to define pertinent spoken vocabulary words such as *burial, cemetery, deceased, funeral, mourning,* and *perish*.
>
> (p. 145)

Although similar strategies may not mitigate the grief experience, CALM or similar curricula may prevent those difficult circumstances which accompany the death of a caretaker from becoming overwhelming to the surviving individual. It provides a potentially useful tool in the individual's repertoire of coping mechanisms, which is often a repertoire comprised of far too few functional skills. An important feature of any such program is to include a component that stresses the falsehood of "magical thinking" in this context. Often an individual can become convinced that somehow a kind word or good deed can (and should be able to) heal the dying, or even bring back the dead. Even worse, some may come to believe that a random bad thought, angry exclamation, or just plain poor behavior played some kind of active role in the death of another person, a form of magical thinking (Yanok & Beifus, 1993). These types of thoughts can be destructive, and lead to inappropriate guilt and related behavior problems.

Instructional programs such as CALM can help incorporate the individual into the death surround process and may help the individual deal with the death of a loved one on a broader basis. In so doing, they not only assist the individual by increasing their adaptive functioning related to bereavement and grief, but also provide the person with a sense of independence and capability in facing death directly. This may help reduce the likelihood of anxiety reactions and depression relating to the concept of death in general, and may even assist the individual in coping with the idea of their own eventual death as a natural process.

Behavior analysts have made tremendous gains in the last 25 years helping people with disabilities and language delays learn to communicate (Michael, 1998). This therapeutic approach has become a standard treatment for children with autism (Higbee & Sellers, 2011; Kodak & Grow, 2011). It has also proven effective with other populations, including individuals with traumatic brain injuries (Sundberg, San Juan, Dawdy, & Arguelles, 1990), and even adults with significant intellectual disabilities. Early phases of this type of instruction typically target teaching functional responses, such as making requests (Shafer, 1994–1995; Yi, Christian, Vittimburga, & Lowenkron, 2006). Training quickly moves to naming or describing items and important environmental features (Gilic & Greer, 2011) and can eventually lead to conversation (Sundberg & Sundberg, 2011). Development of these skills can also lead to the development of highly functional self-management behaviors (Ferris & Fabrizio, 2009). In terms of importance of communication skills in the area of death education and bereavement, it should be clear that we are all more likely to make our way through the winding and sometimes dense forest of grief, while avoiding some significant dark detours along the path, when we can communicate to those closest to us our sense of loss and desolation. In so doing, we take power away from the darkness and more easily find the path back to the light.

Future research examining the death experience for people with ID might focus on identifying and building particular behavioral repertoires relevant to the *death surround* process, and to learning to fully engage in life again, following the death of a loved one. Skills that comprise these repertoires may be identified as well as the range of daily situations in which these behaviors are most likely to be exhibited. Identifying these skills and typical situations could result in frequent instruction occurring outside of the direct experience of death. Skills developed through this training might then generalize to situations in which one actually experiences the death (or impending death) of a parent or significant party. Additionally, researchers might examine existing instructional curricula currently in use with people with ID, to determine if those curricula could be adapted for use in death education contexts. Researchers should also examine methods for and effects of including individuals with ID in the death surround, as well as examining any delayed effects that may be likely to arise at some point in time after the actual date of the death of the loved one.

Needs of people with ID have been generally misunderstood, dismissed, or even ignored when it comes to our social approach to coping with death. We see this when we fail to allow the individual opportunities to say goodbye to a dying loved one; when we hold back information from the individual regarding the actual death; when we prevent the individual from attending the funeral; and when we fail to produce adequate research in behavioral and emotional correlates of the bereavement experience for individuals with ID. Perhaps by combining knowledge and continuing efforts from the fields of thanatology and applied behavior analysis, we can learn to assist these individuals in acquiring tools to more effectively cope with life's natural losses. We can also support persons with ID by helping them find ways to remember their loved ones as they continue their lives as fully as possible in their physical absence.

Key Terms

Death surround—all of the death-related activities and preparations associated with each death.
Intellectual disability—(may also be called intellectual developmental disability or IDD); generalized neurodevelopmental disorder characterized by significantly impaired intellectual and adaptive functioning. It is defined by an IQ score below 70 in addition to deficits in two or more adaptive behaviors that affect everyday activities and general living.
Secondary losses—losses that result from a primary, significant loss or event.

Questions for Reflection

1. "The loss of a loved one represents many actual losses in terms of the survivor's experience of daily life." Consider your own experiences of bereavement, and try to identify as many associated losses as you can. How does this help you to understand the experience of grief and loss for adults with intellectual disabilities?
2. How important is a "reality-based perception of death" in responding to the physical absence of a person who was formerly present? Do we need a new framework for discussing the grief experiences of adults whose intellectual disability may prevent full comprehension of death? Why or why not?
3. To what extent do you believe that increasing understanding of death for adults with intellectual disabilities (via instruction such as that provided by the CALM program) could improve coping mechanisms and reduce the risk of becoming overwhelmed when a death occurs? What other types of proactive death education do you believe might be helpful?

References

Austin, J., & Carr, J. E. (2000). *Handbook of applied behavior analysis.* Oakland, CA: Context Press.
Bihm, E. M., & Elliott, L. S. (1982). Conceptions of death in mentally retarded persons. *The Journal of Psychology, 111*(2), 205–210.
Cathcart, F. (1995). Death and people with learning disabilities: Interventions to support clients and carers. *British Journal of Clinical Psychology, 34*(2), 165–175.
Childers, P., & Wimmer, M. (1971). The concept of death in early childhood. *Child Development, 42*(4), 1299–1301.
Doka, K. J. (1989). *Disenfranchised grief: Recognizing hidden sorrows.* Lexington, MA: Lexington Books.
Emerson, P. (1977). Covert grief reaction in mentally retarded clients. *Mental Retardation, 15*(6), 46–47.
Ferris, K. J., & Fabrizio, M. A. (2009). Teaching analytical thinking skills to a learner with autism. *Journal of Precision Teaching and Celeration, 25,* 29–33.
Gilic, L., & Greer, R. D. (2011). Establishing naming in typically developing two-year-old children as a function of multiple exemplar speaker and listener experiences. *Analysis of Verbal Behavior, 27*(1), 157–177.
Harper, D. C., & Wadsworth, J. S. (1993). Grief in adults with mental retardation: Preliminary findings. *Research in Developmental Disabilities, 14*(4), 313–330.
Higbee, T. S., & Sellers, T. P. (2011). Verbal behavior and communication training. In J. L. Matson & P. Sturmey (Eds.), *International handbook of autism and pervasive developmental disorders: Autism and child psychopathology series* (pp. 367–379). New York, NY: Springer Science.
Hollins, S., & Esterhuyzen, A. (1997). Bereavement and grief in adults with learning disabilities. *British Journal of Psychiatry, 170*(6), 497–501.
Kodak, T., & Grow, L. L. (2011). Behavioral treatment of autism. In W. W. Fisher, C. C. Piazza, & H.S. Roane (Eds.), *Handbook of applied behavior analysis* (pp. 402–416). New York, NY: Guilford Press.
Lavin, C., & Doka, K. J. (1999). *Older adults with developmental disabilities.* Amityville, NY: Baywood.
Lipe-Goodson, P. S., & Goebel, B. L. (1983). Perception of age and death in mentally retarded adults. *Mental Retardation, 21*(2), 68–75.
MacHale, R., & Carey, S. (2002). An investigation of the effects of bereavement on mental health and challenging behavior in adults with learning disability. *British Journal of Learning Disabilities, 30*(3), 113.
Michael, J. (1998). The current status and future directions of the analysis of verbal behavior: Comments on the comments. *Analysis of Verbal Behavior, 15,* 157–161.
Rojahn, J., Schroeder, S. R., & Hoch, T. A. (2008). *Self-injurious behavior in intellectual disabilities.* New York, NY: Elsevier.
Shafer, E. (1994–1995). A review of interventions to teach a mand repertoire. *Analysis of Verbal Behavior, 12,* 53–66.
Sigelman, C. K, Budd, E. C., Winer, J. L., Schoenrock, C. J., & Martin, P. W. (1982). Evaluating alternative techniques of questioning mentally retarded persons. *American Journal of Mental Deficiency, 86*(5), 511–518.
Sternlicht, M. (1980).The concept of death in preoperational retarded children. *The Journal of Genetic Psychology, 137*(2), 157–164.
Stoddart, K. P., Burke L., & Temple, V. (2002). Outcome evaluation of bereavement groups for adults with intellectual disabilities. *Journal of Applied Research in Intellectual Disabilities, 15*(1), 28–35.
Summers, S. J., & Witts, P. (2003). Psychological intervention for people with learning disabilities who have experienced bereavement: A case study illustration. *British Journal of Learning Disabilities, 31*(1), 37–41.
Sundberg, M. L., & Partington, J. W. (1998). *Teaching language to children with autism or other developmental disabilities.* Pleasant Hill, CA: Behavior Analysts.
Sundberg, M. L., & Sundberg, C. A. (2011). Intraverbal behavior and verbal conditional discriminations in typically developing children and children with autism. *Analysis of Verbal Behavior, 27*(1), 23–43.
Sundberg, M. L., San Juan, B., Dawdy, M., & Arguelles, M. (1990). The acquisition of tacts, mands, and intraverbals by individuals with traumatic brain injury. *Analysis of Verbal Behavior, 8,* 83–99.
Yanok, J., & Beifus, J. A. (1993). Communicating about loss and mourning: Death education for individuals with mental retardation. *Mental Retardation, 31*(3), 144–147.
Yi, J. I., Christian, L., Vittimburga, G., & Lowenkron, B. (2006). Generalized negatively reinforced manding in children with autism. *Analysis of Verbal Behavior, 22*(1), 21–33.

14

Social Expectations of the Bereaved[1]

Darcy L. Harris

Jim is a 57-year-old man whose wife, Susan, died a year ago after a lengthy struggle with cancer. They had been married for almost 35 years. Jim was devastated by the loss of Susan. He had worked as a high school teacher for over 30 years. After Susan's death, he took a leave of absence from teaching because he was unable to concentrate and he could not focus on his work well. He found that most of his male friends were uncomfortable around him, and their talk about sports and general banter made him feel worse. Many of them suggested that the answer to his problems was to "drink more beer and get involved in watching hockey." Jim was deeply lonely. He hated eating alone and the house they shared felt very empty. He sometimes would go to the closet and run his hands through Susan's clothes that were still there. He found it difficult to sleep in the bed he had shared with Susan, so he now slept on the couch in front of the TV, which would stay on all night, providing him with noise and distraction so that he could sleep and not feel so alone. When he went to see a grief counselor, he said that he wanted help to "stop wallowing in self-pity" so that he could get back to work and "get on with things."

One day, Jim ran into one of Susan's friends at the grocery store. She invited him to join a group of Susan's girlfriends for coffee the next week. It turned out that they met every week at the same place, and they had supported each other after Susan died. Jim joined them the next week and felt immediate relief that they all liked to talk about Susan and they seemed to be struggling with her loss in the same way that he was. After a few months of meeting regularly with Susan's girlfriends, Jim asked one of the single women if she would like to go to a movie with him. She seemed put off by his request and said that she didn't think it was appropriate to go out with him. After this incident, Jim sensed the women were more cautious around him and that several of them seemed to distance themselves from him. Jim felt lost. He couldn't relate to his old buddies and he didn't know how to just "be friends" with the women with whom he had shared his deepest thoughts and feelings. He felt a great deal of pressure to return to work, with the principal of his school calling him at one point and telling him that he needed to just "get over it and move on." It was suggested that maybe he should ask his doctor for antidepressant medication. The question he kept asking the grief counselor was, "Am I normal"?

This chapter originally began as a point of intersection between a scholarly exploration of social influences on bereavement and the real-life issues that arose in my clinical practice setting with clients who were bereaved. Over time, I have found that one of the more common questions that clients raise in the context of grief counseling is how they *should* grieve after a significant loss (i.e., what is *normal*?) Clients frequently report distress over not just the loss(es) they have experienced, but also to their responses to these losses. Sadly, the distress is often magnified by how these responses are perceived by others with whom they interact on a daily basis, including family, friends, coworkers, and healthcare practitioners. Upon reflection, I realized that much of my work as a grief counselor has been spent attempting to normalize grief responses that are deemed as problematic by unrealistic social norms and expectations, trying to find ways to allow grief to unfold rather than supporting its suppression, and attempting to re-frame the pathology-based approach to grief that seems prevalent in Western society. I've observed many of my grieving clients in a sort of paralysis, caught between attempts to try to conform to unwritten social rules about grief versus entering into the grieving process as it actually needs to manifest in their lives after significant losses. As a result of this reflection on grief and social rules, I wanted to uncover and explore the social context in which grieving individuals have to function in order to help them to better understand themselves, and to hopefully feel a greater sense of freedom and empowerment in the midst of their grief. What follows is my attempt to delve into the social construct of grief as it is experienced in Western-oriented, capitalistic societies.

Death and Loss: A Critical Analysis

Although initially focused on small groups that were mostly white and middle class, bereavement research has broadened in the last 25 years to include many diverse groups of grievers and types of losses, and attempts have been made to engage with the larger social context and underlying assumptions that are part of the response to death and loss in Western society (Breen & Connor, 2007; Irish, Lundquist, & Nelson, 2014; Ng, 2005). There is now awareness that children grieve differently than adults and that their grief is often misunderstood because it is different (Dyregrov, 2008; Oltjenbruns, 2001; Silverman, 2000). The role of gender socialization in grief responses after a significant loss is also better understood (Doka & Martin, 2010; Hockey, 1997; Lund, 2001). It is now known that grief may continue for a long time and, in fact, that it is very common for a relationship to continue with a deceased loved one (Klass, Silverman, & Nickman, 1996). It is also understood that there is a wide variance in how people respond to loss based upon many factors that are both external and internal (Sanders, 1999; Stroebe, Hansson, & Stroebe, 2001: Worden, 2009). However, despite research and anecdotal accounts that confirm the normalcy of many diverse responses to loss, social expectations of uniformity (and conformity) are still placed upon bereaved individuals in current Western society.

Because I see the empowerment of bereaved clients in their subjective experiences as a crucial part of my work, I looked for a framework that incorporates power dynamics into social analysis. I began with critical theory, as it examines social norms and conditions in order to identify and expose power, control, and oppression in various contexts. Oppression is defined as the act of using power to empower and/or grant privilege to a group at the expense of disempowering, marginalizing, silencing, and subordinating another group (Brown, 1994). The root of the word oppression is the key element, *press*. The experience of oppressed people is that the living of one's life is confined by barriers which are not accidental; therefore, they are unavoidable. These barriers are also systematically related to each other in such a way that they feed into each other, resulting in restrictions or penalties for anyone who attempts to circumvent them (Frye, 1998).

One of the cornerstones of critical theory is that knowledge is power. It is assumed that when oppressive forces are identified and understood, the potential exists to enact change, which will allow freedom from these forces (Littlejohn, 1992; Schieman & Plickert, 2008). A critical analysis in a social context will almost always include questions about the ways in which inclusion and exclusion criteria (understood as social norms) serve the interests of the dominant group (which supports an ideology or basic belief held by the elite within a particular social structure). In turn, a critical analysis will also examine how the dominant group utilizes these inclusion/exclusion criteria to oppress those who do not fit into these categories as a means of maintaining dominance (Brookfield, 2005). The underlying premise of this exploration is that if we are aware of the factors that influence our perceptions of an experience, we have the opportunity to consciously act and respond with intentionality and purpose, rather than to simply react or follow rote patterns without reflection. Critical theorists emphasize reflexivity, or the human capacity to reflect upon our history and our actions, as essential for liberating social change (D'Cruz, Gillingham, & Melendez, 2007; Swenson, 1998). In the context of bereavement, dissecting out social and cultural expectations of how bereaved individuals are expected to respond to loss (i.e., how they *should* respond) from the actual reality of their loss experience (how they *actually do* respond) provides an ability to normalize the human response to loss without the oppressive factor of shame and the inhibition caused by external social constraints which may have the potential to suppress adaptive, but socially uncomfortable or stigmatized responses.

For the purpose of this chapter, a working definition of grief will be utilized rather than a theoretical one. Thus, grief will be simply defined as the highly unique, personal response to loss (Harris, 2014). This definition allows for the inclusion of all aspects of the grief response (i.e., emotional, social, cognitive, physical, behavioral, etc.) by focusing on the loss experience as identified subjectively by an individual rather than a specific type of response to be explored, or the internal/external mechanisms which may mediate the grief response (i.e., attachment style, coping style, method of death). This response to loss occurs within the social construction of what is viewed acceptably as "normal" grief in Western society. The use of the term *society* rather than *culture* is intentional. A society is an economic, social, and industrial infrastructure in which a varied multitude of people or peoples are a part, and members of a given society may consist of many different cultural and ethnic groups (Jenkins, 2002). This exploration focuses on the dominant group's views of death and grief within a given society rather than upon those of the specific cultural traditions or ethnic groups of which a society may be comprised.

In general, Western society is basically described as a death-denying and product-driven society whose foundation rests upon capitalism and patriarchal hierarchies in all significant social institutions (Wood & Williamson, 2003). Individuals who are terminally ill are often viewed with pity for their dependency, and avoided by many due to their representation of mortality and inability to control life, serving as a reminder that all of us will eventually die. Death is typically viewed as the failure of medical technology and a source of shame (Reynolds, 2002). This foundation sets the stage for how bereaved individuals are perceived and the standards of acceptability for mourning after a loss.

There are several social rules for grieving in most Western societies that are not stated explicitly, but which are widely known and recognized. These social rules identify who, in a given society, is granted the privilege of any exemption from roles and responsibilities as a result of a socially recognized condition that is legitimized through a political structure or authority figure, such as a physician.

For example, Parsons (1951) described the concept of the *sick role* as a status that is granted by a physician to a patient who is deemed unwell. In response for being diagnosed as "legitimately" sick and therefore relieved of social responsibilities, the patient is also expected to comply with the rules of the sick role, which include following the doctors' treatment recommendations and attempting to get better as quickly as possible. The use of "doctors' notes," which serve to excuse individuals from work, from certain responsibilities, or which give specific benefits to the recipients (such as tax deductions for items that are deemed medically necessary) underscores the power and legitimization of physicians in this society.

Exclusions from work and social responsibilities are legitimized through social rules, as well as the granting of special social support by identification with the prescribed role of mourning in losses that meet the criteria of acceptability. These rules are not posted on the doors of funeral homes and religious centers; they are implicit and imbued with a great amount of power in their ability to ascribe legitimacy to the grief response in a mourner. Doka (1989) defined the social rules of grieving as "A set of norms that attempt to determine who, when, where, how, how long, and for whom people should grieve" (p. 4). These rules are the "shoulds" and "should nots" that govern individual responses to loss (Kalich & Brabant, 2006). In Western society, these rules identify the following:

- *Who has permission to be identified as bereaved and whether or not the relationship to the deceased is valid according to social expectations.* For example, grief is recognized through workplace leave policies as valid if the loss is that of a child or spouse, but not if the deceased is the ex-spouse or a close friend instead of a close family member. One of the functions of any society is to validate the legitimacy of its members, and individual subjective experiences of loss are judged by the social norms of that society. Another example of lack of validation of loss occurs in perinatal loss, which is seen as a different loss than the loss of a child that lived outside of the womb. Because the parents may not actually "hold" their baby or have shared memories of the baby (often referred to as the "products of conception" rather than as a baby), the baby is premature, or has deformities, it is not seen as a "true" loss, although research supports the development of significant prenatal attachment, often at an early gestational age (Klaus & Kennell, 1976).
- *How long grief can last.* Funeral leave for most workplaces is three days for a close family member. In my presentations to public audiences, I often ask the question, "How long do you think grief should last"? The typical responses to this question are that someone is expected to grieve from three months to one year after a significant loss. Many of the clients in my clinical practice reflect this sentiment when they voice concern that they are still experiencing symptoms of raw grief a year (or several years) after their loss. In the case study at the beginning of this chapter, we see that Jim also believed he should be able to move forward and we also see the impatience of others who believe similarly. However, current research in the area of bereavement indicates that the length of time one grieves is dependent upon many varying factors, which may include personal grieving/coping style, cultural affiliation, concurrent stresses, and loss history (Klass et al., 1996; Stroebe, Hansson, & Stroebe, 2001; Worden, 2009). It often takes many years for bereaved individuals to feel they are able to function normally again after a significant loss experience. For many individuals, grief continues to manifest at important milestones throughout one's life (Oltjenbruns, 2001). Grief may never really have a defined point of resolution, or the relationship with the deceased individual continues indefinitely after death, which also has implications for the grieving process (Neimeyer, Baldwin, & Gillies, 2006).
- *How grief can and should be manifest.* For example, women are generally allowed to cry "within reason" and men are generally expected to be "strong," meaning to be stoic and to show very little emotion (Doka & Martin, 2010). Gender socialization and stereotyping are strong social forces that shape the expectations of how individuals should grieve. We see the expectations that Jim experiences in his grief as a man in the case study. It is interesting that as a man, he sought the company of women in order to share his grief openly. Strong emotions of any type are usually stigmatized, and bereaved individuals often express embarrassment for "losing control" of their emotions in front of others.
- *If the manner of death is considered "acceptable" or if it is a loss with some stigma attached to it.* For example, family members of individuals who complete suicide are frequently assumed to be dysfunctional. Deaths through AIDS and through acts of intention (i.e., murder) or volition (i.e, drunk driving or drug use) also have significant social stigma attached to them as well (Doka, 2002). Associated with losses that involve the legal system is the view that the public

has a right to know about the details of deaths, even at the expense of the surviving family members, as the right of the press to expose such details supersedes the privacy and needs of the surviving bereaved individuals (Breithaupt, 2003). Although the detailed coverage of these types of deaths is rationalized by invoking reference to the freedom of the press, the reality is that sensationalized media content sells well, which is another example of how capitalistic values intrude upon the privacy and needs of grieving individuals and the survivors of these events.

Social Conformity in Bereavement

We have already introduced the term *disenfranchised grief* in an earlier chapter to describe grief that does not fit into socially acceptable norms within a given society (Doka, 1989). Violation of any of the social rules of grief can have a deep impact upon the bereaved individual, as these rules govern the social support and public policies that are extended after the death of a loved one. Social support is a very important factor in bereavement adjustment, and bereaved individuals will readily adhere to these social rules about their grief in order to prevent further losses that may occur through the withdrawal of their social support system if they do not conform to these unwritten rules (Nichols, 2001).

Many researchers describe the grief experience as a threat to the attachment system of the bereaved individual. Threats to the attachment system often trigger a heightened activation of that same system, resulting in an increased sense of vulnerability in bereaved individuals and the need to seek the safety of social support (Parkes, 1981, 1997; Weiss, 2001). Another reason that bereaved individuals attempt to conform to social grieving rules can be found in the concept of "social pain," which is described as the "specific emotional reaction to the perception that one is being excluded from desired relationships or being devalued by desired relationship partners or groups" (MacDonald & Leary, 2005, p. 202). These authors state that social pain is felt on many levels and that aversion to this pain is a powerful motivating force for compliance with social norms and rules. In addition, individuals who stray from accepted norms of behavior are often shamed by their social group, which functions as a powerful form of social control to ensure compliance with social norms (Kalich and Brabant, 2006). This sense of shame may also be internalized by the bereaved individual, who describes frustration at his or her inability to "keep it together" or as we saw with Jim in our case study, to "move on and stop wallowing in self-pity." Thus, there are many strong pressures that may influence bereaved individuals to try to conform to social grieving rules, even when adherence to these rules could prolong their personal suffering after a loss.

Capitalism and Grief: The Clash

The undercurrent of these socially-mediated grieving rules can be explored by understanding the values of the society in which they have been created. Reynolds (2002) concludes that it is not enough to state that Western society is basically death denying, and that bereaved individuals are marginalized because they represent the fact that we are mortal beings. Going deeper, he states that the relationship between Western society and death and grief is shaped by the driving forces of the capitalistic economic structure. A capitalistic society is governed by the high value placed upon productivity, competition, and consumerism. In a capitalistic society, the active seeking of economic growth, expansion, consumption, and the view of unlimited possibilities is highly prized. Brookfield (2005) describes capitalistic societies as those which tend to define human worth "in economic terms by the elevation of materialistic values over the human values of compassion, skill, or creativity" (p. 162).

Bereaved individuals are often impaired in their functionality by their grief experience. These same individuals are often not very good consumers of market goods (unless these market goods are targeted for bereaved individuals, such as self-help books and pharmaceuticals). The potential for lack of productivity and inability to perform the socially-expected role of consumer presents a threat to the basic structure of a capitalistic society. If their grief response adheres to the previously described social rules concerning grief, bereaved individuals will be allowed a brief, temporary exemption from functionality and the expectation of being consumers and producers for a limited period of time.

In order to become more socially acceptable, and to counteract the potential for social isolation or exclusion due to lack of conformity to expectations, grieving individuals may try to "mask" their grief in stoicism or find covert ways to grieve that keep their experience out of the public eye. By so doing, bereaved individuals internalize the oppression that is enforced through the social rules of acceptability after a loss occurs. Death and grief signify vulnerability, which is a sign of weakness. In a social system that is based upon competition and acquisition, weakness is not tolerable, and so grief goes underground.

Western society also tends to be a patriarchal society, and patriarchy is perpetuated in capitalistic societies through the hierarchical structure of most large companies and social institutions, and the desire to compete and to "dominate" the market (Hartman, 1995; Rasmussen, 2005). Certainly, a patriarchal society favors the male-dominant patterns of stoicism and denial of emotionality, which are often hard to maintain in acute grief. Many bereaved individuals would share that the most frequent comments they receive from well-meaning others are those that would minimize their loss or offer distraction from their grief in an attempt to help them to regain control over their vulnerability and emotionality. Jim's buddies actively tried to distract him from his grief by telling him to "watch more hockey" and to suppress his feelings by "drinking more beer." This mandate to minimize one's experience and to deny a potentially adaptive grief response in favor of the maintenance of a veneer of control and functionality represents a unique form of oppression. The cost of noncompliance can be very high, manifest through job loss secondary to loss of productivity, loss of support, loss of status, and shame if one appears weak in a competitive market or is not pulling one's weight as expected.

Death and grief represent the ultimate loss of control over one's destiny, one's life, and one's choices. A capitalistic, patriarchal, consumer-driven culture values control and rationality in order to foster productivity (Bottomore, 1985). The large pharmaceutical industry feeds off these values, and quickly offers consumers the hope that they can control their grief through the use of antidepressants, anxiolytics, and sleeping medications. In Western society, the high value that is placed on youth and vitality, the warehousing of elderly or disabled individuals into institutional care out of the public eye, and the fact that most people die in institutional care settings removed from everyday life prevents a more reflexive and normative response to mortality. In addition, we do not have time to deal with death because we are busy producing and consuming, and unless we are personally affected by a loss, we can function efficiently and without hindrance because death is hidden from sight. And when all else fails, we can take medication to overcome our weakness, which is another suggestion that was made to Jim.

The fact that these social norms are so deeply entrenched into every institutional structure and internalized into individuals' identification with the need to "be strong" and "in control" at all times prevents the exposure of these underlying themes and values as unrealistic and often unhealthy. Death is everywhere, but it is also nowhere. Grief is a universal experience, but it is expected to be hidden from sight as if it were a source of shame rather than the result of loving and attaching to others. As stated in the introduction, much of the focus in grief therapy and support is often upon the "un-doing" of these oppressive social norms, which ironically causes prolonged suffering in grieving individuals, by preventing the potentially adaptive aspects of the grief process to unfold naturally without hindrance (Doka & Martin, 2010).

Diagnosis and Grief

As discussed in a previous chapter, another aspect of how death is viewed in Western culture has revolved around the controversy over when grief is to be considered "abnormal" versus "normal," and the ongoing debate about delineating between these two categories. While the newly released *Diagnostic and Statistical Manual of Mental Disorders* (*DSM-5*, APA, 2013) does not list various manifestations of grief as a primary disorder, the removal of the bereavement exclusion from the criteria listed for clinical depression opens up the door for lumping grief into the same category as depression, with the implications for diagnostic labeling and the potential for more pharmacological treatment for bereavement (Iglewicz, Seay, Zetumer, & Zisook, 2013; Kosminsky, 2014; Kupfer, Kuhl, & Regier, 2013). In the past, an individual would not be diagnosed with a major depressive disorder (MDD) if s/he had experienced a significant loss within the previous two months. However, in the *DSM-5*, this qualifier no longer exists. Thus, grief can become equated and folded into descriptions of a MDD and thereby be identified as a disorder instead of a normal reaction to significant loss experiences.

This change posits grief as a medical issue, legitimizing the associated role of the bereaved individual through diagnostic labeling and the resulting medicalization (see Parsons, 1951,) which is purported to assist with coverage from third party insurance when professional support is sought. This change also opens the door to the greater use of pharmacologic intervention with antidepressants in bereaved individuals as well. There is a trade-off: If a bereaved individual meets the criteria for clinical depression by virtue of the fact that s/he is grieving, s/he may receive the social benefits of legitimization and access to resources. However, that same individual must then live with being identified with a certain degree of "abnormality," described as a diagnostic entity indicating a mental disorder, even if his/her experience of grief falls within generally normal parameters. In contrast, bereavement researchers and clinicians generally believe that the majority of bereaved individuals manifest their grief in a myriad number of unique but healthy ways, and that grief is not a disease or illness, even though it may temporarily mimic other conditions such as depression (Wakefield, 2013). Some researchers in the area of bereavement have cautioned that removing the bereavement exclusion could potentially cause an otherwise healthy individual to become identified with psychopathology, and some of these labels may follow that person for the rest of his or her life (Hogan, Worden & Schmidt, 2003–2004; Wakefield, 2013).

Clinical Implications

Explore What's Right About What's Wrong

Bereaved individuals often mention that they feel that they are going crazy or "losing it" because their grief sometimes feels overwhelming or they are not able to function well because of distraction, exhaustion, or intense feelings. Many feel that something is wrong with them, and they hope that in coming for professional support, they will regain their functionality more quickly and be able to enter back into their world as they once did. Clinicians need to contextualize an individual's grief experience within the social rules of grief in Western society, which are based upon market economics rather than true human experience. It is important to help clients to recognize that it is normal to have difficulty focusing, that grief over a relationship that is not socially recognized as valid is still their grief, and deserves to be honored. Often, bereaved individuals may feel that something is wrong with them when the reality of their experience is juxtaposed with what is deemed right socially. The bereaved individual's subjective experience needs to be re-framed as what is "right" against the social rules of grief that are just plain "wrong."

Advocate and Inform Where Possible

Professionals who work in thanatology-related areas (i.e., hospice or palliative care, death education, bereavement counseling or support) are often called upon to provide information to the public as it relates to their area of expertise, and to offer comment upon current events that are relevant to death and grief. In these open discussions, it is possible to raise awareness about specific issues in death and loss that may marginalize bereaved individuals, including disclosure of recent research that speaks to the normal complexity of the grief experience. It is important to remind individuals that the societal pressure to make a quick return to functionality and efficiency can be highly unrealistic, given the amount of reconstruction that a significant loss requires on many different levels. Working with terminally ill and bereaved individuals provides an opportunity to see where the focus on productivity, youth, and consumerism has not served us well. Engaging the academic community in reflective analysis of social structures and their impact upon bereaved individuals is also an important aspect of this process. Finally, in death education, teaching about and discussing issues that relate to social justice and diversity in grief may also help increase awareness of the need to question social rules that oppress instead of support bereaved individuals.

Be Careful With Labels

As stated previously, it is important to be careful with labeling bereaved individuals with disorders through the use of pathology-based diagnostic systems or through subtle alignment with pressure to suppress the experience either through medicalization or adherence to social rules that subvert the normal grief response. Given the hegemonic propensity for the *DSM* to be utilized as a dividing line between those who are "healthy" and those who are mentally ill, great care must be taken when associating a client's distress and pain with a reified set of criteria in a diagnosis code. This is not to say that in some instances, concurrent disorders may exist alongside the grief. It is also not the intent of this article to oppose the use of medication when a client may benefit from or require medication in order to help with daily functioning. However, the focus must remain on the client's experience, feelings, and choices so that the unique grief experience of that client will be allowed to unfold without hindrance and with healthy support from a strengths-based perspective. It is also important to keep in mind that the ability to apply a diagnostic label reinforces the power differential between a client and a clinician, which may have implications for the therapeutic relationship (Brown, 1994).

Conclusion

In this chapter, I have tried to underscore the influence of the capitalistic values in Western society upon attitudes toward death, dying, and bereavement. It is important to recognize that the social rules and expectations for those who are terminally ill and bereaved in this society are grounded in values that are economically based, and not humanistically oriented. The clash of these values with the reality of the experiences of individuals who face terminal illness or who are bereaved often results in the marginalization of these individuals rather than recognition of the situations where a market-based social system does not reflect acceptance or understanding of a normal and universal human experience. The role of individuals who work in thanatology-related areas in Western society is clear: We must not allow the normal and healthy expression of grief to be considered a source of shame. Our imperative is to strive to find ways to normalize death as a natural part of life, and grief as a normal and adaptive response to the losses we encounter as a result of the healthy human connections that are necessary for our survival.

Key Terms

Oppression—the act of using power to empower and/or grant privilege to a group at the expense of disempowering, marginalizing, silencing, and subordinating another group.

Reflexivity—the human capacity to reflect upon our history and our actions.

Social rules of grieving—A set of norms that attempt to determine who, when, where, how, how long, and for whom people should grieve.

Social pain—the specific emotional and physical reaction to the perception that one is being excluded from desired relationships or being devalued by desired relationship partners or groups.

Questions for Reflection

1. Which "unwritten social rules about grief/grieving" do you recognize? How have you experience these personally? Have you ever felt that your grief experience was constrained or criticized due to differing from these unwritten rules? How do you see that you have responded to others' grief based on your own internalization of these rules?
2. Consider the Western view of death as a failure of medical technology and a source of shame. How might this affect perception of bereaved individuals in Western society?
3. Brookfield (2005) describes capitalistic societies as those which tend to define human worth "in economic terms by the elevation of materialistic values over the human values of compassion, skill, or creativity" (p. 162). How might this interact with the individual's experience of their bereavement (self-reflection/self-evaluation)? How might this influence the response of others towards the bereaved individual?
4. "Death is everywhere, but it is also nowhere. Grief is a universal experience, but it is expected to be hidden from sight as if it were a source of shame rather than the result of loving and attaching to others." What is your experience of death awareness in day-to-day life? What has your experience been of day-to-day life immediately after bereavement?

Note

1. This chapter is a revised version of the article, "Oppression of the Bereaved," which was originally published in 2009–10 in *Omega*, *60*(3) 241–253.

References

American Psychiatric Association. (2013). *Diagnostic and statistical manual of mental disorders* (5th ed.). Arlington, VA: American Psychiatric Publishing.
Bottomore, T. (1985). *Theories of modern capitalism*. London: George Allen and Unwin.
Breen, L. J., & O'Connor, M. (2007). The fundamental paradox in the grief literature: A critical reflection. *Omega: Journal of Death and Dying*, *55*(3), 199–218.
Breithaupt, F. (2003). Rituals of trauma: How the media fabricated September 11. In S. Chermak, F. Bailey, & M. Brown (Eds.), *Media Representations of September 11* (pp. 67–81). Westport, CT: Praeger.
Brookfield, S. D. (2005). *The power of critical theory: Liberating adult learning and teaching*. San Francisco, CA: Jossey-Bass.
Brown, L. S. (1994). *Subversive dialogues: Theory in feminist therapy*. New York, NY: Basic Books.
D'Cruz, H., Gillingham, P., & Melendez, S. (2007). Reflexivity, its meanings and relevance for social work: A critical review of the literature. *British Journal of Social Work*, *37*(1), 73–90.
Doka, K. J. (1989). *Disenfranchised grief: Recognizing hidden sorrow*. Lexington, MA: Lexington Books.
Doka, K. J. (2002). How we die: stigmatized death and disenfranchised grief. In K. J. Doka (Ed.), *Disenfranchised grief: New directions, challenges, and strategies for practice* (pp. 323–336). Champaign, IL: Research Press.
Doka, K. J., & Martin, T. L. (2010). *Grieving beyond gender: Understanding the ways men and women mourn*. New York, NY: Taylor & Francis.

Dyregrov, A. (2008). *Grief in children: A handbook for adults*. London: Jessica Kingsley.
Frye, M. (1998). Oppression. In P. S. Rothenberg (Ed.), *Race, class, and gender in the United States* (pp. 146–149). New York, NY: St. Martin's.
Harris, D. L. (2014). A fate less than death: Supporting clients through non-death loss and grief. *New Therapist, 90*, 14–19.
Hartman, H. (1995). The unhappy marriage of Marxism and feminism: Towards a more progressive union. In D. Tallack (Ed.), *Critical Theory: A Reader* (pp. 183–199). New York, NY: Simon & Schuster.
Hockey, J. (1997). Women in grief: cultural representation and social practice. In D. Field, J. Hockey, & N. Small (Eds.), *Death, Gender and Ethnicity* (pp. 89–107). London: Routledge.
Hogan, N. S., Worden, J. W., & Schmidt, L. A. (2003–2004). An empirical study of the proposed Complicated Grief Disorder Criteria. *Omega, 48*(3), 263–277.
Iglewicz, A., Seay, K., Zetumer, S. D., & Zisook, S. (2013). The Removal of the Bereavement Exclusion in the DSM-5: Exploring the Evidence. *Current Psychiatry Reports, 15*(11), 1–9.
Irish, D. P., Lundquist, K. F., & Nelsen, V. J. (Eds.). (2014). *Ethnic variations in dying, death and grief: Diversity in universality*. New York, NY: Taylor & Francis.
Jenkins, R. (2002). *Foundations of sociology: Towards a better understanding of the human world*. New York, NY: Palgrave.
Kalich, D., & Brabant, S. (2006). A continued look at Doka's grieving rules: deviance and anomie as clinical tools. *Omega, 53*(3), 227–241.
Klass, D., Silverman, P. R., & Nickman, S. (1996). *Continuing bonds: New understandings of grief*. Washington, DC: Taylor & Francis.
Klaus, M. H., & Kennell, J. H. (1976) *Maternal-infant bonding*. St. Louis: Mosby.
Kosminsky, P. (2014). Coming to grief: What you need to know about grief in DSM-5. *New Therapist, 90*, 20–24.
Kupfer, D. J., Kuhl, E. A., & Regier, D. A. (2013). DSM-5—The future arrived. *JAMA, 309*(16), 1691–1692.
Littlejohn, S. W. (1992). *Critical theories in theories of human communication* (4th ed.). Belmont, CA: Wadsworth.
Lund, D. (2001). *Men coping with grief*. Amityville, NY: Baywood.
MacDonald, G., & Leary, M. R. (2005). Why does social exclusion hurt? The relationship between social and physical pain. *Psychological Bulletin, 131*, 202–223.
Neimeyer, R. A., Baldwin, S. A., & Gillies, J. (2006). Continuing bonds and reconstructing meaning: Mitigating complications in bereavement. *Death Studies, 30*(8), 715–738.
Ng, B. Y. (2005). Grief revisited. *Annals of the Academy of Medicine Singapore, 34*(5), 352.
Nichols, D. L. (2001). Social support for the bereaved: Some practical suggestions. In J. D. Morgan (Ed.), *Social support: A reflection of humanity* (pp. 33–43). Amityville, NY: Baywood.
Oltjenbruns, K. A. (2001). Developmental context of childhood: Grief and regrief phenomena. In M. S. Stroebe, R. O. Hansson, W. Stroebe, & H. Schut (Eds.), *Handbook of bereavement research: Consequences, coping, and care* (pp. 169–198). Washington, DC: APA.
Parkes, C. M. (1981). *Bereavement: Studies of grief in adult life*. Madison, CT: International Universities Press.
Parkes, C. M. (1997). Bereavement: What most people should know. In J. D. Morgan (Ed.), *Readings in thanatology* (pp. 241–253). Amityville, NY: Baywood.
Parsons, T. (1951). *The social system*. Glencoe, IL: Free Press.
Rasmussen, S. L. (2005). Masculinity and Fahrenheit 9/11. *International Journal of Feminist Politics, 7*(1), 137–141.
Reynolds, J. J. (2002). Disenfranchised grief and the politics of helping: Social policy and its clinical implications. In K. J. Doka (Ed.), *Disenfranchised grief: New directions, challenges, and strategies for practice* (pp. 351–388). Champaign, IL: Research Press.
Sanders, C. M. (1999). *Grief: The mourning after* (2nd ed.). New York, NY: Wiley.
Schieman, S., & Plickert, G. (2008). How knowledge is power: Education and the sense of control. *Social Forces, 87*(1), 153–183.
Silverman, P. R. (2000). *Too young to know: Death in children's lives*. New York, NY: Oxford.
Stroebe, M. S., Hansson, R. O., & Stroebe, W. (2001). Introduction: Concepts and issues in contemporary research on bereavement. In M. S. Stroebe, R. O. Hansson, W. Stroebe, & H. Schut (Eds.), *Handbook of bereavement research: Consequences, coping, and care* (pp. 3–22). Washington, DC: APA.
Stroebe, M., Schut, H., & Finkenauer, C. (2001). The traumatization of grief: A conceptual framework for understanding the trauma-bereavement interface. *Israel Journal of Psychiatry and Related Sciences, 38*(3–4), 185–201.
Swenson, C. R. (1998). Clinical social work's contribution to a social justice perspective. *Social Work, 43*(6), 527–537.

Wakefield, J. C. (2013). The DSM-5 debate over the bereavement exclusion: Psychiatric diagnosis and the future of empirically supported treatment. *Clinical Psychology Review, 33*(7), 825–845.

Weiss, R. O. (2001). Grief, bonds, and relationships. In M. S. Stroebe, R. O. Hansson, W. Stroebe, & H. Schut (Eds.), *Handbook of bereavement research: Consequences, coping, and care* (pp. 47–62). Washington, DC: APA.

Wood, W. R., & Williamson, J. B. (2003). Historical changes in the meaning of death in the Western tradition. In C. D. Bryant (Ed.), *Handbook of death & dying* (Vol 1, pp. 14–23). Thousand Oaks, CA: Sage.

Worden, J. W. (2009). *Grief counseling and grief therapy: A handbook for the mental health practitioner* (4th ed.). New York, NY: Springer.

Part Five
Practice Implications

This part explores potential practice and policy implications for addressing social injustice.

By its very nature, injustice silences voices that are not recognized by those in positions of privilege and power. Injustice robs us of meaning and purpose. Discrimination, marginalization, and oppression undermine the intrinsic value and dignity that defines what it means to be human.

In this section, many possible responses to injustice are portrayed, suggesting various potential ways to enfranchise, empower, and support those who have suffered from injustice and inhumane treatment in some way. Various approaches to address unjust practices are discussed, which may involve meaning making, identification with true spirituality, creative responses, the use of rituals and healing spaces, and advocating for just practices at individual, community, and broader political levels.

Finally, we conclude with a description of two models of compassion that have been developed to assist in cultivating reasoned responses to injustice from a position of awareness, insight, and discernment. Compassion is presented as a protective stance from which to address injustice and the suffering that it causes.

15
Transformation Through Socially Sensitive Experiences

Doneley Meris

Defined by trauma, social injustices and multiple losses, Wilfred's world almost collapsed numerous times but Wilfred learned to find meaning(s) in his challenges and complications and even courage (Attig, 2001; Gillies, Neimeyer, & Milman, 2014; Neimeyer, 2010; Parkes & Weiss, 1983) to change the course of his own life story. This clinical qualitative exploration examines Wilfred's experiences with sudden death, trauma, sexual discovery, and social and community re-integration/transition. It engages a client and clinical practitioner in a partnership to integrate and facilitate life transitions from assessment to exploring and planning interventions (Guess, 2013; Hedges, 2011).

Despite updated laws and protections for individuals in same-sex relationships, in some segments of American society, sexual identity and orientation reassessment continue to be viewed and received with prejudice and stigma (APA, 2007; Spitzer, 2012), leaving individualss alone in reframing social connections with family and attempts to form and engage in new communities. This journey described in this chapter provides a framework utilized in supporting a male client in his difficult roadmap to self-sexual discovery and mixed-race identity while living with the trauma of early sudden death experiences, familial dis-connects, the sudden loss of a child, lifelong effects of bullying and difficult healing experiences.

The traditional concept of marriage between a man and a woman has been challenged for some time In the history of American life, those who stray from this norm are often ostracized and denied constitutional protections (Comer, 2013; Paul et al., 2002). Wilfred addressed these challenges by overcoming his internal conflicts. His story also confronts the conventional threshold of who is acceptable and embraced within the lesbian, gay, bisexual, and transgender (LGBT) communities (Brimlow, Cook, & Seaton, 2003; D'Emilio, 1993). Wilfred's journey provides unique lessons of self-determination, tenacity and resilience.

While some states in America, because of conservative religious beliefs and political ideology, still advocate for reparative or conversion therapy to "reform," "cure," and "repair" same-sex thoughts and persuasions (Watson, 2014; Wolfson, 2014), the work with Wilfred was to support him in his self-exploration rather than attempt to change his awakening sexual identity. The issue of mixed race and ethnicity was equally examined but only addressed secondarily to issues of sexuality. When he initially attempted to integrate within the LGBT community he was faced with gay internal sub-groupings, based not only on race, ethnicity, and socioeconomic realities; in addition, there were also issues related to age, body types, partner, and sexual practices and preferences (Bajko, 2014; Cheng, 2011; *Metro Weekly*, 2013; NGLTF, 2013).

The Therapeutic Relationship

Wilfred came in for an intake counseling assessment in late 2011, 11 months after he moved to New York from Michigan. He claimed to be "overwhelmed" and needing help. A British-Vietnamese financial analyst, his professional life in America started in 1984, when he was sent by his multi-national development firm from Hong Kong to oversee a project in Minnesota. This is where he met and eventually married his wife, Marianne. After two miscarriages, Marianne gave birth to a daughter and two years later, a healthy son. The family moved four times within seven years wherever he was reassigned to oversee company projects.

His formative years included living and studying in Vietnam, Hong Kong, Australia, England, and Switzerland. His British father was an executive banker and his mother a Vietnamese, Paris-educated medical doctor. They met and settled in Hong Kong before he was born. Wilfred has a younger sister who followed the footsteps of their mother and continues to live in Hong Kong working as a medical director in a general hospital.

Wilfred excelled in school and quickly earned his undergraduate degree in Hong Kong and graduate degree in business management in England. He worked for his father's bank since age 14 in Hong Kong and accompanied his father to numerous bank branches in Vietnam before the "global conflict." His mother's entire family fled Saigon when the war broke out. Wilfred was not directly impacted by the political repression of Vietnam and did not witness or experience the horrific plight of his maternal extended family. Through the determined medical work of his mother, he was empathetic and cautiously aware of his interracial connections, which he claims better prepared him in his professional multi-national corporation endeavors.

Wilfred swiftly learned the ropes of the financial world from his well-respected father. It was during his late teen years that Wilfred experienced his first traumatic view of the world. While he filed documents in Hong Kong, three men entered the bank, held five customers hostage, demanding the bank be locked and that all employees empty their cash drawers and the money vault. Panic ensued and the three robbers started firing their guns, killing two employees and wounding dozens more. Wilfred was witness to this horrific incident. During the assessment process, he narrated this story, void of any emotions. This was noted for future conversations.

During a skiing vacation in Switzerland with college friends at age 20, Wilfred was exposed to another tragic event—the death of one of his best buddies. In the middle of the slopes, this friend fell on the side of a mountain, breaking his skull and killing him instantly. Wilfred was designated by the others to relate the news to the family. He shortly stopped seeing the college friends and never returned to his ski gear and equipment again. He did not provide any more information on how and why he abandoned his friends (Park & George, 2013) and skiing—yet this later provided a wealth of information that eventually he permitted himself to explore in his therapeutic work.

Before coming to America, he learned that his parents had decided to divorce as his father had "fallen out" of loving his mother. Wilfred found out later that his father had an affair with one of his bank mates that started while Wilfred was completing his last year in graduate school in England. He stated that he felt badly for his mother, but was comforted by the fact that she had her own career and maintained contact with international friends since medical school. She also managed to cultivate her interests in theater and classical music as well as Vietnam refugee relief and medical-social policy volunteer work. Also, he knew that his sister, who never married, would be a guardian to both his parents in Hong Kong even with their now separate lives.

When asked why he was seeking psychotherapeutic support now, Wilfred hesitated to reveal the primary reason he sought clinical support. Nearly 56-years-old, he had thought about and often questioned his sexual identity and sexual orientation. He revealed that he had been thinking "affectionately" about his 47-year-old co-worker Edsel, who had just got divorced, recently relocated to New York, and with whom he had been sharing time. He confided that he was not eager to go home to his wife who remained in Michigan with the expansion of her interior design business. Their eldest daughter just completed her sophomore year at the university there, majoring in international relations. Their son graduated with honors from high school and was off on a two-month tour of Southeast Asia and New Zealand with a couple of buddies and a new love interest before starting his first year of engineering school.

Three weeks after their son left for his long tour, Marianne received a phone call from the Philippines that her son and his friends went to a bar for drinks and dinner and were involved in a fight as they were leaving. Rushing out of the bar-restaurant, their son was run over by a speeding truck as he and his friends ran away from the group with whom they had an altercation. His friends stood shocked and helpless as they witnessed the accident. Wilfred and Marianne's son was killed on the spot. This devastated Wilfred after Marianne delivered the news to him over the phone. Wilfred flew to fetch Marianne and they both traveled to this foreign soil to retrieve the body of their only son who had just celebrated his 18th birthday before his international tour.

After their son's funeral, the somber and detached time Wilfred had with Marianne only solidified his thoughts that in the midst of this terrible loss, he was now set to move on alone. He emphasized that his love for Marianne and his remaining daughter will be forever but, although scared and confused, he wanted to explore himself in a different light. It was during this time that he decided to seek therapy.

Wilfred's social encounters with Edsel had given him a refuge as he tried to make sense of the sudden end to his son's young life and the tender father–son moments they shared and what they aimed for in the future. Edsel provided Wilfred a different way to spend quiet, quality and physical-leisure time during this mourning period—bowling, long bicycle rides, and excursions on most weekends, indoor rock-climbing and more time at the gym. He added that he and his wife had not had sex for over two years and he had no desire to rekindle the sexual connection. The sudden death of their son further removed him from that possibility. Given that this was the main reason for his outreach for help, it provided a starting point in the clinical counseling work.

Therapeutic Process and Strategies

Concerns Collage

With Wilfred's permission, he was asked to create a collage of all the concerns that he shared during the intake process, starting with his sexuality. This exercise allowed him to visualize the many changes that he had to live with and adjust to, which provided the biopsychosocial context of his traumatic experiences (McFarlane & van der Kolk, 1996). He drew a flower and in each petal and leaf, he wrote down the themes of issues that he had had to confront since his teens. These included being bi-racial; not very good with "any" sports; being bullied as a "bookworm," always staring intently at others and being "too close" to his mother and sister; his nightmares and fears after the bank robbery; his good friend's instant death at the ski slopes; his parents' divorce; the experience of two miscarriages before his first child's birth; his own divorce from Marianne; his daughter off to college; his being alone and lonely during his work-related travels; and what was most recent and so devastating—the death of his young son.

Interestingly and unprompted, Wilfred created a different collage with different concerns that included his internal homophobia; fears of being "in the company of mixed lesbian, gay, bisexual, and transgender (LGBT) crowds; fears of being outed in the corporate workplace; American societal hatred, discrimination and stigma against the LGBT community; and potential fear and sadness of losing Edsel if he did not "perform well" sexually. As he created his flower-collages, he cried uncontrollably and proclaimed that it was the first time he expressively emoted in front of another person. There were many silent moments during this process and he was provided a safe space to take his time and re-engage in the difficult self-exploration collage activity. Through this exercise, Wilfred mapped out and visually illustrated his traumatic narrative (Aldwin, 2009; Konig & Gluck, 2013; Neimeyer, Klass, & Dennis, 2014; Silverman & Nickman, 1996; Ursano & Fullerton, 1997) and his experiences of bereavement and losses (Black, Santanello, & Rubenstein, 2014).

By providing him with a safe space, giving him room to begin and phase his male traumatic survival experience (Mejia, 2005), making sense of his lessons of and the language of his loss (Neimeyer, 2001), and by incorporating his bodily movements and nonverbal indicators (Meris, 2003), Wilfred felt comfortable enough and willing to revisit, make sense of, prioritize, and begin to address ways that his past impacts his here and now. By giving himself permission to dictate the timeline of his self-exploration, we created the "urgency agenda" from his concerns collage that facilitated his traumatic recovery (Rando, 2003; Reece, 2002).

Mixed Race Identity, Global Identification and Early Bullying

To address Wilfred's concern of bi-racial identity, the premise of early encounters with him *briefly* discussed the similarities and differences between him and his therapist, both of mixed-race identities. He was pointedly asked if the potential working dynamic would provide him with comfort or challenges to explore his life transitions. Wilfred digressed from his story to inquire about his clinician's ethnic background and his "professional gates installed to address the enormous challenges of grieving clients." Directly responding to his inquiry, this clinician identified his ethnicity, and explained the clinical concepts of a) client-centered approach, b) issues-driven exchange, c) client-tailored agenda setting, d) emphasis of client timeline, and e) the value of debriefing, employed in each counseling session. After this brief clinical overview, the interaction promptly returned to Wilfred's concern about being born bi-racial.

As a British-Vietnamese, now gay-identified adult, he reviewed his early years as "normal," surrounded by other foreigners and yet deemed "different" in Hong Kong society. His social environment was comprised mostly of similar multi-racial constituents in an international city and he assimilated without many traumatic incidences—except for his lack of sports enthusiasm, his inferior physical agility, and disinterest in anything requiring "physical expenditure." Some of his interactions with other teens were remembered as moderate forms of bullying but did not deter him from achieving his early goal to transition from Hong Kong and consciously draw upon his bi-racial identity to his career advantage. He added that being tri-lingual (English, Vietnamese, and French) was an asset.

Probed further on his more recent interactions with Edsel, he opined that there were fewer critics and monitors of his daily life agenda. He recognized though that within his new LGBT community, he would always be perceived as racially different, taking comfort in positives to his present stature. Yet he was aware and expressed sadness of the blatant discrimination and prejudice within the gay community based solely on one's physical appearance.

Life Loss Review, Cognitive Life Raft, Self-Talk, and More . . .

The process of exploration with Wilfred included cognitive restructuring that incorporated a) self-talk, where he identified and gave voice to emotions that paired his reactions to current events and his past recollections, b) empty-chair dialogs with the deceased where he confronted his emotional landscape (Meris, 2003), c) life loss review (LLR) with each of the individuals he lost (Rando, 2003), and d) the complex and delicate process of a cognitive life raft (Nord, 1996) as he reviewed his relational adjustments, and his entitlements or lack thereof.

Wilfred reluctantly agreed to return to the scene of each loss starting with where, what, and how he reacted to the bank robbery in Hong Kong, who he communicated with, what he witnessed, how he conveyed and expressed his emotion after the incident, and who was supportive of him during this initial traumatic experience. He was also asked to chart his life activities after the incident. Wilfred followed with the loss of his college friend; he claimed this to be an extremely difficult exercise as he finally realized and admitted that at that time he had same-sex feelings for his deceased friend. This exploratory exercise continued with all the other episodes of loss and grief including his separate ties with his parents before and after their divorce, his letting go of his heterosexual sex life, and "editing" his social networks to redefine his social supports.

By cross-referencing his "concerns collage" to his life loss review (LLR), Wilfred was able to piece together the clues and discoveries of his past as a sexual being and his new sexual orientation, behaviors, and practices. After several sessions of agonizing over how his wife and daughter would react, he finally admitted to himself that he had to confront his internal homophobia (Meris, 2002) and courageously pursue his next sexual life chapter. Through his journey of many silent moments in therapy, self-doubt, and self-blame, Wilfred was able to come to terms with the fact that a) he did justice to his heterosexual life as a husband and father, b) he will always continue to love his family, and c) he was now willing and ready to embrace a scary but also exciting new phase of his adult sexual life.

Coed Grief Support Group (Phase I): Grief Exploration

After the initial contracted 12 sessions of individual counseling, it was suggested to Wilfred that he consider participating in a coed grief support group, also facilitated by his therapist. He voiced his reservations about sharing his story with strangers but welcomed the opportunity to hear how others dealt with their grief processes and how they made sense of the meanings of their life traumas (Park & George, 2013). After two more individual sessions of wrestling with his potential communal experience and being assured that any anxieties experienced in group can be further explored in his individual counseling; he enlisted in the 10-session coed grief support group (Phase I), joining seven other men and women (of mixed sexual orientations and gender identities) for the agenda-driven and bereavement-focused journey.

Phase I of the coed grief support group afforded each group member the chance to share their stories of multiple losses and Wilfred was able to establish that his individual story, though unique, was a norm in the human life-death experience. He participated in group exercises that included a) *connection chronologies*, where survivors map out their start-to-finish ties with the deceased, b) *emotional rollercoaster drawings*, where feelings associated with grieving were illustrated in images instead of words, c) *petals of accompanying life events* that allowed for identifying concurrent life events in the midst of grief, d) a *tie exercise* that encouraged group members to illustrate with one sketch on a paper tie all their recent challenging concerns then later wore their paper ties to indicate how heavy their life-load was, e) *first thought*, where initial thoughts upon waking up were jotted down and pondered on their relevance to the grief process, f) *spheres of compatibility*, where here-and-now scenarios are shared that impact on mourning, g) *triggers identified*, where lists of what reminds survivors of the deceased are shared and analyzed, h) *24-hour emotional charts* when a full day's worth of activities are chronicled and dissected in group, i) *letters to loved ones*, where letters were written to the deceased about what they miss most about them—letters were sealed and dropped in a group mailbox, and j) *challenge boxes*. As a home assignment, group members wrote a full-page *reflection* after each group session that they submitted the following session to be later compiled into their individual reflection binders and read by the group facilitator so that any lingering group themes would be incorporated into future agendas.

All activities were shared in dyads and small groups and lessons learned from each exercise were summated and explored in the entire large group. Wilfred expressed in the fourth session of the group process that he had to learn to let go of "intellectualizing" the meanings of these group activities and permit himself to just be in the moment to use the assignment of reflections and his individual counseling sessions to further explore his reactions and the linkages to his own traumatic experiences.

Challenge Boxes

Prior to joining the coed grief support group, Wilfred was assigned to gather objects that represented his life challenges—representations of all the issues he identified in his concerns collage. Mixing objects in a medium-size box over a two-session period, he narrated their associations to his traumatic life experiences. Deaths from the bank robbery were represented by a piggy bank with a crack on one-side. He illustrated the divorce of his parents with their photograph that showed them sitting stoic in a park bench with a shopping bag separating them. A recent ski magazine opened to beaming gentlemen going down ski slopes represented his memories of his last skiing fun turned tragic. Wilfred cried as he tore in half a wedding picture when he spoke about his divorce from Marianne. He admitted the most difficult object in his challenge box was his son's miniature tennis racket from when he was a toddler, which Wilfred kept in his office.

Wilfred brought in his challenge box for the grief support group but with different objects from what he presented in his individual counseling work. Alhough he kept the piggy bank and ski magazine, he replaced the more personal objects with a father-son photo from a magazine, a tassel that represented his children's scholastic transitions, a map of the Asian continent where he identified the places his son traveled to, and a rainbow flag he acquired at an LGBT meet-and-greet event. In his individual counseling after he presented his challenge box to the group, Wilfred explained that he wanted some of the more intimate objects contained in his box to be reserved for his private sessions.

Grief Companioning

The winter–spring of 2012 was difficult for Wilfred as he negotiated familial ties with his ex-wife on finances, time with their surviving child, and the logistics of their separate lives. He also began to enter the gay world with significant fear, excitement, and well-meaning questions. As a man in his mid-fifties, it was tough for him to integrate with a complex, small, and homogeneous group-oriented gay community. He felt lucky to have found Edsel as a co-navigator in his coming-out journey as they both struggled to socialize, cultivate new friendships, and sustain contacts with other gay men in their age group. Wilfred required several counseling sessions to explore and make sense of his new physical ties with Edsel, whom he did not have sex with until seven months after his divorce from Marianne. The desire was there but the mental torture that he put himself through to submit to the sexual act required repeated review of his sexual identity, behavior, and now new practices. The exercise of "companioning grief" (Meris, 2003) where he was asked to review his previous sexual ties with his wife and later with Edsel, identify similarities and differences, then let go of the former and embrace the new provided Wilfred a more present way to be intimate with his male partner (Philippe & Vallerand, 2008).

While making sense of his sexuality, Wilfred also reviewed his collective trauma (Miller, 2003). From his review of the fatal bank incident and skiing death of his college friend, he surrendered to the reality that being witness to and adapting to early traumatic events (Ursano & Fullerton, 1997) made him sensitive to the living and dying processes. He gained strength in knowing the pain of loss(es) (Kauffman, 2010; Robson & Walter, 2013). His readiness to revisit these traumatic experiences engaged him to own up to his remarkable resiliency, resolve, and reconstruction of survival skills (Attig, 2001; Bonanno, 2004; Doka & Martin, 2010).

Coed Grief Support Group (Phase II): Re-Integration

Wilfred had no hesitations participating in the coed grief support group (Phase II) where the focus was primarily on survivors' work to re-engage in the living process. With all the returning group members, Wilfred welcomed genuine interpersonal skills-gains through activities that included: a) *wheel of social networks—then and now*, where they listed their social connections before losses-trauma and their current social ties, b) *update letters*—letters to the deceased about where the survivors are today which were deposited in the group mailbox, c) *triggers now*—identifying and conquering moments of remembrance, d) *self-care agendas*, where lists of how one self-soothes daily and weekly and pinpointing the somatic, mental, and social gains from self-nurturing activities, e) *do the right thing*—where mental redirections are noted when thoughts of the deceased inhabit and overwhelm, f) *readiness to social–sexual revitalization*, where assessment of physical-sexual need requirements are explored, g) *meanings of touch, hugs, and intimacy* where hand lotion is shared between group members through their hands as they discuss and share what and how intimacy means, and h) *opening letters*, where group participants retrieve their letters to the deceased from phase I and their update letter from Phase II to discuss the meanings of these written communications and their relevance to their lives now.

Group members were asked to continue writing their weekly reflections. Another new dimension to this second-stage of group process was encouraging group members to exchange contact information, reach out to each other through email or phone contacts, and chat or meet over coffee, a movie, walk on the esplanade, or any social activity they deemed appropriate. By the fifth session, all group members reported constant email and phone exchanges. The group unanimously decided to arrange their schedules so they could have dinner together after each group session and that the wrap-up last group session must be a "celebration" and volunteered to have a pot-luck dinner. This transformative interaction dynamic engaged Wilfred to recognize that his and his group's collective traumatic life experiences had resulted in a new beginning to human re-integration (Hostetler, 2012).

Moving on: New Beginnings

By normalizing his experience both in his individual counseling sessions and his active participation in the two-phase coed grief support group, Wilfred reconfigured new, authentic bonds with his now remarried father. He also acknowledged a renewed connection with his actively philanthropic and socially integrated mother. The continued close oversight of his sister of both parents reassured him of a freedom to discover his world. The lessons learned from his parents' divorce ultimately helped him to bridge the difficult emotional, financial, psychological and social life adjustments (Cary, Chasteen, & Cadieux, 2014; Hostetler, 2012; Konig & Gluck, 2013) he had to endure with his ex-wife and his daughter. By revisiting and examining his complicated interpersonal connections, identification, and societal reception of his being different (Ross & Mirowsky, 2008), he also explored concerns of oppression, homophobia, disclosure, re-establishing and formulating new supportive networks, and re-assessing both his healthy and dysfunctional ecosystemic scans (LeBeau & Jellison, 2009; Mattiani, Lowery, & Meyer, 2002; Becvar & Becvar, 2006), which afforded him an ability to discover the meanings of his complicated grief (Worden, 2009).

Social Justice and Philanthropic Ventures

Wilfred's learning curves from his individual counseling sessions and his coed grief support group participation—where he gained new allies and friendships—paved his constructive efforts to be fully engaged in "giving" to social justice and human (LGBT) rights advocacy. Acknowledging his "relatively secure financial stature," he started to volunteer with Edsel at an LGBT-focused outreach and anti-violence program where they reviewed policy statements and grant proposal applications, and conducted client intake assessment interviews. They also set aside a night weekly to provide free meals at a homeless shelter that primarily catered to homeless and runaway LGBT-identified youth. They actively contributed to the vital and eventually successful statewide initiative on same-sex marriage equality and legislation.

In spite of all these efforts to be fully integrated in his new LGBT community, Wilfred expressed caution and fear that he and his new partner had not fully embraced their lives as a gay couple since they had not officially come out as gay in their work environment. Several sessions were devoted to prepare him for the potential consequences of this public declaration. It was at this time that Wilfred initiated and suggested that he and Edsel come to couples' counseling to address their crucial joint workplace inclusion and/or rejection. Edsel's willingness to participate in this process only reassured Wilfred of his life partner's commitment. For three sessions, they proactively reviewed and came to terms with any outcomes of their joint workplace coming-out process. To their delight, their corporate-public proclamation was greeted with support and without any negative consequences as they sustained their job–collegial networks and managerial leadership standings. This welcome reception allowed Wilfred and Edsel to entertain the possibility of someday legally documenting their commitment to each other. Both acknowledged that they are bonded by love and would fully entertain the marriage threshold in the future.

Fourteen months after Wilfred marched to fully face his grief, he decided to end his therapeutic journey, equipped with renewed life-skills and ready to embrace what his new complex and exciting world had to offer. It was agreed that his counseling door was left open whenever he needed for further self-examination and wellness discoveries.

Client-Centered Reminders and Practical Strategies for Grief-Trauma Clinicians and Direct-Service Providers

- *Here and now:* Meet your clients in their present state. Yes, review their past trauma but always re-frame the conversation in what is current—they are still alive and your task is to re-engage them in their world today.
- *Silence is power.* Learn the powerful and clinical wonder skill of active listening.
- *"Don't speak!"* It's their story to tell. Let clients fully relate their stories from start to finish without any interruptions from you.
- *Do not edit the narration* when you feel uncomfortable—*sit with your discomfort* and return to listening to your clients in crisis. They are paying you to listen to them—just remember that this is your job.
- *Clients' stories are heavy!* Be prepared to listen to the good and horrific details of their singular and individual worlds.
- *Death anxiety exists*—let it happen.
- *Be present.* Your clients can detect your unattentive body language. Your clients know when you have drifted away as you think of what items to buy in the grocery store after work. Stay focused.
- *It's NOT about you.*—it is about your client's loss (es) and traumatic experiences. Concentrate—stop touching your hair and looking at the clock or your newly manicured fingernails.
- *Mind the gap.* Encourage the grieving process; allow the manifestation of emotions. Your clients will cry, stay quiet for periods of time, may walk out, or change the subject to a more pleasant scenario. Do not stop the outpouring of their grieving and encourage them to return to the difficult details of their mourning narratives.

- *Group work-process helps.* Suggest group counseling participation and do not impose the service program; it is their decision to make.
- *Multiple identities*: Clients are not just grievers—they are fathers, husbands, engineers, cigarette smokers, aunts, cousins, Facebook-addicts. Acknowledge their entire being!
- *Help clients re-channel their present energies.* Remind clients that others continue to rely/expect their active engagement in day-to-day activities. A widow must still prepare breakfast for her children before the school bus arrives at 7:30 a.m., report to her job, pick up her sons/daughters from after-school dance practice after her PTA meeting . . .
- *Encourage grieving clients to execute their self-care agendas.* Walk to the park—it's a form of exercise, window-shop at Macy's department store even when you're broke, seen it a dozen times but watch that episode of *Law and Order: SVU* on TNT anyway—it's your only downtime, go ahead and smell the beautiful roses at Central Park, get that pedicure already, sleep later on Saturday morning—its your day-off, volunteer at the youth shelter once a week, smoke just a pack of cigarettes this weekend instead of three, call your 92-year-old grandma on Sunday—she likes hearing from relatives.
- *Encourage clients to be socially and community involved.* Suggest volunteering at the soup kitchen once a week; say hello to the recently widowed neighbor in the elevator; open the door for the elderly customer at Starbuck's; smile at the frowning little girl seated across in the subway; model for your nephew and recycle all the plastic bottles and soda cans; start a weekly knitting group with the other ladies in the senior citizens center; exercise your civil rights and vote on election day . . . Engage clients in human reconnections/interactions.
- *Leave the work in the office*: Supporting and being present with your clients is your nine to five job! Another world awaits your full and active participation outside of the workplace.
- *You are not getting paid to think about your clients* when you are preparing dinner for your family, helping your son with his homework, making love with your spouse, playing tennis with your best friend, having a father–son discussion about using condoms when he has sex with his girlfriend . . . Current life events require your complete attention outside of work.
- *You are working alone when your client is not in front of you.* Grief work must be done when the client and clinician are both present in the same space and time. Thinking about what you should, must, ought to say to clients when they are not in front of you is wasted and toxic energy.
- *Take care of yourself—laugh.* Listening to stories of death, dying, trauma, and bereavement is only a part of your work life. After your 45-minute session with your first client today, you have six more clients with different, sad stories. Rejoin and enjoy the benefits of laughter each day!

Key Terms

Concerns collage—therapeutic technique of creating a visual representation of various aspects of one's life that cause consternation or stress; usually these are in the form of pictures and words that are either drawn or cut and pasted from magazines or other sources.

Internalized homophobia—refers to negative stereotypes, beliefs, stigma, and prejudice about homosexuality and LGBT people that a person with same-sex attraction turns inward on himself/herself, whether or not they identify as LGBT.

Therapeutic relationship—a professional relationship that exists for the purpose of growth and support of another individual. Therapeutic relationships differ from social relationships in their goals, boundaries, and process.

Questions for Reflection

1. Consider some of the therapeutic exercises described in this chapter. Have you ever engaged in self-exploratory work like this? If so, what was your experience of integrating such reflection with your ongoing experience? If not, do you imagine that such work could lead to meaningful insight? Why might it be valuable to use a range of exploratory processes rather than simply asking or being asked direct questions about oneself?
2. What is the difference between homophobia that is present in society versus internalized homophobia in individuals? How might internalized homophobia be manifest for an individual?

References

Aldwin, C. M. (2009). Gender and wisdom: A brief interview. *Research in Human Development, 6*(1), 1–8.
American Psychological Association. (2007). *Task force research on the impact of reparative therapy, harms caused by societal prejudice.* Retrieved from www.apa.org/pi/lgbt/resources/therapeutic-response.pdf.
Attig, T. (2001). Relearning the world: Making and finding meanings. In R. Neimeyer (Ed.), *Meaning reconstruction and the experience of loss* (pp. 33–54). Washington, DC: American Psychological Association.
Bajko, M. S. (2014, April 20). Black LGBT seniors struggle with double discrimination. *New American Media.* Retrieved from www.newamericamedia.org/2014/04/black-lgbt-seniors-struggle-with-double-discrimination-housing.php
Becvar, D., & Becvar, R. (2006). *Family therapy: A systemic integration.* Boston, MA: Harvard Press.
Black, H. K., Santanello, H. R., & Rubenstein, R. L. (2014). A pragmatic belief system in family meaning-making after death. *Death Studies, 38*(8), 522–530.
Bonanno, G. (2004). Loss, trauma, and human resilience: Have we underestimated the human capacity to thrive after extremely aversive events? *American Psychologist, 59*(1), 20–28.
Brimlow, D. L., Cook, J. S. & Seaton, R. (2003). *Stigma and HIV/AIDS: A review of the literature.* Rockville, MD: US Department of Health and Human Services.
Cheng, P. (2011). Gay Asian masculinities and Christian theologies. *Cross Currents, 61*(4), 540.
Comer, M. (2013, June 13). Gay marriage campaigns taught social justice, unity. *QCityMetro.* Retrieved from www.qcitymetro.com/living/articles/gay_marriage_campaigns_taught_social_justice_unity073719668.cfm
D'Emilio, J. (1993). *Sexual politics, sexual communities: The making of a homosexual minority in the United States.* Chicago, IL: University of Chicago Press.
Doka, K., & Martin, T. L. (2010). *Grieving beyond gender: Understanding the ways men and women mourn.* New York, NY: Routledge.
Gillies, J., Neimeyer, R., & Milman, E. (2014). The meaning of loss codebook: Construction of a system for analyzing meanings made in bereavement. *Death Studies, 38*(4), 207–216.
Guess, P. E. (2013). The power of client engagement: "Contextual healing" research and implications for treatment of depression. *Ethical Human Psychology and Psychiatry, 15*(2), 109–119.
Hedges, L. E. (2011). *Psychotherapy: Sexuality, passion, love and desire in the therapeutic encounter.* New York, NY: Routledge.
Hostetler, A. J. (2012). Community involvement, perceived control, and attitudes toward aging among lesbians and gay men. *International Aging and Human Development, 75*(2), 141–167.
Kang, S., Chasteen, A., Cadieux, J., Cary, L., & Syeda, M. (2014). Comparing young and older adults' perceptions of conflicting stereotypes and multiply-categorizable individuals. *Psychology and Aging, 29*(3), 469–481.
Kauffman, J. (2010). *The shame of death, grief, & trauma.* New York, NY: Routledge.
Konig, S., & Gluck, J. (2013). Individual differences in wisdom conceptions: Relationships to gratitude and wisdom. *International Journal of Aging and Human Development, 77*(2), 127–147.
LeBeau, R. T., & Jellison, W. A. (2009). Why get involved? Exploring gay and bisexual men's experience of the gay community. *Journal of Homosexuality, 56*(1), 56–76.
McFarlane, A., & van der Kolk, B. (1996). Trauma and its challenge to society. In B. van der Kolk, A. McFarlane, & L. Weisaeth (Eds.), *Traumatic stress: The effects of overwhelming experience on mind, body and society.* New York, NY: Guilford Press.
Mattiani, M. A., Lowery, C. T., & Meyer, C. H. (Eds.). (2002). *Foundations of social work practice: A graduate text* (3rd ed.). Washington, DC: NASW Press.
Mejia, X. E. (2005). Gender matters: Working with adult male survivors of trauma. *Journal of Counseling & Development, 83*(1), 29–40.

Meris, D. (2002). Isolation vs. inclusion: Addressing the grief concerns of LGBT individuals. *Proceedings: 24th Annual ADEC Conference*. Portland, OR.

Meris, D. (2003). Gay survivor challenges after 9/11/2001-WTC disaster: John's story. *Proceedings: 25th Annual ADEC Conference*. Cincinnati, OH.

Metro Weekly. (2013). Don't ask: Just tell sexual racism is at the core of what many gay men believe to be *preferences*." Retrieved from www.metroweekly/news/opinion/?ak=5613.

Miller, M. (2003). Working in the midst of unfolding trauma and traumatic loss: Training as a collective process of support. *Psychoanalytic Social Work*, *13*(4), 7–25.

National Gay and Lesbian Task Force. (2013). Study of Asian Pacific American LGBT people reveals high rates of discrimination. Retrieved from www.thetaskforce.org/press/release/pr784_020805.

Neimeyer, R. A. (2001). The language of loss. In R. A. Neimeyer (Ed.), *Meaning reconstruction and the experience of loss* (pp. 261–292). Washington, DC: American Psychological Association.

Neimeyer, R. A., Klass, D., & Dennis, M. R. (2014). A social constructionist account of grief: Loss and the narration of meaning. *Death Studies*, *38*(8), 485–498.

Nord D. (1996). Issues and implications in the counseling of survivors of multiple AIDS-related loss. *Death Studies*, *29*, 389–413.

Park, C. L., & George, L. S. (2013). Assessing meaning and meaning making in the context of stressful life events: Measurement tools and approaches. *The Journal of Positive Psychology*, *8*(6), 483–504.

Parkes, C. M., & Weiss, R. S. (1983). *Recovery from bereavement*. New York, NY: Basic Books.

Philippe, F. L., & Vallerand, R. J. (2008). Actual environments do affect motivation and psychological adjustment: A test of self-determination theory in a natural setting. *Motivation and Emotion*, *32*(2), 81–89.

Paul, J. P., Catania, J., Pollack, L., Moskowitz, J., Canchola, J., Mills, T., . . ., & Stall, R. (2002). Suicide attempts among gay and bisexual men: Lifetime prevalence and antecedents. *American Journal of Public Health*, *92*(2), 1338–1345.

Rando, T. (2003). *Treatment of complicated mourning*. Champaign, IL: Research Press.

Reece, G. W. (2002). Trauma, loss & bereavement. *Self-improvement newsletter*. Retrieved from www.selfgrowth.ccm/form-newsletter.html.

Robson, P., & Walter, T. (2013). Hierarchies of loss: A critique of disenfranchised grief. *Omega: Journal of Death and Dying*, *66*(2), 97–120.

Ross, C., & Mirowsky, J. (2008). Age and the balance of emotions. *Social Science & Medicine*, *66*(12), 2391–2400.

Silverman, O., & Nickman, S. (1996). Concluding thoughts. In D. Klass, P. Silverman, & S. Nickman (Eds.), *Continuing bonds: New understanding of grief* (pp. 349–354). Washington, DC: Taylor & Francis.

Spitzer, R. L. (2012). *Spitzer: Noted psychiatrist apologizes for study on gay cure*. Retrieved from www.nytimes.ccm/2012/05/19/health/dr-robert-l-spitzer-noted-psychiatrist-apologizes-for-study-on-gay-cure.html.

Ursano, R., & Fullerton, C. (1997). Trauma, time and recovery. In C. Fullerton & R. Ursano (Eds.), *Posttraumatic stress disorder: Acute and long-term responses to trauma and disaster* (pp. 269–274). Washington, DC: American Psychological Association.

Watson, B. (2014, June 13). GOP marches backward: 2014 Texas platform veers hard right. *Austin Chronicle*, (editorial page).

Wolfson, E. (2014). Texas republican party adopts discredited 'reparative therapy' for gays. *Newsweek*. Retrieved from www.newsweek.com/texas-republican-party-adopts-discredited-reparative-therapy-gays-254168.

Worden, J. W. (2009). *Grief counseling and grief therapy: A handbook for the mental health practitioner*. (4th ed.). New York, NY: Springer Publishing.

Exam Questions

List and briefly describe X of the client-centered reminders and practical strategies for the grief-trauma clinician.

ANSWERS (pp. 86–8)

Here and now: Meet your clients in their present state.

Silence is Power: Learn the powerful and clinical wonder skill of active listening.

"Don't speak!" Let clients fully relate their stories from start to finish without.

Do not edit the narration when you feel uncomfortable—sit with your discomfort and return to listening to your clients in crisis.

Clients' stories are heavy! Be prepared to listen to the good and mostly horrific details.

Death anxiety exists; let it happen.

Be Present: Your clients can detect your unattentive body language. Stay focused.

It's NOT about you—it's about your client's loss(es) and traumatic experiences.

Mind the Gap: Encourage the grieving process; allow the manifestation of emotions

Group work-process helps. Suggest group counseling but do not impose—it's their decision.

Multiple identities: Clients are not just grievers—acknowledge their entire being!

Help clients re-channel their present energies. Remind clients that others continue to rely/expect their being actively engaged in day-to-day activities.

Encourage grieving clients to execute their self-care agendas.

Encourage clients to be socially and community involved.

Leave the work in the office: Support your clients as your 9 to 5 job; but remember that another world awaits your full and active participation outside of the workplace.

You are not getting paid to think about your client outside of work . . . Current life events require your complete attention outside of work.

You are working alone when your client is not in front of you. Grief work must be done when the client and clinician are both present in the same space and time. Thinking about what you should, must, ought to say to clients when they are not in front of you is wasted and toxic energy.

Take care of yourself—laugh. Listening to stories of death, dying, trauma, and bereavement is only a part of your work life. Rejoin and enjoy the benefits of laughter each day!

16
Spirituality and Social Justice

Neil Thompson

Introduction

Spirituality and social justice are both fields of intellectual inquiry with a large literature base, but there has been relatively little attention paid to how the two areas inter-relate and how one can cast light on the other. This chapter is intended as a small contribution to exploring how there is much to be gained, in both intellectual and professional practice terms, from recognizing more fully the importance of connecting spirituality with social justice.

The chapter focuses first on how religion has a mixed track record when it comes to social justice, with some very positive aspects and some far from positive ones. This leads into a discussion of the importance of recognizing spirituality as a key phenomenon in its own right distinct from religion.

The emphasis then switches to a stronger focus on social justice by way of an examination of the relationship between spirituality on the one hand and equality and diversity on the other. The following section continues this theme, but does so by exploring specific aspects of spirituality as they relate to social justice. Our next focus of attention is on spirituality, social justice, and loss, important topics that are rarely discussed in combination.

The chapter draws on a number of theoretical concepts, but also seeks to cast light on some of the key practice implications of the issues discussed.

Religion and Social Justice: A Mixed Picture

The notion of "Christian fellowship" and good will towards others is a well-established concept. One of the meanings of "Islam" is peace and one of its five pillars is "zatak," the giving of alms to poor and needy people. The humanitarian work of Mahatma Gandhi, rooted in Hinduism, is also well established historically. One of the Four Noble Truths of Buddhism is the cessation of suffering (*dukkha*). A commitment to caring for poor people is a central part of the Sikh faith. It should be clear, then, that "good works" are an important element of the main world religions. Indeed, one of the root words from which the term "religion" is believed to be derived is *ligare*, which means to connect. So, the notion of solidarity can also be closely associated with religion (as is captured in the term, "faith community").

However, it does not follow that that a commitment to humanitarianism encompasses social justice or a rejection of inequality. For example, George Washington, a deeply compassionate and religious man, was a slave owner. The concept of social justice is socially constructed, in the sense that different cultures and different historical eras will have different conceptions of what is socially just. Religions, as major influences on social mores and beliefs, therefore have an important role in shaping conceptions of social justice and thereby influencing in powerful ways people's attitudes to inequality and matters of justice. As Illouz (2008) comments: "if culture matters, it is because of the ways it shapes and orients the meanings and interpretations with which we carry on daily life and make sense of the events that disrupt daily life" (p. 35). For a high proportion of people, of course, their religion is a major feature and component of that culture.

There are at least two mains sets of issues to be considered here. First, a religion's conception of social justice will often be biased by principles and beliefs inherent in the faith itself. For example, religions which adopt an exclusive approach and see themselves in terms of "the one truth" thereby place other religions (and non-religious groups) in a subordinate position. This creates a relationship of dominance and thus of inequality, with little room for ecumenical approaches of mutual tolerance and acceptance. That is, some elements of certain religions are intrinsically rooted in inequality. Second, there are many examples of inequality and unfairness that are not intrinsic to a particular faith, but which have arisen because of how certain groups of people have interpreted a particular aspect of that religion's tenets. For example, Islam, as practiced by many people, involves clear elements of patriarchy in the attitude towards women. However, there is also within the Moslem community itself a feminist critique of such inegalitarian values, which argues that there is nothing in the Qur'an or hadith that justifies the treatment of women as secondary or subordinate (Wadud, 1999). As the Dalai Lama (2013), in a different religious context, puts it: "Though religion certainly has the potential to help people lead meaningful and happy lives, it too, when misused, can become a source of conflict and division" (p. xii).

A further example of how religion and social justice can clash is in the rejection of the validity of same-sex relationships within certain strands of Christianity. There have been many criticisms of this stance from gay liberation groups, but there is also a growing voice from within the Christian church which highlights the injustice and inappropriateness of such discriminatory attitudes and practices. For example, Paris (2011) argues that some Christians counter an oversexualized culture with an undersexualized spirituality which unnecessarily places homosexuality in a subordinate position to heterosexuality, thereby creating social injustice.

In a similar vein, Coulton (2005), writing from a Christian perspective, argues that:

> A sexuality that has to hide itself is demeaning and destructive of the person. Acceptance, by oneself and by others, is needed for integration, wholeness and fulfilment in human relationships. A minority, not deviant but different, will only find fulfilment with people of the same gender. Concealment is alien to Christian understanding of the God who rejoices in those made in God's likeness.
>
> (p. 7)

Rowland (2005) echoes similar concerns in highlighting the dangers of regarding the Bible as a set of laws rather than part of: "discerning what the divine Spirit is now saying to the churches" (p. 30). He warns that Paul was against using scripture as a form of "law code."

Religion can also be problematic in terms of how non-belief is handled. For example, Stephens (2014) points out that, for many centuries, the rejection of religious belief (apostasy, to use the technical term) was punishable by death in Christian communities. This still remains the case to this day in some Moslem communities (Dawkins, 2007). Further examples of inequality being seen as an acceptable part of a religion can be found in Hinduism, which is perhaps better seen as a family of related religions, rather than a single religion in its own right. The caste system of social stratification predefines certain assigned rights and status, consigning some people to the stigmatized and socially unvalued category of what was formerly referred to as "the untouchables," or "Dalit," to use the contemporary term. There is now a strong movement towards challenging this inherently discriminatory system (www.dalitfoundation.org).

Onfray (2011) pulls no punches in highlighting the negatives associated with religion over the centuries. He claims that "In the name of God, as centuries of history attest, the three monotheisms have caused unbelievable rivers of blood to flow! Wars, punitive operations, massacres, murders, colonialism, the elimination of entire cultures, genocides, crusades, inquisitions, and today's global terrorism" (p. 62). But the religious picture is not an entirely negative one when it comes to social justice and equality. There have also been important contributions to challenging discrimination and oppression across faith groups and across history. For example, what came to be known as "liberation theology" was an important movement in Latin America that made strong, decisive, and concerted steps towards tackling poverty, deprivation, social exclusion, and related injustices (Gutierrez, 2010).

We can see, then, that, while religion is a source of much good and value when it comes to humanitarianism in general and social justice in particular, we have to recognize that it is a mixed picture, in so far as religion, whether intrinsically in terms of its very precepts or extrinsically in terms of how those precepts have been interpreted and deployed, has contributed—and continues to contribute—to social injustices on a major scale. Adopting an uncritical acceptance of religion as a plank of social justice is therefore far from wise. If we are to do justice to the complexities of the relationship between religion and social justice, we need a fairly sophisticated understanding of the subtle, multilayered dynamics that are involved.

Spirituality Beyond Religion

For many people there is an automatic association between spirituality and religion—that is, they assume that spirituality is necessarily a religious matter. However, although this is an understandable connection to make, it ignores the fact that, while not all people on this planet are religious, everyone has spiritual needs and faces spiritual challenges. Religion is a very common and well-established basis for addressing spiritual issues, but it is certainly not the only one. In this connection, the Dalai Lama (2013) makes what I am sure many people will see as a very surprising comment when he argues that: "For all its benefits, however—in bringing people together, giving guidance and solace, and offering a vision of the good life which people can strive to emulate—I do not think that religion is indispensable to the spiritual life." (p. 16) Indeed, to assume that spirituality has to be part of religion is to exclude and discriminate against large numbers of people who have no faith allegiance, a step away from social justice in its own right.

Moss (2005) defines spirituality as how we express our chosen worldview. It is how we make sense of who we are and how we fit into the wider world and is therefore concerned with such matters as meaning, purpose and direction, hope and aspirations, wisdom, and 'connectedness'—our sense of being part of something bigger than ourselves, including society. Religions offer predefined answers to our spiritual questions in the form of scriptures, edicts, and pastoral guidance. However, there are other ways of addressing our spiritual needs that do not involve subscribing to a particular faith or religious ideology. For example, existentialism is premised on the need to find our own pathway, to create our own meanings—individually and collectively (in, through, and against culture; Thompson, 2007).

This idea of forging our own path encompasses both religious and atheistic forms of existentialism. The latter, epitomized in the work of Sartre, focuses on avoiding "bad faith," the denial of responsibility for our own actions and choices (Kaufmann, 1988). An example of the former would be Kierkegaard who, although a devout Christian, argued for the need for individuals to serve God by finding their own way forward, rather than relying on religious doctrine to dictate this for them

(Hampson, 2013). Whether, and to what extent, the way forward we choose incorporates a commitment to fairness and equality will shape whether our spirituality contributes to social justice or not. Our path can be selfish and self-centered, concerned with only our own material benefits or it can be rooted in compassion and a humanitarian concern for all as part of a value commitment to social justice which entails promoting equality, valuing diversity, and challenging discrimination and oppression (Thompson, 2011). We will return to these issues below.

Hamilton (2001) highlights connections across spiritual, existential, and social concerns:

> In providing meaning, religion is often said not simply to address existential questions relating to the individual but also to play a central social role. It provides justification for actions and legitimation of practices, customs and social arrangements. Sociological approaches to religion have usually stressed its role in upholding the social order. It is certainly clear that religious systems have generally been locked into the wider social order. To explain the world in ways that make it meaningful, inevitably entails explaining also the social order in a meaningful way and thereby legitimating it. Thus religion has a social as well as an individual dimension.
>
> (p. 273)

We can broaden this out beyond religion to encompass spirituality more generally. That is, religion is just one way—although a very important one sociologically—of addressing existential concerns. Whatever form our spirituality takes—whether faith-based or not—existential questions will be part of it and those existential questions have both socio-political roots and consequences to a certain extent. It is therefore a mistake to assume that spirituality is somehow disconnected from wider social concerns, including social justice concerns.

Spirituality, Equality, and Diversity

Tomikel (2010) argues that people:

> concerned with attaining spirituality may follow one of two paths, or perhaps both, if a selected path does not give satisfaction. One path is the acceptance of our place in society and to operate from that place. The other is to reject society and seek spirituality in complete isolation.
>
> (p. 101)

Tomikel's view reflects two assumptions, both of which I disagree with. First, his approach echoes the common assumption that spirituality is a personal matter (to be carried out in isolation) which can be contrasted with religion as a social matter. However, this is a misrepresentation of spirituality. There is nothing inherent in the notion of spirituality that needs to make it a purely personal matter unconnected with wider social concerns. Indeed, the key spiritual concept of "connectedness" is intrinsically social, a point to which I will return later. I also reject his assumption that, apart from an atomistic spirituality, the choice is quietism—that is, the option of resigning ourselves to our place in society. To accept Tomikel's premise would amount to disconnecting spirituality from social justice.

By contrast, spirituality has the potential to contribute to social justice in a number of ways. Consider, for example, two of the key elements of social justice: equality and diversity. Equality, of course, should not be confused with uniformity—it is a matter of treating people with equal fairness, rather than treating them all the same (Thompson, 2011). Equality, then, entails not discriminating against people because they are in some way different (on the grounds of ethnicity, gender, and so on). Diversity is the other side of the coin, in the sense that the notion of valuing diversity involves recognizing difference as an asset, as a positive to be valued and even celebrated, rather than as a problem to be solved. If diversity is valued, then the tendency to treat certain individuals or groups unfairly on the basis of their difference becomes much less of an issue. Social justice can therefore be seen to be premised on equality and diversity.

The significance of spirituality in this regard lies in the various ways in which our chosen worldview incorporates or marginalizes a concern for the well-being of others, particularly those who are disadvantaged by such destructive forces as poverty, racism, sexism, and other such forms of discrimination that give rise to oppression and social exclusion. Our spirituality and associated values will guide us in how we respond to social injustices. It is therefore important to understand spirituality as a dimension of social justice, rather than as something separate from it. To go down the atomistic road of spirituality (that is, one which focuses narrowly on individual aspects and ignores the wider context) is to ignore the political (and hence social justice) implications of spirituality and, ironically, that is a political step to take, as a claim to be apolitical is, in effect, a bolster to the socio-political status quo, which thereby goes unchallenged. Existing relations of inequality remain untouched when they are accepted as normal and natural and beyond the remit of spiritual inquiry within an atomistic model of spirituality. Indeed, a strong feature of Marx's argument against religious belief was that an emphasis on acceptance of the status quo in this life in exchange for rewards in the next life was a key element of social control to maintain existing socio-political and economic patterns of dominance by the ruling class (Marx, 2008).

Hamilton (2001) also draws links between spirituality (in terms of meaning) and issues of social injustice:

> Questions of meaning, furthermore, often stem from a sense of injustice or discrepancy between what is and what ought to be. Since such matters are bound up with patterns of social advantage and disadvantage, religious answers to such questions inevitably address and reflect aspects of the social order.
>
> (p. 274)

Returning to existentialist thought, we can see the benefits of a holistic view of human experience—that is, one that incorporates psychological, social, and spiritual elements (Thompson, 2012a). Atomism focuses on individual psychological aspects of the situation. As we have noted, spirituality is often viewed from an individualistic point of view. The dimension that tends to be neglected, then, is the social (or, more specifically, the socio-political). As Hall and Janman (2010) explain, in discussing leadership:

> To reconcile the person and the social is a real challenge for psychology and sociology generally, not just the field of leadership specifically. Some of the more experienced authors in this sector have said that 'to speak of personality and social structure in the same breath is as close as one can get to heresy.'
>
> (p. 78)

This reflects a long-standing failure to adopt holistic approaches that go beyond academic disciplinary boundaries to present a fuller, more adequate conception of what it means to be human. It is an example of "silo thinking" in which members of one academic discipline fail to acknowledge the contribution of other perspectives. This problem can also be seen to apply to the relationship between spirituality and social justice. As we shall see, this can be problematic for professional practice in the human services in general, but especially for work involving responding to the challenges of loss and grief (Thompson, 2012a).

Furedi (2004), in a sociological critique of the atomistic approach to social problems which conceives of them in individualistic, therapy-oriented terms, argues that there is a tendency for individuals to interpret the difficulty they have in making sense of their lives as the product of their internal life, rather than as a statement of the inability of society to provide people with a common web of meaning. In such circumstances, the distress that emerges from social conditions can be experienced as a problem of the self. Increasingly, we tend to think of social problems as emotional ones.

(p. 24)

This passage helpfully links spirituality ("making sense of their lives") with social problems which can, in turn, be linked to social justice. This is because there is a close association between the social justice concerns of equality and diversity and the destructive social processes of exclusion, discrimination, and oppression that are so often features of social problems.

Promoting equality and valuing diversity without taking account of spirituality can result in a superficial approach (Moss & Thompson, 2006). Addressing spiritual matters while neglecting wider issues of equality, diversity, and social justice is likely to produce an incomplete understanding of how spiritual matters are rooted in the social world, including its problems and iniquities.

Dimensions of Spirituality

In an earlier work (Thompson, 2010), I identified some of the main elements of spirituality as: meaning, purpose, and direction; connectedness; and awe, wonder, and hope. In this section I draw links between these specific elements of spirituality and social justice, focusing on each in turn.

Meaning

There are, of course, personal, individualized elements of meaning. Each of us is a unique individual, with our own "narratives" or frameworks of meaning built around our unique life experiences. However, it also has to be recognized that we are unique individuals in a social context—we do not operate in a social vacuum (Thompson, 2012b). Our meanings are shaped to a large extent by wider cultural frameworks of meaning or "discourses," which bring with them relations of power (hierarchies of dominance and subordination), that have implications for not only our life experiences but also how we perceive and interpret them—the meanings we attach to them. Meanings, as Illouz (2008) points out: "differ in their ability to constrain definitions of reality: some meanings are more powerful and binding than others" (p. 9). For example, patriarchal discourses will have a bearing on how both women and men experience their lives and how they make sense of them.

In this sense there is very clearly a socio-political dimension to the meaning element of spirituality, and that dimension is very relevant in relation to social justice.

Purpose and Direction

Similarly, our sense of purpose and direction will be unique to each of us, but will also be in part shaped by wider social influences. What we want out of our lives, what form we want fulfillment to take and so on are important elements of spirituality, but are also to a certain extent reflections of powerful discourses at a cultural level and social divisions at a structural level, the role of which we would be unwise to ignore. An important question to ask is: Does the direction we take in our lives contribute to greater social justice or does it reinforce existing inequalities and injustices?

Connectedness

At the heart of spirituality is the notion of connectedness, the recognition that, however individual each of us may be, we are part of a wider society, part of something greater than ourselves. For many people, this "something greater than ourselves" is religion, but it does not have to be. It could be a commitment to saving our habitat from environmental destruction (Zapf, 2010), to a professional calling (health care, for example) or to a political cause. In this regard our spiritual connectedness could well take the form of a commitment to promoting social justice.

The tendency to focus narrowly and lose sight of the wider context is highlighted by Hall and Janman (2010), who argue that human beings struggle to see our connectedness to the world around us and to each other. They emphasize the need to consciously recognize we are all no more and no less than the sum of our relationships with others, what they call our "total social capital." It is therefore important that we go beyond an atomistic perspective on spirituality and recognize its important *social* dimension. Moss (2005) captures this point well when he points out that: "There is no doubt that the themes of religion and spirituality are seen by many as being intensely personal, private even. They touch our lives at the deepest level, and illuminate what some call the 'core of our being,'" (p. 61) but then goes on to argue that there is also a social—and specifically social justice—dimension that needs to be considered.

Awe, Wonder and Hope

Being denied some degree of awe, wonder, and hope can so often be the result of oppression. In keeping with the notion of connectedness, there is a strong argument that these are aspects of human existence that should be available to all and should not be rationed according to hierarchies of power and privilege. Spirituality is also closely linked to identity, our sense of who we are and how we fit into the wider world. Part of this is a sense of security. Clearly, a key part of a sense of security is having a home, and yet the social problem of homelessness is one that continues to haunt even the most affluent of our societies. Barry (2005) links homelessness with social justice when he explains that:

> Homelessness is the most extreme form of social exclusion (with the possible exception of being in prison) in contemporary western societies. Those with "no fixed abode" (whether sleeping rough or in temporary shelters) have no mailing address, which is a minimum condition of participation; they have no way of exchanging hospitality (so it is hardly surprising that they hang out with other people in like circumstances) and they occupy the most despised social status. They thus illustrate strikingly the dependence of behaviour on circumstances. Faced with a bleak and meaningless existence, can it be wondered at that homeless people resort to some reliable means of attaining oblivion? "The research will exacerbate concern that it may be almost impossible for homeless people to kick addictions to drugs and alcohol" [Summerskill and Mahtani, 2002]. So once again, instead of holding individuals responsible, we should apply the public health model and change the circumstances in which they find themselves.
>
> (p. 161)

This is an important passage, in so far as it indicates that a lack of social justice can have significant consequences in terms of spiritual impoverishment. The losses involved in being denied the security of a home can also be seen as spiritual matters (Thompson, 2012a).

Spirituality, Social Justice, and Loss

Loss can be seen as a linking thread between spirituality and social justice. This is because loss raises a number of spiritual challenges in a number of ways (Gilbert, 2013). As the homelessness example from Barry above illustrates, social injustice also involves both spiritual challenges and losses. In particular, how we respond to death has spiritual implications. Sprintzen (2009) captures a key aspect of this when he argues that:

> Here resides the existential root of religion—in that conjoint experience of wonder at being and fear of death to which self-consciousness opens us up. Hence, also the pervasive universality of religious belief and practice. For all humans must ask themselves where do I come from— one of the first questions children ask—and where am I going?
>
> (p. 23)

Our response not only to death and bereavement but also to loss more broadly can be seen to have a strong spiritual dimension. For example, Marris (1996) shows how our frameworks of meaning can be severely disrupted at a time of significant loss:

> When someone is bereft of a crucial relationship, nothing seems to make sense any longer: the world has become meaningless instead of a generalizable structure of beliefs sustaining the bereaved through the particular loss, interpreting it and setting it in a larger context of meaning, the beliefs themselves may invalidated, compounding the sense of loss so, for instance, C S Lewis describes how, on his wife's death, he underwent a bitter crisis of faith; and widows I interviewed in a London study described the same rejection of religious consolations in which they had believed.
>
> (p. 47)

The important work of Neimeyer (2001) on meaning reconstruction theory as a means of understanding grief reactions reinforces this theme, as does that of Tomer, Eliason, and Wong (2008). This is important in terms of the implications for professional practice as it means that practitioners will need to be aware of both the spiritual and social justice aspects of the loss situations they encounter in their work. Marris goes on to explain that grief is a reaction to the disintegration of the whole structure of meaning associated with this relationship, rather than directly to the absence of the person who has died or otherwise been lost from the griever's life. Their intense anxiety and sense of hopelessness are brought about by their sense that their former reality no longer means anything to them. This reflects a process whereby grief undermines the emotional structures that give us our spiritual sense of purpose and direction.

Existentialist thought is again helpful in this connection as it helps us to understand that significant losses bring about a degree of "biographical disruption"—that is, we temporarily lose not only our framework of meaning (or "narrative"), but also to a certain extent, our identity, our spiritual sense of who we are. But it also helps us to understand that these struggles for meaning take place in a social context which, in part, will shape our reactions to the challenges we face (Thompson, 2012a). That social context will not be a level playing field; it will reflect the social divisions that produce unequal relations of power. It is therefore important that professional practice is able to transcend the silo thinking of academic disciplines that focus on one aspect or other of human experience and seek to make sense of our practice more holistically—seeing spirituality and social justice as two sides of the same coin, rather than as distinct fields of study or concern.

The work of Moss and Thompson (2006) is important in this regard. They take PCS analysis (Thompson, 2011; 2012b), which focuses on the three levels of social life (personal, cultural, and structural), and show how spirituality can be seen as an important dimension of each of the three levels. This can be a useful analytical tool for practitioners: To ensure that there is a spiritual dimension to the *personal* aspects of the situations they are working in (cognitive, emotional, and behavioral); to the *cultural* aspects (frameworks of meaning, discourses, and ideologies); and to the *structural* aspects (social divisions such as class, race, and gender). The value of using this analytical framework as a practice tool is that it enables us to incorporate both spiritual and social justice issues and to see how they inter-relate, thereby avoiding the long-standing problem of separating out these two important—and interconnected—dimensions of human experience.

Conclusion

In light of the immense harm inequality, discrimination, and oppression inflicted on a wide range of groups of people (with many of these groups experiencing multiple, simultaneous oppressions; Thompson, 2011), the promotion of social justice is a vitally important endeavor for any group of people—whether religious or not—committed to humanitarian goals. Spirituality has rarely featured in discussions of social justice, but it is to be hoped that this chapter has cast some light on the importance of connecting the two domains of study and their respective implications for practice. We live in a world riven with various conflicts, characterized by a depressing array of personal and social problems and often lacking any sense of purpose and direction other than the dangerous seductions of materialism and consumerism (see Thompson, this volume). The promotion of social justice is not a panacea or magic answer, but it would be short-sighted of us not to recognize that so much of our contemporary malaise is (i) rooted in inequality, discrimination, and oppression; and (ii) largely spiritual also in terms of the causes and the effects.

Reflecting this, Wilkinson and Pickett (2009), in their important work on highlighting the social, financial, and human costs of inequality, argue that:

> It is a remarkable paradox that, at the pinnacle of human material and technical achievement, we find ourselves anxiety-ridden, prone to depression, worried about how others see us, unsure of our friendships, driven to consume and with little or no community life. Lacking the relaxed social contact and emotional satisfaction we all need, we seek comfort in overeating, obsessive shopping and spending, or become prey to excessive alcohol, psychoactive medicines and illegal drugs. How is it that we have created so much mental and emotional suffering despite levels of wealth and comfort unprecedented in human history?
>
> (p. 3)

Their answer to this question is that the structured inequalities of wealth, opportunities, and power their book addresses have a powerfully detrimental approach at a number of levels. To this I would want to add the fact that social injustice stands as an obstacle to meeting spiritual—and thus human—needs, in so far as social disadvantage can be seen to have spiritual consequences. Hamilton (2001) captures this point well in arguing that:

> Inequalities of power affect both vulnerability to bereavement and the ability to recover from it. The fewer resources you control, the less likely you are to protect yourself and those you love from traumatic events—diseases you cannot afford to treat or avoid, accidents due to dangerous work, the violence of urban slums, unemployment, eviction, imprisonment. But this vulnerability itself—as a source of anxiety and feelings of helplessness or dependence—also makes recovery from loss more difficult. Those who are most exposed to loss also tend to have fewer assurances and continuities by which to reconstruct the meaning of their lives.
>
> (p. 118)

One element of spirituality we have not explored but which is worth mentioning by way of conclusion is that of "the sacred." Perhaps what we need to aim for is a spirituality in which social justice is sacred, a worldview that regards circumstances in which certain groups are discriminated against, disenfranchised, disempowered, and oppressed as totally unacceptable as a major affront to human dignity.

Key Terms

Apostasy—formal disaffiliation from, abandonment, and/or renunciation of a religion by a person.

Atomistic spirituality—focuses narrowly on individual aspects/experience and ignores the wider (societal/social justice) context.

Quietism—resigning oneself to one's place in society (without question or resistance).

Silo thinking—problematic pattern of thought in which members of one academic discipline fail to acknowledge the contribution of other perspectives.

Spirituality—the way in which we make sense of who we are and how we fit into the wider world; concerned with such matters as meaning, purpose and direction, hope and aspirations, wisdom, and "connectedness"—our sense of being part of something bigger than ourselves, including society.

Total social capital—the sum of our relationships with others.

Questions for Reflection

- How would you differentiate religion and spirituality? In your experience, how does each of these concepts intersect with questions of social justice, equality and diversity?
- The author proposes that significant losses—including bereavement—may result in some degree of loss of identity, of our spiritual sense of who we are. Have you ever experienced this form of "biographical disruption" personally, or witnessed someone who appeared to be going through such a struggle? What was your experience during this time?

References

Barry, B. (2005). *Why social justice matters*. Cambridge: Polity Press.
Coulton, N. (2005). Does it matter enough, and to whom? In N. Coulton (Ed.) *The Bible, the Church and Homosexuality*, London: Darton, Longmann and Todd.
The Dalai Lama (2013.) *Beyond religion: Ethics for a whole world*. London: Rider.
Dawkins, R. (2007). *The god delusion*. London: Black Swan.
Furedi, F. (2004). *Therapy culture: Cultivating vulnerability in an uncertain age*. London: Routledge.
Gilbert, P. (Ed.). (2013). *Spirituality and end of life care: A handbook for service users. Carers and staff wishing to bring a spiritual dimension to palliative care*. Brighton: Pavilion.
Gutierrez, G. (2010). *A theology of liberation*. Norwich, CN: SCM Press.
Hall, T., & Janman, K. (2010). *The leadership illusion: The Importance of context and connections*. Basingstoke, U.K.: Palgrave Macmillan.
Hamilton, M. (2001). *The sociology of religion: Theoretical and comparative perspectives* (2nd ed.). London: Routledge.
Hampson, D. (2013). *Kierkegaard: Exposition and critique*. Oxford: Oxford University Press.
Illouz, E. (2008). *Saving the modern soul: Therapy, emotions and the culture of self-help*. Berkeley, CA: University of California Press.
Kaufmann, W. (1988). *Existentialism from Dostoevsky to Sartre* (2nd ed.). Harmondsworth, U.K.: Penguin.
Marris, P. (1996) *The politics of uncertainty: Attachment in private and public life*. London: Routledge.
Marx, K. (2008). Introduction to a contribution to the critique of Hegel's philosophy of Right. In D. Roussopoulos (Ed.), *Faith in faithlessness: An anthology of atheism* (pp. 141–154). Montreal: Black Rose Books.
Moss, B. (2005). *Religion and spirituality*. Lyme Regis, U.K.: Russell House Publishing.
Moss, B., & Thompson, N. (2006). Spirituality and equality. *Social and Public Policy Review*, 1(1): 1–12.
Onfray, M. (2011) *Atheist manifesto: The case against Christianity, Judaism, and Islam*. New York, NY: Arcade Publishing.
Neimeyer, R. (Ed.). (2001). *Meaning reconstruction and the experience of loss*. Washington DC: American Psychological Association.
Paris, J. W. (2011). *The end of sexual identity: Why sex is too important to define who we are*. Downers Grove, IL: Intervarsity Press.

Rowland, C. (2005). "The letter killeth, but the Spirit giveth life": Christian Biblical interpretation. In N. Coulton (Ed.) *The Bible, the Church and homosexuality*. London: Darton, Longman and Todd.

Sprintzen, D. (2009). *Critique of Western philosophy and social theory*. New York, NY: Palgrave Macmillan.

Stephens, M. (2014). *Imagine there's no heaven: How atheism helped create the modern world*. New York, NY: Palgrave Macmillan.

Summerskill, B., & Mahtani, D. (2002). Homelessness in drugs epidemic. *The Observer*, July 14, p. 12.

Thompson, N. (2007). Spirituality: An existentialist perspective. *Illness, Crisis & Loss*, 15(2): 125–136.

Thompson, N. (2010). *Theorizing social work practice*. Basingstoke, U.K.: Palgrave Macmillan.

Thompson, N. (2011). *Promoting Equality: Working with diversity and difference* (3rd ed.). Basingstoke, U.K.: Palgrave Macmillan.

Thompson, N. (2012a). *Grief and its challenges*. Basingstoke, U.K.: Palgrave Macmillan.

Thompson, N. (2012b). *Anti-discriminatory practice* (5th ed.). Basingstoke, U.K.: Palgrave Macmillan.

Tomer, A., Eliason, G.T., & Wong, P. T. P. (Eds.). (2008). *Existential and spiritual issues in death attitudes*. New York, NY: Lawrence Erlbaum.

Tomikel, J. (2010). *Spirituality without religion*. Corry, PA: Allegheny Press.

Wadud, A. (1999). *Qur'an and woman: Rereading the sacred text from a woman's perspective* (2nd ed.). New York, NY: Oxford University Press.

Wilkinson, R., & Pickett, K. (2009). *The spirit level: Why more equal societies almost always do better*. London: Allen Lane.

Zapf, M. K. (2010). Social work and the environment: Understanding people and place. *Critical Social Work* 11(3): 30–46.

17

From Violation to Voice, From Pain to Protest

Healing and Transforming Unjust Loss Through the Use of Rituals and Memorials

Carlos Torres and Alfonso M. García-Hernández

It was difficult to ignore the yellow posters covering what appeared to be every other telephone pole in midtown, Memphis. They were the size of a man's chest, giving ample space for the large bold letters on the poster to make its message clear from several feet away: "On August 12, 2011, you killed my son." Alternate posters replaced "son" with "father," "fiancé," and "friend." The image of a bicycle below the text loosely linked them to the mysterious bicycles that appeared almost simultaneously, and in the same neighborhoods, as the posters. Painted in all white and tethered to fences and poles, the bikes produced an ominous presence that cut through the noise and bustle of the busy streets.

Those who could not get information from neighbors and friends found clarity in the media. The article posted on the WMC Action News 5 website was short but to the point: "37-year-old Chris Davidson was hit by a car while riding his bicycle home from Hi-Tone (a music club) just after midnight Friday morning" (Friends say midtown Memphis bicyclist killed by hit-and-run driver, 2011). The details about Chris that the news omitted were provided by the many that knew him and loved him: He was an avid cyclist and supporter of the Memphis music community. Friends and family called him "ManWhat" due to his frequent use of the phrase. They shared stories and honored his memory through the videos they created and posted online, during the ManWhat benefit concert and mass bike ride that raised enough money to cover his funeral expenses, when they showed off their ManWhat memorial tattoos to friends, acquaintances, and strangers, and when they successfully petitioned for the creation of bicycle lanes on midtown's busiest streets.

Looking back on their efforts, Chris' family and close friends explained that his death sparked an anger that led to a call for action: They wanted the person who hit him and left him to die to come forward. The injustice would not go unnoticed. It had to be addressed. Memphis had to know. Their relentless pursuit of justice was an expression of their love. They were also angry that the city's poor regard for cyclist rights had contributed to his death. They wanted to turn their tragedy into a change for Memphis, a change that would have made Chris proud.

Introduction

What makes a loss unjust? A sense of being cheated or robbed is a common feeling shared by many who have experienced the death of a loved one. Grief can feel like an intrusion, one that robs us of our sense of control. In its wake, an attempt to understand why can present as a desire to hold someone or something accountable. Indeed, anger often turns to blame in dealing with the loss: "How could God do this?" "What kind of world would let this happen?" Parkes and Prigerson (2013) observed, "Grief is the price we pay for love," and explained that grief is our love transformed in the face of absence (p. 6). We do not stop loving and we do not stop living, but we do need to learn to connect to our deceased loved one and the world in new ways. This implies acceptance. Minimally, we accept that the world is transient and nothing lasts. If we accomplish this, the world can feel just once again.

A loss narrative is different when a death is perceived as unjust. It maintains that an element of the death is unacceptable. The focus of the painful experience is not solely on the absence of the deceased, but rather shifts to how the death occurred. Thus, the blame is concrete. There is an actual person, or a group of people, who are to blame. Instead of an intrusion, there is a sense of violation. Beyond sorrow, there is rage. What becomes of that rage? For many, anger turns into action. Refusing to let their loved one die in vain, the bereaved become advocates for social change. They tell and retell the story of their loss so that others may understand the injustice they experienced, may see through their suffering, and accompany them in their quest for change.

This chapter examines the use of rituals and memorialization practices among individuals who suffered a death deemed unjust. How do individuals, who have suffered an unjust loss, use memorials and rituals? How are they different from the mourning practices used by others? Grief rituals help us reorganize our lives; they help us live anew without the one we love, without losing our footing in the world at large (Reeves, 2011). They help us close chapters of our lives yet still maintain a connection with the dead, without severing our connections with the living. When the death is deemed unjust, rituals may connect us with the deceased through an attempt to change the world. Rather than accepting and connecting with the world as it is, rituals for the unjustly dead honor their memory by attempting to right a wrong. Thus, rituals for the unjustly dead are visible. They are not silent. There is a message to be seen and heard. They are inherently political, often disruptive, and counter-hegemonic[1] (Holst-Warhaft, 2000).

We will first consider the inner grief experience and then connect it with the outer mourning practices. By considering the psychology of grief first, we hope to make clear what motivates action. By considering the anthropology of mourning, we attempt to recognize the social factors that shape how rituals and memorialization practices are used to satisfy inner psychological needs and maintain social stability among the living. After providing this theoretical background, we will provide examples of rituals and memorialization practices used in response to an unjust loss. We tie the individual with the social by examining the use of rituals and memorialization practices in response to the mourners' relationship with the deceased, with society, and with themselves.

The Psychology of Grief

To understand the uniqueness of grief following an unjust loss, we first examine a broader psychological understanding of grief and provide a current conceptualization of grief that explicates how grief responses relate to the details of the death. Historically, psychologically oriented theorists and researchers have conceptualized grief within an overarching medical model that aims to establish normal trajectories for basic cognitive and emotional processes and palliative solutions for people with pathological symptoms (Charmaz & Milligan, 2006). The result was the promulgation of stage-based models that assumed a universal progression of affective stages that culminate in recovery and a return to normative functioning (Gillies & Neimeyer, 2006). As these models gained popularity outside academic circles and applied medical and mental health settings, a chorus of dissent grew louder. Some argued against the particularities of the model, offering their own alternate conceptualizations (Stroebe, Hansson, Stroebe, & Schut, 2007). Others attacked the philosophical foundations of any such model that claims an all-encompassing explanation for an experience as existentially complex as grief (Cooper, 2013).

Despite the dissent, many scholars still rely on grief models that distinguish between healthy and unhealthy grief symptoms. However, efforts to critique previous models were not in vain. The current complicated grief model proposes diagnostic criteria to assess the duration and severity of a constellation of grief related symptoms, focusing on a subjective assessment of decreased functioning, rather than an objectively measured deviation from an assumed norm (Boelen & Prigerson, 2013). The nucleus of these symptoms is an intense yearning for the deceased, which often leaves the bereaved confused, without a clear sense of self, and feeling helpless. Researchers have found that problematic attachment styles and failure to make sense of the death predict the protraction and severity of the debilitating symptoms (Burke & Neimeyer, 2013). As such, the model opens awareness to our relational matrices and social contexts. The theory, proposing that an inability to make sense of a loss produces distress that can impair us so profoundly, also provides a conceptual bridge between internal affective and cognitive states and our connection to a social world. It will be further described in the following paragraphs.

As proposed by Kelly (1955), a foundational task for all humans is the ability to anticipate the world. As such, Kelly explained that we enter an event with a hierarchical system of personal constructs from which we make sense of, and respond to, that event. Similar anticipatory schemas have been described as basic relationships that orient individuals to the world (Proulx & Inzlicht, 2012) and as *global meanings* that include beliefs about self and the world and sense of purpose (Park, 2010). Meaning making describes the processes that aim to reduce distress when discrepancies arise between specificities related to events and broader global meanings.

Park (2010) describes *meaning making* as both an autonomic and deliberate process that involves cognitive and emotional processes, such as the positive reframing of a situation. For example, a teenager who unexpectedly lost a grandparent may draw on her biological understanding of human functioning and her spiritual beliefs to conclude that her grandfather was granted peace by God and was relieved of his aching and deteriorating body. *Meanings made*, according to Park, are the result of one's effort toward coherency and include acceptance of the event, a sense of growth, and changes in one's global meanings. For example, that same bereaved teen may realize that surviving the distress caused by her grandfather's death has shaped her self-concept as a strong and emotionally mature woman.

The example provided above would be considered a prototypical example of *meaning reconstruction* after bereavement, the healthy navigation through bereavement-related distress that involves making sense of the death, benefit finding, and identity change (Neimeyer, Baldwin, & Gillies, 2006). The meaning reconstruction view of bereavement, contrasting older views of bereavement that proposed a universal, linear, and stage-based model toward resolution, proposes that sense making is a subjective experience (Neimeyer, Prigerson, & Davies, 2002). Moreover, the meaning reconstruction view posits that complicated grief arises when the bereaved individual is unable to make sense of the death. Hence, anger, numbing, and refusal to let go of the deceased manifests from the inability to find meaning in the loss (Neimeyer, 2006).

Consistent with the meaning reconstruction view of bereavement, losses that are unexpected, violent, and deemed unjust can pierce meaning structures profoundly, to the point that individuals may be rendered shocked beyond repair. For many who have experienced an unjust loss, sense making involves identifying injustice, locating the source of the injustice, and making a plan to restore justice. Benefit finding then, includes knowing that death resulted in positive social change.

It may also include an appreciation for those who rallied around the bereaved and shared their time, energy, and money. Identity change, beyond learning to live without the deceased loved one, will frequently include a newfound sense of values and perspectives that are often the result of re-assessing life and clarifying what is most important. Identity change also occurs in the form of discovering or acquiring new competencies in response to losing a loved one (this is especially true if the loved one was the major economic provider within the family) and, of course, in responding to injustice through public protest. Individuals who may have considered themselves shy or meek may find that the anger that fueled their desire to become a social activist has led them to realize they are more socially competent than they ever imagined. They may feel that with the loss of their loved one, their own shy side also died and was replaced by a new, bolder self.

The Anthropology of Mourning

The meaning reconstruction approach opens the door for greater appreciation of how social context influences the meaning someone makes and the resulting feelings they experience. Its hermeneutic approach[2] ties well with social interactionism theory and its use in sociology/anthropology in order to reveal discourses and symbols that guide action and maintain a sense of coherency and stability. According to Hochschild (1979), the matrix of social meaning also contains "feeling rules," that dictate which feelings are supposed to be felt when, and moreover, how they are to be expressed. That "boys don't cry" or that one should keep a "stiff upper lip," and the communal wailing that some cultures require, are well-known examples. Furthermore, such societal rules inform the interpretation of particular deaths such that certain deaths are not viewed as tragic or are made illegitimate and are thus not mourned.

Such instances are captured by Doka's (1989) conceptualization of disenfranchised grief. Grief is disenfranchised when it is "not openly acknowledged, publicly mourned or socially supported" (Doka, 1989, p. 4). Explicating the "serious social failure" that occurs when grief is disenfranchised, Attig (2004) describes disenfranchised grief as "a political failure involving both abuse of power and serious neglect" (p. 200) as well as "an ethical failure to respect the bereaved both in their suffering and in their efforts to overcome it and live meaningfully again in the aftermath of loss" (p. 201). Examples of disenfranchised grief include stigmatized deaths such as suicide or death from AIDS-related complications, where the deceased may be viewed as having committed an act deemed reprehensible in regards to normative religious beliefs and thus, not "deserving" our grief. The silencing of another's bereavement can occur in subtle ways. For example, in an article examining the eventual web-based memorialization of those who participated in the mass suicide in Jonestown in 1978, Moore (2011) explains that Americans initially "denied or suppressed the possibility of grief by adopting the expression 'drinking the Kool-Aid,'" a satirical reference to the method by which the adults ingested the potassium cyanide that killed them (p. 49).

Rituals and memorialization practices exist within the social matrix and thus adhere to and reflect through symbolic behaviors the beliefs, values, and regulatory guidelines of a given society. However, rituals are not simply a show and tell of a culture's norms nor are the symbols meant to be passive reminders of values of which to abide. Turner (1969), an anthropologist who studied rites of passage and ritualization practices among the Ndembu of the Democratic Republic of the Congo, explains that the symbols and behaviors are entryways to direct contact and communication with the divine that remains unseen but energetically present in social life. A less animist, more secular reading of Turner's report may be gleaned if one considers Foucault's (1980) explanation of the creative potentials in social power dynamics. Rituals and memorialization practices may disrupt those disciplinary social processes used to silence "deviant" desires to connect with a loved one whose death was deemed illegitimate or to critique the social structures that made possible an unjust death.

Holst-Warhaft (2000) argues, "grief can always be manipulated for political ends" because "it arouses passion" (p. 5). Lebel and Ronel (2005) explain that public grief responses carry power that can shift policy because bereavement narratives speak to a universal need to sustain life. In that regard then, grief narratives have the potential to uncover repressive power structures that are otherwise unconsciously agreed to and followed. Unjust deaths point to corrupt social scripts.

Our human predisposition to interpret the world via an interconnected web of socially negotiated meanings implies that we live by scripts that are mostly unspoken, guided by a sense of "that's just the way things are," and with an intuitive understanding that those "things" do not have a one-to-one correspondence with material reality. When the corporeal body of our loved one ceases to function and they are rendered unable to look us in the eye with a loving gaze, we do not simply forget about them and cut cleanly the psychological strings of our attachment to them. Rather, we augment the conditions of our relationship in ways that imply a change in our relationship with the world as well as with ourselves. This remains true when the death of our loved one was unjust. The final section of this chapter offers concrete examples of rituals and memorialization practices. We discuss specific practices and their particular functions as they relate to the grieving individual's relationship with the deceased, society, and self.

Memorials and Rituals that Establish and Maintain a New Relationship with the Deceased

The term "continuing bonds" is a fairly recent addition to the bereavement literature and describes the specific practices used by the bereaved to maintain an active relationship with the deceased. Given the ancient use of religious practices that call on ancestors for guidance and strength, it is quite surprising that scholars have only in the last few decades acknowledged such practices as both common and non-pathological. However, academics speak from and reflect larger social beliefs and values as much as any other persons. Marwit and Klass (1994–1995), two scholars who have extensively studied the use of continuing bonds, describe four ways continuing bonds serve to maintain connection between the bereaved and the deceased. The first is through an ongoing identification with the deceased in such a way that the bereaved individual seeks to embody valued qualities of the deceased in their daily life. Individuals who have lost a loved one through unjust means and who have thus become sensitive to the corruption and cruelty that has profoundly disrupted their life may look to their deceased loved one as a teacher or mentor whose positive qualities are a reminder that the world is not all bad. Emulating those qualities is a striving to counter that corruption and cruelty that leads to death and suffering. For example, a father may attempt to engage the world in a more playful and creative way, as his adolescent daughter did before being killed by a drunk driver. He might connect with her further by employing some of her catch phrases or gestures that he found particularly amusing.

The bereaved maintain bonds with the deceased by looking to them for guidance. Navigating through the possible legal, political, and psychological ramifications of trying to right the wrong that killed a loved one can be as distressing as coping with the pain of their absence. If the bereaved is religious and believes in a spiritual connection with the deceased, she or he may turn to prayer or meditation and ask their loved one to guide them through their trials. Individuals who do not hold such beliefs may identify specific qualities their loved one embodied and draw inspiration or guidance from their memory, all the while asking, "What would they do in this situation?"

The deceased continue to clarify the values by which the bereaved want to live. By deciding which of the deceased's many behaviors, beliefs, and personality attributes the bereaved was most inspired by, connects with, or wishes to emulate, personal guidelines by which to live are clarified. This is an important process for those whose loved one died unjustly. The world may feel unstable and threatening and examining what is important in life will aid in reconnecting and re-establishing trust. For example, a teen whose older brother was killed by terrorists while he provided medical care to refugees abroad may realize a profound resonance with courage and compassion embodied by the brother, despite the present grief-related feelings of anger and fear.

Lastly, continuing bonds provide the bereaved with consoling memories. The psychological toll of anger and heavy time-occupying desire to respond to an unjust loss with social activism can, ironically, leave the bereaved with little emotional or temporal space to maintain a relationship with the deceased. The use of "linking objects," such as urns, altars, photographs, personal items belonging to the deceased, or symbolic tokens maintain a space where the memory of the deceased can reside without necessitating arduous effort on the part of the bereaved. The first author encountered one particularly sweet example of a linking object when he spoke to a mother whose son was the unfortunate target of a gang initiation murder. As she described her relentless efforts to counter gang violence through countless hours of community involvement, she grabbed one of her dreadlocks, slightly longer than the others, and explained that she kept her son's spirit close by in the form of his hair. She had taken a snippet of one of his dreads and attached it to her own, so she could enjoy his company and memory as she went out to do some needed good in the world.

Memorial tattoos are another example. The inked commemoration of the deceased rests on the body silently, it's meaning and associated memories waiting to be rediscovered anytime the bereaved catches a glace of it or is asked about it by another. Although memorial tattoos are a static symbol linked to a memory of the deceased, they can serve as sites of active meaning making (Schiffrin, 2009). Through personal reflections when looking at the design and the sharing of memories about the deceased when explaining the meaning behind the piece to those who ask about it, memorial tattoos provide the potential to maintain an active bond to the deceased.

Memorials and Rituals that Establish and Maintain a New Relationship with Society

A public memorialization or ritual practice intends to convey a statement. At its most basic, the statement is a relaying that the death occurred. It assures awareness that the event took place. In this regard, those public practices often make use of the same elements found in that culture's mourning practices in order to relay the information to the public that someone or that a group of people have died. Roadside memorials, for example, convey this information simply by existing as a wooden cross in an unexpected location. The use of flowers, candles, wreaths, coffins, skulls, and religious symbols are common cultural tropes that signal the intention to honor the memory of someone who has died. Placing those items in a public space where they would normally not be found can effectively convert that space into a memorial site. Similarly, a public funeral procession or other common behaviors reserved for death rituals enacted in shared social space make the intentions of those involved at least partially clear.

Though not as common, public memorials and ritual practices that make little or no use of common mourning elements can be just as engaging and emotionally provocative. The use of "ghost bikes," which are bicycles painted completely in white and placed at the site where a cyclist was struck dead by an automobile, is one example that was mentioned in the opening of this chapter. Just like more "formal" memorials, a ghost bike disrupts expectations regarding what will be encountered in a public space and in turn arouses and engages. Furthermore, because their curious presence begs for explanation, ghost bikes relay the death story and generate further discussion among the network of inquiring individuals and knowing others. Similarly, graffiti or wheat pasted posters with ambiguous symbols, when placed in multiple locations throughout a community, generate a sharing of information regarding a particular death, as well as generating discussion regarding death, justice, and policy in general.

Public memorials and rituals are not always impromptu or time-limited. Community-created structures such as memorials statues or benches, rituals such as marches, parades (e.g., Bordere 2008–2009), or observances are all relatively easy to find. However, the memory of the deceased and the message and intention of the space or practice will likely change over time. Their interpretations, and in turn, social effects, will be negotiated within a broader social discourse.

Justice is not just sought through small efforts that only impact local communities. Nationwide organizations have been created in response to unjust loss. The NAMES Foundation, which is responsible for creating and touring the aforementioned AIDS Memorial Quilt, is one example. Mothers Against Drunk Driving (MADD), which was founded by a mother whose daughter was killed by a drunk driver, is another. Organizations such as those, beholden to the memory of the deceased through their commitment to effect positive social change on their behalf, through their size and influence, create different discourses by establishing new policies and laws.

Public space no longer implies material space. Our increasing reliance on the Internet for information and social connectivity makes cyberspace a relatively new location for engaging in memorialization and grief rituals. The Internet allows nearly unlimited and inexpensive space to tell the story of injustice, to rally for change, and to create, maintain, and mobilize a network of sympathetic and committed individuals. Facebook memorial pages have grown in popularity, though memorial websites are common as well (e.g., Sofka, Gilbert, and Cupit Noppe, 2012). An added benefit for the bereaved: Virtual memorial spaces, compared to those that involve brick, mortar, and other materials, afford the opportunity to protest with a much reduced chance of being stripped down, dismantled, and silenced.

Using public space to convey a message is empowering. It allows the bereaved to simultaneous refuse to accept an unjust loss by not remaining silent, calling for change, and rallying support. Beyond making the public aware of an unjust death, the memorial or ritual, both through its call for action as well as through the act itself, can counter-hegemonic metanarratives by calling into question the ethics of their practice. The AIDS Memorial Quilt is a powerful example of this. The quilt can be viewed as a multitude of continuing bonds between thousands of individuals and their deceased loved ones, woven together to make a legitimizing space for the humanity of those who died while calling on society to examine those disenfranchising practices that offer little space to honor the lives of those who contracted HIV. This section focused its attention on public individual or grassroots movements responding to unjust loss. Large-scale memorial structures or public rituals that respond to unjust loss, such as reading the names of those killed on 9/11, exist as well. National mourning practices, by their nature, move in the direction of current political winds though nonetheless afford the same space to connect with the dead as well as the living.

Memorials and Rituals that Establish and Maintain a New Relationship with the Self

If profound loss, especially loss that violates our assumptions of justice, disrupts the coherency of our worldview, it will very likely bring into question assumptions we've held about ourselves. Rose (2000) argues that humans are not "unified subjects" but rather live "in constant movement across different practices that address them in different ways" (p. 319). Adapting to the significant changes that occur after loss connotes engaging in different practices. This is particularly true in the context of an unjust loss, which may lead bereaved individuals, in an empowered state while on their mission to incite social change, to relate differently to the world and demand that others relate differently to them. Whereas bereaved parents whose child died of cancer have discussed feeling isolated from other parents and creating marked boundaries regarding with whom they share their loss stories, parents whose children died due to terrorist acts have described forcing their voice in public arenas in order to incite political change (Lebel & Ronel, 2005).

Calhoun and Tedeschi (2006) noted that the sentence "I am more vulnerable than I thought, but much stronger than I ever imagined" aptly sums up their observations of individuals who have experienced *post-traumatic growth*, or instances when individuals change in positive ways as a result of experiencing traumatic losses (p. 5). The processes involved in continuing bonds and engaging in public memorialization can produce moments of awareness that many things, including the self, have changed. But, what ritual practices can help recognize and celebrate this newfound strength and way of being in the world? In our clinical practice, we have successfully used various expressive and artful therapies with clients bereaved through losses they deemed unjust. We briefly describe a few below.

Strouse (2013) has written beautifully about the power of collaging to heal grief. The first author has found it to be a powerful medium for self-exploration in clinical practice and agrees with Butler-Kisber (2010), who describes collaging as "a user-friendly medium, one in which the basic skills of cutting and sticking that are acquired early in life can be used" by anyone and "evokes embodied responses and uses juxtaposition of fragments and the presence of ambiguity to engage the viewer in multiple avenues of interpretation" (p. 102). Thus, collages allow bereaved individuals to literally reassemble their lives via cut out symbols, images, and words that hold special meaning. The physicality of cutting and pasting can be grounding, and the ability to arrange and rearrange cutouts taps into emotional and cognitive meaning-making processes. Feelings, thoughts, and memories touch and intersect right along with what is moved around and finally pasted on the paper.

Journaling is used in a wide variety of therapeutic contexts and is quite appropriate to use with individuals whose grief journey has been a complex amalgamation of sorrow, anger, and activism. Lichtenthal and Neimeyer (2012) suggest using a directed journaling approach, by which the bereaved are asked to respond to specific prompts, such as "What qualities in yourself have you drawn on that have contributed to your resilience?" or "What qualities of a supportive kind have you discovered in others?" (p. 165). It is suggested that individuals write for 20–30 minutes and that the writing be spontaneous. The intention is to facilitate the meaning-making process by asking clients to focus on the sense they have made of the loss and the benefits they have found, which in turn can clarify what they hold valuable, how they strive to live, and how they can achieve new goals.

Whereas the first technique involved cutting and pasting images in order to explore new connections and subsequent meanings and the second technique involved writing as a method to achieve clarity about values and life goals, this final technique involves visualization to achieve a combination of those results. Sitting comfortably, individuals are asked to take a few minutes to attune their awareness to their breath and then imagine themselves on a path, encountering facilitators and obstacles as they move toward predetermined concrete goals they identity as currently important (such as finishing school, searching for a new job, or starting to date again). The instructions include noting anything that appears on the road, noting its shape, color, and size, as well as the feelings and bodily sensations that arise. The visualization space is meant to allow the images to appear. After 20–30 minutes of sitting and encountering the images, the individual can then write about them, draw them, or talk about them in order to explore their meaning and how they might inform decisions or imply actions to take.

Conclusion

We hope this chapter illuminates the inherent political forces that must be negotiated when individuals experience a death deemed unjust, and that the rituals and memorials that respond to those deaths involve confrontation with those forces. We have aligned with theories of grief that propose that healthy mourning (that is, not protracted and not debilitating) necessitates the ability to make sense of the death, to find benefit in the experience, to realize a change in identity. Making meaning of unjust loss involves making sense of the loss by clarifying the source of injustice, finding benefit through righting a wrong, and sees one's identity change to that of an activist engaged socially in ways that might be totally new.

We also appealed to those current understandings of healthy grieving that promote continued relationships with the deceased. Noting that, in as much as continuing bonds with the deceased implies a restructuring of that relationship, relationships with society and self are restructured as well. Rituals and memorials honor and mark the reconfiguration of those relationships. As such, we focused on rituals and memorials that held space for the grief and the call to activism. Confronting political forces means that those mourning practices align with certain socially sanctioned rules for expressing grief, while countering and opposing others.

We state again Holst-Warhaft's (2000) argument that grief "arouses passion," and that the narratives of an unjust loss can incite movement toward political change (p. 5). Change need not occur on a large scale to be profound. ManWhat's family countered his hit-and-run death with a successful campaign to create bike lanes on busy and unsafe roads. The result of their grief transformed into action literally opened up new paths for progress. We wish similar success to survivors of unjust loss as they come forward to make their voices heard.

Key Terms

Continuing bonds—the specific practices used by the bereaved to maintain an active relationship with the deceased.

Counter-hegemonic—processes that oppose the processes through which dominant cultural ideals maintain power.

Global meanings—include beliefs about self and the world and sense of purpose.

Hermeneutic approach—concerned with understanding and interpretation.

Meanings made—the result of one's effort toward coherency and include acceptance of the event, a sense of growth, and changes in one's global meanings.

Meaning making—both an automatic and deliberate process that involves cognitive and emotional processes, such as the positive reframing of a situation.

Meaning reconstruction—after bereavement, the healthy navigation through bereavement-related distress that involves making sense of the death, benefit finding, and identity change.

Post-traumatic growth—instances when individuals change in positive ways as a result of experiencing traumatic losses.

Unjust loss—a term applied when some element of a death is deemed unacceptable; this may be due to features of how the death occurred, and may involve focus/blame on the person or group of people who are seen as responsible for the death.

Questions for Reflection

1. What makes a loss unjust? Take a moment to reflect on your personal response to this question. Do you believe this is a subjective label, or are there objective criteria to define unjust loss?
2. According to Hochschild (1979), "the matrix of social meaning also contains 'feeling rules,' that dictate which feelings are supposed to be felt when, and moreover, how they are to be expressed." What is your experience of these feeling rules? What has your experience been of social response when your action or expression of emotion fell outside of these rules?
3. "Using public space to convey a message is empowering. It allows the bereaved to simultaneous refuse to accept an unjust loss by not remaining silent, calling for change, and rallying support." What has your response been in seeing publicly located memorials?

Notes

1. Hegemonic processes are those processes through which dominant cultural ideals maintain power. This involves cultural practices that inculcate and reinforce social ideals. Thus, counter-hegemonic practices are those that oppose.
2. Hermeneutic approaches are concerned with understanding and interpretation.

References

Attig, T. (2004). Meanings of death seen through the lens of grieving. *Death Studies, 4*, 341–360.
Boelen, P. A., & Prigerson, H. G. (2013). Prolonged grief disorder as a new diagnostic category in DSM-5. In M. Stroebe, H. Schut, & J. Van den Bout (Eds.) *Complicated grief: Scientific foundations for health care professionals* (pp. 85–98). New York, NY: Routledge.
Bordere, T. C. (2008–2009). 'To look at death another way': Black teenage males' perspectives on second-lines and regular funerals in New Orleans. *Omega: Journal of Death and Dying, 58*(3), 213–232.
Burke, L. A., & Neimeyer, R. A. (2013). 11 prospective risk factors for complicated grief. In M. Stroebe, H. Schut, & J. Van den Bout (Eds.), *Complicated grief: Scientific foundations for health care professionals* (pp. 145–161). New York, NY: Routledge.
Butler-Kisber, L. (2010). *Qualitative inquiry: Thematic, narrative and arts-informed perspectives*. Thousand Oaks, CA: Sage Publications.
Calhoun, L. G., & Tedeschi, R. G. (2006). The foundations of posttraumatic growth: An expanded framework. In L. G. Calhoun & R. G. Tedeschi (Eds.), *Handbook of posttraumatic growth: Research and practice* (pp. 1879–2213). New York, NY: Lawrence Erlbaum.
Charmaz, K., & Milligan, M. J. (2006). Grief. In J. E. Stets & J. H. Turner (Eds.), *Handbook of the sociology of emotions* (pp. 516–543). New York, NY: Springer.
Cooper, R. (2013). Complicated grief: Philosophical perspectives. In M. Stroebe, H. Schut, & J. Van den Bout (Eds.), *Complicated grief: Scientific foundations for health care professionals* (pp. 13–26). New York, NY: Routledge.
Doka, K. J. (1989). *Disenfranchised grief: Recognized hidden sorrow*. Lexington, MA: Lexington Books.
Foucault, M. (1980). *Power/Knowledge: Selected Interviews and Other Writings, 1972–1977*. New York, NY: Random House.
Gillies, J., & Neimeyer, R. A. (2006). Loss, grief, and the search for significance: Toward a model of meaning reconstruction in bereavement. *Journal of Constructivist Psychology, 19*(1), 31-65.
Hochschild, A. (1979). Emotion work, feeling rules, and social structure. *American Journal of Sociology, 85*(3), 551–575.
Holst-Warhaft, G. (2000). *The cue for passion: Grief and its political uses*. Cambridge, MA: Harvard University Press.
Kelly, G.A. (1955). *The psychology of personal constructs*. New York, NY: Norton.
Lebel, U., & Ronel, N. (2005). Parental discourse and activism as a response to bereavement of fallen sons and civilian terrorist victims. *Journal of Loss and Trauma, 10*(4), 383–404.
Litchenthal, W. G., & Neimeyer, R. A. (2012). Directed journaling to facilitate meaning-making. In R. A. Neimeyer (Ed.), *Techniques of grief therapy: Creative practices for counseling the bereaved* (pp. 165–168). New York, NY: Routledge.
Marwit, S., & Klass, D. (1994–1995). Grief and the role of the inner representation of the deceased. *Omega: Journal of Death and Dying, 30*(4), 283–298.
Moore, R. (2011). The stigmatized deaths in Jonestown: Finding a locus for grief. *Death Studies, 35*(1), 42–58.
Neimeyer, R. A. (2006). Complicated grief and the reconstruction of meaning: Conceptual and empirical contributions to a cognitive-constructivist model. *Clinical Psychology: Science and Practice, 13*(2), 141–145.
Neimeyer, R. A., Prigerson, H. G., & Davies, B. (2002). Mourning and meaning. *American Behavioral Scientist, 46*(2), 235–251.
Neimeyer, R. A., Baldwin, S., & Gillies, J. (2006). Continuing bonds and reconstructing meaning: Mitigating complications in bereavement. *Death Studies, 30*(8), 715–738.
Park, C. L. (2010). Making sense of the meaning literature: An integrative review of meaning making and its effects on adjustment to stressful life events. *Psychological Bulletin, 136*(2), 257–301.
Parkes, C. M., & Prigerson, H. G. (2013). *Bereavement: Studies of grief in adult life* (4th ed.). New York, NY: Routledge.
Proulx, T., & Inzlicht, M. (2012). The Five "A"s of meaning maintenance: Finding meaning in the theories of sense-making. *Psychological Inquiry, 23*(4), 317–335.

Reeves, N. C. (2011). Death acceptance through ritual. *Death Studies, 35*(5), 408–419.
Rose, N. (2000). Identity, genealogy, history. In P. du Gay, J. Evans, & P. Redmana (Eds.), *Identity: A reader* (pp. 311–324). Thousand Oaks, CA: Sage.
Schiffrin, E. (2009). "This so clearly needs to be marked": An exploration of memorial tattoos and their functions for the bereaved (Unpublished doctoral dissertation), Smith College School for Social Work, Northampton, MA.
Sofka, C., Gilbert, K., & Cupit Noppe, I. (2012). *Dying, death, and grief in an online universe: For counselors and educators.* New York, NY: Springer.
Stroebe, M. S., Hansson, R. O., Stroebe, W., & Schut, H. (2007). Introduction: Concepts and issues in contemporary research on bereavement. In M. S. Stroebe, R. O. Hansson, W. Stroebe, & H. Schut (Eds.), *Handbook of bereavement research: Consequences, coping, and care.* Washington, DC: American Psychological Association.
Strouse, S. (2013). *Artful grief: A diary of healing.* Bloomington, IN: Balboa Press.
Turner, V. W. (1969). *The ritual process: Structure and anti-structure.* Chicago: Aldine.
WMC News (August 13, 2011) *Friends say midtown Memphis bicyclist killed by hit-and-run driver.* Retrieved from WMC Action News 5: www.wmcactionnews5.com/story/15262340/friends-say-midtown-memphis-bicyclist-killed-by-hit-and-run-driver

18
Restorative Justice Principles and Restorative Practice
Museums as Healing Spaces[1]

Carla J. Sofka

Introduction

Throughout history, tragedies involving terrorism, genocide, or politically-motivated actions have left countless survivors searching for justice and ways to cope with the complicated aftermath of these types of events. One value-based process utilizing a balanced approach to addressing the needs of all stakeholders who are involved in these tragedies—the victims, wrongdoers, and communities—is restorative justice, "a broad term which encompasses a growing social movement to institutionalize peaceful approaches to harm, problem-solving and violation of legal and human rights" (Center for Restorative Justice, 2014). While restorative justice originally provided those who caused a crime the opportunity to be accountable for their behavior (e.g., Eglash, 1977), restorative justice principles and restorative practices are now being used for a wide range of situations (Braithwaite, 2002; Van Ness, 2011; Walker, 2013), providing victims with support and giving them a voice to express their needs in a variety of social and cultural contexts (United Nations, 2006). According to Zehr (2013): "Those who have been harmed need to be able to grieve their losses, to be able to tell their stories, to have their questions answered—that is, to have the harms and needs caused by the offense addressed." (p. 7) Restorative justice gives people opportunities to heal (Zehr, 2011).

Jonas, Chez, Duffy, and Strand (2003) described healing as a unique experience for each person that is a holistic (mental, physical, emotional, and spiritual) and dynamic process of recovery, repair, restoration, and transformation of the mind, body, and soul on the path to becoming more whole. These authors note that healing can occur as a communal process, highlighting the important elements of social support and community. Therefore, a "healing environment" consists of people interacting with other physical, psychological, social, and spiritual components that stimulate and support the inherent healing capacities of the participants, their relationships, and their surroundings (Jonas et al., 2003).

In the light of this definition, is it possible that a museum related to tragedy could serve as a healing environment? Consider the following visitor comments written in a book soliciting feedback after a visit to the World Trade Center Exhibit at the New York State Museum in Albany, New York:

Visitor 1: 'It's been an entire year since the accident but it cannot escape my memory. The exhibition is a great way to help the mourning deal with their pain, and show the rest of the world the feelings of all of us affected. Rest in peace.'

Visitor 2: 'It hurts to recall the images and I can still smell NY but seeing all this is helping me to recover.'

Visitor 3: 'The exhibit touched a part of me that I hadn't felt since the day it happened. Finally, I was able to cry and release.'

Based on comments such as these and several other data sources (e.g., interviews with volunteers and visitors, blogs, observations), this chapter proposes that museums and museum exhibits focusing on tragic events can serve as "healing spaces" for individuals and communities who have been impacted by these events. This is also illustrated through a review of the museums' mission statements as well as comments left by visitors at several memorial museums including:

- the World Trade Center exhibit at the New York State Museum (subsequently referred to as the WTC exhibit);
- the World Trade Center Tribute Center in New York City (subsequently referred to as the Tribute Center);
- the National September 11 Memorial Museum (subsequently referred to as the 9/11 Memorial Museum);
- the Oklahoma City National Memorial and Museum (subsequently referred to as OKC);
- the Holocaust Museum in Washington, DC (subsequently referred to as the Holocaust museum);
- the June 4th Museum Hong Kong (subsequently referred to as the 6/4 Museum).

In this chapter, the use of restorative practices proposes that museums and museum exhibits focusing on tragic events can serve as "healing spaces" for individuals and communities who have been impacted by these events. The use of restorative practices during the development of these museums and ways that they have served as "healing spaces" will be described. The challenges inherent in the creation of these healing spaces will also be summarized. Finally, implications for future research and conclusions will be presented.

Restorative Practices and the Missions of Museums

Cornerstones of restorative justice include the involvement of stakeholders in determining how to best repair harm and in the development of community. Although stakeholders play a vital role in facilitating justice, note that it is only "partly restorative" for survivors when the offender does not participate (Wachtel, 2013). Restorative practices also provide a safe environment for the expression and exchange of emotions and the expression of affect that allow people to communicate feelings (Nathanson, 1998; Wachtel, 2013). Collaborative conversations between the survivors and victims of tragedy and the planners of the aforementioned museums have been a crucial component of these museums' development, and common themes in the mission statements of these museums embody restorative justice principles. These themes include:

- bearing witness to a crime through the dissemination of knowledge by providing opportunities for education and learning;
- preserving the memories of the victims through remembrance and commemoration;
- honoring those who risked their lives to save others or demonstrated compassion in the aftermath of the tragedy;
- describing the consequences of terrorism or genocide on individuals and communities;

- creating a hallowed place and preserving sacred ground associated with great loss;
- providing opportunities for participation through storytelling, reflection, and hope;
- celebrating the triumph of human dignity over human depravity and the perseverance/resilience of the human spirit and inspiring the power of healing and recovery;
- instilling an understanding of the senselessness of violence and conveying an imperative to reject violence.

Examples of restorative justice themes and practices within these museums will now be presented.

Bearing Witness: Learning and the Power of Information

A significant function of a museum is to serve as an institution for learning (Falk, Dierking, and Foutz, 2007). According to Sir Francis Bacon (1597), "knowledge is power," and counselors who work with grieving individuals know that understanding the facts and circumstances of a death is crucial. Therefore, the information received by a visitor to an exhibit dealing with tragedy can be powerful on many levels.

While highly visible tragic events receive intense media coverage, not all museum visitors were old enough at the time of these events to comprehend the information. In fact, some visitors were not born at the time of the tragedies but their lives were forever changed by the death of a family member or family friend whom they will never meet. The educational component of a healing space provides opportunities for visitors to learn the history of an event and may provide caregivers or other relatives with the informational support that will facilitate their children's learning. Having factual information is particularly important for children and adolescents who have reached a new developmental stage that encompasses more advanced cognitive skills and emotional resources, allowing them to understand and cope with loss in a more mature way. Rather than dealing with a life-cycle related need as defined by Moussouri (1997), perhaps these visitors are dealing with a "grief cycle" related need, with the marker event being a tragedy. Consider this comment card left by a visitor to the Tribute Center:

> My husband was killed in the attacks—WTC 2. Our children are now seven and five and a half-years-old. This was their first visit to the site. When my younger son, whom I was pregnant with on 9–11–01, started bawling when he saw his father's picture (holding his older brother), I was surprised. He's never had that reaction before. Now it's real for him and he can heal.

There may also be visitors to a healing space who need to "fill in" pieces of information that were not provided or were unavailable to them at the time of the event. This could include visitors from a foreign country or people from the country in which the event occurred who, for whatever reason, did not learn about the event at that time. While visiting the WTC exhibit, a high school student who was nine years old on September 11, 2001 stated,

> I was too young to know what was going on. I don't even remember what I was doing; I don't even remember school or anything. So it kind of makes me feel like—this is bad, am I a bad person because I'm not like everyone else and I can't remember what I was doing.

Feelings of guilt may be experienced by young adults who were not old enough to understand the significance of the event. After using what he had learned to perform a play about 9/11 in his school, one student stated: "It made me feel good and it made me feel like we got it across—and we had more than just us remembering such a tragic event and honoring the lives that were lost." Having an opportunity to learn about the history and the impact of these events on others is a powerful way to resolve feelings of guilt created by the lack of information.

In some countries, where government censorship prevents information from being widely available, a museum can play a crucial role in providing not only an opportunity for gaining information but also a chance for visitors to experience the healing power of being given a voice. In June of 2014 on the eve of the 25th anniversary of the Tiananmen Square Massacre (i.e., the June 4th incident), the 6/4 Museum opened in Hong Kong. According to Lee Cheuk Yan, head of the pro-democracy group that operates the museum, "The world memory of it [the massacre] is fading and the younger generation doesn't know of it in China, where it's also banned. So we think it's very important for us to preserve the historical truth" (Chan, 2014). While contemplating a visit to this museum with no external signage, prospective visitors may be fearful of being perceived as politically subversive by virtue of simply going. This fear may quickly dissipate and a sense of enfranchisement be restored when presented with the opportunity to voice their opinions and reactions on a chalk board that is placed between the government's accounts of the events and the accounts of observers and those who participated.

Sacred Space: A Place to Go

All cultures have traditional rituals that occur following a death, such as holding a funeral or a ceremony to acknowledge a life and the end of that life as well as choosing an appropriate final resting place for a loved one's human remains. Grieving rituals often involve visiting that final resting place, leaving flowers or other meaningful offerings, and perhaps feeling closer to that loved one than is possible in any other place. However, restorative practices for some victims may occur posthumously (Sofka & Strock-Lynskey, 2011), in some cases many years after a person's death. Because of the circumstances of 9/11, the Holocaust, and the massacre at Tiananmen Square, many bereaved individuals were not able to participate in some or all of these rituals. For these individuals, memorial museums may serve as a "sacred space" if they did not receive physical confirmation of their loved one's death and do not have a cemetery to visit. This particular need—a spiritually oriented, coping-related or potentially therapeutic need—appears to be unique to this type of museum.

The physical spaces and the artifacts in museums can serve as a "proxy" for individuals who do not have a traditional place to go or for those who cannot travel to the actual site of a tragedy. For those whose loved ones were buried in mass graves, the Hall of Remembrance at the Holocaust Museum has an eternal flame and a black marble block, evocative of a coffin, which contains dirt from 38 of the concentration camps in Europe. The 6/4 Museum has maps of Tiananmen Square, noting the locations where identified and unidentified victims died. One case in the WTC exhibit in Albany served this purpose for a family living near Albany, New York. The AON Corporation had offices located on the 92nd floor and floors 98–105 of the South Tower of the World Trade Center. A portion of the sign that hung above the entrance to AON's corporate suite survived the collapse of the building and occupies a case in the exhibit. On one early anniversary of 9/11, a family approached a museum volunteer with a unique request—to place a bouquet of flowers on this case in memory of their father who worked for AON. Since his body was not recovered, the family did not have a cemetery to visit, influencing their decision to come see the exhibit. Finding a portion of the sign that they saw each time they visited their father at work created an unanticipated "object experience" as well as an unexpected opportunity to help them cope with a difficult day.

Because of the individual nature of grief and varying beliefs about burial and memorialization, it is not surprising that disagreements can occur when thousands of people are impacted by a large-scale tragedy such as 9/11. In May of 2014, the National September 11 Memorial Museum opened amid controversy regarding the decision to include a repository for the unidentified remains of 9/11 victims. While some family members hailed the decision to return the remains to the place where they perished in 2001, others were outraged and considered the decision to be inherently disrespectful and offensive (Stepansky, Badia, & McShane, 2014). Until more sophisticated DNA identification techniques become available, the controversy will remain.

Honoring the Memories and Legacies of Victims and Survivors

Museums commemorating tragic events provide an opportunity to honor the memories of the deceased and to validate the memories of survivors (Manderson, 2008). The Tribute Gallery at the Tribute Center has over 1,200 photographs and other memorabilia shared by family members. In OKC, the Gallery of Honor poignantly displays photographs and memorabilia of the 168 people who died on April 19, 1995. Items that belonged to a loved one or are connected to a loved one's life or death (such as the AON case described above) serve as "linking objects," and these objects are powerful tools for documenting what has been lost (Fein & Danitz, 2008). When displayed in a museum, these objects provide a place for remembrance as well as a place for the general public to connect names and faces with the tragedy, making it a bit more personal and "real." Individuals may seek out an object experience connected with a deceased loved one or interact with these exhibits to gain a sense of appreciation for the losses that occurred.

On September 11, 2001, Engine 6 was one of the first fire companies to respond to the attacks on the World Trade Center. This special pumper, capable of shooting water to the top floors of the Towers (110 stories high), was parked under the pedestrian bridge between the North Tower and the World Financial Center located across the street. When the North Tower fell, the pedestrian bridge collapsed and Engine 6 was irreparably damaged. Four of the firefighters from this company were killed when the towers collapsed. In September of 2002, the deceased firefighters' children placed flowers on the bumper of Engine 6, now on display at the WTC exhibit. On subsequent anniversaries of the tragedy, new bouquets have appeared to honor their memories.

It is not uncommon for survivors of various tragedies to use the phrase "never forget" and to express the importance of finding ways to make sure that stories about the people who died are preserved. In addition to displaying the names of victims and exhibiting photographs or personal memorabilia, museums provide this powerful component of a healing space through opportunities for connecting with others, meaning making, and the creation of empathy.

Connecting With Others, Meaning Making, Survivor Advocacy, and Creating Empathy

According to M. Lobel (personal communication, March 3, 2008), a curator at the Tribute Center, it is important "to honor and respect not only the place, but the processes that occur within the walls" of a museum space commemorating tragedy. This includes all of the "connections" that are formed between the people who interact within the space. While it may not be the typical "social experience" described by previous research, museums that focus on a particular tragedy provide an opportunity for visitors and museum volunteers alike to connect with others who have personal experience with the same traumatic event.

Erikson (1995) used the term "spiritual kinship" to describe this type of connection, one that provides reassurance that someone can truly understand what you have experienced, often without saying a word. Commonalities in experiences may include dealing with survivors' guilt, the agony of waiting for confirmation of a loved one's death (and perhaps never receiving it), or becoming "newsworthy" and dealing with high-profile media coverage during an intensely personal time of loss. In addition to helping each other adjust to the consequences of a tragedy, these connections create a support system to help museum volunteers deal with more "normal" challenges that have no relationship to the tragic event (e.g., physical illness or injury as well as subsequent changes or losses in their lives) but are placed in their paths during their volunteer service.

Although it is a sad commentary on our society's ability to provide unconditional support to people who are grieving, a museum may be the only place where it is socially acceptable to shed a tear in public or to express one's thoughts and feelings about the aftermath of a tragedy. Sidewalk chalk in Oklahoma City, comment cards at the Tribute Center, and comment books at most facilities provide a forum for expressing emotions that may have no other outlet. While describing the connection between the work of Csikzentmihalyi & Hermanson (1995) and his own, Falk (2009) noted that "flow learning experiences" contain mental as well as emotional experiences. Comment cards written by visitors to each of these facilities capture the emotional nature of each visit. Would grieving individuals and survivors consider their visits to be peaceful, resulting in a "recharged battery," or would they describe the experience as psychologically necessary, perhaps therapeutic? Is it possible that it could be experienced as both? Falk's (2009) discussion of the construction of meaning and memories following a museum visit has relevance to the premise that museums serve as healing spaces. For people with a survivor identity or who identify themselves as a griever, museums seem to serve as a place to "make meaning" out of the event itself and to explore the impact of this event on their own identities. Holocaust museums and memorials have served this purpose for years, helping first, second, and third generations of Holocaust survivors to deal with the intergenerational legacy of the Holocaust (Chaitin, 2002; Meyers & Zandberg, 2002; van Alphen, 2006; Wiseman, Metzl, & Barber, 2006). Some individuals may come to museums seeking an opportunity to "do something," creating an opportunity to gain control over the impact of an event that may cause them to feel powerless. Meaning-making opportunities may also occur when an individual impacted by tragedy volunteers for a museum.

Person-to-person history events (i.e., first-person history) provide powerful opportunities for visitors to learn about an event from someone who witnessed or was directly impacted by the event, raising awareness of the long-term impact and creating empathy for individuals affected by tragedy. Storytelling is a powerful process, not only for the storyteller, but also for the people who are fortunate enough to hear the stories. Telling one's story repeatedly can be an important component of the healing journey for grieving individuals. When asked why she decided to volunteer at the Tribute Center, one woman whose son died on September 11, 2001 stated that she heard her son's voice in a dream saying that it was important for her to be there. She noted that if she had died, her son would be here telling stories about her! She also noted: "I still can't watch the films (about 9/11), but I can do this!"

Volunteering to speak on panels or interacting with visitors in the galleries provides a way for loved ones and survivors to preserve the legacy of those who died through conversations and storytelling. A small screening room at the 6/4 Museum allows parents to talk about their children who were killed in Tiananmen Square, and visitors from Mainland China can speak freely about an event that has been erased from public discourse in their homeland (Chan, 2014). Volunteers at the Tribute Center as well as in OKC noted the importance of having visitors leave "with a very personal sense" of what was lost. Holocaust survivors in Washington, DC, continue to honor their promises to the men and women who saved their lives by telling their stories, ensuring that the world "never forgets."

For some visitors, meaning making may occur in different ways and for different reasons. For example, members of the military have visited 9/11-related exhibits prior to being deployed to Iraq or Afghanistan. A member of the Navy, who decided after 9/11 that he would join the military, noted after his visit to the Tribute Center: "I am going on my first deployment to Iraq and after being here I am no longer scared."

Museums provide a unique opportunity to help visitors empathize with individuals who have been forever changed by a tragic event and its aftermath. During a visit to the WTC exhibit in Albany, a former NYPD. detective who spent almost a year at the Freshkills landfill sorting debris from 9/11 expressed his gratitude regarding the information provided by videos about the sorting process in which he participated. "I'm so glad that these videos and this exhibit are here. Now I finally have a place that I can bring my family and friends so that they can understand what all those months of my life were like. I just couldn't talk about it with them."

These museums also provide public death education—information to the general public about dying, death, and grief. For example, the "Impact" section of the exhibit in OKC contains videos of survivors and loved ones describing the aftermath of the tragedy. Calendar pages for each month of the year highlight dates of significance, educating visitors about "anniversary reactions," a normal component of grief.

According to the Trauma Foundation (2001), some people who survive the traumatic loss of a loved one channel the force of their grief and shock into preventive action by becoming "survivor advocates" who work to save others from having to experience a similar loss and trauma. Survivor advocacy efforts in OKC (lobbying for policy changes regarding access to federal trials, presenting various perspectives about the death penalty) are described in the exhibit. Participating in educational programs that are designed to prevent future tragedies involving genocide or terrorism instills hope in the hearts of those who have survived them, and survivor advocacy is a powerful tool for healing.

Visitors to tragedy-related exhibits that offer person-to-person history or have components of the exhibit that educate about the impact of tragedy may possess a newfound ability in the future to provide support to survivors and people who are grieving. After viewing the exhibits, a Tribute Center visitor noted:

> It was a very captivating moment to just walk through the halls and see the people's expression on their face, you can actually feel their confusion, their sadness and even surer, actually most were scared. I thank you for having this exhibition, because not until today I realized the pain these people went through.

Through their presence in the galleries or first-person history events, survivors and loved ones of the victims can educate the general public (as well as professionals) about the individual nature of coping with traumatic grief and post-traumatic stress. The mother of a fallen NYC firefighter described how she was coping with the death of her son, stating: "Closure is not a good word—I'm not sure that you can ever get closure." She also was not sure that describing the Tribute Center as a "healing space" was appropriate, noting that she didn't consider this to be a good word either since there's a scab over the wound that will always be there. Finding the "right" language that is comfortable for everyone is indeed a tricky task. It is often best to simply ask a person to describe their journey with grief and listen carefully to the words that are used.

The following comment card beautifully captures the experience of a Tribute Center visitor in September 2007:

> I watched the event of September 11th on television, like so many others. You think you understand—but you don't, can't. The Tribute Center helped share the personal stories that you can only understand via the human contact. TV can report, but only to a certain extent. I will share my experience of this tour with others and hopefully thru the "personal" connection the spirit of this venture, this place, will help others begin to "understand.

Challenges Faced by Museums Serving as Healing Spaces

While recognizing the many benefits of museums as healing spaces, it is equally important to note the challenges that are inherent in their successful creation and maintenance. Some of these challenges are unique to museums that focus on commemorating tragedy, while others are universal to all museums. As noted by Eberle (2005), the development of an exhibit that encourages museum visitors to explore issues related to loss and grief may cause development teams to encounter a range of philosophical, historical, psychological, and therapeutic issues.

Museum staff and volunteers in the galleries must be trained and prepared to handle a potentially wide range of emotional responses among visitors. Involving a mental health professional with expertise in traumatic grief and post-traumatic stress in the planning of this type of exhibits is wise, as is having a trained professional available to assist should a visitor or volunteer experience a crisis.

As previously noted, when working with individuals impacted by tragedy, it is important to respect the power of language. The connotation of the word "healing" must be explored carefully, since this word may not be a universally appropriate or comfortable one. This message was communicated eloquently by survivors of the Holocaust who volunteer at the Holocaust Museum, one of whom noted that "healing" for some people may involve "forgetting." This outcome is one that would never be welcomed by this group of volunteers.

Perhaps the most universal challenge for any museum involves the availability of resources. Unless exhibit space is an unlimited commodity, securing the financial resources required to design, renovate, and maintain the space over time can be a daunting task at a time when the number of "good causes" requesting donor support is overwhelming. Person-power is a potentially difficult challenge in terms of individuals to undertake the administrative responsibilities of creating and maintaining a healing space as well as finding and training volunteers to carry out the numerous tasks and responsibilities for which volunteers are the best choice. Over time, the needs of volunteers may change, resulting in turnover and potential challenges recruiting people with a firsthand connection to the tragedy.

Another challenge involves those that occur during the creation and development of exhibits around topics or events that involve differing perspectives or controversy. Kratz and Karp (2006) labeled these challenges "museum frictions" and include the range of roles, definitions, and cross-institutional relations involving disparate constituencies, interests, goals, and perspectives that produce debates, tensions, collaborations, contests, and conflicts, resulting in both positive and negative outcomes. When museums have multiple mandates with complex and contradictory goals, conflicting demands are placed upon them by a range of stockholders—funders, government officials, professionals, and the intended audiences. This concept acknowledges the complex social processes and transformations that are occurring in the museum world as the types and scale of museums have grown and changed, and recognizes that museums and heritage organizations are becoming sites of political debates and disagreements. Museums have clearly become places where statements about history, identity, and values are being made.

Kratz and Karp (2006) note that in the planning of a museum, curators must deal with cultural, economic, social, and political flows and processes, including how history will be presented and preserved in the space. It is common for exhibits commemorating tragedy to represent points of view and perspectives that vary widely. The challenges inherent in the creation of the Holocaust Museum and in OKC have been well documented. According to Linenthal (2001, 2003), common challenges have included when to begin the timeline of events required to tell the story; whether or not to include information about the perpetrators of the crimes (significant to include factual information vs. perceived as disrespectful/dishonoring the memory of those who died); how to define the word "survivor" in the context of the tragedy; and how to list the names of the victims, if this should even be done. Decisions regarding the appropriateness of displaying sensitive artifacts appear to be a universal challenge.

Implications and Conclusions

This chapter has documented ways in which museums are contributing to the evolution of restorative justice principles and practices that are being used to assist individuals and communities dealing with the aftermath of tragedy. Engaging stakeholders in the development of museum mission statements, discussions about the types of exhibits that should be created, and identification of the artifacts to be displayed are restorative practices that have the potential to contribute to the reparation of harm that has occurred.

Storytelling and remembering are crucial components of grief work, and memory is a powerful tool to help individuals and societies to "never forget" what has happened following a tragic event with widespread impact. How is "memory" captured in a museum designed to commemorate these events? Regarding the role of memory in the creation of the Holocaust Museum, Kaplan (1994) noted: "Memory always entails a form of martyrdom: life sacrificed to a thought, an emotion, to our spiritual substance. For the victims of the Holocaust the issue is no longer death, as death has claimed them, but the manner of it in memory, for in the manner of their dying we face toward the void" (p. 16). When considering how to honor the memory of the victims of highly publicized tragedies, this quote seems relevant. The manner of their deaths receives worldwide attention, and the political aftermath of tragedies or terrorist attacks continues to have an impact on those around the world involved in any subsequent conflicts or wars that may ensue. This significant component of the story, while raising considerable potential for debate and disagreement when designing museum exhibits, must be carefully considered from multiple perspectives.

Theory development relevant to issues of history, memory, and tragedy/trauma has become rich over time. What concepts are important to consider regarding the use of museums as healing spaces? Till (2003) notes the significance of "places of memory," acknowledging the presence of numerous "theatres of memory" where selective histories about people and places have been presented and preserved. She also notes that places of memory are also impacted by the "politics of memory," similar to the political component of "museum frictions" previously described. The concept of "social memory" (Crane, 1997) can have a significant influence on what is displayed in a museum, recognizing that memories can belong to social groups, including families, religious organizations, and even societies. Personal cultural memories, defined by van Dijck (2007) as "the acts and products of remembering in which individuals engage to make sense of their lives in relation to the lives of others and to their surroundings, situating themselves in time and place" (p. 6) could easily be influenced by the types of information gained and the experiences that occur within a museum space.

As younger generations visit museums commemorating tragic events, their recollections will be based on "mediated memories" (van Dijck, 2007) or memories formed as a result of interactions with multiple sources of information, including caregivers and other individuals, the media, various types of technology, and the wide range of possible experiences within a museum. The fact that memories and meanings attached to tragic events are not stable in time or space must also be considered when debating how to update exhibits as time passes and as outcomes within the criminal justice system are determined. Exhibits documenting events surrounded by political controversy or censorship may need to be revisited as those political contexts change over time.

The increased presence and popularity of museums and memorials to commemorate tragic events has already created controversy and debate (e.g., Doss, 2008; Sturken, 2007) and provides a unique opportunity to broaden the types of museums that have been studied in relation to Falk's model. Manderson (2008) describes museums and memorials as providing an institutional means of recalling and retaining the shameful as well as the noble and serving as "therapeutic arenas" for healing and places to acknowledge the suffering and grief of everyone impacted by a tragedy, allowing everyone to move forward. Exploring the ways that museums serve as "therapeutic arenas" merits attention.

According to Elliott (2011), "Restorative justice processes create environments in which reflection on experiences with an event can help everyone affected to learn and grow" (p. 104). The anecdotal evidence presented in this article provides support that museums can serve as healing spaces. However, empirical research documenting the impact of participation in the potentially restorative process of creating or spending time in such a museum has not been conducted. Tools to assess the role of these museums in the lives of survivors and grieving individuals or communities, as well as members of the general public who are less directly impacted by these events, must be developed. Documenting the relationship between museum visits and the role of a "grief cycle" and one's personal identity as a survivor of a tragedy or as a grieving individual will truly expand our understanding of these unique museums. Creating partnerships between thanatologists (individuals who study dying, death, and bereavement), professionals who assist grieving individuals and survivors, and museum researchers to document the motives for visiting or volunteering in museums that focus on a tragic event as well as the outcomes of spending time in these museums would assist museums with the task of creating and maintaining effective healing spaces for visitors, museum volunteers, and the broader community.

Key Terms

Healing environment—physical, psychological, social, and spiritual components that stimulate and support the inherent healing capacities of the participants, their relationships, and their surroundings.

Linking objects—objects that are connected with a deceased loved one or interact with exhibits to gain a sense of appreciation for losses that occurred.

Mediated memories—memories formed as a result of interactions with multiple sources of information.

Museum frictions—challenges that occur during the creation and development of exhibits around topics or events that involve differing perspectives or controversy. These include the range of roles, definitions, and cross-institutional relations involving disparate constituencies, interests, goals, and perspectives that produce debates, tensions, collaborations, contests, and conflicts, resulting in both positive and negative outcomes.

Personal cultural memories—the acts and products of remembering in which individuals engage to make sense of their lives in relation to the lives of others and to their surroundings, situating themselves in time and place.

Restorative justice—a broad term which encompasses a growing social movement to institutionalize peaceful approaches to harm, problem-solving and violation of legal and human rights. Originally provided to those who caused a crime the opportunity to be accountable for their behavior, and expanded to include providing victims with support and giving them a voice to express their needs in a variety of social and cultural contexts.

Social memory—memories belonging to social groups, including families, religious organizations, and/or societies.

Spiritual kinship—a type of connection that provides reassurance that someone can truly understand what you have experienced (discussed in this chapter in the context of survivors or those bereaved by the same tragic event).

Survivor advocates—people who, after the traumatic loss of a loved one, channel the force of their grief and shock into preventive action by working to save others from having to experience a similar loss and trauma.

Theatres of memory—term for places where selective histories about people and places have been presented and preserved.

Questions for Reflection

1. Have you ever attended a museum-memorial such as those described in this chapter? Which of the principles of restorative justice was the most meaningful to you during your visit?

2. What are the sacred spaces in your life? Consider your personal use of such spaces, and the meaning of these spaces for you. What might you miss if these spaces were not available to you? What proxies might you consider?
3. "Memories and meanings attached to tragic events are not stable in time or space." Given the social, political, and individual pressures on memory—which are not stable—what do you consider to be the most important elements as museums strive to represent a particular tragedy?

Note

1. An earlier version of this chapter was published in the *International Journal of the Inclusive Museum* and is reproduced here with permission (see Sofka, 2009).

References

Bacon, F. (1597). *Religious meditations, of heresies*. Retrieved from www.quotationspage.com/quote/2060.html
Braithwaite, J. (2002). *Restorative justice and responsive regulation*. Oxford: Oxford University Press.
Center for Restorative Justice (2014). What is restorative justice? Retrieved from www.suffolk.edu/college/centers/15970.php.
Chaitin, J. (2002). Issues and interpersonal values among three generations in families of Holocaust survivors. *Journal of Social and Personal Relationships*, 19(3), 379–402.
Chan, K. (2014, June 22). Tiananmen memory flickers in tiny Hong Kong museum. *Detroit Free Press*. Retrieved from www.freep.com/apps/pbcs.dll/article?AID=2014306220012.
Crane, S. A. (1997). Memory, distortion, and history in the museum. *History and Theory*, 36(4), 44–63.
Csikzentmihalyi, M., & Hermanson, K. (1995). Intrinsic motivation in museums. Why does one want to learn? In J. Falk & L. Dierking (Eds.), *Public institutions for personal learning*. Washington, DC: American Association of Museums.
Doss, E. (2008). Memorial mania. *Museum*, March/April. Retrieved from www.aam-us.org/pubs/mn/memorialmania.cfm
Eberle, S. G. (2005). Memory and mourning: An exhibit history. *Death Studies*, 29(6), 535–558.
Eglash, A. (1977). Beyond restitution: Creative restitution. In J. Hudson & B. Galaway (Eds.), *Restitution in criminal justice* (pp. 91–99). Lexington, MA: DC Heath.
Elliot, E. (2011). *Security with care: Restorative justice and healthy societies*. Halifax, Canada: Fernwood Publishing.
Erikson, K. (1995). Notes on trauma and community. In C. Caruth (Ed.), *Trauma: Explorations in memory* (pp. 183–199). Baltimore, MD: Johns Hopkins University Press.
Falk, J. H. (2009). *Identity and the museum visitor experience*. Walnut Creek, CA: Left Coast Press.
Falk, J. H., Dierking, L. H., & Foutz, S. (2007). *In principle, in practice: Museums as learning institutions*. Lanham, MD: AltaMira Press.
Fein, J., & Danitz, B. (2008). Objects and memory (DVD). Information about the documentary is available from *www.objectsandmemory.org*.
Jonas, W. B., Chez, R. A., Duffy, B., & Strand, D. (2003). Investigating the impact of optimal healing environments. *Alternative Therapies in Health and Medicine*, 9(6), 36.
Kaplan, H. (1994). *Conscience and memory: Meditations in a museum of the Holocaust*. Chicago, Il: University of Chicago Press.
Kratz, C. A., & Karp, I. (2006). Introduction. In I. Karp, C. A. Kratz, L. Szwaja, & T. Ybarra-Frausto (Eds.), *Museum frictions: Public cultures/global transformations* (pp. 1–31). Durham, NC: Duke University Press.
Linenthal, E. T. (2001). *Preserving memory: The struggle to create America's Holocaust Museum*. New York, NY: Columbia University Press.
Linenthal, E. T. (2003). *The unfinished bombing: Oklahoma City in American memory*. New York, NY: Columbia University Press.
Mancerson, L. (2008). Acts of remembrance: The power of memorial and the healing of indigenous Australia. *Adler Museum Bulletin*, 34(2), 5–19.
Meyers, O., & Zandberg, E. (2002). The sound-track of memory: Ashes and dust and the commemoration of the Holocaust in Israeli popular culture. *Media, Culture, & Society*, 24(3), 389–408.
Moussouri, T. (1997) Family agendas and family learning in hands-on museums. Unpublished doctoral dissertation. University of Leicester, Leicester, U.K.

Nathanson, D. (1998, August). From empathy to community. Paper presented to the First North American Conference on Conferencing, Minneapolis, MN.
Sofka, C. J. (2009). History and healing: Museums as healing spaces. *International Journal of the Inclusive Museum*, *2*(4), 79–90.
Sofka, C. J., & Strock-Lynskey, D. (2011). Utilizing cemetery work as a mechanism for teaching social justice and engaging students in restorative justice efforts. In J. Birkinmaier, A. Cruce, E.Burkemper, J. Curley, R. A. J. Wilson, & J. J. Stretch (Eds.), *Educating for social justice: Transformative experiential learning* (pp. 149–170). Chicago, IL: Lyceum Books.
Stepansky, J., Badia, E., & McShane, L. (2014). Some family members denounce return of 9/11 remains to World Trade Center, others call it "respectful". Retrieved from www.nydailynews.com/new-york/unidentified-remains-9–11-transfered-new-york-world-trade-center-article-1.1787160.
Sturken, M. (2007). *Tourists of history: Memory, kitsch, and consumerism from Oklahoma City to ground zero*. Durham, NC: Duke University Press.
Till, K. E. (2003). Places of memory. In J. Agnew, K. Mitchell, & G. Toal (Eds.), *A companion to political geography* (pp. 289–301). Malden, MA: Blackwell Publishing.
Trauma Foundation (2001). Survivor advocacy. Retrieved from www.traumaf.org/featured/7–01-survivor_advocacy.shtml
United Nations Office on Drugs and Crime (2006). *Handbook on restorative justice programmes*. New York, NY: United Nations. Retrieved from www.unodc.org/pdf/criminal_justice/06-56290_Ebook.pdf
van Alphen, E. (2006). Second-geneneration testimony, transmission of trauma, and postmemory (Holocaust literature and testimony). *Poetics Today*, *27*(1), 473–488.
van Dijck, J. (2007). *Mediated memories in the digital age*. Stanford, CA: Stanford University Press.
Van Ness, D. (2011, May 2). Restorative terminology: A modest proposal. Retrieved from www.restorativejustice.org/RJOB/restorative-terminology-a-modest-proposal.
Wachtel, T. (2013). Defining restorative. Retrieved from www.iirp.edu/pdf/Defining-Restorative.pdf.
Walker, L. (2013). Restorative justice: Definition and purpose. In K. S. van Wormer & L. Walker (Eds.), *Restorative justice today: Practical applications* (pp. 3–13). Thousand Oaks, CA: Sage Publications.
Wiseman, H., Metzl, E., & Barber, J. P. (2006). Anger, guilt, and intergenerational communication of trauma in the interpersonal narratives of second generation holocaust survivors. *American Journal of Orthopsychiatry*, *76*(2), 176–184.
Zehr, H. (2011). Personal correspondence with Lorenn Walker, as cited in L. Walker (2013).
Zehr, H. (2013). Restorative justice? What's that? Box 1 (p. 7) in L. Walker (2013) as previously cited.

19
Critical Social Work in Action

June Allan

The man leans forward in the armchair, forearms resting on his thighs as he quietly recounts his life story. After fleeing as a refugee from an African nation fraught with conflict, he has resettled in Australia and is endeavoring to 'make his way' in his new country. A proud member of a persecuted ethnic group in his homeland, he nevertheless held a good job in a government department in his country of origin. With a change in the political regime he was imprisoned and tortured for his political beliefs. Having fled his homeland, he now works in a manual job, supporting his wife and two young children. One of his children has just died from an illness. He is grieving . . .

(clinical interview)

Introduction

We might ask how it is that a critical social work approach, a progressive approach to practice with its roots in radical social work, is relevant or useful to social work interventions with people who are grieving or bereaved, such as the man in the above scene. I argue here that critical social work has deep significance in our work with grieving and bereaved individuals if we are to work with them in ways that open up rather than limit the possibilities for supporting them in their grief. Oppressive circumstances and the vicissitudes of power impact the lives of those people affected by loss, grief, and bereavement, whether or not we are consciously aware of this. A critical social work approach helps raise awareness of power and oppression underpinned by taken-for-granted assumptions, and reminds us to first and foremost be person-centered in our work with clients.

Underlining the ideas in this chapter is the premise that loss, death, grief, and bereavement are social experiences; it is impossible for us to be unaffected by the social, political, and cultural contexts in which we live and die, a concept well captured in Brabant's notion of "the social self" (2008, p. 103) and discussed by Fowler (2008). If we are to give full respect to the individuals we work with an understanding of social, ecological, biological, economic, and political conditions is essential to well-being (Green & McDermott, 2010).

In this chapter I consider social work practice with grieving and bereaved individuals from a critical social work perspective, an approach to practice that works towards a more socially just life, employing empowering and inclusive ways of working with people, and emphasizing how social forces impact individual experiences through social norms, policies, and social institutions. Through a scenario, I illustrate the importance of attending to the social, political, and cultural context, not only the psychological world of individuals experiencing significant grief and bereavement. Revealing the significance of understanding the concept of socially structured feelings, I also highlight the need to check taken-for-granted assumptions, whether these are our own as professionals, those of the clients with whom we are working, or systemic as defined by social norms—for example, inclusion and exclusion criteria in social policies, as noted by Harris (2009–2010).

Very little has been written on grieving and bereavement from a critical social work perspective. It is thus quite daunting to undertake this task, especially given the diverse understandings of "critical social work." But I believe it is an important task if it helps to enrich the possibilities for those grieving and bereaved individuals with whom practitioners work. In writing this chapter, I draw on my academic and practice experiences in critical social work and grief and bereavement. A first step is to locate my own psychosocial position.

As a white, now urbanized and middle-class Australian woman of Anglo-Saxon origins, my childhood was spent in modest surrounds on a farm in conservative rural Australia. This is where I was living at the age of 15 when my mother died from cancer in a metropolitan hospital some 300 kilometers distant. Despite some of the apparent privileges borne of my socio-political location in Australian society I nevertheless became more aware, over time, of disadvantage, discrimination, oppression, and disenfranchisement in people's lives. This awareness grew not only through personal experiences of financial and social disadvantage when, on moving to the city to embark on tertiary education, I found I did not really fit in with the wealthy, urban, "well-connected" class of many university students at the time for whom various privileges were taken for granted. However, social movements at that time stirred in me a growing consciousness about gender and, later, "race" issues. Additionally, an evolving social work education influenced by the growth of the radical social work movement also continued to raise my awareness of marginalization and oppression. Later, in the social work program in which I was teaching, structural and then critical approaches to social work theory and practice were adopted. Inspired by the "sensible" ideas in these approaches, I went on to co-edit two editions of a book on critical social work (Allan, Pease, & Briskman, 2003; Allan, Briskman & Pease, 2009) and have continued to grapple with praxis through my roles as educator, bereavement counselor, and counselor advocate with refugees. I introduced a course on loss, trauma, and grief into the social work programs at Royal Melbourne Institute of Technology (RMIT) University. Like Fowler (2008), who introduced a thanatology course at the Ramapo College of New Jersey, my course incorporated a socio-political emphasis in the curriculum, a break from the conventional psychological approaches that had been previously utilized.

I begin the chapter with an overview of critical social work and its development, followed by an outline of core principles and concepts in critical social work that shape the ensuing discussion. Reflecting on a particular practice situation involving multiple losses and bereavement, introduced at the chapter's beginning, I illustrate aspects of critical social work in practice. Woven into the fabric of the discussion are important contextual factors that impacted the personal experience of the individual. The discussion addresses analysis of social location and hidden oppressions, social exclusion, discourses and socially structured feelings, felt thoughtfulness, power, collaboration and partnership, a strengths perspective, advocacy, social change activities and reflexive practice.

Critical Social Work

Critical social work as an approach to social work is a relatively recent phenomenon. Variously conceptualized, the approach differs according to the context in which it has developed in different parts of the globe. For this reason there is a diversity of meanings associated with critical social work and globally, multiple theoretical perspectives on critical approaches (Pease, 2009a).

Various published accounts exist of the historical development of the critical tradition in social work (for example, Adams, Dominelli & Payne, 2009a; Adams, Dominelli, & Payne, 2009b; Allan, 2009a; Ferguson, 2008; Ferguson & Woodward, 2009; Fook, 2012; Mendes, 2009; Pease, 2009b; Rogowski, 2013). The early radical and structural approaches recognized the part played by social structures, vis-à-vis social class, in social problems and the day-to-day lives of individuals.

From the 1960s, radical critiques of traditional social work began to appear in the Western world, emerging out of disenchantment with the inequities and social injustices perpetuated by the capitalist system—in the U.K., Bailey and Brake, 1975; Corrigan and Leonard, 1978; in the U.S.A, Galper, 1975; and in Australia; De Maria, 1993, and Fook, 1993 (Fook, 2012; Pease, 2009a) Rees, 1991; Throssell, 1975. These developments were also in response to traditional social work emphasis at the time on individualized conceptions of personal problems and forms of helping. A structural social work approach that developed in Canada from the late 1970s (Moreau, 1979; Mullaly, 1993, 1997, 2007) also emphasized the structural nature of individual and social problems. Radical social work approaches have enjoyed a recent revival in the U.K. out of concern that practitioners are not sufficiently engaging in social change (for example, see Ferguson, 2008; Lavalette, 2011).

A critique of the earlier universal discourses of structural oppression highlighted the diversity of oppressions. Anti-oppressive approaches (Burke & Harrison, 2009; Dalrymple & Burke, 1995; Thompson, 2003), feminist social work approaches (Dominelli & McLeod, 1989; Marchant & Wearing, 1986) and anti-racist approaches (Dominelli, 1988) drew attention to this diversity arising out of the social divisions of social class, race, ethnicity, gender identity, sexual orientation, education, ability, religion, and age (Fowler, 2008; Woodthorpe & Brennan, 2014)—structural determinants of disadvantage and inequality that are evident in systems such as the health, educational, economic, and cultural systems as well as in personal and organizational issues (Burke & Harrison, 2009). Clifford (cited in Burke & Harrison, 2009, p. 211) developed five key anti-oppressive principles for practitioners to heed in their work: Social difference arising from power disparities between the dominant and dominated social groups; linking personal and political by placing personal stories within a broader social context; power and its impact on access to resources and positions of power; the historical and geographical location of individual life experiences; and reflexivity, to be understood psychologically, sociologically, historically, politically, and ethically.

The ideas underpinning these approaches, along with developments occurring in Australia (for a detailed account of these see Mendes, 2009) contributed to the growth in Australia of a critical social work approach. This approach emphasized the structural basis of personal and social difficulties and the need to work at both personal and political levels to challenge oppressive and marginalizing structures (Mendes, 2009). Cornerstones of a critical social work approach include:

- a commitment to working towards greater social justice and equality for those who are marginalized within society;
- attention to power relations that serve to marginalize individuals and groups;
- a commitment to questioning taken for granted and dominant assumptions and discourses, a principle also noted in a version of critical practice in the U.K. context (Adams et al., 2009a) that highlights the importance of practitioners maintaining a critical, that is, questioning attitude to their work, challenging existing ideas and practices;
- consideration of the social structure in the analysis of problems;
- a shift from a focus on individual pathology to individual or group oppression;
- the development of more egalitarian practice relations;
- involvement of the worker in social change activities (Allan, 2009a; Mendes, 2009).

The recent influence of postmodern thought, especially in the Australian literature (Allan et al., 2009; Pease & Fook, 1999) and elsewhere (e.g., Fook, 2012), has opened up greater possibilities to account for difference than was possible through the earlier radical and structural approaches, and opportunities to apply progressive approaches to practice with individual clients. Influenced by the postmodern notion of power, which describes multiple sources that are not only from the top-down, Australian and international scholar Janis Fook critiqued radical and structural approaches for their oversimplification of the notion of power. A structural account was seen to limit the personal agency of individuals and possibilities for change (Fook, 2012). Fook (2012) also expressed disquiet related to the perceived devaluing of 'micro' work with individuals and of social work practice experience, implied by the radical perspective. Similarly, Payne (cited in Mendes, 2009, p. 27) voiced his concern that focusing on material and structural issues and collective action could overlook the immediate personal needs of clients and their emotional and personal problems, critiques of some significance in relation to work with grieving and bereaved individuals.

The preceding discussion shows the tensions in the conceptions of critical social work, especially the social structure/human agency dichotomy that focuses on the extent to which human behavior is influenced by factors external to a person or is the choice an individual (Woodthorpe & Brennan, 2014; see also Ferguson, 2008; Ferguson & Woodward, 2009; Fook, 2012; Pease, 2009a). With awareness of these tensions and debates, for the purposes of this chapter I take an approach to critical social work that is influenced by postmodern thought. While acknowledging the imperative of practitioners and policymakers giving attention to social change at the 'macro' level, my stance in this chapter is to focus specifically on work at an individual level on the basis that many bereaved and grieving individuals who see practitioners for assistance do so at the level of individual intervention. Before considering the particular scenario, I comment on the contemporary socio-political context and some specific concepts in a critical social work approach.

A Neoliberal and Managerial Context

As indicated earlier, a central element of a critical approach is to consider the socio-political context in which services are offered and practice occurs. In the contemporary context, this requires a consideration of the upsurge of neoliberalism and managerialism in the Western world (Ferguson, 2008; Ferguson & Woodward, 2009; Fook, 2012; Lavalette, 2011; McDonald, 2009; Rogowski, 2013). Neoliberalism, a "policy framework emphasizing a shift from the traditional welfare state to a policy framework that focuses on creating the conditions for international competitiveness" (McDonald, cited in Pease, 2009b), has been adopted by many countries, including Australia, in the largely capitalist, globalized world (Rogowski, 2013). Based on a belief in individual freedom and underpinned by the key values of self-interest, self-responsibility, and individualism rather than the value of social justice, individuals are expected to stand on their own two feet with the state having only a minimal role (Rogowski, 2013).

Neoliberalism has had a significant impact on service provision. Goods and services are expected to be distributed effectively, with privatization of government and user-pay services that emphasize freedom of choice, eroding professional discretion (Dominelli, 2009a; Pease 2009b). As a result of neoliberalism and economic market rationality, systems of management are enforced on human service organizations. Under this new managerialism, outcomes-based funding of non-government programs emphasizes efficiency and outcomes-based targets over the values of social justice (Pease, 2009b), lessening opportunities for the implementation of progressive practice approaches. This is a challenge but does not necessarily exclude critical social work practice opportunities. Within such circumstances grief and bereavement are not necessarily an easy "fit" where rationality and efficiency are given priority. As McDonald asserts, "What can be done is inevitably constrained by institutional realities," but "good critical practice is doing the possible in a manner cognisant of the context" (2009, p. 251).

Some Relevant Concepts

Socio-Political Analysis and Power

Looking for hidden oppressions and considering clients' social locations is central in assisting them to view their experiences within a political framework, and power relationships need to be considered through an identification of the social, political, economic, and professional barriers impinging on clients. The use of consciousness-raising (Rogowski, 2013) is helpful to assist people to understand their personal situations within their broader contexts. However, it is important for this to be a collaborative process between practitioner and client, based on respect, shared expertise, and mutual learning that values both professional knowledge and client knowledge and life experiences. Dominelli conceptualizes power as "a negotiated reality in which neither [practitioner nor client] is either completely powerful or powerless" (2009b, p. 28). In this situation there is a choice to reproduce or challenge existing power relations. As practitioners we can choose to assist grieving individuals to be active agents rather than passive victims, allowing them to voice their views and to participate in decision-making (Dominelli, 2009b).

Discourses

Closely connected with the workings of power, discourses can be thought of as "the ways we make meaning of and construct our world through the language we use (verbal and non-verbal) to communicate about it" (Fook, 2012, p. 72). In essence, the ways we talk about our world also construct it (Fook, 2012). As the ways we communicate to interpret ourselves and our world, discourses establish the boundaries of what we can and cannot say at a particular time and in a specific culture, creating the normative and ultimately, shaping the way we see ourselves (Johnson, 2009). Formal theories, for example, can be seen as particular discourses formed by different contexts and power interests; theories about grief and bereavement can become discourses that can help or hinder grieving individuals. Traditionally dominated by psychological and medical theories, especially in the approach to death and dying (Thornton, 2014), theories about grief and bereavement tended to be culture and gender blind, although this has changed in recent times through the work of scholars such as Rosenblatt (2013) on cultural differences and Doka and Martin (2010) on whether or not grief is gendered. Discourses emanating from the Freudian idea of detachment led to popular but not always appropriate discourses of "getting over" bereavement (Currer, 2009, p. 374); yet the contemporary theory of "continuing bonds" (Klass, Silverman, & Nickman, 1996; Rubin, Malkinson, & Witzum, 2012) equally has the potential to become a disabling discourse that excludes or limits conversations about an individual's relationship with a person who has died (Balk, 2014).

Grieving in Western society is governed by several rules, one of which concerns "whether or not the relationship to [those for whom an individual is grieving] is valid according to social expectations" (Harris, 2009–2010, p. 245), which is of particular relevance to the scenario discussed in this chapter. Doka's (2002) notion of disenfranchised grief highlights that where grief is not validated according to social expectations, it can not only lessen needed support for a grieving individual but indeed exacerbate a sense of anguish that can result from invalidation through disabling discourses or policies.

Advocacy

Advocacy plays an important part in critical practice. While there will always be some individuals or groups who will benefit from having a more powerful person to assist in gaining their rights or entitlements, the situation is more complex and we need to ensure that those requiring advocacy are empowered in the process. Critical practice with its questioning attitude and recognition of power relations draws our attention to these complexities. As Fook (2012) points out, inappropriate advocacy by a practitioner on behalf of a client may leave clients feeling inadequate or missing an opportunity to develop and practice valuable skills in asserting themselves. It is important for practitioners not to assume they know best what is actually wanted by the clients, grieving or otherwise, on whose behalf we are advocating. Given there may be a number of competing rights and interests in a specific situation requiring advocacy, a suggested guideline in changing the situation for the client's benefit is to do so in ways that respect as many of these competing rights and interests as possible. This includes ensuring that clients are involved as much as possible in their own advocacy and empowerment (Fook, 2012).

Critical Reflexivity

The principle of critical reflexivity demands that practitioners reflect on the impact of their own background, socio-political, geographical, and cultural location, perspectives on their practice and the ways in which their own social identity and values affect the information they gather and the way they work (Allan, 2009b; Burke & Harrison, 2009). Thus, we reflect on the social divisions we represent (race, ethnicity, class, gender, sexual preference, ability, education, age, and religion)—acknowledging that awareness of our own biases and assumptions is a limitless task (Battersby & Bailin, 2011)—with the utilization of uncertainty serving as a useful catalyst for change.

The Death of a Child . . . but Much More

To illustrate critical social work approaches that endeavor to acknowledge and respond to aspects of power, marginalization, and oppression of different forms, I now turn to the situation of an African Australian experiencing bereavement and multiple losses, past and present, as he resettles in Australia. The scenario is based upon a "composite" story from practice in which identifying details have been altered and disguised and a pseudonym used. The focus is primarily on individual work, my intention being to draw attention to the scope for acknowledging the socio-political context within "micro" work. It is a story that shows the importance of a holistic perspective.

A Situation of Multiple Losses

"Mohamed" was a middle-aged black man from a country in East Africa who had entered Australia as a refugee on humanitarian grounds a few years earlier. Islamic in faith, he was a member of an ethnic group who suffered unrelenting political, social, and economic oppression under the minority ruling group. Despite this, Mohamed was university educated and had worked in a government department. However, detained as a political prisoner for his political views following a change in regime, he was held in detention, eventually fleeing his country alone, leaving all his extended family behind him. In Australia, Mohamed was now living on the outskirts of Melbourne, a large metropolis in south-eastern Australia, in a community where many others of his ethnic group were resettling. Engaged in unskilled employment, he was supporting his wife and two young children and had been successful in securing Australian citizenship. Experiencing physical health problems, some of which related to torture in prison, he required ongoing medical treatment. Following the death from an illness of one of his young children, he and his wife had been referred to a grief organization. However, because of the nature and complexity of his situation he was referred on to an organization that specializes in working with refugees and asylum seekers experiencing loss and trauma. His wife continued to be seen by a worker at the former organization. This is where the story is taken up. It is a story of anguish and frustration due to the impact of social structures and social restraints related to insufficient resources and cumbersome bureaucracy, but also a story of resilience and hope.

I was in a counselor advocate role at the specialist organization when Mohammed was referred to me. The work of this organization is based on a psychosocial model that focuses on the establishment of recovery goals to address the reactions of individuals and families to their loss and trauma. Services provided include counseling/advocacy, specialist therapy, complementary therapies

(Singer & Adams, 2011), and advocacy at organizational and structural levels. Such a model of healing for refugees has been challenged in recent times, with some protagonists favoring a social model of healing in acknowledgment that much of the suffering experienced by people during resettlement is primarily social in nature, related to life in their host country rather than past experiences (Westoby, 2009; Westoby & Ingamells, 2010). Westoby and Ingamells (2010) argue for a socio-political interpretation of situations rather than interpretations of emotions through the lens of pathology or disease. Bridging these two positions, Allan (2014) notes the importance of giving priority to strengthening the resilience of families and communities through the re-establishment and building of support networks. At the same time though, where a person's needs remain unmet through these networks, targeted therapeutic intervention is required that gives full recognition to the inter-relationship between refugees' sense of loss, hurt, anguish, and betrayal and the structural conditions of their lives. And as Rosenblatt (2013) points out, in some cultures for a person to turn away from grief resulting from oppression and injustices may represent to them a betrayal of particular values. These were the sorts of considerations in my mind when I worked with Mohamed.

The ensuing discussion of the work focuses especially on the socio-political and cultural contexts of Mohamed's life; taken-for-granted assumptions and discourses; aspects of power; advocacy; and reflexive practice in relation to the grief and losses Mohamed experienced.

Socio-political and Cultural Contexts

Analysis of Social Location and Hidden Oppressions. An understanding of Mohamed's social, political and cultural contexts, past and present, was fundamental to our work together. An analysis of social location and hidden oppressions is central in helping clients to view their personal experiences within a political framework (Allan, 2009b). Although Mohamed had now become an Australian citizen and was part of a strong social support network in his local community he was still experiencing the problems of resettlement familiar to many refugees (Allan, 2014; Allan & Hess, 2010; Furneaux & Cook, 2008; Meadth, 2010; Miller & Rasco, 2004), including the inability to secure suitable work akin to his graduate employment in his home country. While Australia has benefited over many generations from the experiences brought by refugees to enrich the nation (Hugo, 2011), issues of race, ethnic identity, and difference create difficulties. In Mohamed's situation, he felt discriminated against in terms of employment and racist behaviors towards him in the community, a circumstance that can result in a sense of rejection (Siddiqui, 2011). Recent Australian studies have noted barriers to employment experienced by people in the resettlement phase, especially structural disadvantage in the labor market and discrimination according to race, religion and ethnic origin (Colic-Peisker & Tilbury, in Hugo 2011, p. 145; RCOA, 2010; Tempany, 2009). From the beginning of our work together it was crucial for me to listen to and validate Mohamed's experiences, from his multiple losses to understanding his life experiences laced with stories of oppression and social injustice but also resilience and optimism for a better future.

Social Exclusion, Discourses, and Socially Structured Feelings. Fook (2012) draws attention to cultural domination in which people are socially excluded when they are subjected to ways of communicating in their host culture that are alien to them. Cultural disrespect can also occur where people are excluded through stereotyping within the dominant cultural context. When Mohamed was referred to me shortly after the death of his child, I assumed in my mind that this death was likely to be the primary source of grief for him. On meeting with him I quickly learned that this was not the case, at least at this point of time in his life. While he expressed sorrow and sadness about his child's death that required careful psychological support, he took a spiritual view that "every one of us is going to die one day" and that the death was Allah's will. Typically, the death of a child can be viewed in Western cultures as a significant contributing factor to complications in grieving (Boerner, Mancini & Bonnano, 2013, p. 64). In Mohamed's situation, this was not a good "fit," forcing me to reassess my assumption.

Among the various losses past and present that Mohamed had experienced, including the loss and abuse of his human rights in his country of origin, it became clear that a more pressing source of anguish and grief for Mohamed was the separation from his extended family, particularly his siblings' children for whom he had taken responsibility in his country of origin because of his financial capacity to do so—a common occurrence. It was important to Mohamed for these children to be educated to prevent starvation of the family in the longer term and to provide hope for the future. Aggravating Mohamed's grief was a grave sense of injustice as Australian government policy prevented him from sponsoring these family members to come to Australia, his hope for them to be safe and educated. Because the children still lived with their biological parents inside their home country, they did not meet the criteria to allow sponsorship.

In a consideration of socially structured feelings, or emotions in a political context, the work of Hoggett and Thompson (2012) suggests that a sense of injustice such as that which Mohamed experienced contributes to a sense of loss and associated feelings of grief, sorrow, disappointment, disillusionment, and melancholy. Loss, for example, is seen to accompany domination, and feelings associated with injustice include anger, resentment, grievance, and outrage (Hoggett & Thompson, 2012). Frost and Hoggett's (2008) work suggests that such experiences of loss and hurt become individualized with people feeling isolated and ashamed, profoundly affecting their capacity to act and reach their goals.

Underpinning Mohamed's grief associated with his extended family was his profound sense of responsibility towards the children according to his cultural norms; anguish at the impossibility of being able to sponsor them; and financial pressures and difficult choices in wanting to support both his family in Australia and his family in his country of origin. Each of these issues needed to be addressed in supporting him with his grief and sense of helplessness. They formed basic goals in our work together, along with his goal of improved health.

Felt Thoughtfulness. Frost and Hoggett (2008) call for practitioners to exercise "felt thoughtfulness," empathizing with the people whom they are assisting "to feel the pain of the other," at the same time thinking critically about the injustices that produce the pain (Frost & Hoggett, 2008, p. 455). In order not to risk disenfranchising Mohamed's grief and anguish regarding his extended family and the felt injustice of them not being able to join him in Australia, it was useful for me to acknowledge, empathize with, and validate the circumstances. All avenues were explored in relation to ways of bringing his extended family members to Australia. Sadly, after following up, advocating for, and checking all options, there were no avenues open to Mohamed. Acknowledging and sitting with Mohamed in his anguish and disappointment about these circumstances was essential, as was talking through with him the foundations of the policy with its assumptions based on different cultural understandings of "family" and "family responsibility" from those to which he was accustomed.

Power

When I first met with Mohamed, he was experiencing overwhelming sadness and a sense of hopelessness due to what he perceived as the very powerless position that he was in, because of his various losses, but also his anguish regarding his extended family. Mohamed's capacity to draw on his personal power was compromised because of his experiences and as Frost and Hoggett (2008) assert, social suffering is at the heart of subjective experience, affecting a person's capacity for agency.

Recognizing this profound lack of a sense of power and control, I endeavored to work with Mohamed in ways that enabled him to regain a sense of power and control over his decisions and actions. This follows the idea that power is used and created rather than possessed, with every person exercising and having the potential to create a sense of power (Fook, 2012).

Collaboration and Partnership. With this understanding of power in working with Mohamed, from the beginning it was important to work on the basis that we were "potential allies" (Rogowski, 2013). This meant working in a collaborative, partnership-oriented way, listening to and, wherever possible, acting on his view of the situation (Fowler, 2008; Rogowski, 2013, p. 164). Recognizing that Western reasoning has subjugated personal experience as expert knowledge (Hanrahan, 2013), this collaboration extended to us informing each other from our respective knowledge bases—I informed and discussed with him, for example, definitions of "family" underpinning government policy, as described earlier; how "the system" works; and especially how his grief and anguish related to the broader socio-political and cultural factors impacting his life. He, on the other hand, informed me about his country of origin—its history, politics, religious and cultural mores, and his extended family's religious and cultural mores. These mutual learnings fostered an open discussion about the impact of the difficulties and injustices he was experiencing and enabled a fuller exploration of the ways in which his feelings and experiences interrelated with social-political and cultural factors.

Strengths Perspective within a Critical Social Work Approach. It was also important that the work we undertook together drew on a strengths perspective within a critical framework. Given the adverse pre-flight and resettlement experiences on a person's sense of self, a focus on what they want and their aspirations in life—a source of hope—is important (Allan, 2014). An attitude of curiosity, focusing on how the person is responding to their experiences (Marlowe, 2010), and the drawing out of sources of resistance and resilience to identify what has sustained the person can be employed (Allan, 2014). The skill of "double listening" to the ordinary in a person's life and not just the extraordinary (Marlowe, 2010, p. 192), can assist in thickening their narratives and enable a holistic approach that encompasses the emotional, cultural, political, spiritual, and social domains of their lives, opening up stories about their hopes and aspirations in their lives (Allan, 2014).

Such an approach encouraged Mohamed to develop a new goal of further study in Australia to enhance suitable job prospects. Through intensive brokerage and advocacy on my part and supporting Mohamed to advocate for himself as an empowering act (for example, by helping him to write a letter to support his tertiary education application), Mohamed was eventually successful in being granted a tertiary place. He subsequently had to defer this place when his physical health deteriorated and his material circumstances changed after losing his job, placing him under financial stress and requiring him to attend rehabilitation. While extremely disappointed at having to defer his studies, Mohamed's resilience showed through when he took from the situation that he now knew he could achieve entry into a tertiary program. This "success" assisted him in some small way to address his loss of self-esteem and his conflict about his capacity to provide for his families in Australia and his country of origin, another significant loss, especially felt when he lost his job.

Advocacy and Alliances. As just described, advocacy formed an important part of our work together, to access needed services and resources, to push for Mohamed's rights, and to help him manage his grief in ways other than simply talking with a practitioner. An important means to achieve these things was the formation and/or sustenance of alliances—between Mohamed and me, as noted in the discussion of collaboration and partnership; between Mohamed and the team of professionals within and outside the organization; and between Mohamed and his social network.

Over the course of our work together, Mohamed was linked in with numerous services to assist with financial pressures, physical health treatments, and employment possibilities. This involved significant advocacy work in which I as the practitioner "walked alongside" him in helping him access needed resources. When Mohamed and I began work together, I referred him to the complementary therapists within the organization to assist him with ongoing physical health problems. Physiotherapy and massage became part of his treatment regime. Together as a multidisciplinary team sharing similar values, we paid attention to Mohamed's physical and social circumstances and liaised with other professionals in Mohamed's life including doctors, specialists, and rehabilitation staff.

The impact of disabling dominant discourses through the influence of managerialism and goals of efficiency was encountered in services providing rehabilitation and re-employment assistance—a frustrating experience for Mohamed that did not encourage him in his efforts to work towards being able to provide for his families and hence address the loss of self-esteem and loss of role as primary provider within his family. Workers in these services tended to see Mohamed through a single lens: somebody to be placed in a job, as rapidly as possible to help meet targets. Lacking in this service provision was an empathic understanding of him as an individual impacted by his experiences of grief, anguish, and frustration. On occasion, some of these personnel expressed frustration with Mohamed, tending to see him as "resisting" treatment options through not wanting to help himself sufficiently—in other words, he was not "fitting" the neoliberal ideology of being self-responsible and standing on his own two feet, maximizing opportunities seen to be available to him. This required me to engage in discussions with the personnel concerned about the client's circumstances from a holistic perspective, in an endeavor to influence a shift in attitude and understanding about the normality of his attitudes, given his circumstances—a matter of exploring what's right about what's wrong (Harris, 2009–2010). Advocacy in this way can at least give pause to the set of attitudes and discourses that imparts the message that clients—especially those from other countries—ought to "fit in" and be grateful for what is being offered to them. It can also help to counter the dominant discourse that loss, grief, and bereavement is something to be put aside, of "nuisance value" in a society valuing rationality, efficiency and achievement of goals.

Such disabling experiences help to highlight the value of the support that can come from people's own support networks. Mohamed had a strong network of friends from his ethnic community and took an active role in sustaining alliances with those like-minded people in his community. He was emotionally and materially supported and sustained by this strong network and I consistently and actively encouraged this connection. In accordance with Westoby's (2009) social model of healing, the building of support networks is an important way in which grief can be supported, in ways that do not have to pathologize the grief, anguish, and grievances a person may hold. At the time Mohamed and I worked together there was no formal support group for his people, although one has subsequently been established. His informal support network was of central importance to him.

Social Change Activities

Service provision shaped by neoliberal attitudes and managerialist discourses are deeply entrenched and as commented on earlier, we do what we can to challenge disabling practices, policies and structures within the given context of the times. An issue with working in this way from a critical perspective is the sense that very little may be occurring by way of ultimate social change. But as Rogowski (2013) states in his own reflections using a critical perspective, it is better to aim at small steps towards a more socially just and equal society.

> Social work is unlikely to be at the vanguard of fundamental social change, but critical social work's emphasis on critical analysis and practice that is person-centred, with work wherever possible focusing on problems and difficulties as defined by users, makes a small contribution to making the world we inhabit a better place.
>
> (Rogowski, 2013, p. 8)

My challenge to the resistant attitudes of the service providers who saw Mohamed as resisting their efforts was one small way in which this occurred.

At an indirect level of intervention, in my role as an educator in the field of loss and grief and in social work practice more generally, I actively endeavor to promote a critical approach to practice in the hope of raising awareness and changing attitudes that fail to question taken-for-granted assumptions, and systems and discourses that oppress and perpetuate marginalization and disadvantage.

Reflexive Practice

Reflexive practice is ongoing; here, due to space constraints, I will focus on only a couple of issues. As a white Western woman I was cautious about entering into work with Mohamed—would my own social location impinge too greatly on our work together? Before accepting the referral I checked that it would be acceptable to Mohamed to work with a white female from a Western background—an important first step. Culturally (from his perspective), my status as an older woman was a positive factor. I drew confidence from a critical social work approach as a socio-political analysis was integral to working collaboratively with him. Mohamed valued having a space in mainstream society where he could talk freely about his experiences past and present without fear of judgment and persecution for his beliefs—having an ally bear witness to his life's story from a socio-political perspective was an important psychological support for him.

I observed that Mohamed had a matter-of-fact approach to life and the issues he was facing. Although he sought help psychologically as well as practically, his grief followed what Doka and Martin (2010) define as an instrumental style that "focuses on practical matters and problem-solving" (Corr & Corr, 2013, p. 144). This was perhaps one of the most important factors for me to recognize in our work together. Many times during our work I questioned myself on whether I should be focusing more directly on his specific losses (including the death of his child). Western discourses suggested to me that I "should" be revisiting and exploring the death of his child and his other losses in a more direct and focused way than I was. Working collaboratively with Mohamed, respecting his cultural and religious views and being person-centered acted as firm principles underpinning when and how I broached these issues. After the initial work of firmly grounding Mohamed's experiences within a social-political framework, as well as attending to his feelings of loss and anguish, focusing on the instrumental issues and making links and connections between Mohamed's losses and his circumstances when opportunities arose, seemed an appropriate way to proceed.

Ways Forward

At the time our work together ended Mohamed was receiving assistance from a rehabilitation service. A number of problems chiefly related to health, secure employment and finances remained but his grief related to his multiple losses of relationships, home country and extended family had eased significantly through his opportunity to talk these issues through in their social, political and cultural contexts and through the support from his own social networks.

The question remained open whether Mohamed himself might have been more actively engaged in any collective possibilities for social change. At the time of writing it is heartening for me to learn that a support group for Mohamed's people has now been established in Australia and is planning to send a representative from Australia to the United Nations Human Rights Council to provide accounts of human rights violations committed on Mohamed's people (Diaspora Action Australia, 2014).

Conclusion

In this chapter I have outlined core components of a critical social work approach and applied the approach to a composite situation of an African Australian who was experiencing grief and bereavement. As challenging and complex as a critical social work approach is, it endeavors to respond to people's lives in their entirety. Important is the practice of understanding people's grief and bereavement within the socio-political and cultural contexts of their lives, and working collaboratively with them in ways that acknowledge the interwoven nature of these dimensions.

The use of a critical social work approach highlights the importance of being open to possibilities for fostering and advancing a person's rights. It challenges taken-for-granted assumptions and shifting attitudes and discourses that can serve to disenfranchise grief and work against a person using and building their power in order to help them to live with their losses and give energy to their life circumstances. I hope that this chapter makes some small contribution to the developing understanding of how a critical social work approach might assist practitioners to work in ways that acknowledge the integral part socio-political and cultural factors play in the experiences of those who are grieving and bereaved.

Key Terms

Critical social work approach—a progressive approach to practice with its roots in radical social work; one that attempts to raise awareness of power and oppression underpinned by taken-for-granted assumptions, and reminds us to first and foremost be person-centered in our work with clients.

Cultural domination—a process by which people are socially excluded when they are subjected to ways of communicating in their host culture that are alien to them.

Felt thoughtfulness—empathizing with another person ("to feel the pain of the other") while at the same time thinking critically about the injustices that produce the pain.

Gender blind/culture blind—failing to consider differences that may occur based on unique features/experiences of individuals or groups (e.g., gender, culture).

Inappropriate advocacy—action undertaken by a practitioner on behalf of a client may leave clients feeling inadequate or missing an opportunity to develop and practice valuable skills in asserting themselves.

Instrumental style of grieving—focusing on practical matters and problem-solving.

Neoliberalism—a "policy framework emphasizing a shift from the traditional welfare state to a policy framework that focuses on creating the conditions for international competitiveness." Based on a belief in individual freedom and underpinned by the key values of self-interest, self-responsibility, and individualism rather than the value of social justice, individuals are expected to stand on their own two feet with the state having only a minimal role.

Questions for Reflection

1. The author begins by locating her own psychosocial position. What is yours? How can awareness of this inform your interactions with others (and with the material in this chapter)?
2. Consider the socio-political context in which you live, work, attend school, engage in hobbies, and more. To what extend does this context influence your experience of these activities?
3. Have you experienced the "dominant discourse that loss, grief and bereavement is something to be put aside, of 'nuisance value' in a society valuing rationality, efficiency and achievement of goals" (p. 234)? What do you think is needed in order to challenge this dominant view?

References

Adams, R., Dominelli, L., & Payne, M. (Eds.). (2009a). *Social work: Themes, issues and critical debates* (3rd ed.). Basingstoke, U.K.: Palgrave Macmillan.

Adams, R., Dominelli, L., & Payne, M. (Eds.). (2009b). *Critical practice in social work.* (2nd ed.). Houndmills, Basingstoke, U.K.: Palgrave Macmillan.

Allan, J. (2009a). Theorising new developments in critical social work. In J. Allan, L. Briskman, & B. Pease (Eds.), *Critical social work: Theories and practices for a socially just world*. (2nd ed). Crows Nest, NSW, Australia: Allen & Unwin.

Allan, J. (2009b). Doing critical social work. In J. Allan, L. Briskman, & B. Pease (Eds.), *Critical social work: Theories and practices for a socially just world*. (2nd ed). Crows Nest, NSW: Allen & Unwin.

Allan, J. (2014). Reconciling the 'psycho-social/structural' in social work counselling with refugees. *British Journal of Social Work*. doi: 10.1093/bjsw/bcu051

Allan, J., & Hess, L. (2010). The nexus between material circumstances, cultural context and experiences of loss, grief and trauma: Complexities in working with refugees in the early phases of resettlement. *Grief Matters*. 13(3), 76–80.

Allan, J., Pease, B., & Briskman, L. (2003). *Critical social work: An introduction to theories and practices*. Crows Nest, NSW, Australia: Allen & Unwin.

Allan, J., Briskman, L., & Pease, B. (Eds.). (2009). *Critical social work: Theories and practices for a socially just world*. (2nd ed). Crows Nest, NSW, Australia: Allen & Unwin.

Bailey, R., & Brake, M. (Eds.). (1975). *Radical social work*. New York, NY: Pantheon Books.

Balk, D. (2014). Getting researchers and clinicians to play nice together: Building a bridge to span the gap separating practitioners and researchers. Conference presentation at Australian Grief and Bereavement Conference, March 26–28, 2014, Melbourne.

Battersby, M., & Bailin, S. (2011). Critical inquiry: Considering the context. *Argumentation*. doi 10.1007/s10503-011-9205-z

Boerner, K., Mancini, A., & Bonnano, G. (2013). On the nature and prevalence of uncomplicated grief. In M. Stroebe, H. Schut, & J. Van Den Bout (Eds.), *Complicated grief: Scientific foundations for health care professionals*. Hove, East Sussex: Routledge.

Brabant, S. C. (2008). Clinical sociology and bereavement. In J. M. Fritz (Ed.), *International Clinical Sociology*. New York, NY: Springer.

Burke, B., & Harrison, P. (2009) Anti-oppressive practice. In R. Adams, L. Dominelli, & M. Payne (Eds.), *Critical Practice in Social Work* (2nd ed.). Basingstoke, U.K.: Palgrave Macmillan.

Corr, C., & Corr, D. (2013). Historical and contemporary perspectives on loss, grief and mourning. In D Meagher & D. Balk (Eds.), *Handbook of thanatology* (2nd ed.; pp. 135–148). New York, NY: Routledge.

Corrigan, P., & Leonard, P. (1978). *Social work practice under capitalism: A Marxist approach*. London: Macmillan.

Currer, C. (2009). Care at the end of life and in bereavement. In R. Adams, L. Dominelli, & M. Payne (Eds.), *Critical practice in social work* (2nd ed.). Houndmills, Basingstoke, U.K.: Palgrave Macmillan.

Dalrymple, J., & Burke, B. (1995). *Anti-oppressive practice: Social care and the law*. Buckingham, U.K.: Open University Press.

De Maria, W. (1993). Flapping on clipped wings: Social work ethics in the age of activism. *Australian Social Work*, 50(4), 3–19.

Diaspora Action Australia. (2014). Retrieved from www.crisishub.org.au/content/our-work

Doka, K. (2002). *Disenfranchised Grief: New directions, strategies and challenges for practice*. Champaign, IL: Research Press.

Doka, K., & Martin, T. (2010). *Grieving beyond gender: Understanding the ways men and women mourn* (rev. ed.). New York, NY: Routledge.

Dominelli, L. (1988). *Anti-racist social work*. Basingstoke, U.K.: Macmillan.

Dominelli, L. (2009a). Introduction: Repositioning social work. In R. Adams, L. Dominelli, & M. Payne. (Eds.), *Social work: Themes, issues and critical debates* (3rd ed.; pp. 19–31). Basingstoke, U.K.: Palgrave Macmillan.

Dominelli, L. (2009b). Values in critical practice. In R. Adams, L. Dominelli, & M. Payne. (Eds.), *Critical Practice in Social Work* (2nd ed.). Basingstoke, U.K.: Palgrave Macmillan.

Dominelli, L., & McLeod, E. (1989). *Feminist social work*. Basingstoke, U.K.: Macmillan.

Ferguson, I. (2008). *Reclaiming social work: Challenging neo-liberalism and promoting social justice*. London: Sage.

Ferguson, I., & Woodward, R. (2009). *Radical social work in practice: Making a difference*. University of Bristol, Bristol: Policy Press.

Fook, J. (1993). *Radical casework: A theory of practice*. Sydney: Allen & Unwin.

Fook, J. (2012). *Social work: A critical approach to practice*. (2nd ed.). London: Sage.

Fowler, K. (2008). "The wholeness of things": Infusing diversity and social justice into death education. *Omega: Journal of Death and Dying*, 57(1), 53–91.

Frost L., & Hoggett, P. (2008). Human agency and social suffering. *Critical Social Policy*, 28(4), 438–460.

Furneaux, S., & Cook, K. (2008, March). The experience of temporary protection and the resettlement of refugees within a socio-political context. *Just Policy: A Journal of Australian Social Policy*, 47, 6–13.

Galper. J. (1975). *The politics of social services*. Englewood Cliffs, NJ: Prentice Hall.

Green, D., & McDermott, F. (2010). Social work from inside and between complex systems; Perspectives on person-in-environment for today's social work. *British Journal of Social Work, 40*(8), 2414–2430.

Hanrahan, C. (2013). Critical social theory and the politics of narrative in the mental health professions: The mental health film festival as an emerging postmodern praxis. *British Journal of Social Work, 43*(6), 1150–1169.

Harris, D. (2009–2010). Oppression of the bereaved: A critical analysis of grief in Western society, *Omega: Journal of Death and Dying, 60*(3), 241–253.

Hoggett, P., & Thompson, S. (2012). *Politics and the emotions: The affective turn in contemporary political studies.* London: Continuum.

Hugo, G. (2011). *Economic, social and civic contributions of first and second generation humanitarian entrants.* National Centre for Social Applications of Geographical Information Systems, University of Adelaide, Adelaide. Retrieved from www.crc.nsw.gov.au/__data/assets/pdf_file/0009/19728/2011_The_Economic_Civic_and_Social_Contributions_of_Ist_and_2nd_GenerationHumanitarian_entrants.pdf

Johnson, K. (2009). Disabling discourses and enabling practices in disability politics. In J. Allan, L. Briskman, & B. Pease (Eds.), *Critical social work: Theories and practices for a socially just world* (2nd ed.; pp. 188–200). Crows Nest, NSW, Australia: Allen & Unwin.

Klass, D., Silverman, P., & Nickman, S. (1996). *Continuing bonds: New understandings of grief.* Washington, DC: American Psychological Association.

Lavalette, M. (Ed.). (2011). *Radical social work today: Social work at the crossroads.* University of Bristol, Bristol: Policy Press.

McDonald, C. (2009). Critical practice in a changing context. In J. Allan, L. Briskman, & B. Pease (Eds.), *Critical social work: Theories and practices for a socially just world* (2nd ed). Crows Nest, NSW, Australia: Allen & Unwin.

Marchant, H., & Wearing, B. (1986). *Gender reclaimed: Women in social work.* Sydney: Hale & Iremonger.

Marlowe, J. (2010). Beyond the discourse of trauma: Shifting the focus on Sudanese refugees. *Journal of Refugee Studies, 23*(2), 183–198.

Meadth, K. (2010). On arrival support for refugees and Special Humanitarian Visa holders. *Victorian Social Work Newsletter, 4*(2), 4–5.

Mendes, P. (2009). Tracing the origins of critical social work practice. In J. Allan, L. Briskman, & B. Pease (Eds.), *Critical social work: Theories and practices for a socially just world* (2nd ed.; pp. 17–29). Crows Nest, NSW, Australia: Allen & Unwin.

Miller, K. E., & Rasco, L. M. (2004). *The mental health of refugees: Ecological approaches to healing and adaptation.* New Jersey: Lawrence Erlbaum.

Moreau, M. (1979). A structural approach to social work practice. *Canadian Journal of Social Work Education, 5*(1), 78–94.

Mullaly, B. (1993) *Structural social work: Ideology, theory and practice.* Toronto: McLelland & Stewart.

Mullaly, B. (1997). *Structural social work: Ideology, theory and practice* (2nd ed.). Toronto: Oxford University Press.

Mullaly, B. (2007). *The new structural social work.* (3rd ed.). Toronto: Oxford University Press.

Pease, B. (2009a). From radical to critical social work: Progressive transformation or mainstream incorporation? In R. Adams, L. Dominelli, & M. Payne (Eds.), *Critical practice in social work* (2nd ed.) (pp. 189–198). Houndmills, Basingstoke, U.K.: Palgrave Macmillan.

Pease, B. (2009b). From evidence-based practice to critical knowledge in post-positivist social work. In J. Allan, L. Briskman, & B. Pease (Eds.), *Critical social work: Theories and practices for a socially just world* (2nd ed.; pp. 45–57). Crows Nest, NSW, Australia: Allen & Unwin.

Pease, B., & Fook, J. (Eds.). (1999). *Transforming social work practice: Postmodern critical perspectives.* Sydney: Allen & Unwin.

Rees, S. (1991). *Achieving power: Practice and policy in social welfare.* Sydney: Allen & Unwin.

Refugee Council of Australia (RCOA). (2010, February). *Economic, civic and social contributions of refugees and humanitarian entrants: A literature review.* Commonwealth of Australia.

Rogowski, S. (2013). *Critical social work with children and families: Theory, context and practice.* University of Bristol, Bristol: Policy Press.

Rosenblatt, P. C. (2013). The concept of complicated grief: Lessons from other cultures. In M. Stroebe, H. Schut, & J. Van Den Bout. *Complicated grief: Scientific foundations for health care professionals* (pp. 27–39). Hove, U.K.: Routledge.

Rubin, S., Malkinson, R., & Witzum, E. (2012). *Working with the bereaved: Multiple lenses on loss and mourning.* New York, NY: Routledge.

Siddiqui, S. (2011). Critical social work with mixed-race individuals: Implications for anti-racist and anti-oppressive practice. *Canadian Social Work Review, 28*(3), 255–272.

Singer, J., & Adams, J. (2011). The place of complementary therapies in an integrated model of refugee health care: Counsellors' and refugee clients' perspectives. *Journal of Refugee Studies, 24*(2), 351–375.

Tempany, M. (2009). What research tells us about the mental health and psychosocial wellbeing of Sudanese refugees: A literature review. *Transcultural Psychiatry, 46*(20), 300–315.

Thompson, N. (2003). *Promoting equality: Challenging discrimination and oppression in the human services*. Basingstoke, U.K.: Palgrave Macmillan.

Thornton, T. (2014). Medicalization. In M. Brennan (Ed.), *The A-Z of death and dying: Social, medical and cultural aspects* (pp. 302–304). Santa Barbara, CA: Greenwood.

Throssell, H. (1975). Social work overview. In *Social work: Radical essays* (pp. 3–25). Brisbane: University of Queensland Press.

Westoby, P. (2009). *The sociality of refugee healing: In dialogue with Southern Sudanese refugees resettling in Australia—towards a social model of healing*. Retrieved from www.ondiversity.cgpublisher.com/product/pub.190/prod.2

Westoby, P., & Ingamells, A. (2010). A critically informed perspective of working with resettling refugee groups in Australia. *British Journal of Social Work, 40*(6), 1759–1776.

Woodthorpe, K., & Brennan, M. (2014). Sociology. In M. Brennan (Ed.), *The A-Z of Death and Dying: Social, medical and cultural aspects* (pp. 386–389). Santa Barbara, CA: Greenwood.

20
Navigating Social Institutions and Policies as an Advocate and Ally

Sandra Joy

When I first met Brian Steckel, he was in shackles and handcuffs. Brian had finally agreed to meet with me three months after I started to visit the men on Delaware's death row. Brian was among those who had initially refused to meet with me, yet he was later convinced by a fellow inmate to accept my visit. I was particularly anxious about meeting Brian after reading about his case. The nine inmates I had met before him were not the monsters that death row inmates are typically portrayed to be, yet the gruesome details of Brian's crime led me to expect that this time I had finally found a death row inmate who fit the stereotype of the sociopath. Brian's crime was arguably one of the most gruesome committed by the men on Delaware's death row, at least in the way that it was portrayed by the media. I was familiar with the procedures for visiting death row inmates by that point, which are very secure, so I was not afraid for my safety. I was, however, nervous that I would have trouble maintaining a conversation with this man who, in print, had been painted as truly monstrous.

When the guard led Brian into the visiting room of the maximum security unit, he would not look me in the eye. Handcuffed with his hands in front of him and shackled at his feet, he shuffled into the small, narrow room that was completely separated from my side of the room by concrete and a glass window. He was visibly nervous about meeting with me. I broke the awkward silence between us as I thanked Brian for agreeing to meet with me. I proceeded to inform him of the purpose of my research, as I told him that I wish to tell the stories of the family members of death row inmates. I told him that I intended to trace the grieving process that these families go through from the time of the alleged crime of their loved one, all the way up to the execution and beyond. Brian commended me on my commitment to the death row families, yet suggested that I may not want to include him and his family in my research as he said, "You know that *I am guilty*, right? Did you read about what I did? I'm no choir boy!" He presented as somewhat skeptical of my intentions when I replied, "Your crime and whether or not you are guilty is irrelevant to my research." I told him that his family's story deserves attention, as they are experiencing grief that has largely been ignored by the surrounding community, criminal justice system, and research community. When I left my first visit with Brian, I had a very different impression of him than I expected to find. He had presented as very respectful and humble, so humble, in fact, that he appeared to feel undeserving of sharing the same space with me.

Over the next year and a half, I continued to visit Brian every couple of months, as I rotated my visits with the other men on death row. He seemed to have difficulty believing that I really cared about him and his family and offered me several "outs" in his letters and visits, assuring me that he would not blame me if I would rather not include him in my sample of death row inmates. He continued to accept my visits. However, it was clear to me that something within him wanted to believe that someone else, outside of his family, could see another side to him than that which had been portrayed in the media. Eventually, he became more confident in his interactions with me, greeting me with a smile on his face and his head held high. It had taken longer than any other man on death row, but Brian had finally begun to trust that I genuinely cared about him and his family.

Brian rarely called me on the telephone, so when I received a call from him on October 6, 2005 I became worried. Brian told me during our phone call that he had been taken to the warden's office earlier that fall day in order to receive the official word that he was being issued a death warrant carrying an execution date of November 4, 2005. When I began my research with death row inmates approximately two years earlier, I had not been naïve enough to deny that executions were likely to claim the lives of the inmates who I would come to know through my research. Having been an anti-death penalty activist even before I moved to Delaware in 1995, I had become acutely aware that this state had become known for executing more people *per capita* than any other state in the country. It just so happened that the period over which I had been gathering my research was the longest that Delaware had gone without executions since 1992, when the first death row inmate in nearly 40 years was executed. Brian was to become the 14th inmate to be executed within 13 years. Not only had I entered my research project equipped with knowledge of the reality of frequent executions in Delaware, but over the time that I visited the men on death row, I had also been made aware of several death warrants that had been signed for them. However, each time a death warrant had been signed during the time that I was conducting my research, a *stay* had been granted, allowing the inmate to escape execution, if only temporarily. Despite my experiences witnessing other inmates survive death warrants, somehow I knew when Brian called me to tell me about his death warrant that he was not going to be that lucky. Somehow *I just knew* that I would soon lose one of the men whom I had befriended through my research to a state execution.

The time soon came for Brian to identify the two people he was entitled to have with him in the "death chamber," where he would be executed. Both his mother and his cousin Mary had expressed a desire to be there for him that night. These were the two women who had stood by Brian and provided him with the most support throughout his time on death row. I felt honored to be associated with these dedicated, loving women when he referred to the three of us as his "dream team." Marlene wished to be there for her son during his execution, reasoning, "I was with him when he came into this world and I must be there for him when he leaves." However, Brian was adamantly opposed to having his mother witness his execution, as he knew that the image she would be left with of his death would be more than she could bear. Marlene was disappointed that he wouldn't allow her to be there for him, but she agreed to honor his wishes. She worried that he would be alone during his execution, since Mary was too afraid to be there without someone else to lean on. When Brian and Marlene asked me to be a witness to Brian's execution, I realized that by agreeing to do so, I would be helping not only Brian, but also Marlene and Mary. Brian would be able to have the support of a friend during such a scary time for him, Mary would have someone to lean on, and Marlene could rest knowing that her son would have two friendly faces to look upon during his final moments. For all of these reasons, I agreed to witness Brian Steckel's execution.

Bridging Identities: Role Compatibility of Multiple Roles

When I began my research with death row inmates and their families, I felt whole for the first time in many years. I had finally found a way to bridge three very integral parts of my identity: Clinician, activist, and academic. Over the many years leading up to the moment that I decided to conduct research with death row inmates and their families, I had dealt with the subject of the death penalty on separate occasions as a clinician, as an activist, and as an academic. While I had focused most of my prior research on various aspects of the death penalty, this time I had finally chosen to research an aspect of the death penalty that allowed me to harmoniously merge all three of these parts of my identity at once. As a therapist, I was able to use my therapeutic skills to generate research that would allow my peers in the professional mental health community to understand the grieving process of death row families. This would enable them to provide more effective treatment for these families. As an activist, I was able to use my position and connections within the anti-death penalty movement to gain the trust of death row inmates and their families. This would allow me to generate research that would allow their voices to be incorporated within the movement's message. The voices of murdered victims' family members have already been heard, due to the gains of the victims' rights movement, yet with my study I would give voice to the *forgotten victims*, those who go through the excruciating experience of having a loved one on death row.

As I progressed throughout this research project, I found that the roles of therapist, activist, and academic complemented one another. It was not until Brian's execution approached that I realized these parts of my identity were not as compatible as I had originally thought. The roles of therapist and activist began to conflict with that of academia. The roles of therapist and activist further conflicted with one another as well. These forms of role conflict that I began to feel after Brian received his death warrant significantly complicated my ability to carry out the functions of the multiple roles that I was previously able to fulfill simultaneously. Institutional barriers erected by the criminal justice system and the university presented me with additional challenges as I aimed to advocate for Brian and his family throughout this critical period.

Navigating the Activist and Academic Roles

To the extent that I had ever felt conflict between my roles of activist and academic in the past, it was primarily the factor of time that had caused such conflict. The demands of each role are typically such that it is very difficult for me to find enough time to fulfill the level of my expectations for each role. This usual conflict between the competing roles of activist and academic initially was not a problem when I began my research with death row inmates and their families. My research goal of examining the grieving process of death row families is compatible with my aim as an anti-death penalty activist to humanize death row inmates. Conflict between the two roles was initially avoided, therefore, since the same activity was able to satisfy typical expectations for both the activist and the academic. However, once Brian's death warrant was signed, all of that changed. I was no longer able to satisfy the expectations of both activist and academic simultaneously. I found myself having to choose between what I would ordinarily do as an activist and what I needed to do as a researcher. As an activist, I had been involved in planning and carrying out many activities organized by the local anti-death penalty organization. Executions are an all too frequent reality in Delaware; therefore, this local anti-death penalty organization was particularly busy anytime there was an active death warrant. Ordinarily, when a death row inmate is in immediate danger of execution, I was in the practice of picking up a bullhorn and a protest sign, and hitting the streets. However, this time, I had elected to be there for Brian's family instead. This was the first time I had removed myself from the frontlines of protest demonstrations during such an urgent time. I opted instead to host Brian's Pennsylvania-based family in my Delaware home to more easily allow for daily visits with Brian, as I assisted them through this stage of their grieving process. Within my academic role, I was also gathering data throughout this period. This data would contribute tremendously to my research focused on the grieving process confronting death row families.

Several obstacles that arise have been noted when efforts are made to integrate the roles of activist and academic. One such obstacle has been deemed the "paralysis of analysis," which refers to the frustration that activists feel with academics who feel the need to gather more research before taking action (Divinski, 1994, pp. 3–24). In their quest to pursue social change, activists feel the need to act, yet academics who are "engaged in the search for 'Truth' do not believe that it is ethical to act before finding 'The Solution'" (Divinski, 1994, p. 19). For those who identify as both activists and academics, these conflicting orientations can create tension within them as they attempt to reconcile the need to act and the need to find out more. I can certainly identify with this internal struggle, as I fought off my activist urges to take action in order to find out more about how Brian's impending homicide was impacting upon his family.

Another difference found in the orientations between academics and activists has to do with the tendency of the academic to focus more on ideas than people. Activists, on the other hand, are oriented more often toward people. Striving to mobilize people toward action, activists argue that ideas only carry power when people are mobilized to back them (Biklen, 1983; Staples, 1984). Particularly during a time of crisis, activists must focus on mobilizing people while helping to channel their anger about the predicament at hand. Academics often maintain a very different orientation at such a critical time, for they "may feel a responsibility for exercising 'appropriate restraint' as they engage in reasoned argument to persuade others" (Divinski, 1994, p. 20). When critical times arise for death row inmates, activist academics may find it easier to exercise restraint when they discuss the cases of some inmates rather than those of others. When the cases of particular inmates contain strong claims of innocence or at least questionable issues with the initial trial proceedings, the facts around these cases are able to speak for themselves. When people are presented with such compelling cases, they are easily persuaded to oppose the death penalty, if only for these particular inmates. On the other hand, when the men facing execution are obviously guilty and/or the circumstances surrounding the murder of their victims are particularly gruesome, activist academics have a much more difficult time presenting reasoned arguments that will persuade others to oppose the death penalty for these men. This was the case with Brian Steckel. From the time that he was arrested for murder, he consistently admitted his guilt and the media took every opportunity throughout his 11 years on death row to demonize him. As a result, it was especially challenging for me to exercise "appropriate restraint" in my efforts to mobilize people to support a man who had been painted as truly monstrous.

Tough cases like Brian's require more than reasoned argument to persuade people to mobilize in opposition to his execution. Impassioned appeals to moral sensibilities, including pleas for mercy and/or forgiveness, are typically called for with such tough cases. As Brian's execution date approached, I wished to spend time persuading people to take action to stop the execution. Having already committed myself to attending to the needs of Brian and his family, however, very little time or emotional energy remained for me to hit the streets as an activist.

When I discuss the death penalty within the classroom, I make certain to emphasize the complexities that exist with this issue. Both sides of the debate around the death penalty are discussed, bringing out all of the subtleties that make this issue such a hotly contested one in American society. However, as an activist, I am most effective in winning support for my cause if I am able to simplify the issues involved with the death penalty for the public. The goal is not to clarify all sides of the debate, rather to argue unapologetically *against* the death penalty. Arguments are often reduced to slogans on protest signs and chants at demonstrations. Activists are expected to present their arguments in a biased manner, particularly during periods of crisis when it is crucial to win support for their cause. When the date of a scheduled execution approaches, I am in my activist role as I present all arguments from my collection of arguments against the death penalty. When acting within my academic role, on the other hand, my presentation of this issue, like *any* subject of my instruction, is expected to occur in a manner that is as objective and non-biased as possible.

Sandra Joy

Navigating the Roles of Clinician and Academic

Once Brian's execution became imminent, another tension arose between two previously compatible roles that I had assumed during my research with death row families. Initially, my roles as both clinician and academic were compatible as I worked with the men on death row and their families. The clinical skills that I had acquired during my years as a graduate student of social work and the nearly dozen years of experience I had working as a licensed clinical social worker had served me well as I began my research with those condemned to death row. I established rapport with these men very quickly, in large part due to the many years I had spent as a mental health therapist and substance abuse counselor with people from various backgrounds, including numerous adult ex-offenders and incarcerated juveniles.

Once Brian's death warrant was signed, I suddenly felt torn between what I felt led to do as a therapist versus that which I had been encouraged to do as an academic. The clinician in me felt the need to attend to the emotional needs of Brian and his family as they entered a new stage of the grieving process. The trauma that comes from the knowledge that a family member is about to be killed by the state carries unspeakable grief. Over the last few weeks leading to Brian's execution, as I opened my home to his family and transported them to and from the prison for their final visits with Brian, I witnessed the agony they felt as they dealt with the realization that their loved one was losing his legal battle to the state. I slipped quite easily into my clinician role as I served as a sounding board for them and attempted to comfort them. The feedback that I received from Brian at that time and that which I have received from his family over the years that have passed since the execution confirms that my support during that time was a great source of comfort to them. The more successful I was as I acted within this clinician role, however, the greater the risk of interference with my role as an academic.

When I went through this experience as a researcher, I was gathering my data primarily through the method of participant observation. As the date of Brian's execution approached, I became less of an observer and more of a participant within my role as a researcher. The problem posed by my participation was its effect on the data that I gathered. While my therapeutic skills were helpful to Brian and his family, my actions within the clinician role interfered with my ability to produce unbiased results from my study. As a therapist, I am expected to offer comfort and solace to grieving family members, yet as an academic engaged in research; I am expected to gather my observations without biasing "the data." Indeed, an ethical dilemma arises by "the fact that as we encourage people to tell their stories, we become characters in those stories, and thus change those stories" (Shaw, 2008, pp. 400–414).

Brian told me several times in his final days that he would not have been able to face his execution with the level of peace that he maintained if I had not helped him to have the regular contact he needed with his family in order to say his goodbyes to each of them. His family members shared similar sentiments with me. Their remarks made it clear to me that if I had simply observed Brian and his family throughout this stage of their grieving process, and not become a participant in the process, my study would have yielded very different outcomes. Without the opportunity to stay closer to the Delaware prison, the family members would have had much less time with Brian in his final days, thus less time to work through their anguish with him. Without a clinician on hand to help them process their feelings each evening after their visits with Brian, they would have had much more difficulty expressing their emotions when appropriate (i.e., with each other and with Brian) and containing their emotions when necessary (i.e., resisting the urge to express their anger toward the guards and/or warden of the prison).

Another conflict that I experienced between the roles of clinician and academic during the weeks and moments leading up to Brian's execution involved the orientation of each role toward Brian and his family. Acting within the clinician role in my interactions with Brian and his family, I was there *for them*, to help them through their grief as much as possible. Yet as an academic, I am oriented more toward seeing how these "research subjects" can *help me*, as they provide me with data and enable me to complete my research project. My role as an activist further exacerbated this conflict in orientation, as a similar conflict is found to exist within activist academics. Cancian (1993) submits that "activist research," which challenges the status quo and promotes social change, is "for" relatively powerless groups, yet "academic research" that is aimed solely at increasing knowledge is "for" colleagues (Cancian, 1993, pp. 92–106). The conflict lies with the likelihood that the sociologist who directs her energy to "activist research" will encounter challenges as she strives to build a successful academic career. Cancian argues, "In most sociology departments, academic standards devalue essential elements of activist research: advocacy of particular social goals, social change projects, and active involvement with community groups" (Cancian, 1993, pp. 92–106). I have been fortunate enough to have colleagues in my sociology department who value my activist research with death row inmates and their families. I have not always felt that same level of support, however, throughout the university, particularly at the administrative levels. As Brian's execution became imminent, the urgency of the crisis at hand led me to put any concerns that I had about my academic success aside as I responded to the needs of Brian and his family.

The clinician in me chose to exist "in the moment" with Brian and his family as they went through the anticipatory grief of the looming execution. The time that I spent with them as they went through this excruciating process often ran counter to the expectation that, as an academic, I would focus exclusively on my research agenda and adhere to a timeline for the collection and reporting of my data. Perhaps the chief irony of the situation is that at the same time that my therapeutic skills enabled me to assist Brian and his family during such a grave time, Brian's impending execution and my exposure to his family had presented me with an "opportunity" to enrich my study of death row families. As a clinician, I wished to curtail the pain of this family, yet as an academic engaged in research, I had a vested interest in observing the many layers of their grief. My realization that Brian's scheduled execution would add depth to my study of death row families created a degree of conflict within me. The clinician within me took precedence over my academic persona during this critical time, as I was more concerned with trying to assist Brian and his family than with advancing my research agenda.

Navigating the Clinician and Activist Roles

The decision that I made during the weeks leading up to Brian's execution to prioritize my clinician role over the role of academic was a choice that I made with little hesitation or guilt. On the other hand, a great deal of inner turmoil arose when it became most crucial for me to assume the clinician role over that of the activist. I have already noted above that a conflict arose between the activist in me wishing to be there on the frontlines of a protest to try and stop the execution and the academic in me that had a research agenda to fulfill. My experience as a therapist enabled me to negotiate this conflict and helped me to accept that it was best that I remove myself from the frontlines of protest with this particular execution. I reasoned that doing so would not only allow me to gather data for my study, but also permit me to offer therapeutic support to Brian and his family.

Over the two years of my data collection that preceded the day that Brian was served a death warrant, the two roles of clinician and activist had been fairly compatible with one another. Whenever the time that I committed to my research with death row inmates interfered with my ability to devote energy toward my activism, I was comforted by the realization that my research not only feeds the demand of academia that I publish scholarly works, but it also provides the movement against the death penalty with an important tool. As my fellow activists frame their position against the death penalty, they must work hard to combat the common view that the men on death row are "monsters" who must be exterminated. My study offers a valuable resource that activists can use to counter the dehumanization process that occurs from the time that death row inmates are arrested, incarcerated, and eventually marched to their death. My research humanizes them through multifaceted descriptions of their lives in the years prior to and since their incarceration, as well as the tremendous grief their death sentence brings to their families. Knowledge of the utility of my research for those in the trenches of the movement consoled me whenever I felt as though I was slighting the time that I would typically exert within my role as activist.

During the time that passed from the moment when Brian's death warrant was signed through to his execution a month later, it became increasingly more difficult for me to deny the urge I felt to hit the streets in protest of the pending execution. I was appalled that the state of Delaware was planning to carry out an execution and I needed an outlet to vent my outrage in an effort to build public opposition, yet I was devoted to my clinician role as I attended as best I could to the emotional needs of Brian and his family. I did not wish to get Brian or anyone in the family riled up as they struggled to come to terms with the brutal reality of the situation. As a result, I suppressed my outrage and focused instead on helping them deal with the intensity of their grief.

The most challenging time for me to reconcile this conflict that I was feeling between the activist and clinician roles came on the night that Brian was executed. Immediately before Brian's cousin Mary and I filed into the death chamber to witness the execution, along with the over thirty other witnesses, we were instructed to remain silent. How on earth would I be able to stand silently by and watch someone very methodically being killed without speaking up in protest? The activist in me would never sit silently by and watch such an atrocity. The period of time that I was in the death chamber witnessing the execution of Brian Steckel required more restraint from me than I have ever had to exercise in my life. I wanted to cry out *Stop! Murder!!*—just anything to disrupt the carefully premeditated homicide that was being carried out right before my eyes. I knew that the prison guards would escort me out of the building if I became disruptive, but more importantly, I had made a commitment to be there for Brian and for Mary too. The therapist in me would have to win this particular conflict against my activist urges in order to uphold my agreement with Brian and his family to be an emotional support to them during this horrendous event.

Suppressing my activist urges, I stood by and watched my friend being executed by the state of Delaware. After the execution I was in the process of gathering the family when someone who worked for the prison came over to us and offered Mary and me the opportunity to speak to the press in order to give a reaction to what we had just witnessed. I hesitated initially, as I was feeling an urgent need to leave the prison grounds, yet Mary expressed a strong desire to speak to the press. I suddenly realized that this was an opportunity for me to release the activist within me that I had grown tired of holding back. In fact, my activist consciousness reminded me that after witnessing what I considered to be a disgrace, a grave injustice, I was obligated to speak about what I had just seen firsthand. To remain silent would make me complicit in the homicide that had occurred within the death chamber. The time had come for the activist in me to boldly emerge and take center stage. I justified that doing so need not contradict my therapeutic relationship with Brian's family; rather, it could empower them as they began their healing process to also speak out unashamedly against what the state of Delaware had done to their loved one.

Although my outrage about Brian's execution remained after I stepped away from the press conference, I felt somewhat vindicated, having taken advantage of the opportunity to distinguish myself from those who seemed to have reveled in what had occurred within the death chamber that night. The activist in me had reemerged, and as I spoke with Brian's family back at the hotel afterwards, it was apparent that my words had therapeutic value for them as well. I stayed up talking with the family for most of the night, offering them therapeutic support, sprinkled with activist sentiment. Both the therapist and the activist in me were once again having their voices heard. As both a socio-political activist and a narrative therapist, I had effectively linked their personal story to the oppression that results from dominant discourses around the issue of the death penalty. Monk and Gehart (2003) have observed that through the process of "externalizing," clients are allowed to locate problem stories within a community's dominant discourses rather than within themselves. As Brian's family began to work through the grief they felt upon their loss, they used words similar to those that they had heard me speak to the press moments earlier. They moved from expressions of anger and sadness about their own personal loss to concerns about this happening to other families, as they articulated a renewed, intensified outrage about the death penalty. I had essentially offered Brian's family socio-political intervention as a narrative therapist. I externalized their story and placed it within the dominant discourse of the community. Monk and Gehart (2003) describe the way that this process can benefit clients of narrative therapy. Because clients are viewed as agents in their life narratives from the outset, the therapeutic process is focused on eliciting lived experiences that can be pulled together to dispel what has now been constructed as an identifiable target. When people gain a full appreciation of the toll that damaging cultural prescriptions can foster, there is often a heightened degree of motivation among clients to address their pain.

Brian's family would need ongoing extensive therapy to assist them through the grieving process that was certain to continue long after the execution of their loved one, but it became apparent on the horrific night that Brian was executed that as the family moved through this process, their "identifiable target" was the institution of the death penalty. They were responsive to the words of comfort that I offered them as I alternated between activist and therapeutic approaches to the pain that they expressed.

Navigating Consequences of Advocacy

The response that I received from the prison officials following Brian's execution was not a favorable one. The warden immediately issued a *lifelong ban* against me ever returning to the prison, claiming in a letter addressed to me that I had "voiced statements that threaten the safe and secure operation of the institution." The only words I had uttered to the press which may be viewed as inflammatory were those that I opened with before going on to share my concerns for Brian's grieving family: "I just witnessed a premeditated homicide carried out by the state of Delaware." The response of the warden to my comments about the execution can be explained by interactionist theories of deviance that focus on the process by which sociologists who challenge the status quo are labeled by those in power as deviant (Becker, 1973). In *Outsiders: Studies in the Sociology of Deviance*, Howard Becker (1973) argues that when sociologists take an interactionist approach with their attempt to expose the mechanisms of power, they

> question the monopoly on the truth and the "whole story" claimed by those in positions of power and authority. They suggest that we need to discover the truth about allegedly deviant phenomena for ourselves, instead of relying on the officially certified accounts which ought to be enough for any good citizen. They adopt a relativistic stance toward the accusations and definitions of deviance made by respectable people and constituted authority, treating them as the raw material of social science analysis rather than as statements of unquestioned moral truths.
> (Becker, 1973, p. 207)

Becker continues with an account of the response of those in power to sociologists who offer bold analyses of official views: "The authorities whose institutions and jurisdictions become the object of interactionist analyses attack those analyses for their 'biases,' their failure to accept traditional wisdom and values, their destructive effect on public order" (Becker, 1973, p. 208). This response that Becker finds among officials who are challenged is similar to the response that I received after I witnessed Brian's execution and spoke at the press conference that followed. My subsequent ban from the prison came at the height of the role conflict that I had been experiencing from the time that Brian's death warrant was signed a month earlier.

The role conflict that I experienced from the execution that I witnessed and the cost of *suffocated grief* (Bordere, 2014) of speaking out against it only served to exacerbate the grief that I had already expected to experience if any of the death row inmates in my study were to be executed. I had somehow managed to navigate the roles of therapist, activist, and academic with relative success, at least concerning my ability to support Brian and his family through such a traumatic event, as well as my ability to gather data that would simultaneously help the anti-death penalty movement and satisfy the research demands of academia. In spite of these successes, I did not escape the traumatic event of Brian's execution unscathed. I went through my own grieving process, which was complicated by the effects of vicarious trauma and disenfranchised grief. As a witness to a state execution, I was traumatized by viewing the killing of the man I had befriended, particularly because the execution was considered botched by most of the witnesses present.

The grief that I felt as a result of witnessing an execution is best referred to as *disenfranchised* grief because it was outside of the grieving rules for a researcher. Doka (1989) has argued that someone experiences disenfranchised grief when their loss is not recognized, the relationship between the griever and the deceased is not recognized, and/or the griever is not recognized. In all three ways that Doka (1989) submits, and through all three of my identities discussed within this chapter, my grief was disenfranchised. The relationship that I had with Brian and his family was not recognized, in that they would be viewed as "research subjects" by academics, as "clients" by therapists, as "victims of the system" by activists, and as a "monster" (Brian) and "guilty by association" and/or "better off without him" (family) by many people in society. Most people are simply not likely to recognize my relationship with Brian and his family as "friends," for whom I might grieve.

Brian's execution in itself was also not recognized as a loss by most. Academics are likely to view Brian's execution as an opportunity for me to gather data. Therapists are likely to view Brian's execution as a loss to his family, but not necessarily as a loss to anyone else. Activists are likely to view Brian's execution as an injustice that offends all of us in society, yet they are less likely to view it as a personal loss to anyone outside of his family. Many people in society view Brian's execution as good for the functioning of society, not at all a loss for anyone.

Not only did I feel disenfranchised because the loss of Brian and my relationship with him both were not recognized, but I was further disenfranchised in that I was not recognized as a griever. As a researcher, I am not supposed to become personally involved with my research subjects. As a therapist, I am expected to be a support to my clients, yet maintain boundaries that prevent me from becoming personally involved with them. As an activist, I am supposed to educate the public about issues that affect people, but not become so intimately involved with the people affected by these issues that it interferes with my activism in any way.

Traditionally, researchers have been expected to maintain a level of detachment from the subjects of their studies, avoiding emotional interchanges between researcher and subject. Increasingly more academics are indicating an appreciation for the value of the "emotional work" that researchers put into their qualitative studies of marginalized groups (Rowling, 1999). It has been found that researchers who maintain a level of detachment during their interviews are unlikely to be viewed in a positive manner by participants, yielding less meaningful data as a result (Rowling, 1999). Instead a new role is proposed, the role of "being alongside" or "with" the participant as a way to manage the emotionality that surfaces throughout the research process, particularly when participants are dealing with loss and grief. In order to elicit the most meaningful data, "what is required is compassionate analysis which intertwines the researcher's and participant's emotions, as long as the emotions do not interfere with 'real listening'" (Rowling, 1999, p. 177).

While I have not been permitted to enter the prison since the night that I witnessed Brian's execution, I have continued to engage in my work with death row inmates and their families as both an activist and a researcher. I am no longer able to transport the families to the prison, yet I have maintained frequent contact with many of the family members that I interviewed for my research. My research was recently published as a book that both describes the grief process of death row families and offers clinical interventions that can be utilized by mental health professionals who work with the families at various stages of this process (Joy, 2014). Occasionally, the clinician reemerges in my work when I get a phone call from a distraught family member regarding a failed court appeal and/or the looming threat of an execution. When family members express a desire to externalize their pain, situating their stories within a larger context of oppression, they often become empowered to fight against the political machine that seeks to kill their loved one. Presented with these newly empowered family members, I help to connect them to the anti-death penalty movement.

It is a delicate task to balance the demands of the roles of clinician, activist, and academic. All three roles are essential components of my identity and I found that they each served valuable roles in my qualitative research with death row inmates and their families. The conflicts that I have focused on in this chapter are typical of those that tend to emerge between various roles when applied academics attempt to integrate their activism and/or their clinical work with their scholarship. Despite the disenfranchised grief and vicarious trauma that I experienced as a result of witnessing an execution, the advantages that my experience as both an activist and a therapist have brought to my research have enriched my data tremendously. Activist academics, as well as those who possess clinical skills, must continue the discussion of various ways to address the conflicts that arise among their roles in order to maximize the potential advantages that they each bring as we strive to create progressive social change.

Key Terms

Advocacy—is typically a political process by an individual or group with the goal to influence decisions within political, economic, and social systems and institutions.
Externalizing—a process by which clients may locate problem stories within a community's dominant discourses rather than within themselves.
Paralysis of analysis—the frustration that activists experience towards academics who feel the need to gather more research before taking action.

Questions for Reflection

1. What are your personal beliefs regarding the death penalty? How do these beliefs affect your response to the material presented here?
2. What preconceptions do you have about the people—and about the families of the people—who are on death row?
3. Clinician, activist, academic. Which of these roles do you most identify with? Which of these roles do you anticipate participating in during your lifetime? Where (i.e., what areas/issues) do you feel most passionate about applying your skills/interests?
4. The chapter explores many ways in which the roles of clinician, activist, and academic may interact to augment or conflict with each other. As you arrive at the end of the chapter what are your thoughts on the intermingling of these roles?

References

Becker, H. (1973). *Outsiders: Studies in the sociology of deviance*. New York, NY: Free Press.
Biklen, D. P. (1983). *Community organizing: Theory and practice*. Englewood Cliffs, NJ: Prentice Hall.
Bordere, T. C. (2014). Adolescents and homicide. In K. Doka & A. Tucci (Eds.), *Helping adolescents cope with loss* (pp. 161-181). Washington, DC: Hospice Foundation of America.

Burnett, C. (2003). "Passion through the profession: Being both activist and academic." *Social Justice, 30*(4), 135–150.

Cancian, F. M. (1993). Conflicts between activist research and academic success: Participatory research and alternative strategies. *The American Sociologist, 24*(1), 92–106.

Divinski, R. (1994). Social change as applied social science: Obstacles to integrating the roles of activist and academic. *Peace and Change, 19*(1), 3–24.

Doka, K. J.(1989). *Disenfranchised grief: Recognizing hidden sorrows*. Lexington, MA: Lexington Books.

Joy, S. (2014). *Grief, loss and treatment for death row families: Forgotten no more*. Lanham, MD: Lexington Books.

Monk, G., & Gehart, D. (2003). Sociopolitical activist or conversational partner? Distinguishing the position of the therapist in narrative and collaborative therapies. *Family Process, 42*(1), 19–30.

Rowling, L. (1999). Being in, being out, being with: Affect and the role of the qualitative researcher in loss and grief research. *Mortality, 4*(2), 167–181.

Schlosser, J. A. (2008). Issues in interviewing inmates: Navigating the methodological landmines of prison research. *Qualitative Inquiry, 14*(8), 1500–1525.

Shaw, I. (2008). Ethics and the practice of qualitative research. *Qualitative Social Work, 7*(4), 400–414.

Staples, L. (1984). *Roots to power: A manual for grassroots organizing*. New York, NY: Praeger.

21
Care for the Caregiver
A Multilayered Exploration

Darcy L. Harris

Introduction

I am frequently asked to provide presentations and workshops on the topic of "care for the caregiver" to professional groups that consist mostly of hospice/palliative health care and service sector workers. During one session in which I was the speaker, one participant raised her hand and said,

> I can soak in a bubble bath until I am a prune and I can do all the relaxation exercises in the world to reduce my stress, but the bottom line is that I can't change the fact that I am literally running off my feet from the time I start my shift until I finally finish seeing my last patient, and I am paid less than someone who works as a waiter in a diner. No bubble bath, wine, massage, or 'me' time is going to make that better.

She was absolutely right. Typical self-care strategies often fail to take into account the operational and structural policies that have created the highly stress-laden environments in which these caregivers work. In fact, Thompson (2011) accurately describes the very problematic focus upon individualistic factors in workplace stress as being counterproductive,

> leading people who experience stress feeling guilty and blaming themselves for a situation in which at least part of it (and possibly all of it) will be due to broader social and organization factors, rather than individual ones. This can lead to stigma (stress comes to be seen as a sign of a weak or inadequate individual), shame, and a reluctance to address or even acknowledge the issues. This, in turn, can make the situation worse, unnecessarily increasing levels of stress.
> (p. 27)

Finding a balance between personal/individual factors and the organizational/structural forces affecting workers in caring contexts can be tricky. On the one hand, there may actually be personal, internal characteristics that influence how a caregiver perceives the workplace and how s/he fits into that environment. On the other hand, there may be significant external, workplace-induced factors that have a profound impact upon the individual caregivers who work in health care contexts. It is important to consider the interactional nature of these variables to create a more complete picture of the caregiver embedded within the "culture" of the workplace and socio-political ideation that surrounds the delivery of care.

Rezenbrink (2011) described the phenomenon of "reciprocity" between the individual care provider and the workplace as a key element to the caregiver's ability to work effectively with those in her/his care. An analysis of stress in the workplace must include not just the unique characteristics of the health care provider, but also the culture and context of the work environment in which that caregiver works, and the social messages and political forces that determine many of the policies that exist within that workplace. Vachon (1995) described the "person-environment fit" premise of stress in palliative care workers. The goodness of fit between the individual characteristics and values of the care providers (including their perceptions of what good patient care entails) needs to be congruent with the organizational goals and resources that are present within the work environment.

In this chapter, we will explore specific variables that are related to working in the environments that serve those who are terminally ill and bereaved. We will then discuss the implications for both individual caregivers and the society in which they serve. Finally, we will examine the external and overarching social/political factors that may significantly affect the experience of those who work with individuals who are dying and/or bereaved.

Individual Factors

There is a plethora of literature and research on the topic of caregiver stress. Maslach is probably the best known researcher to describe the syndrome of worker exhaustion. He and his colleagues developed the Maslach Burnout Inventory as a measure to document burnout in individual workers (Maslach & Jackson, 1982). Figley introduced the concept of compassion fatigue, describing a constellation of symptoms that resulted from the traumatic overlay in caregivers who acutely identify with the pain, suffering, and horrific circumstances of their patients (Figley, 1995). Other writings and research have included the exploration of secondary traumatization, vicarious trauma, and caregiver syndrome (Devilly, Wright, & Varker, 2009; Newell & MacNeil, 2010). In this section, we will explore some of the unique characteristics of individuals who regularly work with people who are facing losses of many different types, and how these characteristics have an impact upon the perception and experience of stress for these workers.

Studies of personality characteristics of caregivers who work in hospice/palliative care settings have shown several commonalities within this group. For instance, most of the nurses who work in hospices tend to be motivated to "make a difference" in the care that they offer, and many of those who work and volunteer in this area feel their choice is akin to a religious calling or sense of mission that draws them to this particular type of work (Ablett & Jones, 2007; Claxton-Oldfield & Claxton-Oldfield, 2005; Claxton-Oldfield, Jeffries, Fawcett, & Claxton-Oldfield, 2004; Dougherty et al., 2009). Vachon (1995) states that many hospice caregivers

> came into the field with a sense of purpose and commitment borne out of personal experience with death, a sense of disenchantment with the dehumanization of dying persons within the hospital setting, and a desire to avoid the use of technology in prolonging the dying process by focusing on quality of life, as opposed to quantity of life.
>
> (p. 96)

Although less described in the literature, the characteristics of professional caregivers who provide therapeutic support to bereaved and traumatized individuals are similar to those who care for dying patients and their families. The concept of the "wounded healer" is often cited as one reason why clinicians who work with bereaved individuals are drawn to this particular specialty area of practice (Jordan, Kosminsky, & Neimeyer, 2014; Papadatou, 2009). These clinicians will often speak of having experienced significant losses in their lives, which then informs and motivates them to provide therapeutic support to others with similar experiences (Papadatou, 2009; Rappaport, 2009).

In general, professionals who choose to work in this area tend to be highly empathetic and readily identified with their profession. They are often passionate about their work, have consciously chosen to work in this field, and they tend to be uncompromisingly committed to providing high quality care to patients and families who are vulnerable and are often experiencing terminal illness and death as a crisis in their family system (Claxton-Oldfield & Banzen, 2010; Kearney, Weininger, Vachon, Harrison, & Mount, 2009). Several studies of hospice workers have reinforced the view that most of the professionals in this area view their work as much more than "just a job" (Ablett & Jones, 2007; Kearney et al., 2009; Whitebird, Asche, Thompson, Rossom, & Heinrich, 2013). It is interesting to note that in studies of hospice and palliative care workers, the main sources of stress cited were not related to chronic exposure to death and dying. Rather, hindrances and environmental distractions that prevented the caregivers from being able to provide the level of care and attention to patients and family members that they felt was indicated were the most commonly cited sources of stress and frustration (Dougherty et al., 2009; Kearney et al., 2009; Vachon, 1995).

It can be said that the greatest strengths of these caregivers may also be their Achilles' heel. Their deep commitment to their work and their highly compassionate, empathic tendencies might make them more sensitive to issues related to short staffing (and the resulting lessened time to spend with their patients and families), and the imposition of external constraints upon their perceptions of good care (which may be in conflict with their sense of reward for their work), could interfere with their sense of work as a calling in line with their personal views of meaning and purpose. These same tendencies are protective to many of these workers, providing a philosophical and existential perspective from which they are able to care for dying and bereaved individuals without being overwhelmed by a sense of hopelessness and powerlessness. Thus, these core characteristics, which may make these professional caregivers vulnerable to environmental and structural pressures, are ironically the very same factors that allow them to thrive in the daily care of a population that is highly vulnerable and often medically and socially disenfranchised.

Social Influences and Context

Although there is certainly more awareness and openness in the general population about issues related to death now than even a decade ago, most people are still uncomfortable talking openly about their wishes at the end of life and most families do not discuss funeral arrangements until the need for such arrangements is imminent (Carstairs, 2010; Corr & Corr, 2013). While the popular media might explore high-conflict issues such as the controversy surrounding euthanasia and physician-assisted suicide, openly talking about my death with friends and family members is uncommon unless there is a terminal illness or impending death. In general, current Western social thinking continues to deny death by the emphasis on conquering disease with technology, the focus on youth and productivity, and the ability to distance oneself from death by institutional care. This death denial, whether subtle or overt, means that open discussions about mortality are typically awkward, uncomfortable, and strained. By extension, people who work with terminally ill or bereaved individuals are often considered to be either "saints" for doing this type of work, or distrusted for choosing work that involves death, an example of which might be with the frequent jokes and dark humor that surrounds funeral directors and their fees. Papadatou (2009) describes social discrimination towards "death" professionals who work in this field as manifest through 1) dismissal of the services that they provide, as well as lack of recognition of their significance, 2) attempts by others to avoid or shut down discussions pertaining to this work because of the stigma surrounding death and bereavement, 3) overt or subtle forms of aggression or negativity directed at caregivers whose work reminds others of their mortality, and 4) unrealistic, idealized views of individuals who work in this area, leading to professional isolation and alienation.

Most medical school curricula do not include in-depth discussions about how to talk with patients and families about end of life care and choices. Palliative care is often viewed as "end of the line" care, when there is nothing more that can be done for a patient with a terminal illness. In addition, the professional socialization process, especially for health care workers, is shaped by three very important social influences:

1. the focus on treatment of disease, reductionism, and the emphasis on super-specialization, which tends to produce feelings of powerlessness and helplessness when cure is not possible;
2. young health care professionals are often traumatized in their training and early practice through unrealistic demands and demeaning attitudes about caring and through power plays and bullying at the hands of senior staff members, resulting in an inability to handle normal human suffering that occurs in the context of terminal illness;
3. a clinical environment that is often cold and uncaring, with the imposition of corporate values and financial austerity measures that result in lack of time and attention to shared meaning, identity, and purpose within the culture of the health care setting.

(Youngsen, 2011)

In a fact sheet that describes nursing care at the end of life, the End of Life Nursing Education Consortium (ELNEC), a division of the American Association of the Colleges of Nursing (AACN), states:

People in our country deny death, believing that medical science can cure any patient. Death often is seen as a failure of the health care system rather than a natural aspect of life. This belief affects all health professionals, including nurses. Despite their undisputed technical and interpersonal skills, professional nurses may not be completely comfortable with the specialized knowledge and skills needed to provide quality palliative care to patients.

(End of Life Nursing Education Consortium (ENLEC), 2014)

Even with the growth of hospices and palliative care specialty units in the last three decades, there is still an association of death with failure and the implied sense that "there is nothing more that can be done" when a patient's prognosis is terminal. Palliative medicine was only granted the status as an official specialization by the American Board of Medical Specialties in the United States in 2013, and in the same year by the Royal College of Physicians and Surgeons in Canada (Giddings, 2014; Quill & Abernethy, 2013). Specialty status increases the chances that medical students will choose to enter the field as a formalized program of study. Specialty status also increases the visibility and acceptance of palliative care, hopefully ushering in better access to and provision of palliative care to those who would benefit from its implementation. This recognition has taken decades of argument, advocacy, and gathering of evidence for the important role of palliative care within these two medical systems. Indeed, this difficulty is not confined to North America. Dr. Ghauri Aggarwal, head of Palliative Care at Concord Hospital in Sydney, Australia states, "Palliative care is not seen as a 'sexy' specialty as yet. Often junior doctors are still very nervous about engaging in end-of-life discussion, communication and symptom control" (Murray, 2014). The fact that this recognition has taken so long and has encountered so much opposition along the way attests to the lack of understanding and appreciation for the role of end of life care within the purview of modern medicine.

In combination with the social stigma that still surrounds death and care of terminally ill patients is the social disenfranchisement of emotions and the strong emphasis on stoicism and productivity that is extended to the experience of many bereaved individuals and the clinicians who provide support to them (Harris, 2010). In general, emotions are seen as demonstrating weakness, lack of control, and are an embarrassment to those who openly express them. Likewise, those who provide counseling support to bereaved individuals are often seen as encouraging dependence and weakness, and "preying" upon those who are weak by providing these services for a fee (Konigsberg, 2011). While the current research indicates that most bereaved individuals do not require professional treatment in order to find meaning in their lives after a significant loss, there is resounding evidence to support professional therapeutic intervention for those bereaved individuals who experience varying forms of complicated grief (Neimeyer, 2012; Shear, Frank, Houck, & Reynolds, 2005).

Although some hospices and outpatient clinics receive subsidy to provide bereavement support to clients after a death has occurred in the family, most counseling and therapy services are typically provided to bereaved clients through a fee for service, private pay system. The fact that this type of therapeutic support is often not covered by insurance companies produces hardship for clients who could benefit from it, and care providers who may have specialty training in working with complicated grief are often not on the "approved" reimbursement list by insurance companies or by workplace employment assistance plans (EAPs), leaving a large gap in the ability of the people who need this care to be able to access it. The "bigger picture" view here is that therapeutic support is devalued because of the association with emotional weakness, and professionals who possess specialty training in working with complicated grief and trauma are often not recognized for their specialty training because of the stigma attached not only to the field, but also to the sense of failure and helplessness identified with it due to the emphasis in medical care on cure instead of care. This devaluing occurs not just socially, but also financially.

Political and social systems within a society are interrelated. Politicians are elected by the members of their jurisdictions; both the politicians and their constituents are influenced by and internalize the dominant discourse about productivity, stoicism, and the resulting denial and/or avoidance of topics related to death and grief. These same politicians enact legislation that determines funding towards care, and public policies regarding workplace treatment of individuals who are ill and family members who are either caring for a terminally ill loved one or who are bereaved after the death of a loved one. Occasionally, politicians will have had personal experiences with their own health issues or perhaps even have exposure to hospice care through the terminal illness of a relative or friend to sensitize their views about the need for governmental support of policies that will address the needs of an aging population base. The emphasis on quick return back to work, lack of tolerance for emotions, and the valuing of people by their productivity becomes embedded in the social milieu and can make for very oppressive and inflexible social norms around death and responses to loss (Harris, 2010).

Consider this case example: Janice is a social worker in a downtown counseling center that receives governmental and private funding to subsidize counseling for clients whose financial situations do not enable them to seek counseling through private means. The subsidy comes from a small provincial governmental budget that has been designated to assist individuals to return to work after experiencing significant stressful or traumatic life events. The private part of the subsidy comes from the United Way campaign, and the combined amount from these two sources is stretched to cover counseling services for clients whose incomes are lower or whose personal situation is deemed amenable to counseling support through published guidelines that are set forward by the funding sources each year. Each client who qualifies for the subsidy is offered eight sessions with one of the counselors at the center, and clients who apply for subsidized counseling usually wait three to four months to start their sessions due to the limited amount that is available to cover these services. Janice's area of specialization is loss and trauma, and she usually is assigned clients who are bereaved or who have experienced traumatic losses.

Alice is assigned as a client to Janice. Her husband died six months ago as a result of suicide. She found him when she returned from a weekend visiting her ill mother, who lives five hours away from her home. He had closed the garage door, placed a rag in the tailpipe of the car, and kept the car running until he passed out and then died. When Alice found her husband in his car in the garage when she returned from visiting her mother, he had most likely been dead for two days.

For the first few sessions, Alice focused mostly on the incident of finding her husband and the reactions of her grown children and their neighbors when they realized that her husband had died by suicide. She described feeling that she was "living in a fog" and she had difficulties talking about what had happened. Janice assumed that since the death was unexpected and Alice had been the one to find her husband's body, there was probably some traumatic overlay, which could make talking about what happened more difficult. On session number six, Alice started talking, but then became very quiet. Janice gently coaxed her to share what was on her mind. Alice began recounting scenarios of serious physical and emotional abuse by her husband over the course of their 26-year marriage. She told Janice that she had never told anyone about these incidents before. The session seemed to fly quickly and when it ended, Janice realized that the grief over Alice's husband's suicide was just touching the surface of her traumatic experiences. The next session was equally intense, with Alice recounting more incidents of abuse and trauma, in addition to telling Janice that she was now having nightmares and had been unable to sleep for the past week. She described feeling acutely anxious and having a sense of "something dark and ominous" hanging over her head. She finally told Janice that she had also been having thoughts of her life ending, although she denied active suicidal ideation. Janice was in a quandary. This was her seventh session with Alice, and she was allowed to only have one more session before their time was to end. However, she felt that Alice was in a very vulnerable place and needed more therapeutic support than the one more session that was allotted. She knew that Alice could not afford to seek private counseling elsewhere, and she also knew that Alice had taken a very big step to trust her with the disclosure of the abuse, and she felt they had established a strong therapeutic alliance.

The executive director of the counseling center told Janice that she could not authorize extended sessions for her client due to financial constraints and the fact that the center had a long waiting list with people who had been waiting to be seen for several months. She reminded Janice that the limited funds they received for clients who required subsidized counseling needed to be stretched over many people, and others needed to access the service as well. Janice felt like she had somehow betrayed Alice by encouraging her to open up and trust her because she would now have to abandon her at a very pivotal time in her therapeutic process. Janice felt a great deal of anxiety terminating with Alice at a time when termination felt wrong. She wondered about her professional and ethical obligations in this situation, but none of these seemed to matter because she had been told by her agency that she could not schedule more sessions with Alice. She also could not try to work with Alice outside of the agency setting due to the conflict of interest policy that was in the contract with all therapists in the agency.

If you were Janice in the above scenario, what would you do? If you had more than one or two of these experiences with clients, where you felt moral distress regarding premature termination based upon the institutional policies in place, how do you think you would cope?

Addressing Caregiver Issues

As discussed throughout this chapter, self-care strategies aimed only at individual practices may be helpful, but in isolation of addressing the larger organizational and political contexts in which care occurs, they will be inadequate. With this premise in mind, we will attempt to explore practices that might help to foster caregiver resilience along with recognition of overarching social messages and political/organizational policies that are counter to the focus of the professional caregiver in the context of caring for those who are terminally ill and bereaved. A question of balance occurs at this juncture: How much should we focus on cultivating individual resilience and hardiness in the individual workers who provide care to these individuals versus how much energy and strategizing should focus on changing the social messages and resulting policy-making for political and organizational structures where this care is provided? As mentioned earlier, Papadatou (2009) states that organizations/institutions and the individuals who work within their systems have a dynamic relational interplay, whereby each affects and changes the other. Thompson and Bates (2009) posit that it is essential to recognize the organizational roots of stress while also focusing on individual self-care strategies. Thus, we will explore both of these factors, with suggestions for strengthening resilience within the caregivers, following with an exploration of the role of advocacy and public awareness as a key to enact political and social changes that have an impact upon these same caregivers and those who receive this same care.

Holistic Self-Care Strategies

Drawing upon the research that has reported a propensity for caregivers who work in this field to be passionately dedicated to their work and ideals, a few strategic practices may be of benefit to enhance the inherent resilience and strength that is present in many of these individuals. These strategies are aimed at depersonalizing the stress and frustration that occur in practice within organizational structures, recognizing that there will be times where caregivers will feel stretched, stressed, and torn between priorities not because of their inability to organize or manage their workload properly, but because of the inevitability of times when these things can't be controlled or approached in a way that is ultimately rewarding for the professional caregiver.

Mindful Awareness. Cultivating mindful awareness involves learning how to remain engaged with an intense or difficult situation while not being "drawn into" the drama that surrounds the experience. Many individuals who work and volunteer in hospice and palliative care areas already practice some form of mindfulness, which allows them to deeply engage with people who are dying without being overcome with grief and sadness due to multiple losses of the people within their care. Suffering is viewed as an inevitable part of the human condition, and the offering of oneself to try to relieve suffering while at the same time accepting that death and suffering might not be preventable is balanced through acceptance and nonjudgment of situations as they occur on a moment to moment basis (Kearney et al., 2009).

The key component of mindful awareness that can be of benefit to professional caregivers in this field especially is the ability to recognize that some types of suffering occur due to clinging to certain expectations regarding outcomes, scenarios, and basic beliefs. If we look at some of the stresses that have been discussed in this chapter related to hospice/palliative care workers, we might address the tendency of workers in this field to be passionate and focused upon the highest standards of care and accept that despite the best intentions, not all suffering can relieved, not all terminally ill patients will have a peaceful death, and the intrinsic rewards of caring in this context may not always be the ability to provide the most and the best in every situation. Rigidly holding on to original ideals (even if they are founded in very good intentions) can engender frustration, self-doubt, and burnout. Alternatively, a balance exists between remaining open to the opportunities to enable aspects of the "good death" for patients, while also accepting that not everyone will have such a "good death," and that there are many aspects of the human condition that are outside of one's control. This means encountering hospice clients and their families with open and curious minds, developing skills to delve into reasons underlying their choices, revising goals, valuing small successes, and becoming experts at tapping into what sustains them. Hindrances to compassion, such as the caregiver's personal situation and experiences, short staffing, and highly anxious and stressed clients and family members all become seen as "grist for the mill" in the daily reality of impermanence and the awareness that we can't control many things that we wish that we could.

Professionals who work with the terminally ill and bereaved must develop ways to maintain motivation in the face of obstacles to the good death and to some facets of what they view as supportive care, such as inadequate resources, ageism, patients referred too late for needed services, long-standing complicated situations, and being the objects of displaced anger and guilt. Additionally, being fully present from moment to moment to patients and family members in their current situation as it unfolds offers a powerful potential to cultivate equanimity and well-being, even in the midst of very challenging circumstances. Professional caregivers can provide valuable healing or peace to clients by being keenly attuned and present in brief interventions or even nonverbal connections:

> Mindfulness, the core of everything that we do in being with dying, is a practice of giving deep attention to what is happening in the present moment—what is happening in the mind and body of the observer and also what is going on in our surroundings. We might practice being mindful of the body, the breath, or the experience of physical change (including sickness and pain). We can also experience being mindful of our responses—the feelings that arise in reaction to pleasure or discomfort—and watching them arise and disappear. Trust and patience combined with openness and acceptance—qualities nurtured by mindfulness practice—enable us to sustain ourselves in being with dying.
>
> (Halifax, 2008, p. 11)

There are training programs available to assist with learning more about the application of mindful awareness to stressful work and life situations. The Mindfulness-Based Stress Reduction Program (MBSR), developed by Jon Kabatt-Zinn and his colleagues at the University of Massachusetts and the Being With Dying training (BWD) offered through the Upaya Zen Center in Santa Fe, New Mexico, are examples. In addition, there are many published and online resources available for incorporating mindful practice into the care of those who are dying and bereaved, which is cited to be of great benefit to professional caregivers who work in this field (Goodman & Schorling, 2012; Irving, Dobkin, & Park, 2009; Levine & Levine, 1989; Praissman, 2008).

Reflective Practice. Reflective practice is an approach that enables professionals to understand how they use their knowledge in practical situations and how they combine action and learning in a more effective way. The ability to reflect on one's professional practice can be considered a form of competence for any health care or mental health professional, and many regulatory bodies require that their members demonstrate that they have engaged in some form of reflective practice as a requirement for their registration renewal.

Reflective practice is more than "navel gazing" or emotional processing. To *critically* reflect on one's practice involves cultivating awareness and understanding of the interplay that occurs between the various personal characteristics of the caregiver and the organizational and environmental context in which the care occurs. Kearney et al. (2009) propose the need to develop multiple levels of awareness, where the clinician is able to simultaneously attend to and monitor the needs of the patient/client, the work environment, and his/her subjective experience. It is important to note that reflective practice is not just for the benefit of the practitioner; it may also be an important means of positively influencing the organization and workplace culture as well:

> Given the key role of organizational factors in either helping or hindering reflective practice, there is much to be gained by trying to think of tackling obstacles as a collective challenge as well as an individual one, with people pulling together to promote critically reflective approaches wherever possible.
>
> (Thompson & Thompson, 2008, p. 132)

For many, the ability to reflect is second nature—a way of being that is a natural extension of their personality and daily practice. However, for others, reflection needs to be learned and structured (at least in the beginning). Reflective practice has been linked to enhanced professional competence and to more effective delivery of care, which is why it has become a requirement for many professionals in their ongoing practice. When first introduced into a professional competence program, reflective practice is often seen as an indulgent luxury for those who do not have heavy workloads or tight schedules. It can also be seen as a nuisance or even threatening to those who resist change. In contrast, proponents argue that engaging in reflective practice might allow professionals to use their time more effectively while at the same time enhance their capacity to look at the overall picture of the workplace in order to plan and act more expeditiously (Thompson & Pascal, 2012).

According to Thompson and Thompson (2008), reflective practice involves the following skills:

- *Analytical abilities*—being able to look through complex, multilayered issues to identify patterns, similarities, and functioning systems from a broad-based perspective. To do this, the professional has to be able to disengage from the emotionality around certain situations and have the ability to observe and consider many factors in an open-ended, non-judging way.
- *Self-awareness*—this skill involves cultivating an understanding of how an individual professional processes information and how personal experiences, beliefs, and perspectives inform his/her practice. Being self-aware also means that an individual is consciously aware of the impact of his/her interactions with others and the organization as a whole.
- *Critical thinking*—being able to think critically involves being able to look below the surface, identify underlying beliefs and values (both individually and in groups), and recognize where there are potential (and real) power differences, discriminatory practices, and oppressive policies that have an impact upon the delivery of care.
- *Communication*—learning how to reflect and to share reflection with others can be a step towards making positive change within a workplace culture. Reflection can occur with others in the context of supervision or mentoring, as well as in professional development courses, workshops, and staff debriefings. Shared reflection can be a powerful way to develop stronger cohesion within workplace settings, and it may also decrease negativity between coworkers that has been attributed personally, but is more likely a consequence of social or organizational issues that are not as personal in nature.

There are many ways to reflect. Some individuals find it helpful to talk with a trusted colleague about situations or issues. Many therapists utilize regular supervision with a mentor or senior therapist to discuss issues that arise for them when working with clients or to reflect on personal or professional reactions that surface in specific situations. Others find writing may be a good way to reflect on practice—focusing on their reactions, concerns, and related issues that they associated with specific situations, people, or events. Chris Johns, a complementary therapist in palliative care in the United Kingdom, has developed a model of reflective practice that includes asking specific questions and cues in her various experiences with palliative patients (Johns, 2010). What is important to note is that in critically reflective practice, the reflection includes 1) exploring beyond what is experienced and perceived by a particular individual, 2) awareness of the underlying issues and organizational dynamics that have a bearing on practice, and 3) not just an intellectual analysis, but also an exploration of the emotional (and some would argue, spiritual) components that are part of the process as well. Starting with a mentor or a small group of professionals who are involved in similar work might be the best way to learn how to critically reflect upon one's practice. An added benefit of reflective practice is the ability to situate the personal within the socio-political context of care, so that if there is a need for advocacy or to lobby for change, these requests and the rationales for change come from a balanced, well-considered position.

Political and Social Strategies

Robin Youngson, a U.K.-trained anesthesiologist who now resides in New Zealand, initiated a campaign to incorporate the human dimension of compassion into the current biomedical model of health care. He began this campaign after watching his 18-year-old daughter suffer from dehumanizing treatment after being involved in a serious road accident. He delved into the underlying processes and explanations for why the care his daughter received and the culture of care in which he worked were so dehumanizing, despite the fact that the medical diagnosis and treatment of his daughter's injuries were excellent. In response to this experience, he founded the group, *Hearts in Healthcare*, which advocates for the return of compassion into the medical treatment of people in all aspects of their care (Youngson, 2011, 2012). This organization sponsors web-based learning for clinicians, patients, and the general public. The website, www.heartsinhealthcare.com, has been highly successful as a vehicle for education, a platform for public policy change, and an interactive resource for practitioners from many different disciplines.

Youngson has also written numerous articles, book chapters, in addition to a book on the topic of re-humanizing health care (Youngson, 2012). He was a founding member of the national Quality Improvement Committee in New Zealand and also has been an advisor to the World Health Organization on strategies for patient safety and putting people at the center of healthcare. By virtue of the fact that he is a medical specialist, Youngson has used the power and status of his training and position to draw attention to the way that people have been treated in the bio-medically focused health care system that is prevalent in most Western industrialized countries. Likewise, this type of advocacy and position can be used to draw attention to the need to provide compassionate end of life care and bereavement support to those whose loved ones have died.

All contexts of care, including those which provide health care and therapeutic support, occur within the broader context of the political and social milieu in which they are offered. Governmental policies determine how care is funded, who provides care and to whom, and the environments in which that care occurs. Whether or not people have access to quality palliative care is a political issue. If there is access to this care, how the funding for that care occurs and how it is distributed are also political issues. Regulatory bodies that govern the practice of professionals are also bound by legislative policies and laws. In essence, all aspects of care provided to terminally ill and bereaved individuals are politically determined and managed in some way, shape, or form.

Many of the stresses cited by care providers in the context of hospice and palliative care in addition to therapeutic support of the bereaved occur as a result of the enactment of decisions that are made at the legislative level, either federally, provincially (state), or municipally. The influence of the governmental role in determining the care and consideration of those individuals who are terminally ill and their bereaved families can't be underestimated. In a study utilizing a critical analysis of power relationships in home-based palliative care, almost all of the nurses who were interviewed cited feelings of powerlessness that stemmed from fiscal pressures and constraints related to the rules and regulations under which they worked. These systemic pressures were experienced as a form of political power that undermined their professional autonomy, and their sense of powerlessness further contributed to the feelings of powerlessness of their patients and family members (Oudshoorn, Ward-Griffin, & McWilliam, 2007). Bosma et al. (2010) undertook an exploration of what defining competencies should be included in social work practice in the palliative care context. Citing that the Canadian Senate Committee for Palliative and End of Life care has emphasized the importance of national standards and competency for end of life care and the need for specific training in these areas, the authors stated that there should be evidence-based norms and standards of professional practices in the field that will help to inform legislators of the specific needs of this population and the requirements for competent practice by the professionals who care for them, including the time and expertise required to address the significant psychosocial care needs for patients and families during this time in their lives.

In June, 2010, the document, *Raising the Bar: A Roadmap for the Future of Palliative Care in Canada* was released by The Honorable Sharon Carstairs, a member of the Senate of Canada. In the executive summary, she states:

> There are still Canadians dying in needless pain because health care providers do not know what a good death is. We need to build capacity throughout our health care system with increased research, better knowledge translation, implementation of best practices, better education for our health care providers and a health human resources staffing plan to address future needs. Caregivers are fundamental in our health care system. We need to provide them with adequate supports to keep the family unit functioning as they experience loss.
>
> (Carstairs, 2010, p. 3)

This is the type of leadership at the governmental level that must occur, with achievable goals and the necessary support to achieve these goals in reasonable time frames. It is apparent that Senator Carstairs is highly informed and has utilized her office to advocate for better provision of palliative care and better education and care of the professionals who provide palliative care and bereavement support. However, it is important for the general public to be aware of the importance of voting for representatives at all levels of government who have this same understanding and insight so that the decisions made at these levels occur within a sound understanding and appreciation of the unique needs of the individuals who need these services and the professionals who provide them. Advocacy for death education and the normalization of the diversity in grief responses needs to occur in popular media, public forums, and in the formation of public policy. Local and national associations dedicated to hospice, palliative care, and bereavement support can be powerful sources of public education and advocacy for caregivers and patients alike. As the population base ages, these issues will become more apparent and relevant, and preparation for the care needs of the growing number of aging individuals is an important topic for discussion at the political and public policy level. Professional caregivers may have the very best training and the highest intentions, but if they do not receive the support they need at the macro level, these high standards and best intentions can readily be undermined by oppressive systemic constraints and organizational bureaucracy.

Conclusion

All too often, strategies to address stress and burnout in professional caregivers mistakenly take an individualistic focus without looking at the contextual and structural elements in which the caregivers work. Most professional caregivers in this field tend to possess strong, passionate views about the end of life care and bereavement support that they provide. In turn, these views enable these individuals to thrive in caring for those who might otherwise be socially marginalized and neglected. However, this same passionate investment in the work can lead to greater vulnerability when environmental and organizational policies interfere with the high standards of care that are an extension of these values. Professional caregivers can enhance their innate resilience through specific practices that allow for meaningful engagement with patients while disengaging from feelings of powerlessness and disappointment that frequently occur in managed care settings. The broader view of the organizational and political policies that have been enacted and which directly affect professionals in this field occur at the level where advocacy, voter awareness, and social awareness of appropriate care norms can have the greatest impact.

Key Terms

Compassion Fatigue—a constellation of symptoms that resulted from the traumatic overlay in caregivers who overly identify with the pain, suffering, and horrific circumstances of their patients.

Mindfulness—a practice of giving deep attention to what is happening in the present moment.

Reciprocity—in the context of this chapter, intermingling of caregiver characteristics with the culture and context of the work environment in which that caregiver works, creating an interactional dynamic between both to provide care to those who need it.

Reflective practice—cultivating awareness and understanding of the interplay that occurs between the various personal characteristics of the caregiver and the organizational and environmental context in which the care occurs.

Questions for Reflection

1. The author suggests a sort of double-edged sword associated with the characteristics of service providers working with the dying and the bereaved, particularly their deep commitment to their work and highly compassionate, empathetic tendencies. What would you suggest to someone embarking on work in this field who wish to retain their passion and their compassion while avoiding burnout?
2. Reflect on the comment by the American Association of the College of Nursing: "People in our country deny death, believing that medical science can cure any patient. Death is often seen as a failure of the healthcare system rather than a natural aspect of life." How prepared do you believe you are to accept death as a natural aspect of life? How does your current belief—whatever it is—influence your comfort with the topic of palliative care?
3. Consider the question posed by the author:
   How much should we focus on cultivating individual resilience and hardiness in the individual workers who provide care to these individuals versus how much energy and strategizing should focus on changing the social messages and resulting policy-making for political and organizational structures where this care is provided?
   Where do you believe the primary responsibility lies?
4. Reflective practice challenges the clinician "to simultaneously attend to and monitor the needs of the patient/client, the work environment, and his/her subjective experience." What is your experience with maintaining multiple levels of awareness? How might this enrich your experience, personally and professionally?

References

Ablett, J. R., & Jones, R. S. P. (2007). Resilience and well-being in palliative care staff: A qualitative study of hospice nurses' experience of work. *Psycho-Oncology, 16*(8), 733–740.

Bosma, H., Johnston, M., Cadell, S., Wainwright, W., Abernethy, N., Feron, A., . . ., & Nelson, F. (2010). Creating social work competencies for practice in hospice palliative care. *Palliative Medicine, 24*(1), 79–87.

Carstairs, S. (2010). *Raising the bar: A roadmap for the future of palliative care in Canada.* Ottawa: Senate of Canada.

Claxton-Oldfield S., & Claxton-Oldfield J. (2005). What coordinators of palliative care volunteers in New Brunswick, Canada have to say about their programs, themselves, and their program management practices. *Journal of Volunteer Administration, 23*(3): 30–35.

Claxton-Oldfield, S., & Banzen, Y. (2010). Personality characteristics of hospice palliative care volunteers: The "big five" and empathy. *American Journal of Hospice and Palliative Medicine, 27*(6), 407–412.

Claxton-Oldfield S., Jefferies J., Fawcett C., & Claxton-Oldfield J. (2004). Palliative care volunteers: Why do they do it? *Journal of Palliative Care, 20*(2), 78–84.

Corr, C. A., & Corr, D. M. (2013). *Death and dying, life and living* (7th ed.). Belmont, CA: Wadsworth.

Devilly, G. J., Wright, R., & Varker, T. (2009). Vicarious trauma, secondary traumatic stress or simply burnout? Effect of trauma therapy on mental health professionals. *Australasian Psychiatry, 43*(4), 373–385.

Dougherty, E., Pierce, B., Clement, M., Panzarella, T., Rodin, G., & Zimmerman, C. (2009). Factors associated with work stress and professional satisfaction in oncology staff. *American Journal of Hospice & Palliative Medicine, 26*(2), 105–111.

End of Life Nursing Education Consortium (ENLEC). *ENLEC Fact Sheet*. Retrieved from www.aacn.nche.edu/elnec/about/fact-sheet

Figley, C. R. (Ed.). (1995). *Compassion fatigue: Coping with secondary traumatic stress disorder in those who treat the traumatized*. New York, NY: Brunner/Mazel.

Giddings, G. (2014). Opportune timing for palliative care specialty designation. *CMAJ: Canadian Medical Association Journal, 186*(6), 190.

Goodman, M. J., & Schorling, J. B. (2012). A mindfulness course decreases burnout and improves well-being among healthcare providers. *The International Journal of Psychiatry in Medicine, 43*(2), 119–128.

Halifax, J. (2008). *Being with dying: Cultivating compassion and fearlessness in the presence of death*. Boston, MA: Shambhala Press.

Harris, D. L. (2010). Oppression of the bereaved: A critical analysis of grief in Western society. *Omega: Journal of Death and Dying, 60*(3), 241–253.

Irving, J. A., Dobkin, P. L., & Park, J. (2009). Cultivating mindfulness in health care professionals: A review of empirical studies of mindfulness-based stress reduction (MBSR). *Complementary Therapies in Clinical Practice, 15*(2), 61–66.

Johns, C. (2010). Reflective practice in cancer and palliative care education. In L. Foyle & J. Hostad (Eds.), *Illuminating the diversity of cancer and palliative care education* (pp. 94–109). New York, NY: Radcliffe.

Jordan, J., Kosminsky, P., & Neimeyer, R. (2014, April). *Our work, ourselves—reflecting on our own losses as thanatologists*. Concurrent session presented at the Association for Death Education and Counseling 36th annual meeting, Baltimore, MD.

Kearney, M. K., Weininger, R. B., Vachon, M. L. S., Harrison, R. L., & Mount, B. M. (2009). Self-care of physicians caring for patients at the end of life. *Journal of the American Medical Association, 301*(11), 1155–1164.

Konigsberg, R. A. (2011). *The truth about grief*. New York, NY: Simon & Schuster.

Levine, S., & Levine, O. (1989). *Who dies? An investigation of conscious living and conscious dying*. New York, NY: Anchor.

Maslach, C., & Jackson, S. E. (1982). Burnout in health professions: A social psychological analysis. In G. S. Sanders & J. Suls (Eds.), *Social psychology of health and illness* (pp. 227–251). London: Lawrence Erlbaum.

Murray, R. (2014). Record medical intern numbers do no favours for palliative care. *ehospice Australia*. Retrieved from www.ehospice.com/australia/ArticleView/tabid/10688/ArticleId/8710/language/en-GB/View.aspx

Neimeyer, R. A. (2012). The (half) truth about grief. *Illness, Crisis, & Loss, 20*(4), 389–395.

Newell, J. M., & MacNeil, G. A. (2010). Professional burnout, vicarious trauma, secondary traumatic stress, and compassion fatigue. *Best Practices in Mental Health, 6*(2), 57–68.

Oudshoorn, A., Ward-Griffin, C., & McWilliam, C. (2007). Client–nurse relationships in home-based palliative care: A critical analysis of power relations. *Journal of Clinical Nursing, 16*(8), 1435–1443.

Papadatou, D. (2009). *In the face of death: Professionals who care for the dying and the bereaved*. New York, NY: Springer Publishing.

Praissman, S. (2008). Mindfulness-based stress reduction: A literature review and clinician's guide. *Journal of the American Academy of Nurse Practitioners, 20*(4), 212–216.

Quill, T. E., & Abernethy, A. P. (2013). Generalist plus specialist palliative care—creating a more sustainable model. *New England Journal of Medicine, 368*(13), 1173–1175.

Rappaport, N. (2009). *In her wake: A child psychiatrist explores the mystery of her mother's suicide*. New York, NY: Basic Books.

Rezenbrink, I. (2011). Introduction. In I. Rezenbrink (Ed.), *Caregiver stress and staff support in illness, dying, and bereavement* (pp. xiii–xviii). New York, NY: Oxford.

Shear, K., Frank, E., Houck, P., & Reynolds, F. (2005). Treatment of complicated grief: A randomized controlled trial. *Journal of the American Medical Association, 293*(21), 2601–2608.

Thompson, N. (2011). Workplace well-being: A psychosocial perspective. In I. Rezenbrink (Ed.), *Caregiver stress and staff support in illness, dying, and bereavement* (pp. 25-36). New York, NY: Oxford.

Thompson, N., & Bates, J. (Eds.). (2009). *Promoting workplace well-being: A critical approach*. New York, NY: Palgrave Macmillan.

Thompson, N., & Pascal, J. (2012). Developing critically reflective practice. *Reflective practice, 13*(2), 311–325.

Thompson, S., & Thompson, N. (2008). *The critically reflective practitioner*. New York, NY: Palgrave Macmillan.

Vachon, M. L. S. (1995). Staff stress in hospice/palliative care: A review. *Palliative medicine*, *9*(2), 91–122.

Whitebird, R. R., Asche, S. E., Thompson, G. L., Rossom, R., & Heinrich, R. (2013). Stress, burnout, compassion fatigue, and mental health in hospice workers in Minnesota. *Journal of Palliative Medicine*, *16*(12), 1534–1539.

Youngson, R. (2011). Compassion in health care—the missing dimension of healthcare reform? In I. Rezenbrink (Ed.), *Caregiver stress and staff support in illness, dying, and bereavement* (pp. 37–48). New York, NY: Oxford.

Youngson, R. (2012). *Time to care: How to love your patients and your job*. Raglan, New Zealand: Rebelheart.

22

The Liberating Capacity of Compassion

Mary L. S. Vachon and Darcy L. Harris

Introduction

Both of us worked for many years in health care and we have also had a good deal of experience being on the "other side of the table" as recipients of care in the same system in which we worked. Each of us also came to crossroads in our work and personal lives that required us to deeply reflect on our values, ideals, and intentions for ourselves and the patients/clients who were in our care. At times, we each have had to carefully consider how to respond to clashes of our values versus specific policies and practices in some of the places where we've worked. Many of the choices we made around these factors focused on the relief of our own suffering so that we could continue in the path that we were meant to follow. Although our processes were different, occurring at differing times and in different contexts, the common thread of compassion emerged out of our life experiences as we each searched for meaning and tried to make sense of these difficult situations and times. The personal learning from our (sometimes painful and stressful) experiences were then readily applied to our working lives. Over the years, we each found that responding to our internal distress and to our external circumstances with compassion allowed for a greater sense of discernment and clarity.

In this chapter, we begin by sharing our personal narratives and how these personal experiences opened us to a deeper and more compassionate awareness of both ourselves and others. We then proceed to explore the nature of compassion and its attributes, and then review two training programs that support the integration of compassion into caring professions. We will then discuss how compassion can enhance caregivers' resilience and provide necessary discernment for workplace contexts. Finally, we discuss the range of compassionate responses at the individual, social, and structural levels, and the possibility of compassion as the best foundation from which to respond to injustice and moral distress.

Images of Compassion

I (MLSV) have always been conscious of the concept of compassion, but a few images served to powerfully enhance my awareness. The first was soon after my diagnosis of stage four Non-Hodgkin's lymphoma and my first chemotherapy treatment. I was scheduled to lecture in Shanghai and Hong Kong and figured that since I was likely going to be dying within a short time, and this was a major family trip in which I would be doing some of my lectures with my son (who had just graduated from University), what could be better than to "pass on the torch." In Shanghai, we were taken to the Buddhist temple garden. It was the annual day of healing. I was five days post my first chemotherapy treatment. On our tour we were shown a statue and asked to comment on what we saw. I said I saw a beautiful woman. My husband said, "She is smiling." The monk sitting at the statue said, "Ah, if you see that she is smiling that means that whatever you ask for you will receive." We were then told that she was Quan Yin, the Buddhist figure that represents mercy and compassion. Perhaps my husband asked for my good health, because almost 20 years later I am alive and well, despite my initial prognosis of having a one in four chance of surviving.

The second image is that of the wounded healer. Michael Kearney's book *Mortally Wounded* (Kearney, 1996) accompanied me on my journey through chemotherapy. Daniel Sulmasy (1997), a physician, philosopher, and former Franciscan friar, contends that

> all health care professionals are wounded healers. They cannot escape suffering themselves. Moments of pain, loneliness, fatigue, and sacrifice are intrinsic to the human condition. The physician or nurse's own bleeding can become the source of the compassion in the healer's art. From the physician or nurse's own suffering can come the wine of fervent zeal and the oil of compassion . . . The physician's or nurse's wounds can become resources for healing.
>
> (p. 48)

However, Sulmasy (1997) warns that wounded healers must not become so overwhelmed with the suffering of others that they are unable to offer effective care:

> Competence remains the first act of compassion. Wounded healers do not ask their patients for help, but recognize the unity between their own neediness and the needs of their patients. Wounded healers issue an invitation to patients to enter into the space of the healing relationship.
>
> (p. 48)

Very early in my career, as I began consulting at Princess Margaret Hospital, a cancer hospital in Toronto, I remember one of the oncologists introducing me to Henri Nouwen's book, *The Wounded Healer* (Nouwen, 1972). His perspective provides interesting reflections for caregivers in the field of illness, loss, grief, and trauma. From Nouwen's perspective, the wounded healer must look after his/her own wounds, but at the same time be prepared to heal the wounds of others. The signs that characterize the healing of those aware of their own woundedness are hospitality, concentration, compassion, and perspective (Vachon, 2001).

I was introduced to the third image by a chaplain at my previous place of employment. She was aware of some challenges I was having in my work environment and reached out to be of service. She introduced me to Mathew Fox's book *Sins of the Spirit, Blessings of the Flesh* (Fox, 1999). In it, I read of the Man in Sapphire Blue, an illumination that was received by the twelfth century mystic, St. Hildegard of Bingen. Fox (1999) writes of this image and states that the color of the heart chakra is green. Hildegard built her entire theology on *viriditas*, the marriage of two Latin words, green and truth (Verititas Botanicals, 2015). She felt that all creatures contained the greening power of the Holy Spirit, which makes all things creative and nourishing. In her picture of the Man in Sapphire Blue, the man's hands are outstretched in front of his chest. This gesture is an ancient metaphor for compassion, because compassion is about taking heart energy and putting it into one's hands—that is, putting it to work in the world. When I visited the parish church of St Hildegard in Eibingen Germany, I was privileged to see the mosaic of the Man in Sapphire Blue. Information in the church states that this is St. Hildegard's image of the Trinity. What Fox described as the energy field around the body is described there as the Holy Spirit, which is "always making waves."

The Liberating Capacity of Compassion

So, from the Buddhist and Christian perspectives, I found images of compassion that included the characteristics of equanimity and faithfulness. These same images taught the need for self-compassion, indicating that we must tend to our own wounds before being able to care for the wounded other, as well as the understanding that competence is the first act of compassion. Through a friend I learned that the Latin root for blessing is "to wound." Our wounds can become our blessings. I also became aware of the need to allow for the "space" of the healing relationship, and of course, the poignant image of compassion as taking the energy of the heart and putting it into the hands, and then putting it to work in the world, in the process of healing and assisting. I also could see that there are "waves" of suffering, but the Holy Spirit is with us during these times.

I (DLH) once worked as a staff nurse on a 36-bed medical surgical unit on the night shift. Many of the patients were acutely ill and required dressing checks and intravenous (IV) medications through the night. We also had several patients on telemetry to monitor their heart. For these 36 patients, I was the only registered nurse, which meant that I was also the charge nurse and the person responsible to ensure that all of the patients received the care they required. Working with me was usually one licensed practical nurse and a nursing assistant. Many of the patients needed frequent doses of pain medication, which was my responsibility to administer. Night was often the time when patients became afraid or when they would reflect on their situation, and it was a common occurrence for me to walk into a patient's room to check on an IV only to sit down to speak with the patient who was wide awake and needing to talk. In the best of times, when things ran smoothly and there wasn't a crisis or a new admission, I would manage to leave the workplace just a little late. Most of the time, I stayed way past the time when my shift ended in order to complete the documentation that was required for each patient.

I tried to speak up for an increase in staffing or a redistribution of job descriptions to allow more flexibility for my time to tend to the patients' needs, but I was repeatedly told that I should be able to do the work like the other nurses did. When I spoke with the other nurses about my concerns, several told me of short cuts they had learned in order to be done quicker. Many of them felt the answer to patients who were anxious and awake at night was to give them medication for sleep because they didn't have the time to talk with them. Over time, I began to dread going to work. I felt shame that I was not able to "keep up" with my coworkers on this busy floor and I began to wonder if something was wrong with me. I finally left this job when my husband was transferred and we moved away from this community. I never felt like I resolved the feelings of failure. I felt ashamed that I could not rise up to the expectations of the administration of the hospital, and (more importantly), that I had failed many of the patients who truly needed me to do more than just administer their nightly medications.

Years later, I began to experience similar feelings of exhaustion and dread in another job where I was expected to work 50+ hours per week plus take call on weekends. This time, however, I entered into therapy to explore the recurring feelings of shame and disappointment that I felt towards myself as a result of not being able to leave the workplace stresses at work. Through this process, I began to appreciate the difference between realistic and unrealistic expectations in the workplace and my self-critical tendencies. I came to realize that my wounding in the workplace was not because I had some basic flaw, but because I cared deeply about my patients and could not numb myself enough to tune out their human needs for basic comfort and presence in the midst of their suffering. In essence, I learned that there was something "right" about what was being perceived as something "wrong" with me. It was through this process that I began to identify with the gifts of the *wounded healer*, and I also learned that the compassion I felt for others was incomplete without a compassionate stance towards myself as well. This time, it was self-compassion and not shame that gave me the permission to change jobs without feeling like I had failed. And the new position I took afterwards was in a much more humane environment, allowing my work to be meaningful and fulfilling.

Many years after this last experience, I began to see how professionals in managerial and administrative roles in the places where I worked were also wounded by a system that had reduced patient care down to commodities, defined only in quantified objective outcomes and fiscal restraint. I began to see that those in front line care felt the pressure of unrealistic expectations from administration, and that those in administration were placed in positions of enforcing these unrealistic expectations for staff because of the social pressures, norms, and fiscal policies that had been enacted by people at a level where there was no understanding or connection to the people in our care. While this recognition was frustrating to the advocate inside me, the ability to see without being blinded by reactionary, defensive anger provided me with a freedom to reflectively choose my responses and maintain a sense of congruence with my deepest intentions.

Models of Compassionate Response

We have both just provided examples of how compassion has been manifest in our personal and professional lives. Mary described how the images of compassion became particularly important to her both personally and in her work after her diagnosis. This awareness led to her recognition and value of the wounded healer; Darcy experienced profound grief over the loss of innocence and burnout in an overburdened health care system, which then allowed her to see the common humanity that we share with those who may consciously or unconsciously oppress us as well as with those who are oppressed. In each of these descriptions, compassion was the common thread that gave each of us the capacity to be open to the suffering of ourselves and others in a way that allowed for healing to occur. Both of us became interested in a deeper exploration of the nature and attributes of compassion after these and other experiences. In this section, we will define compassion, and look at the elements that comprise compassionate responses.

For the purposes of this chapter, the definitions and models of Roshi Joan Halifax (2011, 2012, 2013a, b; 2014) and Paul Gilbert (2009, 2010, 2013a, 2013b; Gilbert & Chodon, 2014) will be used. We have both attended workshops that were facilitated by Roshi Joan Halifax on the cultivation of compassion in end of life care and we have each incorporated much of her work into each of our practices. We have also both drawn richly from the work of Dr. Paul Gilbert, who introduced the approach of Compassion-Focused Therapy (CFT), which has also provided a description of how compassion can be a venue for healing in therapeutic work. We will explore each of these approaches in more detail in this section.

Roshi Joan Halifax: The ABIDE Model of Enactive Principled Compassion

Roshi Joan Halifax received a fellowship to study at the Library of Congress as a Distinguished Visiting Scholar for several months. She used this time to develop her insights into compassion and how it can be taught. Her initial thinking on the topic was published in an article in *Current Opinion in Supportive and Palliative Care* (Halifax, 2012) at my (MLSV) invitation, in an issue that I co-edited with Drs. Ben Corn and Harvey Chochinov (Corn, Vachon, & Chochinov, 2012). Halifax deepened her understanding of compassion, later describing a model of compassion with the acronym ABIDE In her work, Halifax cites two large categories of compassion. The first is *referential*, or *biased compassion* (i.e., compassion directed toward an object), and the second is non-referential or unbiased compassion (i.e., compassion that is objectless and pervasive; Halifax, 2011). Both of these types of compassion are important for clinicians to actualize in clinician/patient interactions. Non-referential compassion is also called universal compassion. It is compassion without an object, "where compassion pervades the mind of the experiencer as a way of being" (Halifax, 2013a, p. 212).

The ABIDE model of compassion developed by Halifax describes compassion as relational, mutual, reciprocal, and asymmetrical (Halifax, 2013a, p. 208). This view of compassion can have important consequences in the clinical setting and for addressing social injustice that may be the source of suffering (Halifax, 2013a). Halifax defines compassion as "the capacity to be attentive to the experience of others, to wish the best for others, and to sense what will truly serve others" (Halifax, 2014, p. 1). Compassion (and responses that are compassionate) are viewed as extensions of several specific elements that come together to create the ability to respond with intention and attention, for the purpose of relieving the suffering of others (and oneself). Each of the individual elements of compassion are amenable to development through training; and the model identifies key areas that, when cultivated through practice, will lead to a deeper understanding and ability to respond in any given situation with compassion. The specific components of compassion are as follows:

- *Attention and Affectual Balance*—these two key areas involve the ability to hold one's attention without distraction or loss of one's sense of grounding, and the ability to regulate one's emotions in the face of distressing or intense experiences. Halifax suggests that cultivating attention through practices such as mindfulness may enhance one's ability to perceive the reality of suffering more accurately, without being overwhelmed by the magnitude or intensity of that suffering (Halifax, 2013a). In the context of social justice, the cultivation of attention and attunement are necessary to be able to focus and look broadly with compassion upon the many sources of suffering—both internal and external. For example, it might seem obvious when a nurse or doctor acts in a way that seems uncaring or indifferent to a patient's pain and to blame these individuals for their poor attitude. However, being able to focus attention and to attune with others might allow us to better understand and have compassion for the health care providers who may have their own wounds from their past and who also might be chronically overburdened or pressured by social mandates and professional expectations, leading to protective disengagement from a deeper connection with patients. This same stance may also provide a better opportunity to appreciate how past experiences for our patients and clients inform their responses and reactions in the here and now.
- *Intention, Insight, and Discernment*—in the cognitive domain, the cultivation of intention and insight supports discernment in difficult situations. This dimension helps to regulate affect so that reactionary responses are limited and there is more space for reflective responses instead. An important aspect in the cognitive domain is the ability to let go of one's attachment to outcome, which is often very difficult for clinicians. Compassion aspires to transform suffering or end suffering; however, the cognitive dimension provides us with the reasoned realization that our primary focus is upon our *intention* to relieve suffering, rather than upon a specific, desired outcome occurring.

    The *intention* to transform suffering is one of the features that distinguish compassion from empathy (Schmidt, 2004). Key to the concept of compassion is that if one is to practice compassion for others, one must first start with self-compassion (Gonzalez, 2012). In other words, the heart must first pump blood to itself (Kearney, Weininger, Vachon, Mount, & Harrison, 2009). *Insight* helps us to override habitual responses, appraise realistically, and learn how to down-regulate our emotions, thus increasing our ability to tolerate difficult and triggering scenarios more readily. Developing our insight through self-awareness, and staying focused on our intention to relieve the suffering of others, we can more readily shift away from thoughts and behaviors that are destructive. We would be less likely to abandon patients because we are overwhelmed or feel powerless; less inclined to engage in moral outrage that is not channeled in a healthy way, and we would have the ability to be more fully present to the suffering of others. This type of insight provides us with a broader, more open perspective, and it nurtures hardiness and resilience. Insight allows us the ability to decide how to respond to suffering in a realistic and intentioned manner (discernment).
- *Embodiment, Engagement, and Equanimity*—once we are aware of and sense the suffering of others, we often experience *inter-subjective resonance*, wherein another's experience feels as if it

is happening in our own body. (Think of a time when you've seen a cut or wound on another person's body and then felt a sense of resonance from your own body in the same place). Compassionate action arises from the base of a mind that is focused, one's awareness of the reality of suffering, the ability to attune to ourselves and others, and the recognition of our interconnectedness with others. Neuroscience research shows that the ability to tune into oneself and the ability to tune into another, referred to as *interoceptivity*, is located in the same brain circuits in the insula cortex. We are essentially wired to connect (Halifax, 2012).

- "One of the key mental features that arise when all these components are activated is equanimity. Equanimity is characterized by a calm, even, balanced state of mind; it is also supported by the realization of the truth of impermanence and holding things in equal regard" (Halifax, 2013b, p. 220).

Halifax notes that compassion does not lead to fatigue. Rather, it can become a well-spring of resilience to allow our natural impulse to care for another to become a source of nourishment rather than depletion (Halifax, 2013a, 2014). Crucial to the concept of compassion is that we cannot practice compassion for others if we do not practice self-compassion. Recent research shows compassion helps us by reducing physiological stress and promoting physical and mental well-being (Halifax, 2014). Dr. Robin Youngson (2012, 2013), an anesthesiologist who founded *Hearts in Healthcare*, an organization dedicated to the cultivation of compassion in health care contexts, speaks of his revelation about compassionate care:

> There is a widespread belief among doctors that we need to limit our emotional connection with patients because all of our compassion will run out. This one-sided view of compassion is a peculiarly Western belief. In the Buddhist world, every act of compassion is seen as providing compassion equally for the caregiver as the receiver. This has been my recent experience; the more I bring open-hearted compassion to the care of my patients, the more love I have to give. It is a mutually sustaining practice.
>
> (Youngson, 2013, p. 335)

The second thing Youngson (2012, 2013) learned from one of his patients was to choose his attitude (which in Halifax's model represents attentional and affective balance): "If Jessie could choose humor, laughter, and compassion in her awful circumstances, then what excuse could I have for grumpiness or self-pity?" (Youngson, 2013, p. 336) This insight led him to refocus on his intention, (which is the cognitive domain in Halifax's model). For example, instead of being irritated about being called out in the middle of the night to attend a delivery, he chose

> to focus on the extraordinary privilege of being invited to participate in childbirth, one of the most intimate events in our lives. It was a very deliberate process of choosing the thoughts and attitudes I would bring to the patient, replacing grumpiness with gentleness and compassion.
>
> (Youngson, 2013, p. 336)

As he changed his approach, the midwives in the delivery room also changed in their responses to him. They assisted him more willingly and his rate of complications and calls back for inadequate pain relief also decreased.

Paul Gilbert and Choden: Mindful Compassion

Coming from a Buddhist psychological perspective, Gilbert suggests that compassion involves two different psychological processes. The first is the ability to be aware of suffering and to engage with it without being emotionally overwhelmed by it. The second process relates to the wisdom to know how to hold, alleviate, and prevent suffering (Gilbert, 2009, Gilbert & Choden, 2014). He notes that each process is more complex than it might at first seem. Prevention is about removing the causes of suffering, so we need to make an effort to train our minds to relieve suffering when we see it, but also to prevent it from arising where possible (Gilbert & Choden, 2014). "Alleviation and prevention are about creating the conditions for clear insight and change, and that often means facing and accepting what is painful and difficult rather than turning from it" (Gilbert & Choden, 2014, p. 104). These two authors also draw from the work of Matthieu Ricard (Ricard, 2014) stressing the importance of not only opening our minds to suffering, but also opening our minds to loving kindness or friendly kindness, expressing genuine wishes for the happiness of self and others, and embracing the desire that suffering and the sources of suffering cease (Gilbert & Choden, 2014). These concepts are very much in alignment with those of Halifax that we described in the previous section.

Gilbert's work is rooted in neuroscience (Gilbert, 2013a; Gilbert & Choden, 2014) and builds on the evolution of our brains towards flexibility, which allows us to fit into particular social contexts. As mammals, our basic motive systems are very old and designed for gene replication. Like other mammals, we seek safety, prefer to find our lunch rather than to be lunch, engage with sexual partners in order to reproduce, form attachments to our offspring and tend to favor our offspring over those of others, and we often compete for status and position within our social groups and try to avoid being marginalized or rejected (Gilbert, 2013a). This latter insight can help us to see that staff conflict can be a product of what Gilbert and Choden refer to as the "old brain." Gilbert's Compassion-Focused Therapy (CFT; Gilbert, 2010; Gilbert 2013b) defines motives that focus on various types of social relationships and provides a guide for how to navigate different types of relationships as social mentalities. When other individuals respond in a reciprocal manner, then a social role is created and the motivation is fulfilled. Without motivation, there is no means to trigger these attention, thinking, feeling, and behavioral competencies in the social context. A social mentality is more complex than a motive in that it is reciprocal, dynamic, and co-regulated through the unfolding relational process in an ongoing way. Gilbert describes compassion as being rooted in our caring system and is a form of social mentality, arising from signals in the outside world that trigger motivational states, communication, and social behavior within the self. He also states that our evolved brains can create and block compassion (Gilbert 2013a). Central to compassion is the fact that evolution has created styles of relating where individuals have an interest in the well-being of others, are able to understand the feelings and needs of others, and therefore act to reduce distress and increase well-being.

Motivation is described as the first attribute of compassion. Motivation leads to openness to discover the causes of suffering and then anticipate and prevent further suffering. Gilbert states this motivation to care is fundamental to the expression of the other attributes of compassion. For example, experiencing empathy (the ability to sense others' feelings and views) without a desire to be caring to another person could be used for exploitation or manipulation (Gilbert & Choden, 2014). The motivation to care needs to be shaped and tempered by wisdom and insight. Wisdom and insight inform compassion so that compassionate responses are guided by the awareness and understanding of the deeper reality of how things are. The response is both considered and appropriate to the situation (Gilbert & Choden, 2014). Motivation needs to be accompanied by effort, so these authors stress the importance of training and practice in mindfulness and compassion skills, which is congruent with Halifax's stance.

In addition to motivation, there needs to be sensitivity and openness to the moment-by-moment flow of our experiences, not turning a blind eye or using denial or justification to avoid dealing with things that we find painful. This type of sensitivity and awareness allows us to be open to sadness and suffering without becoming overwhelmed. Gilbert and Choden (2014) emphasize that mindfulness practices are helpful in learning to pay attention to what is going on in our minds and bodies, allowing us to recognize that certain emotions are present. Sympathy "is the emotional ability to be moved by distress in ourselves and others" (Gilbert & Choden, 2014, p. 109). Sympathy can be confused with empathy. "[S]ympathy can be taken to be our immediate emotional reaction, without conscious thought or reflection" (Gilbert & Choden, 2014, p. 111). Sympathy may not be helpful because we can be overwhelmed by our own feelings, or we may have difficulty distinguishing them from what is going on in the other person(s). In this event, we can lose perspective and rush in without thinking in a desperate attempt to alleviate our own distress, or turn away from the distressed person because we can't bear his/her pain. Carl Rogers (1957) described empathy as the ability to imagine oneself in the minds of other people and to experience walking in their shoes. Gilbert and Choden (2014) note that empathy allows us to contain our own emotions, so in that respect it can be connected to distress tolerance.

Distress tolerance enables us to stay with the experience of being emotionally tuned into suffering. "Being able to bear and cope with distress allows us to actively listen and work out what it helpful." (Gilbert & Choden, 2014, p. 112) This quality can be seen as related to Halifax's attention and affectual dimensions (Halifax, 2012, 2013a). Gilbert and Choden (2014) point out that this tolerance does not mean that one is masochistic; distress tolerance is based "on a caring motive that facilitates long-term recovery or development" (Gilbert & Choden, 2014, p. 112). For example, sometimes self-compassion might dictate that one leave one's place of employment or career. A recent study of oncologists (cancer specialists) found that only one third of those surveyed were satisfied with their work–life balance (Shanafelt et al., 2014). This finding was lower than other medical professionals; more than a quarter of the oncologists reported a moderate to high likelihood that they would reduce their hours of work in the next year and a third reported a moderate to high likelihood that they would leave their current employment within the next two years. More than a quarter planned to retire before age 65. Women oncologists and those who devoted more time to patient care were less likely to be satisfied with work–life balance. The implication here is that self-compassion may lead us to recognize that there are times when we must take care of ourselves first, despite a desire to care for others.

Compassion fatigue has previously been thought of in association with an empathic process. Elsewhere, the idea that the construct of compassion fatigue is actually measuring empathy has been discussed and the point made that what is possibly operating between compassion fatigue and empathy is a process known as *disruption in empathy* (Vachon, Huggard, & Huggard, 2015). Wilson and Lindy (1994) described this as an "intrusive" empathic strain between the clinician and client that can result in over-identification and pathological bonding and, an "avoidance" empathic strain characterized by being distant and avoiding contact with the patient. These two states are not empathic in the therapeutic relationship; rather, they are dysfunctional processes. This may be what others have been describing in their discussion of the relationship between empathy and compassion fatigue (Vachon, Huggard, & Huggard, 2015). Klimecki and Singer (2012) have suggested a change in terminology to *empathic distress fatigue* rather than compassion fatigue. Gilbert and Choden (2014) note that empathy and compassion are not the same and empathy is not always compassionate. Empathy is a very important attribute of compassion, "but empathy can be used in all kinds of non-compassionate ways. The worst torturer to have is an empathic one. The non-empathic one puts the gun to your head, but the empathic one puts it to your child's head" (Gilbert & Choden, 2014, p. 117).

Klimecki, Ricard, and Singer (2013) write about compassion from the first and third person, using insights from the real-time functional magnetic resonance imaging (MRI) measures taken of Matthieu Ricard, an individual with a long-standing meditative practice. These authors sought to explore the neural signature of Ricard during meditation. Ricard was asked to immerse himself in different states of compassion: non-referential compassion, compassion for the suffering of others, and loving kindness. To their surprise, all of these states elicited activation in rather similar networks. However, these compassion-related networks did not resemble the empathy-for-pain network previously seen and frequently observed in meditation-naïve subjects when exposed to the suffering of others (Klimecki et al., 2013).

To test the intuition that empathy for the suffering of another may be very different to developing benevolent or compassionate motivation towards others, Matthieu Ricard was scanned again, but this time asked only to engage in emotionally sharing the suffering of others without going into any form of compassion. And here it was: the researchers outside of the scanner witnessed the appearance of the empathy-for-pain network similar to what Tania Singer and other colleagues had observed many times before in non-practitioners (Klimecki et al., 2013, p. 275).

These authors concluded that empathy is often misunderstood as compassion. Whereas empathy can lead to burnout, compassion can help foster resilience. Empathy and compassion rely on different biological systems and brain networks (Klimecki et al., 2013). Compassion, the voluntary generation of feelings of warmth and benevolence in humans, may activate areas of the brain which are associated with affiliation, love, and reward (Klimecki et al., 2013). Compassion is good for our brains.

In a YouTube video, Matthieu Ricard (2014) differentiates affective empathy, which resonates with another person's emotional state of happiness, sadness, or suffering, from cognitive empathy, which puts oneself in another's shoes, to imagine how that person feels and his/her state of mind. Ricard warns that stand-alone empathy is risky; indicating that resonating with suffering clients on a daily basis may lead to burn out. One needs to bring in the warmth and fire of compassion. He uses the analogy of empathy being like an electric pump running without water. We need the mental state of love and compassion to prime the pump, so empathy is not left on its own to burn out.

Finally, compassion involves being nonjudgmental in the sense of being non-condemning. In both Buddhism and Christianity, not acting out on others or not seeking to harm people out of anger or vengeance are seen as important parts of kindness and compassion (e.g., let he who is without sin cast the first stone; Gilbert & Choden, 2014). Our brains are always making judgments. The focus here is to not act out on our automatic judgments, but to be more reflective, so our choices are based on compassion, wisdom, and insight.

> . . . nonjudgment is a mindfulness skill that allows the flow of the mind to reveal itself without fighting with it. This stance gives us the ability to clearly discern what is happening and to make choices about how to act wisely.
>
> (Gilbert & Choden, 2014, p. 119)

Bringing the Attributes Together

From the perspective of Gilbert and Choden, if you remove any of the above attributes compassion will begin to struggle. Removing the motivation to be caring causes the ability to demonstrate compassion to fall apart. In addition, if you lose sensitivity and don't pay attention to suffering because you simply don't see it, or you see it but you are so overwhelmed by it that you have to turn away from it, your motivation for caring will be stymied. Finally, if you do actually see it and turn toward it but you don't accurately understand it, you don't have wisdom, or don't know how to respond because your empathy is blocked, then you will also not be able to follow through with a compassionate response (Gilbert & Choden, 2014). When we begin to cultivate mindful awareness and open ourselves to the possibility of compassionate responses, the attributes of compassion

> tend to co-arise, they tend to build and support each other. As we build empathic awareness, this helps distress tolerance; and as we become more tolerant, and able to stay with, contain and explore our emotions and those of others, we become more empathic and open.
>
> (Gilbert & Choden, 2014, pp. 120–121)

To bring this into the practical realm, one of my (MLSV) young clients is dealing with her fourth recurrence of cancer. She is a small woman and usually the nurses use a small needle and there are no problems with chemo. Recently a nurse came in, started to use a large needle, was not sensitive to my client, and began to get upset when she couldn't get the needle inserted. My client, who is very deeply connected and on a spiritual path said, "My body spoke to me and said. I'm not letting her in." She told her body to relax and open her veins. But her body said "No, I'm not doing it." She said it was the first time she had actually heard her body speak in that way. A skillful and compassionate nurse came in, used the right needle, and the chemo went in.

Skills of Compassion: Alleviation and Prevention

Gilbert and Choden use mindfulness meditation practices to develop the attributes they associate with compassion. This is similar to Halifax's recommendation that contemplative practices strengthen the mind, allow for greater focus and discernment, and increase tolerance for distress (Halifax, 2008). Becoming mindfully aware allows for a familiarization with the workings of the mind, which then assists us to cultivate specific qualities and potential that form the basis for compassion training. In other words, there is insight based on observation that leads to a wise discernment of what to do. Pictured as a small circle placed inside a larger circle, the inner circle represents the tuning into suffering so that we can understand it and tolerate it, while the larger circle in which it is embedded focuses on what to do about it, namely using our developed skills for responding in the best way possible to alleviate suffering. In the Buddhist tradition, there is talk about skillful means, which is learning to competently relate to suffering once we have become aware of it (Gilbert, 2009, Gilbert & Choden, 2014). See Figure 22.1 for a comparison of Gilbert's Compassion-Focused Therapy with Halifax's ABIDE model of compassion.

Compassionate Responses to Structural Stresses

Individual Interventions

Gilbert and Choden's book (2014) provides step-by-step meditation practices for quieting the unsettled mind, working with attention and focus, grounding and body awareness, enhancing acceptance, building compassionate capacity, and cultivating compassion within ourselves. The emphasis is upon recognizing that what we focus on has a significant impact upon how we are and what we feel, which in turn, highlights the need to train our ability to focus our attention more specifically and consciously. It is their belief that

> In learning how to choose what to cultivate we can focus on our innate caregiving motives so that they flourish and become a guiding force for the kind of mind we wish to have and the self we wish to become.
>
> (Gilbert & Choden, 2014, p. 301)

More information about this training can be found at www.compassionatemind.co.uk.

Physicians who engage in self-care and have some form of contemplative practice are more empathic (Shanafelt et al., 2005), and less prone to burnout and compassion fatigue (Huggard, Stamm, & Pearlman, 2013; Kearney et al., 2009). In a study of proactive practices in experienced trauma therapists (Harrison & Westwood, 2009) one theme stood out—*exquisite empathy*. Unlike previous studies, these researchers found that empathic engagement with traumatized clients appeared to be a protective practice for clinicians working with these clients. Exquisite empathy

	Compassion-Focused Therapy (Gilbert)	**ABIDE model of Compassion** (Halifax)
Compassion is...	Behavior that aims to nurture, look after, teach, guide, mentor, soothe, protect, and offer feelings of acceptance and belonging in order to benefit another person; is rooted in the caring system and is a form of social mentality, arising from signals in the outside world that trigger motivational states, communication, and social behavior.	An emergent process that arises out of the interaction of interdependent attentional, affective, cognitive, and somatic processes. Involves recognizing suffering, understanding the nature of suffering, and having a desire to alleviate suffering.
Cognitive	a. Attention/Sensitivity to Suffering and the Causes of Suffering b. Reasoning, Wisdom, Insight	a. Attention/Metacognition related to the Presence and Nature of Suffering b. Intention, Insight, Discernment
Affective	a. Empathy/Sympathy/Sensitivity b. Distress Tolerance	a. Emotional Attunement b. Affective Balance
Behavioral	Motivation to care for Well-Being of Self/Others	Ethical Engagement and Embodiment
Social	Sensitivity and Nonjudgment	Interoceptivity and Prosociality
Training	Compassionate mind training, which teaches the skills and attributes of compassion.	Contemplative practices that cultivate the elements of compassion.

Figure 22.1 Comparison of the CFT and ABIDE Models of Compassion

required a sophisticated balance on the part of the clinician as s/he simultaneously maintains clear and consistent boundaries, expanded perspective, and maintains a highly present, intimate, and heartfelt interpersonal connection in the therapeutic relationship with clients without fusing or losing sight of the clinician's own perspective.

(Harrison & Westwood, 2009, p. 214)

Trauma therapists who engaged in exquisite empathy were "invigorated rather than depleted by their intimate professional connections with traumatized clients" (Harrison & Westwood, 2009, p. 213) and protected against compassion fatigue and burnout. The idea that trauma therapists can be both invigorated and protected in their work has also been referred to as bi-directionality (Kearney et al., 2009). Youngson (2013) makes a similar observation when he notes that he came to understand that care and compassion are a two-way street. The practice of exquisite empathy is facilitated by clinician self-awareness (Kearney et al., 2009; Vachon et al., 2015), which can be cultivated through contemplative practices.

Group Interventions

Gilbert and Choden's approach is congruent with Halifax's ABIDE model (Halifax 2012, 2013a). The ABIDE model grew out of Halifax's earlier work with the Being with Dying Program

(BWD; Halifax, 2008, 2013b). The BWD program is an eight-day residential program for health care professionals who work in end of life care contexts. Through the training, emphasis is placed upon the ethical, spiritual, existential, and social aspects of palliative care. In conjunction with the training, various contemplative practices are incorporated for clinicians to learn how to regulate attention and emotion and develop a meta-cognitive perspective on the suffering of their patients as well as themselves. The training also integrates research in neuroscience as it relates to the clinical, contemplative, and conceptual content of the training (Halifax, 2013b).

The premise of the Being with Dying Program, based on the development of mindfulness and receptive attention through contemplative practice, is that cultivating stability of mind and emotions enables clinicians to respond to their environment, others, and themselves with compassion (Halifax, 2008). The program provides skills, reflection on attitudes and behaviors, in addition to tools that change how caregivers work with the dying and bereaved. Halifax's skill training in compassionate responses is described in the GRACE. model that she and her colleagues developed to prime compassion in clinicians for compassion-based clinician–patient interactions. The acronym GRACE. stands for:

G—Gather your attention.
R—Recall your intention.
A—Attune by checking in with yourself, then the patient.
C—Consider what will really serve by being truly present in the moment.
E—Engage, enact ethically, and then end the interaction.

The program was developed to help prevent burnout and secondary trauma in caregivers including doctors, nurses, human rights activists, and others working in stressful situations. The practice offers a simple and efficient way to open to the experience of the suffering of others, to stay centered in the midst of difficult situations and environmental stresses, and to develop the capacity to respond with compassion (Halifax, 2013b, 2014).

Organizational Interventions

Interventions to teach compassion can start at the individual or organizational levels. Obviously, it would be helpful for organizations to be committed to being compassionate places of work and care, and (albeit slowly) progress is occurring in several areas. Early work in organizational intervention was done by Cohen-Katz, Wiley, Capuano, Baker, & Shapiro (2004), who conducted an eight-week Mindfulness-Based Stress Reduction (MBSR) program for nurses within a hospital-based system. Work had already been done to improve employee satisfaction and retention; a nursing advisory council had been set up; there was work to enhance the model of self-governance and increased opportunity for education and professional development. Mindfulness is defined as being fully present to one's experience without judgment or resistance. Its emphasis on self-care, compassion, and healing makes it relevant as an intervention for nurses. The results of the study showed that the treatment group's scores on the Maslach Burnout Inventory decreased significantly, and these changes were still evident three months later.

As mentioned earlier, Robin Youngson, an anesthesiologist, was compelled to re-humanize health care after an experience with his 18-year-old daughter, who was hospitalized after a serious injury in a car crash. As he tried to understand how health care services and practitioners could neglect the basic human needs of patients, he came to understand how professionals also experienced a lack of compassion from the systems in which they work. He developed a model that emphasizes the integration of three important elements in the re-humanization of health care:

1. the development of inner resources, such as empathy and nonjudgment;
2. strategies to strengthen our sense of human togetherness;
3. the creation of a sense of place where people find a renewed sense of shared identity and purpose.

(Youngson, 2011; www.compassioninhealthcare.org)

Very important, systematic research is being carried out in Quebec by Lise Fillion and her colleagues working with meaning-centered interventions combined with mindfulness meditation in palliative care and intensive care units. Based in part on the Being with Dying Program (Halifax, 2008, 2013b, 2014), these researchers note that their goal is to improve the conditions in which palliative care is provided, including end of life care in the intensive care units (Fillion et al. 2013). They seek to validate a conceptual framework to better understand work satisfaction and the well-being of nurses in the palliative care field. They will then be able to offer decision makers at the systemic level a choice of models to be considered before implementing training or service programs for caregivers and managers (Fillion et al., 2013; note that this research report is in French but an English translation is given).

Accelerated Recovery Program for Compassion Fatigue

The Accelerated Recovery Program (ARP) for Compassion Fatigue was established in 1997 as "a five-session individual treatment model for treating professional care providers who had become overwhelmed by the demands of their work" (Baranowsky & Schmidt, 2013, p. 211). In the ARP, self-reflective and self-care skills are taught to establish a non-anxious presence and to reinforce self-validated caregiving. The emphasis is upon learning how to sit comfortably and remain fully present with compassionate intention when working with patients who are in distress. This model may involve a paradigm shift for physicians from the focus on treatment and cure of disease to learning how to maintain presence with their patients as they treat them. In this context, the emphasis on the healer paradigm replaces the technical focus on the physician as the curer of disease. Physicians learn that being non-anxious and fully present can be healing in and of itself to a patient possibly facing the most terrifying time in his or her life. Through this practice, physicians may also learn a more spiritual lesson: that healing and being successful as a healer do not necessarily entail the cure of disease.

Implications. It is important to accurately understand what compassion actually is and its necessity in the contexts of care delivery. The stereotypical image of compassion is of someone who is loving, kind, and accepting; however, that image often doesn't include the underlying strength and discernment that is required in order to sustain compassion in everyday life situations. Halifax states that in order to meet the world, one needs a *strong back and a soft belly*:

> All too often our so-called strength comes from fear, not love; instead of having a strong back, many of us have a defended front shielding a weak spine. In other words, we walk around brittle and defensive, trying to conceal our lack of confidence. If we strengthen our backs, metaphorically speaking, and develop a spine that's flexible but sturdy, then we can risk having a front that's soft and open, representing choiceless compassion. The place in your body where these two meet—strong back and soft front—is the brave, tender ground in which to root our caring deeply when we begin the process of being with dying. How can we give and accept care with strong-back, soft front compassion, moving past fear into a place of genuine tenderness? I believe it comes about when we can be truly transparent, seeing the world clearly—and letting the world see into us.

(Halifax, 2008, pp. 17–18)

Compassion is not a passive state; rather, it is an active and fluid response that occurs when all of its constituent attributes are nurtured. In any given situation, there are a multitude of possible responses. Compassionate responses may involve social activism and engagement to change an unjust law or oppressive political policy. The discernment and balance that comes from contemplative practice may invoke a self-compassionate response to leave a work environment that is potentially harmful to self and others and unamenable to change. The individual who has cultivated the attributes of compassion will be positioned to respond to injustice, marginalization, and disenfranchisement with loving kindness, understanding, and wisdom. Indeed, compassion is a necessary professional competence that can be cultivated through the training and fostering of its constituent elements so that those who deliver care can remain true to their deepest intentions to relieve suffering without fatigue, burnout, or depletion.

Rushton (2013) describes the concept of *principled moral outrage*, where violations of one's values, ethics, and conscience in work place situations can be handled from a compassionate stance, with the choice regarding how to act based in a grounded, clear appraisal of the situation. Possible responses may include:

(1) finding a compromise that preserves integrity particularly when there is factual confusion, uncertainty, conceptual ambiguity, and moral complexity; (2) raising a conscientious voice to bring awareness to or criticize a practice or violation of an ethical standard; (3) refusing to participate on the basis of conscience violations; (4) responsible whistleblowing arising from clarity, nonreaction, and ethical resolve rather than anger and retaliation; and (5) conscientious exiting from institutions or situations where efforts to address isolated or repeated instances that result in moral outrage are unaddressed, unresolved, or continue to compromise integrity.

(p. 85)

The key point here is that cultivating a compassionate stance opens up many possibilities for responding to violations of conscience and injustice that allow for the preservation of one's intention, caring capacity, and integrity.

Summary

This is a very poignant time in the field of teaching compassion. The models of compassion developed by Halifax and Gilbert presented in this chapter draw on the latest in neuroscience and clinical research. Halifax's ABIDE model consists of three interdependent experiential areas that can be taught and that prime compassion: attentional and affective balance; the cognitive domain relating to the cultivation of intention and insight; and embodied and engaged responses to the presence of suffering that and foster ethical grounding and equanimity. This model was compared with the Compassion-Focused Therapy developed by Gilbert (2013a; Gilbert & Choden, 2014). All of these authors describe the attributes of compassion and offer insights regarding the contemplative practices that can be used to cultivate compassionate responses.

Drawing upon the current findings in neuroscience, Fillion and her colleagues demonstrated that meditation and skills training can enhance resilience and expand compassion directed towards the self and others. Some of these findings demonstrate that compassion can activate parts of the brain associated with love and reward; whereas empathy, particularly if there is empathic strain, can lead to feelings of exhaustion and burnout (Singer & Bolz, 2013). The free downloadable electronic book by Singer and Bolz (2013) www.compassion-training.org is an incredible resource that explores a variety of ways in which neuroscience and mindfulness meditation can be integrated into personal and organizational settings to improve health and resilience, and to eventually make the world a better and kinder place.

Conclusion

This chapter provides an ending to a book that describes many situations where people are hindered in their ability to access, receive, and provide appropriate care due to social policies, issues, racism, discrimination, and other forms of injustice. We offer this chapter on the topic of the cultivation of compassion because our view is that a compassionate stance provides us with choices in the face of situations of injustice and pain, either as a patient/client/family member or as a professional/clinician. We all share our interconnectedness and our suffering, even as it occurs in many different forms. The choice to cultivate compassion provides us with the ability to recognize suffering, act to relieve that suffering, and accept when the suffering can't be relieved.

It is easy to feel overwhelmed by the many systemic factors that can cause additional suffering to those who receive care and also those who provide that care. It is easy for us to feel the huge wave wash over us and to get mired down in how wet we got rather than looking at the way the waves move and how these waves form a part of the entire ocean. We need the insight, discernment, equanimity, and engagement that are cultivated within a compassionate stance in order to choose how to respond to suffering (our own included). In many ways, we see the cultivation of compassion as an "inoculation" against burnout and fatigue. We can talk and write about all those who are wounded by the situations in which they reside and feel the heavy burden and powerlessness that can accompany this awareness; however, we can also choose to look at situations in an expansive way that allows us to see the "bigger picture" and then to consciously choose our responses as those who wish to relieve suffering whenever it is possible to the extent that is possible. A compassionate response may include bearing witness silently and with an open heart. It also might include advocating for people who are unable to do so for themselves, deciding that we need to stay to offer a contribution to an environment, or leave a certain situation because the suffering it is causing to either ourselves or those in our care is untenable. We may find ways to increase awareness of an unjust situation through various means. There are a myriad number of other responses that might be possible from this particular stance; what is important is that the stance allows us the balance and equanimity to respond in a way that honors our deepest intentions rather than leaving us open to empathic distress.

By cultivating a compassionate stance through the various means described in this chapter, caregivers can accurately recognize the sources of suffering at multiple levels and choose how to respond to that suffering based upon their insight and awareness. Rather than dwelling on how powerless and helpless we are in the face of a large materialistically driven system, we begin to see all the forces that are in play, recognizing the inevitability of suffering even as we are determined to relieve it. The freedom to choose our response and to stay true to our intention releases us to make conscious choices as to how we respond to injustice and suffering. In essence, compassion provides us with a very liberating capacity to recognize and respond to injustice and the suffering that results from unjust practices.

Key Terms

Discernment—exercising wisdom and good judgment in situations—is seen as a result of cultivating insight and following one's intention.

Embodiment—the felt sense of another's suffering through the experience of inter-subjective resonance, wherein another's experience feels as if it is happening in the subject's own body.

Equanimity—a process of stability or mental balance that is characterized by mental composure and an acceptance of the present moment.

Exquisite empathy—a sophisticated balance by a clinician who maintains clear and consistent boundaries, expanded perspective, and a highly present, intimate, and heartfelt interpersonal connection in the therapeutic relationship with clients without fusing, over-identifying, or losing sight of his/her own and the client's perspective.

Non-referential/unbiased compassion—compassion that is objectless and pervasive; a stance or intention in regards to compassion; also called universal compassion.

Referential/biased compassion—compassion directed toward specific, identified person, place, or thing.

Questions for Reflection

1. Respond to the statement "Competence remains the first act of compassion." What does this mean to you?
2. The authors of this chapter acknowledge that "compassion was the common thread that gave us the capacity to be open to the suffering of ourselves and others in a way that allowed for healing to occur" (p. 268). What is your experience of compassion? What do you consider to be its defining qualities and common effects?
3. Key to the concept of compassion is that if one is to practice compassion for others, one must first start with self-compassion. Reflect on your practice of self-compassion. Do you tend to include yourself when considering the expression of compassion?
4. How do you respond to the suggestion that embodiment—actually feeling another's suffering in your own body through the experience of inter-subjective resonance—forms the fundamental base for an engaged compassionate response?
5. The case is made that empathy may be misunderstood as compassion. How have you traditionally differentiated these terms? How do you understand them following your reading of this chapter?
6. Reflect on Halifax's suggestion that: "in order to meet the world, one needs a strong back at a soft belly." How does this match or challenge the stereotypical image of compassion?

References

Baranowsky, A., & Schmidt, D. (2013). Overcopers: medical doctor vulnerability to compassion fatigue. In C. R., Figley, P. K. Huggard, & C. Rees (Eds.), *First do no self-harm* (pp. 203–215). New York, NY: Oxford.

Cohen-Katz J., Wiley S. D., Capuano T., Baker D., & Shapiro S. (2004). The effects of mindfulness-based stress reduction on nurse stress and burnout: A quantitative and qualitative study. *Holistic Nurse Practitioner, 18*(6), 302–308.

Corn, B. W., Vachon, M. L. S., & Chochinov, H. M. (Eds.). (2012). Psychosocial care inpatients with metastatic cancers. *Current Opinion in Supportive and Palliative Care, 2*(6), 226–227.

Fillion, L., Truchon, M., L'Heureux, M., Dallaire, C., Langlois, L., Bellemare, M., & Dupuis, R. (2013) *To improve services and care at the end of life: Understanding the impact of workplace satisfaction and well-being of nurses.* Rapport R-794, Montreal, IRSST. Retrieved November 5, 2015 from www.irsst.qc.ca/-projet-vers-l-amelioration-des-services-et-des-soins-de-fin-de-vie-mieux-comprendre-l-impact-du-milieu-de-travail-sur-la-satisfaction-et-le-bien-etre-des-0099–6050.html

Fox, M. (1999). *Sins of the spirit, blessings of the flesh: Lessons in transforming evil in soul and society.* New York, NY: Three Rivers Press.

Gilbert, P. (2009). *The compassionate mind.* Oakland, CA: New Harbinger Publications.

Gilbert, P. (2010). *Compassion focused therapy.* London: Routledge.

Gilbert, P. (2013a). The flow of life: An evolutionary model of compassion. In T. Singer & M. Bolz (Eds.), *Compassion: Bridging practice and science ebook* (pp. 126–149). Munich, Germany: Max Planck Society.

Gilbert, P. (2013b). Compassion-focused therapy working with arising fears and resistances. In T. Singer & M. Bolz (Eds.), *Compassion: Bridging practice and science ebook* (pp. 66–80). Munich, Germany: Max Planck Society.

Gilbert, P., & Choden. (2014). *Mindful compassion.* Oakland, CA: New Harbinger Publications.

Gonzalez, M. (2012). Mindful leadership: *The 9 ways to self-awareness, transforming yourself, and inspiring others.* San Francisco, CA: Jossey-Bass.

Halifax J. (2008). *Being with dying: Cultivating compassion and fearlessness in the presence of death.* Boston, MA: Shambhala.

Halifax, J. (2011). The precious necessity of compassion. *Journal of Pain and Symptom Management, 41*(1), 146–153.

Halifax, J. (2012). A heuristic model of enactive compassion. *Current Opinion in Supportive and Palliative Care*, *2*(6), 228–235.

Halifax, J. (2013a). Understanding and cultivating compassion in clinical settings: The ABIDE compassion model. In T. Singer & M. Bolz (Eds.), *Compassion: Bridging practice and science ebook* (pp. 208–226). Munich, Germany: Max Planck Society.

Halifax, J. (2013b). Being with dying: Experiences in end-of-life-care. In T. Singer & M. Bolz (Eds.), *Compassion: Bridging practice and science ebook* (pp. 108–120). Munich, Germany: Max Planck Society.

Halifax, J. (2014, February 12). *GRACE: Training in cultivating compassion in interactions with others* [Web log post]. Santa Fe, NM: Upaya Zen Center.Retrieved from www.upaya.org/2014/02/practicing-g-r-c-e-bring-compassion-interactions-others-roshi-joan-halifax.

Harrison, R., & Westwood, M. (2009). Preventing vicarious traumatization of mental health therapists: identifying protective practices. *Psychotherapy: Theory, Research, Practice, & Training*, *46*(2), 203–219.

Huggard, P. K., Stamm, B. H., & Pearlman, L. A. (2013). Physician stress: Compassion satisfaction, compassion fatigue and vicarious traumatization. In C. R. Figley, P. K. Huggard, & C. Rees (Eds.), *First do no self-harm*. (pp. 127–145). New York, NY: Oxford University Press.

Kearney, M. K. (1996). *Mortally wounded*. New York, NY: Scribner.

Kearney, M. K., Weininger, R. B., Vachon, M. L. S., Mount, B. M., & Harrison, R. L. (2009). Self-care of physicians caring for patients at the end of life: "Being Connected . . . A Key to My Survival". *Journal of the American Medical Association*, *301*(11), 1155–1164.

Klimecki, O., & Singer, T. (2012). Empathic distress fatigue rather than compassion fatigue? Integrating findings from empathy research in psychology and social neuroscience. In B. Oakley, A. Knafo, G. Madhavan, & D. S. Wilson (Eds.), *Pathological altruism* (pp. 368–383). New York, NY: Oxford.

Klimecki, O., Ricard, M., & Singer, T. (2013) Empathy versus compassion: Lessons from the 1st and 3rd persons. In T. Singer & M. Bolz (Eds.) *Compassion: Bridging Science and Practice* (pp. 272–287). Munich, Germany: Max Planck Institute.

Nouwen, H. (1972). *The wounded healer*. Garden City, NY: Doubleday.

Ricard, M. (2014). Empathy explained. Retrieved June 2, 2014 from www.youtube.com/watch?v=khjPsVG-6QA

Rogers, C. (1957). The necessary and sufficient conditions of therapeutic personality change. *Journal of Consulting Psychology*, *21*(2), 95–103.

Rushton, C. H. (2013). Principled moral outrage: An antidote to moral distress? *AACN Advanced Critical Care*, *24*(1), 82–89.

Schmidt, S. (2004). Mindfulness and healing intention: Concepts, practice, and research evaluation. *The Journal of Alternative and Complementary Medicine*, *10*(S1), S7–S14.

Shanafelt, T. D., West, C., Zhao, X., Novotny, P., Kolars, J., Habermann, T., & Sloan, J. (2005). Relationship between increased personal well-being and enhanced empathy among internal medicine residents. *Journal of General Internal Medicine*, *20*(7), 559–564.

Shanafelt, T. D., Raymond, M., Kosty, M., et al. (2014). Satisfaction with work-life balance and the career and retirement plans of US oncologists. *Journal of Clinical Oncology*, March 10, 2014. doi: 10.1200/JCO.2013.53.4560.

Singer, T., & Bolz, M. (Eds.). (2013). *Compassion: Bridging practice and science ebook*. Munich, Germany: Max Planck Society.

Sulmasy D. P. (1997). *The healer's calling*. New York, NY: Paulist Press.

Vachon, M. L. S. (2001). The nurse's role: The world of palliative care nursing. In B. R. Ferrell & N. Coyle (Eds.), *Textbook of palliative nursing* (pp. 647–662). Oxford: Oxford University Press.

Vachon, M. L. S., Huggard, P. K., & Huggard, J. A. (2015) Reflections on occupational stress in palliative care nursing: Is it changing? In B. Ferrell, N. Coyle, & J. Paice (Eds.), *Oxford textbook of palliative nursing* (4th ed.) (pp. 969–986). New York, NY: Oxford.

Vericitas Botanicals. (2015, July). The Meaning of "Veriditas." Retrieved November 5, 2015 from www.veriditasbotanicals.com/about-us/the-meaning-of-veriditas/

Wilson, J. P., & Lindy J. L. (1994). *Countertransference in the treatment of PTSD*. New York, NY: Guilford.

Youngson, R. (2011). Compassion in healthcare—the missing dimension of healthcare reform. In I. Renzenbrink (Ed.), *Caregiver stress and staff support in illness, dying and bereavement* (pp. 37–48). Oxford: Oxford University Press.

Youngson, R. (2012). *Time to care: How to love your patients and your job*. Raglan, NZ: Rebelheart.

Youngson, R. (2013). Anesthesiology: Personal reflections. In C. R. Figley, P. K. Huggard, & C. Rees (Eds.), *First do no self-harm* (pp. 331–338). New York, NY: Oxford University Press.

Conclusion

Darcy L. Harris and Tashel C. Bordere

In this book, many different issues related to social justice in the contexts of care delivery, disenfranchised groups, and political policy-making have been explored. It is easy to feel discouraged and powerless when the magnitude and impact of social injustice is exposed. In light of the deeply embedded social messages and norms that perpetuate ongoing difficulties for people who are disenfranchised or marginalized in their experiences of death and loss, how can we make a difference? In addition, how can we support those who care for people within workplaces that are driven by materialist-based policies?

There is a story that has been adapted and modified over many years about a boy and a starfish. The modified story goes that a boy and an older man were walking together on the beach. Thousands of starfish had washed up on the shore. As the boy walked, he paused every so often and bent down to pick up a starfish to throw it back into the ocean. When the man asked what he was doing, the boy paused, looked up, and replied, "Throwing starfish into the ocean. The tide has washed them up onto the beach and they can't return to the sea by themselves. When the sun gets high, they will die unless I throw them back into the water." To that, the man replied, "But there must be thousands of starfish on this beach. I'm afraid you won't really be able to make much of a difference." The boy bent down, picked up yet another starfish and threw it as far as he could into the ocean. Then he turned, smiled, and said, "It made a difference to that one" (Eiseley, 1978). And so we look to do what we can, where we can, and when we can. In the last section of the book, several recommendations were made that will be briefly reiterated here.

Cultivate Awareness

A recurring theme throughout this book has been the importance of being able to recognize when oppressive or socially unjust practices are occurring. Sometimes, these practices are so ubiquitous and commonplace that we don't even notice them because of their familiarity or due to our privileged position. Consider the telling of a joke in your presence that denigrates a specific group or individual. Stop and consider the implications of laughing at such a joke and the impact of that joke and its underlying message to the person(s) who may be the brunt of that joke. As stated in the introduction, becoming aware of power, privilege, internalized social messages, and the way that our formative years have shaped our attitudes, beliefs, and responses to those around us is not optional if you desire to integrate just and empowering practices into your interactions. Another aspect of awareness is the development of the ability to choose how to respond to situations rather than to react from a place of conditioned and unconscious reactivity.

Recognize Your Role in Oppressive Practices and Historical Oppression

While you may have the highest and best intentions, your position at work or your racial and ethnic identity may trigger reminders of oppressive practices perpetuated by others who are similar to you in some way. Be aware that you can't control others' perceptions. You may never have intentionally acted in a way that is oppressive or controlling, but you still may represent these things to those who have experienced such treatment by others who are perceived as similar to you. Be respectful of these times. Remind yourself of your good intentions to respect others. Be aware of privilege and of ways to form alliances, and choose compassion over reactionary confrontation. With time, your desire to serve will hopefully become apparent. However, if that does not happen, don't let your inability to change the past interfere with your intention to serve and respect those in your proximity in the here and now.

Further, while not being able to change the past, it is important to remain cognizant that oppressive forces of the past continue to have implications for individuals and groups today. That is, various groups continue to benefit, consciously or unconsciously, at the expense of others due to historical discrimination. It is of paramount importance to recognize ways in which we all move through cycles of privilege and oppression in our daily lives based on our social locations, and to understand how social position has an impact upon our interactions and service to others.

Acknowledge the Significance of Rituals, Symbols, and Healing Spaces

It is important to recognize that we are meaning-seeking and meaning-making creatures. While some rituals and symbols can signify oppression and brutality (for example, the Confederate flag in the United States), the same can be said for rituals, symbols, and healing spaces that liberate by openly identifying oppression, bearing witness to injustice and its effects, unifying and creating solidarity among those who have endured cruelty and atrocious acts, and validating the ability of the human spirit to overcome these obstacles—often at a significant price for those who initially stood up against oppression and injustice. Learn to recognize the importance of telling one's story and the need to find meaning in the face of senseless and inhumane treatment. The ability to make meaning allows for the re-assertion of the voice that has been silenced by unjust practices. It is likewise important to recognize that some may be unable or unwilling to derive meaning from death or non-death loss experiences perceived as unjust. In either case, bearing witness with your full presence can be enfranchising and empowering.

Think Critically About Power, Privilege, and the Social Underpinnings of Individual Experiences

It is important to begin to see everyday events through a critical lens that recognizes the presence and impact of social messages, overtones, and expectations that affect attitudes, beliefs, actions, and policies. Consider the messages in your work place, your social world, your personal choices, and think about how these messages reflect compliance with established social norms and expectations. Be aware of how social biases towards certain people, relationships, groups, and systems affect you and the people in your world, both personally and professionally. When you are confronted with a situation that causes you to feel uncomfortable, stop and consider why you are uncomfortable and allow yourself the time and space to thoughtfully look below the surface to the social and structural issues that are in play at that time. Find trusted colleagues and friends to engage in dialog around issues of concern.

Develop Ways to Engage in Reflective Practice

Whether you engage in regular discussions with colleagues or you use a personal journal to reflect upon events in your work, provide yourself with regular time each day to consider the impact of social messages on your ability to follow through with your intentions in your work and other contexts. Take time to think about your deepest and best intention in your work and in your life. What are the things that interfere with your ability to follow through with that intention? What are the things that nurture your ability to express your best intention? Reading about how others engage in reflective practice may assist you with ways to incorporate reflective practice and meaningful contemplation (versus rumination) into your daily world.

Nurture the Various Elements of Compassion in Your Life

Only you will know how to best respond to situations of unjust practice and oppression after you have:

- taken the time to learn how to focus your attention;
- learned how to regulate your emotional reactions;
- adopted a perspective that incorporates the "bigger view" of a situation;
- clearly delineated your intentions;
- discerned what is needed in a given situation.

Some may feel the impetus to engage in some form of activism or advocacy to initiate social change. Others may become better informed voters so that they choose policymakers who may have a better understanding of issues related to care, service, and compassionate practice. Finally, those who quietly listen with full and open attention are not passive bystanders; they may be giving what is truly needed and will serve best in a given moment as well. In order to know how to best serve in situations of suffering, it is important to have the ability to respond with awareness, insight, and intention. Contemplative practices help us to cultivate these key elements of compassionate response.

    The suffering of others through social injustice and oppressive practices hurts us all. The gifts we bring need to be offered not from a place of pity, but from the deep recognition that none of us escapes this world without pain. We can each work to relieve the suffering that occurs through social injustice and we can offer our presence to others in ways that can be incredibly healing. It is our hope that this book will provide readers with the opportunity to arrive at a deeper awareness and understanding of these concepts. Both of us were surprised to find that on many occasions when we shared that we were working on a book exploring the principles of social justice in the context of loss and grief, we were often told that people didn't see the relationship between these topics. Dying, death, grief, and loss all occur within social contexts and social norms that can affirm or invalidate these experiences and their significance in our lives. With the rich descriptions that are delineated in each of the chapters within this volume, we hope that we have opened this dialog, highlighted implications for practice, and increased awareness of the importance of promoting social justice in these common human experiences.

Reference

Eiseley, L. (1978). *The star thrower*. New York, NY: Houghton Mifflin.

Index

6/4 Museum, Hong Kong 216
9/11 disaster 213–219

ABIDE Model of Enactive Principled Compassion 268–270, 274–276, 278
aboriginal title 88–90
absolute wealth 34, 38
abuse: "care for the caregiver" 256; critical social work 232; First Nations People, Canada 90–93; iatrogenic harm 126; older women prison inmates 140, 147–148; rituals in unjust loss 205
academic role navigation 242–245
Accelerated Recovery Program (ARP) 277–278
"acceptable" death 168–169
access aspects: dying with dignity 36; global perspectives 36; infant mortality 50–51
accountability 80
activist role navigation 241–243, 245–247
addressing caregiver issues 256–259
admission delays 55
advocacy: critical social work 229–230, 233, 236; museums as healing spaces 217–219, 222; social expectations: bereavement 172; social institution navigation 240–250
affectual balance 269
"affluenza" 42, 44–46, 48
African Australians 230–235
African infant mortality 51, 54
age group studies 157–158
Aggarwal, Ghauri 254
aging populations: end of life care 100–108; older women prison inmates 138–153
AIDS Memorial Quilt 208
alleviation 40–41, 45, 272, 274
alliances 12, 233
allopathic medicine 22–23, 27–29
ally/advocate policies 240–250

alternative medicine 22–23, 27–29
Amnesty International 93–94
anthropology of mourning 205–210
anti-anxiety drugs 117
anti-death penalty organizations 241–243, 245–247
antidepressants 117
anxiety 117, 158
AON Corporation 216
apostasy 192–193, 200
applied behavior analysis 155
ARP see Accelerated Recovery Program
assimilation 85, 87, 90, 96–97
assumptive worlds 24, 29
atomism 43–44, 48, 195–196, 200
attention, compassion 269, 276
Auditor General of Canada, 2008 92
Australia 226–235, 254
autism 162
awareness 257–258, 262, 282–283
awe 197

Barry, B. 44–45, 197–198
bearing witness 214–216
Beaucage, John 93
Becker, Howard 247
bedside visits 145
behavioral influences 50–52
Being with Dying Program (BWD) 275–276
Bell, L. A. 9–10
bereavement: critical social work 225–236; exclusion 112; infant mortality 50–63; social expectations 165–175; therapy 159
biased compassion 268, 280
bicycle fatalities 202, 207
"biographical disruption" 198
Bradford (UK), infant mortality 53, 60
Brecht, Bertolt 36

285

Index

bridging: death row prisoners 241–247; infant mortality 52–53, 60–61
British Columbia 88–90, 94
British-Vietnamese populations 180–186
broad viewpoints, grief & loss 21–30
Buddhism 191, 266–267, 270, 273–274
bullying 182
burnout: "care for the caregiver" 257; compassion 274, 276–278; iatrogenic harm 132, 136
BWD *see* Being with Dying Program

CALM *see* Communicating About Loss and Mourning
Canada: "care for the caregiver" 254; First Nations Peoples' 85–99
Cancian, F. M. 245
capitalism 40–48, 169–170, 227
"care for the caregiver" 251–264
care choices 22–23, 27–29
care delivery/provision: cultural mistrust 75–82; dignity protection 101–107; end of life care 75–82, 101–107; global perspectives 33–38; iatrogenic harm 125–137; materialist world 40–48; objectification 125, 129–136
caregivers: "care for the caregiver" 251–264; resilience 265
Care Quality Commission 102
Caribbean mothers 51
Carstairs, Sharon 261
case studies: conceptualizations in grief and loss 16–17; critical social work 230–235; developmental disabilities 154–155, 157, 160–161; end of life care 75–76; iatrogenic harm 127–133; infant mortality 53–61; older women prison inmates 140–142; same-sex unions 179–186; social expectations: bereavement 165; socially sensitive experiences 179–186
Cauce, A. M 10–11
censorship 216
"center" benefit 10–11
ceremonies 86–87, 95–96, 202–212, 214, 216–217, 283
CFT *see* Compassion-Focused Therapy
challenge boxes methods 184
children: child care issues 25–26, 126; critical social work 230–235; First Nations People, Canada 90–93, 96; infant mortality 50–61
China 100–101, 216, 218
Choden's mindful compassion 268–276, 278
Christianity 90–93, 96, 191–193, 266–267, 273
church run schools 90–93, 96
class 21–22, 24–29
client-centered reminders 186–187
clinical implications, social expectations: bereavement 171–173
clinician role navigation 244–247
closure 219

coed grief support groups 183–185
cognitive life rafts 182–183
"cognitive understanding" 156
collaboration 233
collaging 181–182, 187, 209
colonial practices 85–99
Communicating About Loss and Mourning (CALM) 162
communication: "care for the caregiver" 259; developmental disabilities 162; palliative care: iatrogenic harm 135
community networks: cultural mistrust 81–82; dignity protection 105; end of life care 81–82, 105; infant mortality 51–53, 56–57, 60–61; medicalizing grief 121
comorbidity surveys 118
"companioning grief" 184
compassion: ABIDE Model 268–270, 274–276, 278; attributes 265, 268–274; "care for the caregiver" 252–253, 257, 260, 262; definitions 40–41; dignity protection 104–105; empathy 272–275; end of life care 104–105; group interventions 275–276; images 265–268; individual responses 265, 274–275; liberating capacity 265–281; materialism 40–49; nature of 265; nurturing 284; organizational factors 276–277; palliative care 104–105; problems with 43; responses to 268–279; self-care strategies 274–275; structural influences 265, 274–278
"compassion fatigue": Accelerated Recovery Program 277–278; "care for the caregiver" 252, 262; liberating capacity 272; materialism 43, 48
Compassion-Focused Therapy (C.F.T.) 268, 271, 275, 278
competence, cultural humility 67–74
competition, social expectations 169–170
complementary therapy 22–23
complicated grief 112–114, 116–119
comprehension assessments 156
computers, healing through rituals & memorials 208–209
conceptualizing grief and loss 9–20
concerns collage creation 181–182, 187
confidence, end of life care cultural mistrust 75–82
conformity 169
connectedness 196–197, 217–219
consciousness 25–29, 40–48, 78–79
consequence aspects 214, 247–249
conspicuous consumption 43–44, 46, 48
consumerism 34, 43–48, 169–170
contextual factors 125–137, 253–255
"continuing bonds" 206–207, 210
control losses 138
Conway, E. M. 36
coroner's cases 16–17

Index

correctional institutions 138–153
counseling 22, 58, 116–117
counter-hegemonic processes 203, 208, 210
critical analysis 166–169
critical consciousness 25–29
critical reflexivity 230
critical social work in action 225–239
critical thinking 21–30, 259, 283
Crown, First Nations People, Canada 88–89
cultural competence 67–74
cultural domination 231, 236
cultural humility 67–74
culturally conscientious practices 16–18, 78–79
cultural memories 221–222
cultural mistrust 75–84
culture: broad views 21, 24, 28; "care for the caregiver" 251–252, 254, 258–260, 262; conceptualizations 10, 18; First Nations People, Canada 85–97; spirituality & social justice 192–193
culture blind 229, 236
curators 220
cyclist fatalities 202, 207

Dalai Lama 192
dams 89
dance 86–87
daycare services 105
death: broad views 21–23, 29; conceptualizations 9–10, 13–17; critical social work 225–236; developmental disabilities 154–163; global perspectives 33–39; healing through rituals & memorials 202–212; infant mortality 50–61; older women prison inmates 141–143
"death chambers" 241, 246
death rituals 95–96
death row 240–249
"death surround" 158, 160–161, 163
death warrants 241
Deaton-Owens, D. 148
deep feeling 40, 45–46, 48
dehumanization 86, 96–97, 245
Delaware's death row 240–249
delayed grief 146, 149
democracy 36
Democratic Republic of the Congo 205–206
depersonalization 139, 149
depression 112–122
deprivation, infant mortality 50–52, 60
detachment maintenance 248
developmental disabilities 154–164
diagnosis and grief 171
Diagnostic and Statistical Manual (DSM) of Mental Disorders 112, 171
dignity: global perspectives in death 35–36; museums as healing spaces 214–215; protection: end of life care 100–108

dimensions, spirituality 196–197
direction, spirituality 196
direct-service providers 186–187
disadvantage, privilege and power 11
discernment 269, 279
Discipline and Punish (1977) 118
discourses, critical social work 229, 231–232, 234
discrimination: broad views 21–24, 28–29; conceptualizations 14; end of life care 75–82; infant mortality 50–61; spirituality 192–196, 199
disenfranchised grief: conceptualizations 14–15, 18; death row prisoners 248; healing through rituals & memorials 205, 208; older women prison inmates 143, 149
disenfranchised populations 154–164
diversity: conceptualizations 9–10; critical social work 227; grief and loss 9–10; spirituality & social justice 191, 194–196
divorce 180
"doctors' notes" 167
domination 231, 236
"double-bind" 11, 18
double-consciousness 12
DSM *see* Diagnostic and Statistical Manual
DuBois, *Souls of Black Folk* 12
dying conditions, global perspectives 33–38

Economic and Social Research Council (ESRC) 53
education: developmental disabilities 160–163; end of life care 77, 80; First Nations People, Canada 90–93; museums as healing spaces 219
elective systems 86–88
embodiment, compassion 270, 279
emotion valuation aspects 22, 26–27, 138–153
empathy 217–219, 272–275, 279
empowerment 28–29, 166, 173
enactive principled compassion 268–270, 274–276, 278
Enbridge pipeline 89
end of life care: "care for the caregiver" 253–255, 260–261; cultural mistrust 75–84; dignity protection 100–108; trust-building strategies 75–84
End of Life Nursing Education Consortium (ENLEC) 254
energy consumption 34
engagement 270, 276, 284
ENLEC *see* End of Life Nursing Education Consortium
entropy aspects 36–37
environmental losses 138–149
equality 191–200; *see also* inequality
equanimity 270, 279
ESRC *see* Economic and Social Research Council

287

Index

ethnicity 50–61, 179, 230–235
exclusion, infant mortality 50–63
execution sentences 240–249
existentialist thought 195, 198
exquisite empathy 274–275, 279
externalizing, death row prisoners 246–247, 249

faith communities 191–201; *see also* religion
families: death row prisoners 240–249; infant mortality 50–63; older women prison inmates 138, 140–143; rights 16–17
fear 158
feelings 231–232
felt thoughtfulness 232, 236
feminist therapy 21
Fillion, Lise 277–278
finances 145
First Nations People, Canada 85–99
Five A's of Culturally Conscientious Care 78–79
follow up care 131–133
Fook, Janis 226–231, 233
Foucault, M. 118
Fox, Mathew 266
France 100
freedom 35, 138, 141
friendships 139–146, 180
Furedi, F. 195–196
furlough policy decisions 145

Gandhi, Mahatma 191
gender: broad views 21–22, 24, 28–29; social expectations: bereavement 166; spirituality & social justice 192, 194
gender blind 229, 236
genetics 52, 56
George, Erin 141–143
ghost bikes 202, 207
Gilbert, Paul 270–276, 278
global health perspectives/state 33–39
global identification 179, 182
globalized world inequities 33–39
global perspectives in death 33–39
Goebel, B. L. 156–158
governance: First Nations People, Canada 87–88; older women prison inmates 138, 141–142; social expectations: bereavement 170
governments: "care for the caregiver" 251–252, 255, 259–262; censorship 216; First Nations People, Canada 85–97
GRACE model 276
Greer, K. 144
grief: broad viewpoints 21–30; conceptualizations 9–20; critical social work 225–236; cultural competence/humility 67–73; death row prisoners 240–249; developmental disabilities 154–164; First Nations People, Canada 85–99; healing through rituals & memorials 202–212; medicalization 111–124; older women prison inmates 138–150; pathologization 111–122; social expectations: bereavement 165–175
grief companioning 184
group sessions/work 146, 183–185, 275–276
guilt 11

Halifax, Roshi Joan 258, 268–270, 274–278
hallowed places 215, 216–217
Hames, R. D. 43
Hamilton, J. B. 194–195, 199
Harrison, M. T. 275
healing: losses through rituals & memorials 202–212; museums as healing spaces 213–224; older women prison inmates 147; significance acknowledgement 283
healing, opportunity, peace, and emotion (HOPE) 50, 54–61
health: global perspectives 33–39; inequities 33–39; older women prison inmates 138, 142–143; social/societal determinants 34–35, 38
health care provision: cultural mistrust 75–82; dignity protection 101–107; end of life care 75–82, 101–107; global perspectives 33–38; iatrogenic harm 125–136
helicopter research 81–82
hereditary rule 87–88
hermeneutic approaches 205, 210
hidden oppressions 231
Hinduism 191–193
historical oppression 283
HIV/AIDS pandemic 37
holistic approaches 195, 230–235, 257–259
Holocaust, museums 216, 218
homelessness 197
homophobia 181–188
honor aspects 214, 217
HOPE *see* healing, opportunity, peace, and emotion
hope, spirituality 197
hospice care: broad views 22, 25–26; "care for the caregiver" 252–257, 260–261; end of life care cultural mistrust 75–84; iatrogenic harm 125–137
housemates, loss of 159–160
housing provision 96
human dignity 214–215
humanitarianism 191, 193
humanitarian refugees 230–235
human rights 35–37, 100–108
humility: acquiring 70; concept of 71; cultural competence 67–74; definitions 70; myths/stereotyping 70–71; respect 71–72; making trouble 71–72
husbands, infant mortality 53

iatrogenic harm 125–137
identity: older women prison inmates 138, 141–142; sexual identity 179–190, 192, 194

images, compassion 265–268
immigrant women/populations 50–61
inappropriate advocacy 229–230, 233, 236
income 22, 25–26
India, aging populations 100
Indian Acts from 1868–1951 86
Indian population, Canada 85–99
indigenous peoples 85–99
individual factors: "care for the caregiver" 251–255, 257–259, 262; compassion 265, 274–275; social underpinnings 283
inequality: compassion & materialism 42; conceptualizations 15; infant mortality 50–63; spirituality & social justice 191–200
inequities 33–39
infant mortality 50–63
information valuation 26–27, 172, 215–216
inmates, prisons 138–153
inner grief experiences 203
insight, compassion 269
instructional programs 160–163
instrumental style of grieving 235–236
integrity 75, 77
intellectual disabilities 155–164
intention, compassion 269, 276
interaction practices 67–73, 79–80
internalized homophobia 181–188
Internet 208
"interpersonal economy" 42, 48
interviews 68–69
involvement aspects, infant mortality 55
Islam 191–192
isolation, infant mortality 57–58

James, O. 44–46
journaling 209

Kasser, T. 44
Kaveny, M. C. 132–133
Kellehear, A. 106
Keller, Helen 40
key people losses 93–94
Kinder Morgan Trans Mountain pipeline 89
Knaevelsrud, C. 116
knowledge valuation 26–27, 56–57
The Korean Declaration 103

labels 172
lack of confidence 75–82
lands, loss of 85–86, 88–92, 96–97
language 13, 85, 88, 90–93, 96
"Latina paradox" 52
leadership 47
Leeds (UK), infant mortality 53, 57, 60
legacy honoring 214, 217
lesbian, gay, bisexual, and transgender (LGBT) communities 179–186

liberating capacity, compassion 265–281
life loss reviews 182–183
life rafts 182–183
"linking objects" 207, 217, 222
Lipe-Goodson, P. S. 156–158
listening aspects 50–61, 186
living conditions 33–38
location aspects 81–82
longevity 101
loss: broad viewpoints 21–30; conceptualizations 9–20; critical social work 230–235; First Nations People, Canada 85–99; indigenous peoples 85–99; older women prison inmates 138–150; social expectations: bereavement 165–175; spirituality & social justice 191, 195, 197–200
loss of control 171–173

Maciejewski, P. K. 112
McNeal, C. T. 10–11
MADD see Mothers Against Drunk Driving
Maercker, A 116
magnetic resonance imaging (MRI) measurements 272–273
major depressive disorders 115
male relatives, infant mortality 53
managerial contexts 228, 234–235
marginalization 12–14, 44–45, 50–61, 75–82
marriage 179
Marris, P. 198
Marxism, materialism 42
Maslach Burnout Inventory 276
materialism 40–49
material possessions 138, 140
maternal health 50–61
Maternity Services Liaison Committee (MSLC) 59
meaning making/reconstruction 196, 198, 204–210, 217–219
media portrayals, death row prisoners 240–241, 243
mediated memories 221–222
medicalizing grief 111–124
medical racism 77, 80
medication care choices 22–23, 27–29
memorial feasts 95–96
memorials 202–212, 214, 217
memory preservation 214, 217
"mental age equivalent" scores 156
mental health 44–46, 53
Millennium Development Goals 37
mindful awareness 257–258, 262
mindful compassion 270–278
Mindfulness-Based Stress Reduction (MBSR) 276
minority populations 50–61, 75–82
misery 40–48
missing women 93–94
Missing Women Commission Inquiry (MWCI, 2013) 94
missions, museums 214–215

Index

mistrust 75–84
mixed race 179, 182
monetary resources 37
moral distress 128–136, 265
mortality rates 50–63, 95–96
mortification 139
Moslem communities 191–192
mothers, infant mortality 50–63
Mothers Against Drunk Driving (MADD) 208
motivation: compassion 271, 273–274; medicalizing grief 116–118
mourning practices 118–121, 203, 205–210
MQCI *see* Missing Women Commission Inquiry
MRI *see* magnetic resonance imaging
MSLC *see* Maternity Services Liaison Committee
multi-generational impacts 92, 97
multilayered explorations 251–264
multiple loss suffering 230–235
multiple role compatibility 241–247
murdered women 93–94
"museum frictions" 220, 222
museums as healing spaces 213–224
myths, cultural humility 70–71

NAMES Foundation 208
National Health Services (NHS) 102
National Perinatal Epidemiology Unit 50, 52
National September 11 Memorial Museum 216–217
nationwide foundations 208
Native Women's Association of Canada 93–94
navigating social institutions 240–250
Ndembu, Democratic Republic of the Congo 205–206
neoliberalism 44, 47, 228, 234, 236
neuroscience 271, 278
New York State Museum in Albany, New York 213–219
New Zealand 254, 260
NHS *see* National Health Services
Nietzsche, Friedrich 40
non-referential compassion 268, 272, 280
"normal grief" 112
"Not Gonna be Laid Out to Dry" 75–84
Nouwen, Henri 266
nurturing compassion 284

objectification 125, 129–136
offending, conceptualization 12–13
older women prison inmates 138–153
one-sided conversations 135
openness 72
Open Society Foundation 103
oppression: broad views 22–24, 28–29; critical social work 227, 231; end of life care 75–82; privilege and power 11; role recognition 283; social expectations: bereavement 166–167, 170, 172–173; spirituality 193–197, 199

Oreskes, N. 36
organizational factors 251–252, 256–262, 276–277
outer mourning practices 203, 205–210
outpatient clinics 255
outside connections 138–146
ownership issues 80

pain: healing unjust losses 202–212; total pain 26, 29, 133
"pains of imprisonment" 139
Pakistani mothers 51–54
palliative care: broad views 22, 26; "care for the caregiver" 252–257, 260–261; compassion 104–105; dignity protection 101–107; end of life care 101–107; iatrogenic harm 125–137; provision challenges 101–102
"paralysis of analysis" 243, 249
parenting models 90–93
partnerships, critical social work 233
past life losses 138
paternalism 43, 87, 97
pathologizing grief 111–122
patient's experiences 130–131; *see also* case studies
patriarchy 67, 170
pediatric palliative care 126
Peloquin, S. M. 126
perinatal loss 50–61
permission issues 168
person, defined as "an individual other than an Indian" 86
personal accounts, infant mortality 53–61
personal cultural memories 221–222
personal factors, "care for the caregiver" 251–255, 257–259, 262
personal losses, older women prison inmates 138–149
pharmaceutical industry 117–118
philanthropic ventures 185–186
"physician-induced" harm 125–137
Piagetian stage of development 156
Pickett, K. 199
Pickton, Robert 94
"piece of cake phenomenon" 135
pipelines 89
pity 40, 48
policy aspects, infant mortality 50, 59–61
political forces/influences: broad views 23–24; "care for the caregiver" 251–252, 255, 259–261; healing through rituals & memorials 203, 205–209; socially sensitive experiences 179
population: end of life care: dignity protection 100–108; globalized world 33
postmodern thought 227–228
postnatal mental health 52
post-traumatic growth 204–210
potlach banning 86–87
Poulter, Dan 59–60

poverty 34–35, 50–52, 60
power: broad views 23–29; conceptualizations 10–11, 13; critical social work 228–229, 232–234; critical thinking 283; social expectations: bereavement 166–168, 172–173
prejudice 14, 18
presence 81–82, 186
Prigerson, H. G. 112
prison inmates: death row 240–249; older women 138–153
privacy issues 138
privilege: broad views 24–29; conceptualizations 10–11; critical thinking 283; end of life care 77–78; global perspectives 34–37; health determinants 34–35; humility 71
problem identification issues 134–135
productivity, social expectations: bereavement 169–170
programming design/implementation 146–148
prolonged grief disorders 113–114
protecting dignity 100–108
protests 202–212
psychological counseling 116–117
psychological iatrogenic trauma 126, 128–129, 136
psychology of grief 203–205
psychotherapeutic support 70–71, 180–181
psy-construction of grief 119
public health priorities, end of life care 105–106
public memorials/rituals 202, 207–208
public space 202, 207–208
purpose, spirituality 196

quality of care 56–57
quality of life 96, 102–107

race 21–29
racism 52–53, 56–57, 60, 67, 69, 77, 80
radical social practices 227
"reciprocity" 46, 252, 262
reconciliation aspects 91–92
Rees, S. 126
referential compassion 268, 280
reflection 77–78
reflective practice 27–30, 258–259, 262, 284
reflexivity 167, 170, 173, 230, 235
refugees 230–235
rehabilitation services 235
rehearsal techniques 161
relationships, healing through rituals & memorials 206–209
relative wealth 34–35, 38
religion: broad views 24, 28; conceptualizations 16–17; First Nations People, Canada 90–93; older women prison inmates 147–148; socially sensitive experiences 179; spirituality & social justice 191–201; *see also individual religions*

remembrance 213–224
research literature, infant mortality 53, 60
residential schools 90–93, 96
resistant attitudes 234–235
resources: global perspectives 36–37; loss of 85–86, 88–92, 94, 96–97; museums as healing spaces 220
respect 68–72, 85–86, 89, 95–97
responses, compassion 268–279
restorative practice/principles 213–224
result's presentation 80
Ricard, Matthieu 272–273
rights 12, 16–17, 35–37, 100–108
rituals 86–87, 95–96, 202–212, 214, 216–217, 283
road accidents 202, 207
Rodriguez, M. M. D. 10–11
Rogowski, S. 234
role compatibility 241–247
Royal Proclamation of 1763 88–89
Rushton, C. H. 278

"the sacred" 199
sacred grounds 214, 216–217
same-sex unions 12, 179–187, 192
schools 90–93
science advances 35
secondary losses 163
self-advocacy education 80
self-awareness 77–78, 259
self-care strategies 251, 256–259, 274–275
self-governance 138, 141–142, 170
self-injury 157
selfless tenderness 41–42, 46
self-relationships 208–209
self-talk techniques 182–183
self-trust 76
sense of self 138, 141–142
sensitivity 54, 56–57, 68–73, 271–272
service access aspects 50–51, 81–82
sexism 67, 69, 71
sexual identity 179–190, 192, 194
sick role 167
Sidewalk chalk in Oklahoma City 218
Sikh faith 191
silenced emotion 138–153
silo thinking 195, 198, 200
Site C Dam, Canada 89
Slate survey 116, 119–123
social capital 44, 48, 52, 60–61, 197, 200
Social Care Institute of Excellence 103
social change activities 234–235
social conformity 169
social determinants of health 34–35, 38
social exclusion 50–63, 227, 231–232
social expectations, bereavement 165–175
social factors/influences: broad views 23–24; "care for the caregiver" 251–255, 259–261;

Index

health determinants 34–35, 38; iatrogenic harm 125–137; individual responses 283
social institution navigation 240–250
social location analysis 231
social losses 138–149
social memory 221–222
social networks/support: infant mortality 50–61; medicalizing grief 121–122
social pain, social expectations: bereavement 169, 173
social responses, compassion 265
social responsibilities 167
social rules of grieving 166–173
social strategies, "care for the caregiver" 251–255, 259–261
social work 225–239
socially just practice 15
socially sensitive experiences 179–190
socially structured feelings 231–232
society relationships 34–35, 38, 207–208
socioeconomic status 51–52, 179
socio-political aspects 228–229, 231–232, 251–252, 255, 259–261
song and dance 86–87
speeches, museums as healing spaces 218
spirituality 191–201; atomism 195–196, 200; beyond religion 193–194; dimensions 196–197; discrimination 192–196, 199; First Nations People, Canada 85–88, 95–97; museums as healing spaces 217, 222; oppression 193–197, 199; spiritual consciousness 40–48, 79–80; "spiritual intelligence" 46, 48; "spiritual kinship" 217, 222
stakeholders, museums as healing spaces 214
Steckel, Brian 240–249
stereotyping 13, 18, 70–71
Sternlicht, M. 156, 158
stigma issues 168–169, 205
stolen children 91–93
storytelling 218, 221
strengths perspectives, critical social work 233
"stress of conscience" 128–136
structural influences: "care for the caregiver" 251–253, 261–262; compassion 265, 274–278; iatrogenic harm 125–137; infant mortality 50–52
student bereavement leave policies 14–15
suffering: compassion & materialism 40–48; First Nations People, Canada 85–97; global perspectives 33–39
suffocated grief 14–15, 18
suicides 94–96, 205, 256
Sulmasy, Daniel 266
Sun Dance 86–87
support groups/networks: critical social work 235; infant mortality 53–54; socially sensitive experiences 183–185

survivor advocacy 217–219, 222
survivor legacy honoring 214, 217
Sweden 100
symbolic meaning 79–80
symbols 79–80, 205, 207, 209, 283
sympathy 272

taking of children 90–93, 96
tattoos 207
team palliative care 134
technology aspects, global perspectives in death 35
teenage mothers 51, 54
temporary inequality 15
tenderness 41–42, 46
terminal illnesses: broad views 21–23, 25–26, 28–29; "care for the caregiver" 252–260; cultural mistrust 75–84; dignity protection 100–107; end of life care 75–84, 100–107
thanatology 15, 155
theatres of memory 221–222
therapeutic programming 147
therapeutic relationships 180–184, 187
therapy 22–23, 159
Thompson, S. 258–259
thoughtfulness 232, 236
Tiananmen Square Massacre 216, 218
time issues, social expectations: bereavement 168
timely care aspects 58
tolerance, compassion 272
Tomikel, J. 194
total pain 26, 29, 133
total social capital 197, 200
tragedy 41–42, 46
training programs 80, 265
transformational compassion 47–48
Trauma Foundation 219
Tribute Gallery, Tribute Center 217
The True Grit Model at the Northern Nevada Correctional Institution 147
trust-building strategies 75–84, 146
Truth and Reconciliation 91–92
Twin Towers, New York 213–219

UK see United Kingdom
unbiased compassion 268, 272, 280
uncertainty 76–82
unearned advantages/entitlements 10–11, 18
UNITAID 37
United Kingdom (UK) 50–63, 100, 102
United Nations (UN) 37, 100, 102
United States (US) 100, 102, 138–153, 179–181, 254
unjust loss 202–212

victim legacy honoring 214, 217
violation issues 202–212
violence, museums as healing spaces 215

virtual spaces 208
voice/protests 202–212
volunteer programs 185–186
vulnerability issues 41–42

Wagner, B. 116
wealth 34–35, 38
Weissman, D. E. 129
WHO *see* World Health Organization
Wilkinson, R. 199
witnessing: death row prisoners 241, 246–249; museums as healing spaces 214–216
women: immigrant populations 50–61; infant mortality 50–63; missing/murdered women 93–94; Native Women's Association of Canada 93–94; older women prison inmates 138–153
wonder 197
word association reactivity 158
work exclusions 167
workplace factors: "care for the caregiver" 251–262; compassion 265, 267–268; iatrogenic harm 127–129
World Health Organization (WHO) 100–103
World Trade Center Exhibit, New York State Museum 213–219

Youngson, Robin 254, 260, 270, 275–277
youth suicides 94–96

Taylor & Francis eBooks

Helping you to choose the right eBooks for your Library

Add Routledge titles to your library's digital collection today. Taylor and Francis ebooks contains over 50,000 titles in the Humanities, Social Sciences, Behavioural Sciences, Built Environment and Law.

Choose from a range of subject packages or create your own!

Benefits for you
- Free MARC records
- COUNTER-compliant usage statistics
- Flexible purchase and pricing options
- All titles DRM-free.

Benefits for your user
- Off-site, anytime access via Athens or referring URL
- Print or copy pages or chapters
- Full content search
- Bookmark, highlight and annotate text
- Access to thousands of pages of quality research at the click of a button.

REQUEST YOUR FREE INSTITUTIONAL TRIAL TODAY | **Free Trials Available** We offer free trials to qualifying academic, corporate and government customers.

eCollections – Choose from over 30 subject eCollections, including:

Archaeology	Language Learning
Architecture	Law
Asian Studies	Literature
Business & Management	Media & Communication
Classical Studies	Middle East Studies
Construction	Music
Creative & Media Arts	Philosophy
Criminology & Criminal Justice	Planning
Economics	Politics
Education	Psychology & Mental Health
Energy	Religion
Engineering	Security
English Language & Linguistics	Social Work
Environment & Sustainability	Sociology
Geography	Sport
Health Studies	Theatre & Performance
History	Tourism, Hospitality & Events

For more information, pricing enquiries or to order a free trial, please contact your local sales team: **www.tandfebooks.com/page/sales**

 The home of Routledge books

www.tandfebooks.com